COLONIAL LAW IN INDIA AND THE VICTORIAN IMAGINATION

Situated at the intersection of law and literature, nineteenth-century studies and postcolonialism, *Colonial Law in India and the Victorian Imagination* draws on original archival research to shed new light on Victorian literature. Each chapter explores the relationship between the shared cultural logic of law and literature, and considers how this inflected colonial sociality. Leila Neti approaches the legal archive in a distinctly literary fashion, attending to nuances of voice, character, diction, and narrative, while also tracing elements of fact and procedure, reading the case summaries as literary texts to reveal the common turns of imagination that motivated both fictional and legal narratives. What emerges is an innovative political analytic for understanding the entanglements between judicial and cultural norms in Britain and the colony, bridging the critical gap in how law and literature interact within the colonial arena.

LEILA NETI is an associate professor of English at Occidental College. Her published articles have appeared in *Differences: A Journal of Feminist Cultural Studies*, *Interventions: International Journal of Postcolonial Studies*, *Law and Literature*, and in various edited collections.

CAMBRIDGE STUDIES IN NINETEENTH-CENTURY LITERATURE AND CULTURE

General editors
KATE FLINT, *UNIVERSITY OF SOUTHERN CALIFORNIA*
CLARE PETTITT, *KING'S COLLEGE LONDON*

Literature, Print Culture, and Media Technologies, 1880–1900
RICHARD MENKE

Aging, Duration, and the English Novel
JACOB JEWUSIAK

Autobiography, Sensation, and the Commodification of Identity in Victorian Narrative
SEAN GRASS

Settler Colonialism in Victorian Literature
PHILLIP STEER

Mimicry and Display in Victorian Literary Culture
WILL ABBERLEY

Victorian Women and Wayward Reading
MARISA PALACIOS KNOX

The Victorian Cult of Shakespeare
CHARLES LAPORTE

Children's Literature and the Rise of 'Mind Cure'
ANNE STILES

Virtual Play and the Victorian Novel
TIMOTHY GAO

Colonial Law in India and the Victorian Imagination
LEILA NETI

COLONIAL LAW IN INDIA AND THE VICTORIAN IMAGINATION

LEILA NETI
Occidental College, Los Angeles

CAMBRIDGE
UNIVERSITY PRESS

CAMBRIDGE
UNIVERSITY PRESS

University Printing House, Cambridge CB2 8BS, United Kingdom

One Liberty Plaza, 20th Floor, New York, NY 10006, USA

477 Williamstown Road, Port Melbourne, VIC 3207, Australia

314–321, 3rd Floor, Plot 3, Splendor Forum, Jasola District Centre, New Delhi – 110025, India

79 Anson Road, #06–04/06, Singapore 079906

Cambridge University Press is part of the University of Cambridge.

It furthers the University's mission by disseminating knowledge in the pursuit of education, learning, and research at the highest international levels of excellence.

www.cambridge.org
Information on this title: www.cambridge.org/9781108837484
DOI: 10.1017/9781108938280

First published 2021

A catalogue record for this publication is available from the British Library.

ISBN 978-1-108-83748-4 Hardback

For Narayan, who is my everything.

Contents

Acknowledgments *page* viii

Introduction 1

PART I CRIMINALITY 31

1 "Power Able to Overawe Them All": Criminality and the Uses of Fear 33

2 The Social Life of Crime: Charles Dickens's *Great Expectations* and Philip Meadows Taylor's *Confessions of a Thug* 63

PART II TEMPORALITY 95

3 Injurious Pasts: The Temporality of Caste 97

4 On Time: How Fiction Writes History in Wilkie Collins's *The Moonstone* 122

PART III ADOPTION AND INHERITANCE 147

5 The Begum's Fortune: Adoption, Inheritance, and Private Property 149

6 Foundlings and Adoptees: Filiality in the Novels of George Eliot 176

Afterword 209

Notes 220

Bibliography 272

Index 289

Acknowledgments

Over the years spent writing this book, I have accrued countless intellectual and personal debts, which I can only begin to name here. Though this project did not grow out of the work I did for my dissertation, the mentoring I received from my Ph.D. committee at the University of California, Irvine, provided a strong foundation from which to begin. Gaby Schwab, J. Hillis Miller, David Lloyd, and Lindon Barrett have been excellent teachers and even better friends throughout my graduate school years and beyond. Hillis has always embodied unfailing generosity. His attention to detail in reading, his kindness, and his willingness to offer his help have provided a model I can only hope to emulate. David is a loyal friend and ally, always ready to share his wisdom and his whiskey without hesitation. Gaby has been a confidante and collaborator, weaving me into her life and her family with warmth and affection. The tragic loss of Lindon left a huge void, not just for me, but for everyone who benefited in so many ways from his presence in the world, and even more for those who will never have the opportunity to do so.

At Irvine, Lindon founded the cultural studies group, which provided a space for radical thinking, rigorous analysis, and unwavering companionship. I continue to benefit from the wisdom of that group and am grateful to its members: Bruce Barnhart, Mrinalini Chakravorty, Naomi Greyser, Ginger Hill, Linh Hua, Janet Neary, Arnold Pan, Amy Parsons, and Rajagopalan Radhakrishnan. A lifeline at the time, the friendships forged in this group continue to sustain me now. For years of fun and friendship, Cyndi La, Barbara Antoniazzi, Lan Duong, Patricia Pierson, Bond Love, Linda Nichols, Jim Ziegler, and Rachel Meyer, whose passing leaves yet another hole in our lives, deserve special thanks.

Conversations with a community of scholars have influenced the project at different stages along its path. I would like to thank Steve Arata, Maria Aristodemou, Nancy Armstrong, Zahid Chaudhary, Kirstie Dorr, Peter Goodrich, Yogita Goyal, Graham Huggan, Sara Kaplan, Bernie Meyler,

Asha Nadkarni, Vasukhi Nesiah, Jahan Ramazani, Sangeeta Ray, Sarita See, Sandhya Shukla, Joey Slaughter, Simon Stern, Marco Wan, Julian Wolfreys, and Robert Young. Portions of the book have been presented at the Annual Conference on Law, Culture, and Humanities at Stanford University (2017), the Annual Conference of the American Comparative Literature Association at the University of California, Los Angeles (2018), and at the Institute of the Humanities and Global Cultures at the University of Virginia (2018). The organizers and audiences at these events have helped shape the contours of the project. An earlier version of Chapter 5 appeared in *Interventions: International Journal of Postcolonial Studies* (vol. 16, no. 2, 2014).

I have been very lucky to enjoy the spirited encouragement of my friends and colleagues at Occidental College. Dan Fineman, James Ford, Ross Lerner, Warren Montag, Eric Newhall, John Swift, and Jean Wyatt have been ideal comrades with whom I am fortunate to share a department. Their support has nurtured my thinking and given me the opportunity to explore and innovate in both teaching and research. Thanks are also due to Donna Maeda, Robert Ellis, Amy Lyford, Salvador Fernandez, and Kristi Upson-Saia. My students at Oxy deserve a special acknowledgment. Their willingness to think with me, their openness to being challenged, and their generosity of spirit are a constant source of inspiration, and an invitation to always do better. This project has also benefited from institutional resources provided by the college. I am grateful to Deans Jorge Gonzalez and Wendy Sternberg for the Macarthur International and Faculty Enrichment Grants that have enabled me to conduct archival research in India and England, and for the generous support of the Brown Humanities Book Publication Fund. The many librarians at the reading room of the India Office Records at the British Library in London and the National Library in Kolkata have patiently helped me find my way through their vast archives. Thank you, as well, to my cousin Bhasker Annavarapu for driving all around the state of Andhra Pradesh to make sure I had access to the books I needed.

Bethany Thomas at Cambridge University Press has been the perfect editor, keeping the project on track with the utmost efficiency and professionalism. I would like to express my sincere gratitude to the anonymous readers, whose careful attention to this manuscript has improved its quality immeasurably. Their thorough, detailed, and constructive suggestions for revision have exemplified the highest standards of peer review, and I am very fortunate to have benefited from their expertise and deep knowledge of the multiple fields that come together in this book. I thank

Kate Flint and Clare Pettitt, the series editors for Cambridge Studies in Nineteenth-Century Literature and Culture, for their willingness to take this project on and to see it through.

Writing a book is never a purely intellectual endeavor, and I am grateful for the support and encouragement I have received from my family along the way. My parents arrived in the United States in 1960, during the era of quotas before the Immigration Act of 1965. They made a life in an unfamiliar and often hostile environment, holding on to their old identities and taking on new ones as the situation demanded. My mother Suseela is a constant flurry of energy. I admire her ready trust of strangers, her joy in small things, and her daily hours spent tending her fabulous garden. She has always been my strongest advocate, ready to indulge my intellectual curiosity when others met it with skepticism. My father Radhakrishna Murty Neti, the original Dr. Neti, has modeled a dedication to his profession that I can never hope to match. Though I dreaded his nudging when he felt the project was moving too slowly (which was often), I have always appreciated his interest in my work, and his desire for my success. His fierce determination continues to take him forward, and every day I learn from his patience, indefatigable sense of perseverance, and general good attitude. Jaya Leslie, my sister, has always looked out for me and brought order to chaos. She has supported me in countless ways throughout my life and has my profound gratitude for everything she continues to do. I am also grateful to Brian, Jhansi, and Neel Leslie for raucous conversations, spirited teasing, and all-around joy.

As immigrants, my parents learned to make family where blood ties were absent. This has taught me to think of kinship in more flexible and innovative ways, informing both my work and my life. I could not be more thankful to my family of choice – Mrinalini Chakravorty, Jeffrey Atteberry, and Narayan Atteberry Neti. Perhaps not always eagerly, but always with good spirits, Jeff and Lini have pored over every word of this manuscript, through all of its many iterations. The final product is worlds better for their insights and interventions. Lini has talked me down from what she wisely recognized as disastrous arguments (though some, I'm sure, have made it past her astute gaze), and Jeff, with his characteristic intellectual precision, has prodded me into thinking about the law in new and more nuanced ways. Their tireless efforts on my behalf are sincerely appreciated. But it is the frolic, forays into new and exciting places, eating tasty meals and treats, laughter, and bearing fears and sorrows together, for which I am most deeply grateful. I am inspired by Lini's infectious sense of wonder, her brilliance, and her willingness to share it all. Jeff's courageous imagination finds a rare match in his constancy and genuine kindness. I could not wish for better human beings with whom to share this journey. I am also grateful to those who have cared for and nurtured us along the way: Joba and Milan Chakravorty, Earline Hammer, David L. Atteberry, and Meenakshy Chakravorty. Finally, Narayan, to whom this book is dedicated, amazes me daily with his curiosity, intelligence, earnestness, and wit. I am in awe of his boundless enthusiasm and his unfailingly happy disposition. He is my most ardent supporter, always ready with an encouraging word and unalloyed in his belief that this book would, one day, be done. I promised him a puppy when that day finally came, and we are glad for the newfound companionship of Jimmy. I look forward to the years ahead with this crew and cherish every moment we have had so far.

Introduction

Colonial Law in India and the Victorian Imagination reads works of fiction from the nineteenth century alongside three legal cases heard before the Judicial Committee of the Privy Council (henceforth the Privy Council or JCPC), which was the highest court of appeal for colonies within the British Empire. By pairing legal judgments with novels by prominent Victorian authors such as Charles Dickens, Philip Meadows Taylor, Wilkie Collins, and George Eliot, I show how crosscurrents between literature and the law shaped, and were shaped by, the broader ideals of imperial expansionism during the nineteenth century. Rather than thinking of the legal and literary realms as distinct, I read the judicial opinions as instances of narrative that share many of the same tropes and strategies typical to the nineteenth-century novel. The legal cases in the study are summarized in *Moore's Indian Appeals*, a fourteen-volume catalog of appeals from Indian courts to the Privy Council from 1836 to 1872. The written summaries of the cases, consumed as texts, were the main avenue through which an English audience could become acquainted with legal disputes in India. And, as is clear from my readings of the judicial opinions, the Privy Council used modes of narrativity (to organize temporality, character, plot, etc.) that were also commonplace in Victorian literature. Reading the legal texts as literature allows us to explore the division between reality and fiction, and to look at the ways in which legal opinions created norms that intersected, often unpredictably, with other forms of cultural representation. As this book demonstrates, reading the archives of the JCPC and the Victorian novel together opens up a series of questions. Does fiction shape materiality in ways that are similar to how materiality shapes fiction? Does reading a text as fiction create different strategies and avenues of interpretation? Is what we think of as reality possible outside of the turns of imagination that we recognize in fiction? These are some of the questions that motivate this study and which *Colonial Law in India and the Victorian Imagination* seeks to answer.

By reading these colonial legal opinions in a study of nineteenth-century literature and culture, I foreground both the narrativity of the law and the disciplinary function of literature. Like literature, the law takes shape at the intersection of representation, narrative, and claims to truth and reality. And as in the broader cultural turns envisioned in literature, the law provides a critical index of the imaginative possibilities available to subjects under its jurisdiction. In particular, by looking at the archive of the JCPC, this study examines how colonial legal appeals from India resonated with, reflected, shaped, reframed, and even obscured the ideological questions raised in the nineteenth-century novel. While *Colonial Law in India and the Victorian Imagination* contributes to a broader discussion of law and literature, its primary focus is on how the specific archive of the Privy Council appeals relates to these Victorian novels. One of the main arguments of the book is that the opinions of the JCPC not only reveal critical intersections between the law and literature but also enliven new interpretations of canonical nineteenth-century novels. As its title indicates, its real interest is in the ways that these realms work together to shape the broader cultural imagination of both India and England. In other words, reading the novels alongside these colonial judicial opinions illuminates critical insights about the Victorian imagination in both the texts and contexts of the novels and legal cases that I discuss.

The Privy Council

I begin with the observation that similar historical forces and cultural anxieties attending the rise of British imperialism not only produced the nineteenth-century novel but also shaped the narrative practices of the JCPC.[1] In this regard, I read colonial law as part of a larger network of narrative practices, developing alongside the literary form of the novel, which furthered a particular notion of English selfhood and sovereignty.[2] The reconstitution of the JCPC in England in 1833 was central to the evolving performative nature of British sovereignty, both at home and in the colonies. A popular narrative that was often recounted by Privy Counselor Lord Haldane involved an Englishman who purportedly came upon a tribal sacrifice in India. When the Englishman enquired about the god to whom the sacrifice was being made, the worshipper replied that he didn't know much about the god, but that its name was the JCPC and it had intervened with the government and restored their lands to the tribe.[3] The story is suggestive of both its mythical, or literary, quality and the absolute authority that the Privy Council sought to invoke.

As I discuss in detail in Chapters 3 and 4, over the period between the 1830s and the 1870s, which forms the historical backdrop for all of the legal cases I consider in this volume, Britain was embracing parliamentary democracy at home, while the Government of India, and later the Crown, was implementing principles of absolute sovereignty abroad. This reverse trajectory for domestic and colonial state forms and governmentality began in the seventeenth century and continued through the early twentieth century.

In Britain, though, the path to national unity was long and brutal. Nevertheless, the deposing of Charles I, the Interregnum, and the bitter economic and sectarian strife that characterized the beginnings of a united Britain in the seventeenth century, produced valuable lessons for the expansion of the empire in other parts of the world. As Linda Colley observes, after 1707, the British "came to define themselves as a single people not because of any political or cultural consensus at home, but rather in reaction to the Other beyond their shores."[4] The same types of conflicts that threatened British unity in the seventeenth century were made useful in the scramble to secure British colonies in the eighteenth and nineteenth centuries.[5] Sudipta Sen brings this history of British state formation to bear on Indian colonial expansion. "Along with the concerns of profit and investment for corporations and spoils of trade and war overseas for individuals," Sen observes, "colonial wars were certainly being projected, if not fought, as national wars... India as an arena of struggle for colonial possession provided an equally significant imperial *and* patriotic arena for the realization of a Greater Britain."[6] Turning back to a past before the period of internal strife helped craft a narrative of unity and progress within the domestic context. If in the British literary arena the medieval romance was a source of influence for the nineteenth-century novel, colonial law also looked to the Middle Ages for inspiration in constituting new modes of governance.[7]

A holdover from earlier legal formations, the Privy Council originates in the medieval Curia Regis, or royal court. Following the Norman Conquest, the Privy Council was established as a group of advisors to the monarch to enable the exercise of royal prerogative. During the fifteenth and sixteenth centuries, the Privy Council occupied an important position in British judicial and administrative governance. For example, the monarch, in consultation with the Privy Council, was permitted to enact laws, inflict punishment (with the exception of death), and hear appeals. In the wake of the English Civil War at the end of the seventeenth century, however, the Privy Council's jurisdiction over England was abolished and the exercise of royal prerogative seriously curtailed.

Yet, the Privy Council's role in the colonies follows a different trajectory. Models of absolute sovereignty that were decisively rejected in England in the seventeenth century took on a productive afterlife through the management of judicial appeals from the colonies in the eighteenth and nineteenth centuries. While the Privy Council ceased to adjudicate most legal matters in England, by the early eighteenth century the Council decided all judicial appeals from British overseas territories.[8] Although initially the jurisdiction of the colonial courts, including the Privy Council, was limited to British subjects and Indians residing within the presidencies of Bombay, Calcutta, and Madras, over the course of the eighteenth and nineteenth centuries, colonial expansion extended its reach. A statute passed in 1726 provided for appeals from the colonial Mayor's Court within the presidencies to the governor-in-council and then to the King's Privy Council. This change in appellate jurisdiction brought Indian colonial courts into alignment (though unevenly) with English law and systems of justice.[9] From this point forward, civil matters in the presidencies in excess of a particular sum were eligible for appeal to the Privy Council.[10]

In 1772, during the British and Mughal era, Warren Hastings, then governor general of Bengal, established in Calcutta the *Sadr Diwani Adalat* (civil and revenue court) and the *Sadr Nizamat Adalat* (criminal court), which served as the colonial civil and criminal high courts.[11] He also replaced Persian with English as the language of the courts. In practice, the *adalats* served to align local laws with colonial ideologies, instituting pandits and muftis (Hindu and Muslim legal practitioners) on the one hand, but subordinating their authority to Orientalist interpretations of scriptures on the other.[12] While nominally endeavoring to preserve local Hindu and Muslim judicial practices, colonial law often worked in practice to invent tradition rather than to accommodate it.[13]

As the empire expanded, the volume of cases heard by the Privy Council grew, and in the nineteenth century the jurisdiction of the JCPC was established statutorily.[14] The Judicial Committee Act of 1833 outlined the rules governing it as a final court of appeal for the colonies.[15] Also in 1833, the Government of India Act sought to normativize the terrain relating to Indian criminal law by appointing a law member to oversee the development of a uniform penal code. Thomas Babington Macaulay was the first law member, and the main author of the Indian Penal Code, which ultimately came into force in 1860. Both Acts worked to bring colonial law increasingly into the fold of English legal norms, one by exporting

English legal principles abroad, and the other by importing colonial legal disputes for resolution in England. At this point a civil code was also considered, but was ultimately rejected.

As the court of final appeals for the colonies, during the nineteenth century the JCPC served a parallel function to the House of Lords for English appeals. In his speech before the Cambridge Law Society in 1938, Sir George Rankin raised the question of this discrepancy between the domestic and international contexts. "How comes it that for these islands jurisdiction in an appeal became vested in one only of the two Houses of Parliament, and why in Parliament at all?" Rankin asked.[16] And relatedly, he also wondered, "How is it that to the Dominions overseas the highest judicial determination comes in the form of an Order in Council, the very voice of executive authority?" These questions, Rankin speculated, "will press strongly for an answer."[17] Throughout the nineteenth century, however, the JCPC's absolutism remained occluded by its apparent reliance on Indian custom and religion in its deliberations.

The Heteroglossia of Colonial Law

Continuing the tradition of the local colonial courts, the JCPC adjudicated cases based on indigenous laws. This created the odd situation in which British judges in London, who were often largely ignorant of the legal traditions under which they were operating, were attempting to apply Hindu or Muslim law, for example, to cases originating from India. Early colonial law was in this sense as thoroughly heteroglossic as the novel in Mikhail Bakhtin's analysis of it. As Lauren Benton, Mitra Sharafi, Rohit De, and others have shown, the application of Indian law by the Privy Council judges was "variegated" and uneven.[18] Yet, just as Bakhtin describes the novel's tendency to draw heteroglossic elements into alignment with an overarching narrative, colonial legal heteroglossia afforded the Privy Council the opportunity to shape the story of the subjects it legislated over while at the same time appearing neutral and objective. A 1917 article in *The Canadian Law Times* praised the Privy Council for its cultural objectivity:

> It is by thus divesting itself of its own particular brand of *Kultur* that the Privy Council successfully interprets the multifarious varieties of law – Hindu, Mahomedan, Canadian-French, Roman-Dutch, and English common law transmuted by the statutes of scores of local legislatures – with which it has to deal; and its practice is an education in the elements of empire.[19]

In this manner, the Privy Council was celebrated for its capacity to convert the heteroglossia of local laws into a coherent narrative of legal rationality. Indeed, as the recurrent themes across the various cases discussed in this volume indicate, JCPC opinions often drew on stock narratives about Britain's colonial populations.[20]

Consequently, under the rubric of opening itself to colonial difference, the law, through the appeals process, reworked native forms of sovereignty into colonialist ones. The paradox between the rhetorical construction of the law as accommodationist and its despotic material practice is a definitive, and by now well-known, feature of British colonial rule in India.[21] One of the foundational points that Radhika Singha makes in *A Despotism of Law* is that the colonial legal system represented itself as embodying a direct relationship to the sovereign on the one hand, and the colonial subject on the other. Despite the unwieldy and varied reality of the legal system, the narrative crafted was one of cohesion and hierarchy. Singha shows how across a range of social issues the narrative of the law sought to bring cumbersome, and implicitly dangerous, Indian practices under the rational "rule of law." In the paradigmatic example of thuggee, which inspired the Criminal Tribes Act of 1871, English fictions about hereditary Indian criminality resulted in material laws.

Nevertheless, like the heteroglossic novel, colonial jurisprudence was neither univocal nor uniform. It varied across history and over different regional and religious contexts. At times, especially over the course of the appeals process, as the cases discussed in this volume indicate, British colonial jurisprudence even worked in alliance with Indian assertions of sovereignty. Lauren Benton, Mitra Sharafi, and others have shown that the pluralism of colonial law offered the occasion for litigants to "forum shop" for the most advantageous venue in which to present their cases. Not only did litigants shop for different courts in which to argue their cases, but, as Elizabeth Kolsky has demonstrated, different categories of subjects were acted upon differently under the law. In short, it is important to state that from early Company-administered courts to the apex of imperial law, there never existed a fully coherent and intentional legal master plan.

Yet, as Jane Burbank and Frederick Cooper argue, jurisdictional complexity and multiplicity did not necessarily undermine legal cohesion. Burbank and Cooper show that "even in situations of local empowerment, obstructionism, and self-serving interpretation – all common phenomena – an underlying assumption for most people involved was that the emperor (the king, the queen, the sultan, etc.) was the head of state and responsible for its provision of legal governance."[22] The "verticality" that "imbued even the controversies over imperial law and its potential" is inescapable, even if the narrative generated by the law was not univocal.[23] Dating back to its medieval origins, the Privy Council reflected the notion that "The King is the fountain of all justice throughout his Dominions, and exercises jurisdiction in his Council, which act in an advisory capacity to the Crown."[24] The absolute sovereignty of the king was mirrored in the sovereignty of the Privy Council, and this model continued to inflect the administration of justice in the colonial era.

As Lauren Benton and Richard Ross point out, historians "have noted a long-nineteenth-century turn away from jumbled jurisdictions to the imagination of a more hierarchical and streamlined legal administrative order."[25] While iterations of colonial law were not necessarily cohesive, over time increasingly vertical pronouncements worked to create and perpetuate ideological norms. The narrative of colonial jurisprudence thus reflects the ways in which, at least in popular imagination (both British and Indian), the law came into increasing alignment with a more vertical administration of justice.

Making Law

The Privy Council was central to this project of streamlining colonial jurisprudence by harnessing and shaping the narrative from above rather than evaluating evidence and testimony on the ground. As is common in appeals processes, in deciding its opinions the Privy Council relied on narratives about cases (provided by lawyers, case records, and law reports from earlier rulings) rather than on direct evidence or witness testimony. But, in addition to filtering the narrative representation through the voice of attorneys and lower court judges, the judgment in a Privy Council appeal during the colonial era, as Mitra Sharafi notes, was univocal, with no dissenting opinions allowed.[26] The JCPC, Rohit De explains, "was premised on the fiction that its judgment was advice to the King" and therefore, "they could not offer divided counsel."[27] The immense heteroglossia of colonial law, then, was rendered at least partially monologic through the judicial opinion of the Privy Council.[28] The univocal nature of the opinion, and the analogy with counsel to the king, further highlight the absolutism of the JCPC in particular. The tension between the heteroglossic nature of the law on the one hand and the monologic judicial opinion on the other was not unique to the JCPC or the colonial context, but it was heightened by the diversity of legal terrains and the externally imposed sovereignty of the judgment.

Writing about appellate judicial opinions as a literary genre, Robert A. Ferguson observes that they are "the most creative and generally read literary form in the law."[29] Like Victorian novels, legal opinions were produced in relation to the larger historical, political, and cultural context from which they arose. Unlike their literary counterparts, however, legal opinions also immediately shaped materiality. The legal opinion, then, bears an interesting relationship to fiction, insofar as it is an utterance that is both representational and real.[30]

In particular, Ferguson examines the question of voice and the monologic quality that the judicial opinion seeks to project: "the speaking judge in the act of judgment and after is profoundly monologic in voice and ideological thrust."[31] As Ferguson observes, the judicial opinion is monologic, but not purely personal. Instead, sifting through the multiple and often contradictory perspectives in the courtroom, "the judicial voice works to appropriate all other voices into its own monologue. The goal of judgment is to subsume difference in an act of explanation and a moment of decision."[32] Ferguson further draws a connection between the monologic tone and voice of the legal opinion and the overarching monologism of the law's ideology as a framework within which the legal opinion is always situated.

The paradoxical nature of the judicial opinion, then, is that it must be both entirely monologic and sovereign in its pronouncement yet at the same time "appear as if forced to its inevitable conclusion by the logic of the situation and the duties of office, which together eliminate all thought of an unfettered hand."[33] "Free from direct interference," Ferguson explains, "the monologic voice nonetheless assumes a larger persona that is enmeshed within the social machinery of decision-making. The voice speaks alone, but the persona behind it accepts and moves on a stage of perceived boundaries, compelled narratives, and inevitable decisions."[34] As Ferguson shows, even though the judge's monologism is absolute in a legal opinion, the encompassing umbrella of the law's rationality works to channel decisions away from individual whim or bias and toward a fixed matrix of norms and standards, mirroring the ways in which, in Michel Foucault's terms, the juridical gives way to the normative.

The normative impulse of the law, including the monologism of judicial opinions, can be seen in relation to larger claims about the law's inherent rationality and objectivity. The judicial opinion's monologism thus works to obscure the law's inherent recourse to fiction and ambiguity. Yet, as the earlier discussion reminds us, fictions of nationalism and selfhood constitute the foundational narrativity of the law. This was true in the domestic British context, and perhaps even more so in the colonies, where narratives about the objective rationality of colonial law were not part of any collective national or cultural interest. Nevertheless, the narrative of the law's rationality, fictional as it might be, served a powerful function in cultivating and reproducing disciplinary norms.

Often, especially in the colonial context, the disciplinary force of the law masqueraded (via broader cultural and literary narratives) as a liberatory structure. As my readings of the cases in this volume show, the law thus both enables the imagination of certain novel possibilities and constrains those possibilities in meaningful ways. This tension within colonial appeals to the Privy Council and the Victorian novels is one of the central threads of the argument across the book. The movement between disciplinary and liberatory models manifests differently in each thematic pairing of literary and legal texts, though there are certain recurring qualities such as the focus on the individual in the English context and the collective in the Indian; material or financial forms of value in the English example as opposed to religion or ideology in India; and the primacy of psychological ties in the English instance in contrast to the recourse to normative modes of family and inheritance in the Indian context. Throughout the book I consider how the Victorian novel and colonial law frame one another's imaginations and create an entwined narrative of ideas and practices. Broadly speaking, in each of the three pairings I examine, the nineteenth-century novel posits the imaginative horizons of imperial subjectivity, while the judicial appeal explains why, and ensures that, those under its jurisdiction fall short of the possibilities represented in the literary texts. Although this may seem to confer a utopian idealism upon literature, while consigning the law to the realm of the real, my objective is rather to emphasize the ways in which colonial law, no less than Victorian literature, is engaged in imagining political subjectivity, of both subject and sovereign, into being.

Like Ayelet Ben-Yishai, I read the disciplines of law and literature "not as two discourses on opposite sides of an imaginary divide but as two discourses and practices taking part in a shared endeavor."[35] Especially when read in relation to popular literary works, the archive of the JCPC's opinions offers insight into how colonial law drew upon certain ideological frameworks to subtend its narrative claims. As historical artifacts, the opinions rendered by the JCPC are in many ways more relevant today for their narrative performativity than for their influence on legal doctrine.

While examining the doctrinal effects of judicial opinions is one method of engaging the legal archive, my interest here is in how narrative structures invoke and make possible certain realities, legal and otherwise, while foreclosing others. In *Colonial Law in India and the Victorian Imagination*, I read the legal opinions of the JCPC as brief glimpses into the psychic lives of individual characters, as well as a window into the functioning of an empire where subjects wrangled with sovereigns. I treat each judicial opinion as a self-contained narrative that deploys many of the recognizable tropes of nineteenth-century novels. By virtue of their selection for appeal before the Privy Council, the cases in this study are exceptional. The characters are eccentric, the turns of plot are unexpected, and the stories they tell are often didactic. In short, these cases share many qualities with the novels with which I pair them, but they are crafted narratives that have a unique relationship to materiality.[36] Reading the colonial appeals alongside these Victorian novels allows us to see how the law's explicit orientation toward material outcomes intersects with the literary texts' capacity to engender real and meaningful changes in what is possible to imagine, and in turn, to be and do.

In my consideration of Privy Council appeals and Victorian novels, therefore, the two categories of law and literature are not separable, but they are also not the same. The "and" within the model of colonial law and nineteenth-century literature that I describe delimits the two spheres while at the same time bringing them together as two components of a single concept category. This relationship can be conceived of in spatial terms, as a model of adjacency. The judicial opinion and the novel can be seen as beside each other, but at the same time, the differences that separate them are in many ways beside the point. Both colonial law and Victorian literature, I show, function within the larger arenas of culture and ideology.

José Muñoz offers a useful way of conceptualizing the relationship I describe. Citing a manifesto written by "a group calling itself Third World Gay Revolution," Muñoz draws attention to the nature of the "we" that forms the collective advocating for rights. Within the manifesto, the group calls for "a new society – a revolutionary socialist society" that would bestow fundamental rights "regardless of race, sex, age or sexual preferences."[37] Theorizing the orientation of the "we" identified in the manifesto, Muñoz shows that the "particularities that are listed – 'race, sex, age or sexual preferences' – are not things in and of themselves that format this 'we'; indeed the statement's 'we' is 'regardless' of these markers, which is not to say that it is beyond such distinctions or due to these differences but, instead, that it is *beside* them."[38] The "beside" that Muñoz articulates does not suggest that the "particularities," here of law and literature, are immaterial, but rather that they are both strategically proximal and that the differences between them are also, again, beside the point.

Relatedly, Eve Kosofsky Sedgwick calls attention to the "beside" that serves as a structuring principle for her brilliant analysis, and performance, of "nondualistic thought" in *Touching Feeling: Affect, Pedagogy, Performativity*. Sedgwick's concept of nondualism informs this project, shaping the way I think about the relationship between law and literature within the broader terrain of culture. Arguing against the "origin" and "telos" oriented critical models of "*beneath* and *beyond*" that inform much cultural theory, Sedgwick instead advocates for a practice of thinking "*beside*."[39] "*Beside* is an interesting preposition," she asserts, "because there's nothing very dualistic about it; a number of elements may lie alongside one another, though not an infinity of them."[40] Importantly, for Sedgwick, and for my purposes here, "*Beside* permits a spacious agnosticism about several of the linear logics that enforce dualistic thinking: noncontradiction or the law of the excluded middle, cause versus effect, subject versus object."[41] Despite opening avenues for thinking in nonbinary or non-oppositional terms, however, the concept of "beside" is not dependent "on a fantasy of metonymically egalitarian or even pacific relations" but instead "comprises a wide range of desiring, identifying, representing, repelling, paralleling, differentiating, rivaling, leaning, twisting, mimicking, withdrawing, attracting, aggressing, warping, and other relations."[42] Sedgwick's insistence on the untidiness and multiplicity that the concept of "beside" enables, or even necessitates, is central to how I conceptualize the relationship between law and literature throughout this volume as well. Thinking about the JCPC appeals and the Victorian novels as "beside" one another helps us see how they share underlying logics, assert their differences, influence one another, and derive certainty from the other's presence. Though colonial law and nineteenth-century literature are relational, the relationship between the two spheres is nimble and diffuse rather than oriented around a single axis of influence. In acknowledging my intellectual debts to Muñoz and Sedgwick, I hope to signal how their work has shaped the methodological, as well as the political, contours of this project.

The aim of *Colonial Law in India and the Victorian Imagination* is thus to place and read these instances of colonial legal appeals *beside* similar themes explored in their literary interlocutors. In the spirit of this model of adjacency, and by way of dismantling any temptation toward a binary structure, I consider the past, present, and future history of colonialism as intrinsic to the way in which this project conceives of the relationship between the legal and literary texts and contexts. To this end, colonialism is not incidental, but rather is central to both the literary and legal narratives of the period. Nevertheless, the ways in which colonialism relates to and influences the law are not always identical to how it intersects with literature. Within this constellation, my argument focuses on the fact that both literature and the colonial appeal are, in their own ways, acts of representation in Gayatri Spivak's dual sense of the term. In the case of Indian appeals to the JCPC, British lawyers represented Indian litigants and British justices adjudicated their cases. Similarly, nineteenth-century English novels represented both English and Indian characters, plots, and themes. While the Indian appellants were material subjects in their own legal narratives, they were, in a sense characters within a broader British narrative of justice and legalism. This central fact of British representation of Indian subjects informed and shaped narratives in both literary and legal contexts, such that both modes of representation are encompassed within the cultural logic of colonialism.

Colonial Law as Narrative

By focusing on the judicial opinion in instances of appeals, I aim to highlight (1) its unique relationship to questions of sovereignty, and (2) its emphasis on narrative. Both of these features of the appeal are central to the project of this book, and are worth briefly situating at the outset. As the legal review of what is otherwise the final judgment in a case, the adjudication of an appeal is a discrete performance of sovereignty.[43] In the case of colonial appeals to the sovereign through the JCPC, the subject's relationship to the sovereign is concretized through the appeal, and the sovereignty of the Privy Counsellors is rendered absolute through the final arbitration of the law. The appeal thus holds the ability to translate the abstract administration of the law into the materiality of lived experience. It also marks the capacity of legal pronouncements to adjudicate life-worlds. In this respect, the notion of the appeal serves both a theoretical and practical organizing principle for this book in terms of its focus on judicial sovereignty. But the appeal also serves a conceptual purpose in joining the literary and legal terrains of this project. If the task of the trial court is to decipher truth from fiction on the basis of testimony and material evidence, the charge of the appeals court is largely to determine which narrative is to be validated as legitimate. In Peter Brooks' terms, appellate courts are "the enforcers of rule-governed story-telling" because their task is to sort through competing narratives.[44]

In their richly suggestive work *Minding the Law*, Anthony Amsterdam and Jerome Bruner examine the narrative basis of the law. Using features of drama to think through the operations of the law, Amsterdam and Bruner suggest that narratives enter into the discourse of law to eventually become entrenched as scripts. If narratives are about negotiating what to do in instances when scripts are inadequate, scripts, they argue, are constructed in relation to expected norms. Over time, narratives often come to reinforce the normativity of scripts:

> *Narratives* serve to warn us of the ever-present dangers that beset our scripts, of the fragility of the ordinary. Yet, in two important ways, narratives also work to reinforce the scripts. First, narrative's very reminder of the inevitability that scripts will sometimes be broken is what enables the scripts to retain their coherence despite those breakings. Second, narrative has a way of domesticating the breakings themselves. Told often enough, any particular narrative version of norm-violation founds a tradition, becomes the kernel of a genre, of an accounting of "how the world is."[45]

The interplay between scripts and narratives characterizes, for Amsterdam and Bruner, the normative impulse of the law. The law persistently engages with narratives, eventually turning them into scripts. Building on Amsterdam and Bruner's assertion that narrative persuasion in legal arguments "is far more powerful than just as a device for convincing people to *do* something," but instead becomes the means "by which a story shapes reality," I argue that the appeal is where the force of this reality takes shape.[46] The capacity of the appellate process to convert a narrative into a scripted reality situates it at the threshold of fiction and materiality, or more pointedly, reveals fiction *as* materiality, and hence opens the law usefully to the scope of literary criticism. Questions of narrative bracket both ends of the legal judgment: there is the narrative that generates a particular legal opinion, as well as the narrative to which the opinion itself gives rise.

One of the central claims of *Colonial Law in India and the Victorian Imagination* is that the narrative crafted through the administration of law helped to shape, or script, affective and expressive dimensions of colonial life. The appeals adjudicated by the Judicial Committee of the Privy Council reveal how certain kinds of narratives were adapted and invented by institutions of law so as to become scripts for colonial life. These authorized narratives, I suggest, circumscribed the imaginative worlds of the colonizers and colonial subjects whose lives were limited by the subject positions available to them within these legal narratives. As well, the legal narratives of the nineteenth century continue to influence contemporary interpretations of the archives. Insofar as colonial law embodies the performative space between what is possible to imagine and what can be made real through the force of its articulation, reading its narratives is central to deciphering the complex consequences and afterlives of colonial rule.[47]

Law and Literature

In reading legal opinions as literature, and beside more traditional works of fiction, this project explores how the particular archive of JCPC opinions intersects with cultural representations enacted in the Victorian novel. It also, however, aims to contribute to the established field of "law and literature." A rich and varied interdiscipline, "law and literature" has embraced a wide range of textual objects, interpretive methodologies, and intellectual concerns. This proliferation of approaches has predictably led to considerable epistemological anxiety and inaugurated a subgenre of meta-commentary on the field and its future. Jane Baron, for instance, has surveyed the field and divided it into three camps: the humanist, the hermeneutic, and the narrative.[48] Baron's schematization contends that, across these various approaches, all forms of "law and literature" have taken the "law" as a stable and unified object of study and, as a result, have failed to recognize sufficiently the degree to which the law itself might be "contingent or created."[49] Baron's critique was later adopted and amplified by Julie Stone Peters, who argues that the relationship between "law" and "literature" was critically constituted as a binary that the field itself has been unable to dialectically resolve. The desired resolution has been lacking, she suggests, because, in the historical genesis of the field, each side of the law and literature divide held a "view of the other discipline as somehow possessing the real."[50] In Peter's analysis, literary scholars sought access to the "real" world of political engagement in the study of law, while legal scholars hoped literature would provide the law with access to the realities of human experience.[51] The taxonomies offered by Baron and Peters, however, are limited both in their representation of various approaches and in their capacity to capture the complexity of the historical and geographical breadth of the field, not all of which identifies itself explicitly with the law and literature movement.

One of the most significant developments in the field is its increasingly global orientation. Examining a variety of literary encounters with legal regimes, new and important research seeks to bring the unique dialogues between law and literature to a broader array of geopolitical contexts. Indeed, the field of colonial and postcolonial studies, within which much of this work is taking place, has always had an implicit focus on the twin impulses of law and literature. For example, Gauri Viswanathan's pioneering work on the legal and legislative arguments for introducing the discipline of English within the Indian university set the stage for understanding the intertwining of law and literature on the Indian subcontinent. Building on work such as Viswanathan's, Uday Chandra reads the hermeneutics of legal documents, paying "particular attention to continuities and shifts in their languages and concepts" in order to historically situate constructions of primitivity from British India to the present.[52] As these scholars show, employing literary methodologies to read legal texts and acts opens the law to interpretations that exceed both its intentionality and its narrow legal context.

More recently, this interest has been brought to the fore within postcolonial literary and legal studies, shifting the contours of the law and literature movement as a whole, and unsettling some of the more entrenched viewpoints about how its two constituent parts interact. Stephen Morton's sweeping analysis of state violence and its relationship to legal frameworks and justifications, for example, makes a cogent argument for thinking across various geopolitical spaces to look at common biopolitical structures. By examining invocations of states of emergency in Ireland, India, Kenya, Algeria, and Palestine, Morton "considers what the law-preserving violence of colonial governmentality can tell us about the founding violence, or law-making violence, of colonial sovereignty."[53] *States of Emergency* thus gives us the tools to think about violence as an organizing principle inherent in discrete, though related, legal formations across the postcolonial world. Nathan Hensley's *Forms of Empire* likewise focuses on the role of violence in legal and literary forms, tracing its development within the realm of the Victorian imagination. Grounding his readings of Victorian literature within a richly researched framework of imperial legal discourse, Hensley exposes the constitutive violence at the heart of the liberal state's self-conception. Hensley's essential contribution to the burgeoning field of postcolonial law and literature performs the vital work of demystifying the logic of imperial governmentality while also revealing its networks across discursive contexts.

Both Hensley and Morton, in different ways, focus on the legal and literary rhetoric that authorizes colonial violence. Equally important, however, is the discourse of nonviolence that has been used to describe the British colonization of the subcontinent. From the popular notion that the East India Company was a primarily mercantile operation (despite its sizeable armies and frequent military campaigns), to the idea that decolonization occurred exclusively as a result of civil disobedience (despite numerous armed conflicts), the idea of nonviolence has played a powerful role in shaping the imagination of the colonial encounter in India from its inception to its end. Much of the logic underlying claims to nonviolence is rooted in the belief that the "rule of law" was the driving force of Britain's colonial pursuits during the era of the Raj. This mythology of *Pax Britannica* secured through the "rule of law" is implicit in literary and legal texts alike, of the nineteenth century and beyond.

Yet, as *Colonial Law in India and the Victorian Imagination* also recognizes, the imagination of justice as implicitly nonviolent often obscures the law's violent impulses. As my discussion of criminality and personhood in Chapters 1 and 2 reflects, legal frameworks for recognizing subjectivity have profound effects on subjection to state violence such as penal transport and execution. Within this context, the question of who can make the transition from symbolic to real personhood has material consequences. While in the law and in literature the Indian criminal is consigned to serve as a figure of deterrence, the English criminal is allowed to emerge as a rehabilitated human. In both the novel and the appeal, legal and literary representations have traveled along a common trajectory that evolves out of a shared colonial ideology. Similarly, in Chapters 3 and 4, we see how reframing historical narratives around normative Western temporalities reorients matters of worth, value, and identity. And, lastly, in Chapters 5 and 6 we encounter the contrast between the law's violent suppression of the affective dimensions of adoption and Eliot's more sympathetic depiction of adoptive love. In each of the thematic pairings, the law's narrative prospectively casts its colonial subjects as incapable of fulfilling the promise of the literary imagination. Evolving beside the logic of the law, the literature of the period often affirms colonial law's disciplinary impulses by imagining a more generous set of possibilities for English lives.

What this book shows, then, is that legal and literary texts share a similar subtext that is rooted in the literary origins of colonial law. In *Archaeology of Babel: The Colonial Foundation of the Humanities*, Siraj Ahmed enables us to see just how humanistic inquiry in the nineteenth century advanced along the same axis as the normativization of colonial law. In particular, Ahmed shows how "late eighteenth-century colonial scholars had already reorganized Indian society on a philological model" by choosing particular religious narratives, or literature, as the basis of Indian law.[54] These philologists "decided which religious manuscripts would become authoritative; translated, edited, and printed them; and made their precepts binding law."[55] In this way, Ahmed argues, "the historical mission of philology reached fulfillment with the establishment of colonial law."[56] Building on works such as Ahmed's, *Colonial Law in India and the Victorian Imagination* traces the ways in which legal cases and novels work within a shared cultural logic that buttresses, and often endorses, colonial motives and methodologies. As I show, aesthetic representations emerge out of, and in relation to, the organizational strategies of the law.

While crucial conversations have been inaugurated by Morton, Hensley, Ahmed, and others, postcolonial approaches have also encountered resistance from within the law and literature interdiscipline. And, perhaps as a result, a large body of work that brings law and literature into conversation with postcolonial studies has yet to develop.[57] Elizabeth Anker has suggested that "the dominant horizons of postcolonial theory have begun to appear increasingly circumscribed and constraining."[58] Yet Anker's critique of postcolonial theory's methodology, which she distills to its affinity with poststructuralism, also sidelines many of its political interventions. [59] In her more recent work, Anker takes aim at legal scholarship and literary texts that interrogate the law's troubled history of racism in the aftermath of colonization and slavery. In Anker's view, such approaches to law and literature often represent the law as "constitutively fraudulent and corrupt," resulting in "inaccurate, simplistic, and exaggerated accounts of law that miss or gainsay the nuances of its real-world operations."[60] Curiously, Anker focuses her criticism substantially on M. NourbeSe Philip's *Zong!*, a poetic dramatization of the eighteenth-century legal case in which the owners of the titular slave ship sought an insurance payment for the 130 enslaved people whom they murdered by drowning in 1781. The poem critiques, in part, the English legal system's willingness to consider the merits of the shipping company's claim. Without elaborating on how the case may be read otherwise, Anker dismisses what she sees as Philip's "affectively charged denunciation of the legal system," the likes of which, she argues "can encourage reductive, unidimensional, and clichéd understandings of law that downplay or neglect its virtues and accomplishments."[61] In my view, however, the complicated work of deciphering and interrogating the law's historical and present failures in relation to questions of race is both necessary and enabling. Sadly, despite its inclusion in a volume entitled *New Directions in Law and Literature*, there is nothing "new" in Anker's move to characterize a forceful critique of the law's racism as "reductive" or "simplistic."

In fact, the suspicion that Anker accurately identifies within postcolonial readings of the law reflects the difficult and highly complex questions – of access to legal remedies and subjection to legal policies and prohibitions – that structure the broader conversation about the law.[62] Examining the incongruencies between the field of legal and literary possibilities available to English and colonial subjects is often disheartening. The purpose of this recognition, however, is not stagnant pessimism, but an endeavor to use the analysis of history in the service of what José Muñoz identifies as "the idea of hope, which is both a critical affect and a methodology."[63] Actualizing the luminous "horizon" of hope, however, also involves contending with the past and its continuities with the future and present. This is not simply to document and explain historical and present failures of liberalism and its associated legal maneuvers, but to imagine new ways of intervening in them.[64] This involves conceding that the paradigmatic subject of postcolonial studies is one whose lived, and embodied, experience has been both actively and passively written out of cultural institutions such as law and literature. Consequently, a postcolonial approach to the literary qualities of judicial opinions begins with the acknowledgment that both the law and literature are forms of discourse that produced colonial subjectivity often in the absence of any material encounter. As colonial administrator Thomas Babington Macaulay's central role in drafting both the Indian Penal Code and the "Minute on Indian Education" attests, the law often works in concert with literature and other cultural forms. In foregrounding these concerns, my project be can be understood as part of a recent trend of turning away from the old dichotomies of "law and literature" toward a more open inquiry into shared ideological operations that take place at the intersection of law, literature, cultural theory, and history.[65]

At the same time, postcolonial approaches to law and literature are also evolving alongside scholarship on Victorian literature and law, bringing the two interrelated areas of study into dialogue.[66] Within Victorian studies, attention to various domestic and colonial sites of violence has called familiar narratives about the "Age of Equipoise" into question. Jan-Melissa Schramm's argument "that there is plenty of evidence to suggest that the mid-Victorian period was indeed characterised by social inequality, anxiety, and constitutional disequilibrium" makes it possible to think about the linkages between unsteady legal structures in Britain and their colonial counterparts throughout the Empire.[67] If the law serves to quell the perception of instability that Schramm identifies, the novel provides a kind of alibi for such legal endeavors. Indeed, as Jonathan

Grossman notes, the storytelling structures of law and literature in the Victorian era were deeply entwined. For this reason, Grossman's work "is about how readers and authors became immersed in this trial-oriented culture as never before and about how their novels were shaped by the complementary and competing storytelling structure of the law courts."[68] Within this growing body of work on Victorian literature and law, a particularly rich area of study has emerged around literary representations of gender and sexuality in relation to the law. Christine Krueger's *Reading for the Law*, for example, traces the relationship between law and literary feminism, and Sharon Marcus examines relationships between women in Victorian law and literature in *Between Women*. While the issue of colonialism skirts the margins of many of these and other texts, with the exception of Hensley's *Forms of Empire*, it is not the central point of interest for any of them.

Adding to this body of work, *Colonial Law in India and the Victorian Imagination* focuses on the colonial era in order to examine how literature and the law share similar impulses, and are often motivated by common goals. Toward this end, this volume examines the larger historical forces that animate legal and literary production in the nineteenth century, and analyzes in turn the effects that those productions have had on spheres such as sociality, culture, the economy, criminality, sexuality, and kinship.

Reading the Archives

In this respect, I look to the archive of colonial jurisprudence to read the process by which narrative,[69] under the mask of facts and evidence, shaped what it was possible to imagine. I argue that colonial jurisprudence – especially in the appeals process – was instrumental in rendering real the fictive life of Empire. Mouthed in the voice of the law, fictions about Indians came to be transformed into realities for them. Thinking about the legal opinion as a narrative, or short story, thus helps to interpret the performative nature of a judicial event.

In 1985, Gayatri Spivak proposed to "read" the archives of the Rani of Sirmur through the lens of literary theory.[70] "To me," Spivak writes, "literature and the archives seem complicit in that they are both a cross-hatching of condensations, a traffic in telescoped symbols, that can only too easily be read as each other's repetition-with-a-displacement."[71] Since Spivak's rejoinder to debates inaugurated within the discipline of history by Dominic LaCapra and Hayden White, the critic's relationship to the archive has continued to evolve. Natalie Zemon Davis' seminal work

Fiction in the Archives makes the case that "the 'fictional' aspect" of the archives should "be the center of analysis."[72] "By 'fictional,'" Davis clarifies, "I do not mean their feigned elements, but rather, using the other and broader sense of the root word *fingere*, their forming, shaping, and molding elements: the crafting of a narrative."[73] Following Davis's enticement to look for and read stories, I approach the legal archives as narrative texts. Building on the foundational work of theorists such as Ann Stoler, Ranajit Guha, Lisa Lowe, and Gayatri Spivak on the fictions of the colonial archives more broadly, *Colonial Law in India and the Victorian Imagination* explores the fictionality of the law and the narratives enacted in legal proceedings.

In framing colonial judicial opinions as narratives, I am invested in probing the cases and their judgments for their imaginative afterlives rather than for their historical facticity or their legal rationale. My purpose in doing so is threefold: (1) to highlight the constructedness of both the narratives themselves and any interpretations we may attach to them, (2) to examine the ways in which these narratives served to shape the imaginary worlds of Empire, and (3) to reveal the plot structures and narrative arcs that underwrite the material practices of the law. The legal opinions are significant, then, not simply for what they reveal about what the British judges and lawmakers thought of Indians, but rather for their ability to reach back in time and reframe "tradition" in order to influence how Indians would come to think of themselves.

In the context of criminal law, the Indian Penal Code continues to inflect the contours of Indian public and private lives, legislating still over broad questions of sociality and subjectivity. Until recently, for example, section 377 of the Penal Code that dates back to 1860 was invoked to justify continued discrimination against queer subjects.[74] In 2009 the Delhi High Court, presiding over the case of *Naz Foundation* v. *Govt. of NCT of Delhi* ruled that in criminalizing consensual sex between adults, Section 377 violated the Constitution of India. However, in 2013 the Supreme Court of India overturned the Delhi High Court decision, controversially arguing that the matter was of parliamentary concern rather than judicial. In February 2016, the Supreme Court once again agreed to hear a petition against Section 377 brought by the Naz Foundation before a five-member bench since it involves matters of constitutionality. On September 6, 2018, the Indian Supreme Court finally struck down Section 377. The role of the law in shaping imaginative and lived possibilities in postcolonial India is crucial in this instance, particularly because few cases of homosexuality have actually been prosecuted in India in recent history. Rather, the legal prohibition serves to structure social norms, ensuring that an aura of illegality, immorality, fear, and shame continues to be cast over expressions of queerness in the public imaginary. The archive of colonial law consequently functions less as a relic of past practices, but rather as a means of contextualizing present cultural formations. In short, the legacy of Section 377 does more than simply police what individuals *do*, in order to effectively police whom they *are* or can imagine being.[75] By turning toward the narrative underpinnings of instances of legal reasoning, I aim to engage the fictions that continue to undergird how the law shapes materiality.

Legal Fictions: The Law as Text

The role of narrative in the law is neatly captured in the concept of the legal fiction. Historically, a legal fiction was "chiefly applied to those feigned statements of fact which the practice of the courts authorized to be alleged by a plaintiff in order to bring his case within the scope of the law or the jurisdiction of the court, and which the defendant was not allowed to disprove" (*OED*). A legal fiction is, therefore, an assertion that the court takes as true for the purposes of the matter at hand. In English law, legal fictions were used to craft unexpected points of entry into cases. For example, a legal fiction may be a hypothetical possibility that served to open up new ways of approaching and thinking about the facts of a case. The legal fiction, in this sense, is a metaphor that served as an explanatory device. The interesting quality of the legal fiction is that it makes use of a known fabrication in order to bring about a material reality in the form of an actionable judgment. An iconic example from American law is the legal fiction that corporations are people. Legal fictions also nicely demonstrate and reveal the performative nature of the law, insofar as the decisions that arise out of legal fictions convert fiction into reality through the force of their utterance.[76] For our purposes here, the concept of the legal fiction serves as a reminder not only of the narrative at work in administering the law, but of the ambiguous relationship to truth that sustains both fictional narratives and the law. The legal fiction also helps to reveal how ancillary structures of colonial ideology become central to the narrative of legal reasoning.

In both England and the colonies, advocates of the law's rationalism sought to diminish the influence of fiction on the law. Legal positivists such as Jeremy Bentham, for example, wished to eliminate what he described as "the pestilential breath of Fiction," which he believed "poisons the sense of every instrument it comes near."[77] While Bentham's critique was of the specific practice of using legal fictions in the common law tradition, his wariness of the fictionality of the law was more expansive. As Robert Yelle notes, "Bentham's proposal for the 'codification' of the law, a term he invented, was closely connected with his critique of linguistic 'fictions' that were to be expelled from the legal code, or even from language itself. His goal was to fix the meaning of terms and produce a language that was not only unambiguous, but also devoid of synonyms."[78] Bentham's distaste for the ambiguity of fiction was thus not limited to its use in jurisprudence, but extended to include the disorder and turns of imagination in language itself.

In an effort to rid the law of its "pernicious fictions," Bentham sought to develop a "pannomion," or a uniform code of law based on scientific rationalism that would remove the ambiguity and irrationality he believed plagued the common law tradition. While Bentham's plans for a pannomion were sidelined in England, in the colonies his ideas formed the basis of the Indian Penal Code. The attempt to rid the law of its uncertainties and ellipses might seem to bring greater clarity and objectivity; however, it also fueled a more authoritarian aspect of the law by limiting the terms by which it could be queried and challenged through imaginative interpretation. In India, the implementation of codified law certainly heightened colonial legal sovereignty. Yet, as the cases I read reveal, despite the attempt to disentangle law from fiction, not only do foundational fictions remain in the law, they constitute the narrative terrain upon which acts of law are grounded. In fact, the legal cases I examine can be readily mapped onto familiar genres of fiction, such as the bildungsroman, the mystery, and the realist novel.

Canonical nineteenth-century novels can thus be read as literary analogs for the kinds of representations I argue colonial law generated. Chapters 1 and 2, for example, approach the question of criminality from literary and legal perspectives to show how the movement toward rehabilitation in England corresponded to an opposite impulse in India, where capital punishment and penal transport were commonplace in the nineteenth century. Similarly, in Chapters 3 and 4, Indian notions of temporality become central to the philosophy of history unfolded in the mystery genre. Finally, the questions of kinship and inheritance raised by Begum Sumroo that I examine in Chapter 5 demonstrate how colonial law dealt with some of the issues raised by the unconventional parental relationships that George Eliot explores in her adoption novels. In this respect, genres of fiction that were central to the narration of English national identity became ready templates for the story of colonial law. Yet, unlike the fictions of law that were officially recognized as such by the courts, fictional fabrications in the colonial legal context were not openly acknowledged as untrue. Rather, as I show, fiction taken for reality was often the founding basis for the sovereignty of colonial law. In addition to the legal appeals I discuss, more prominent narratives of sati and thuggee, for example, created the ideological subtext for the exercise of colonial juridical and political sovereignty. In effect, colonial law relied on a double metaphor: the fiction invoked to adjudicate the case at hand, and the larger structuring fiction of the rational sovereignty of colonial law. By engaging the narrativity of the colonial legal appeal, my goal is to add a new dimension to the existing body of scholarship that primarily engages the legal archive through history, and the literary archive through fiction or the novel.

In its turn toward the literary formations of the law, *Colonial Law in India and the Victorian Imagination* supplements, and complicates, important recent contributions to the analysis of colonial law. The works of Radhika Singha, Indrani Chatterjee, Lauren Benton, Elizabeth Kolsky, Rachel Sturman, and Mitra Sharafi, for example, are grounded more firmly in historical methodologies and, as such, provide a crucial archaeology of the contested archives of colonial law. While building upon this body of scholarship, *Colonial Law and the Victorian Imagination* is not concerned with the historicity of the archive *per se*. Rather, the legal archive provides a snapshot of the turns of *imagination* that were necessary to broker the sovereignty of colonial law. Despite its relationship to fiction, however, the legal archive also documents the processes by which material realities are imagined, produced, managed, and sedimented. By analyzing the role of narrative in these material and psychic processes, I explore the fictions that animate acts of law.

The Archive

"Colonial archives," as Ann Stoler writes, "were both sites of the imaginary *and* institutions that fashioned histories as they concealed, revealed, and reproduced the power of the state."[79] Cautioning against the too-quick tendency to read against the archival grain, Stoler asserts that we "need to read for its regularities, for its logic of recall, for its densities and distributions, for its consistencies of misinformation, omission, and mistake – *along* the archival grain."[80] In taking up the legal archive as narrative, I aim to approach the opinions generated by the Privy Council "not as sites of knowledge retrieval but of knowledge production."[81] The legal opinion is a unique form of narrative because it quite explicitly straddles the line between imagination and reality. Each case, founded upon a fictional conceit, reveals something different about Empire's cast of mind.

I look to the literariness of colonial law to emphasize the law's shared capacity with literature to break down the firm distinction between imagination and lived experience, reader and agent.[82] As Wolfgang Iser notes, "in reading we think the thoughts of another person."[83] Though guided by the text, "It is the reader who unfolds the network of possible connections, and it is the reader who then makes a selection from that network."[84] For Iser, the act of reading is an ethical negotiation, an opening of oneself to the thoughts and life of another.

Likewise, for Gayatri Spivak, "Literary reading teaches us to learn from the singular and the unverifiable. It is not that literary reading does not generalize. It is just that those generalizations are not on evidentiary ground."[85] The "singular and the unverifiable" quality that Spivak assigns to literature, and by extension literary reading, is one aspect of the ethical force of texts. Literature breaches the boundary between subject and object, individual and collective, as does, of course, the law. Yet, in the types of literary readings of legal opinions with which I am concerned here, something in excess of either the singular or the collective is at stake. In its capacity to act as a sovereign pronouncement, the legal opinion takes something singular and unverifiable (for example, evidence used to adjudicate a particular case) and makes it systemic and codifiable. Privy Council judges essentially were tasked with consuming narratives and converting their interpretations into material judgments.

In this sense, what is interesting and remarkable about the judicial opinion in colonial law is its capacity to adopt and transform the ethical impetus of fiction. If fiction's value is that it is always unverifiable and in being so, it holds a radical skepticism of empirical claims – the law's rendering of fiction as fact in the colonies reverses this effect. The legal opinion verifies and validates a particular reading while simultaneously invalidating others. Legal opinions are thus precisely those kinds of narratives that hover between facticity and fictionality to produce new forms of obstinate sovereignty that shaped colonial life in enduring ways.

In English literature of the eighteenth and nineteenth centuries, as Edward Said remarks, references to Empire are both everywhere and nowhere. Aside from a few exceptions (Aphra Behn's *Oroonoko*, William Thackeray's *Vanity Fair*, Walter Scott's *The Surgeon's Daughter*, and Wilkie Collins's *Moonstone*, for example) the literary presence of Empire remains sparse and oblique in the works of prominent writers from the

Restoration through the Victorian periods. In fact, Empire as a sustained and overt theme in literature did not gain significant momentum until the twentieth century in the hands of authors such as Rudyard Kipling, Joseph Conrad, George Orwell, and E. M. Forster.[86] That something so foundational to British material life and national consciousness should be so scant in its cultural production is striking. If the literary archives falter in their representation of Britain's colonial activities, perhaps we must look elsewhere for Empire's fictions.

Periodization

All of the legal cases discussed within this volume were adjudicated between the 1830s and the 1870s. While *The Queen* v. *Eduljee Byramjee* was relatively short (with the original trial and appeal occurring in 1844 and 1846, respectively), the other two cases have more prolonged histories with various court proceedings unfolding over several decades. Begum Sumroo's treaties with the East India Company, and her attempts to bequeath her fortune to her adopted son David Ochterlony Dyce Sombre, began before the 1830s but were not finally resolved until 1872, well after both the Begum and Dyce Sombre's deaths. Similarly, the Privy Council heard *Ramaswamy Aiyan* v. *Venkata Achari* in 1863, but the series of disputes leading up to the appeal to the JCPC began in 1835. This historical period is also responsible for much of the literature that I consider. While temporal proximity does not necessarily suggest shared political goals, both the literary and legal texts arise from within a similar epistemic environment.

The periodization of this study centers on two primary events, the Government of India Acts of 1833 and 1858. The Act of 1833, also known as the Charter Act, extended and reframed the East India Company's royal charter, converting it from a commercial enterprise to an administrative one. The Act consolidated the various presidencies under the authority of the newly created governor general of India and instituted the Law Commission with the intention of streamlining legal processes and oversight. As discussed earlier, the Law Commission ultimately would endeavor to develop a set of codified laws to bring the disarray of multiple legal systems into uniform cohesion. These acts bracket the novels and legal cases that this volume explores and provide a framework for situating the literature in reference to the law.

The Government of India Act of 1858 transferred the administration of India from the East India Company (under the regulation of Parliament) to the Crown. The Queen's Proclamation to the "Princes, Chiefs and People of India" bestowed upon "the Natives of Our Indian Territories" the same rights as "all Our other Subjects." While pledging to be faithful to the "Customs of India," the Proclamation also promised that "all shall alike enjoy the equal impartial protection of the Law." The tension between the rhetorical aims of this promise and the material legal history is the object of my analysis in this project. To this end, a note on organization is warranted. I have chosen to organize each chapter pairing in chronological order, which has resulted in the discussions of the legal cases preceding the novels. This does not represent any primacy accorded to the law over literature, nor does it privilege a directionality of influence beyond the temporal fact of one instance preceding the other.

On Appeal: The Docket

The main body of the text is organized into three sections focused on the themes of criminality, temporality, and inheritance. Each section comprises two chapters that deal with legal cases and novels respectively. The first chapter, "'Power Able to Overawe Them All': Criminality and the Uses of Fear," begins with a discussion of criminality in *The Queen* v. *Eduljee Byramjee* (1846). At the heart of the case was the question of whether criminal convictions could be appealed to the Privy Council. On the one hand, to limit appeals to the Queen would implicitly serve to undermine her absolute sovereignty. On the other hand, granting the right to appeal would undermine the authority of the colonial courts and intervene in the social, political, and economic uses to which Indian criminals were put. Also in this chapter, I show how the fiction of Indian criminality became useful to the exercise of British sovereignty. In many ways, the specter of Indian criminality served to motivate British unity in the colonies. W. H. Sleeman's highly influential portrait of "thuggee" culture, for example, became a kind of standard-bearer for assertions of British moral, cultural, and intellectual superiority over what was seen as the inherent degeneracy of the Indians. At the same time, the Indian criminal body performed a crucial material function in the quotidian operations of Empire. One of the central arguments of the judicial opinion, for example, was that the disciplinary value of capital punishment would be undermined if appeals were allowed. Moreover, as the last ready supply of working bodies after the abolition of slavery, and the end of British penal transport, Indian criminals provided essential physical labor for the territorial expansion of

Empire. The rhetoric of Indian degeneracy, then, was central to both the ideological and material terms by which the British consolidated and expanded their sovereignty.

Turning from the legal instance of Eduljee Byramjee to the fictional realm, Chapter 2, "The Social Life of Crime: Charles Dickens's *Great Expectations* and Philip Meadows Taylor's *Confessions of a Thug*" reads the oppositional evolution of criminal justice in England and India by comparing the two novels. The novel's thematic concerns with criminality, I show, are inextricable from their relationship to the generic qualities of the bildungsroman, bringing together representations of individual and national development. I begin with the observation that the movement toward rehabilitation and the humanization of the criminal in nineteenth-century England occurs in tandem with the rise of corporal punishment and penal transportation in India. Taking the two novels as instances of this contradictory impulse, I examine the figure of the thug as a cipher for racialized fears of Indian criminality. In particular, I look at representations of paternity and masculinity within both novels. I show that Abel Magwitch becomes humanized in Dickens's novel by taking on the mantle of fatherhood for Pip. By contrast, Ameer Ali is condemned for his paradigmatic inability to foster a viable childhood. I argue that criminality emerges within a Victorian matrix of race and patriarchy in which to be a father, or father figure, is to be properly human.

The idea of Indian degeneracy or stagnancy was crucial as well to the case of *Ramaswamy Aiyan* v. *Venkata Achari* (1863), which is the focus of Chapter 3. While the actual substance of the case concerned the distribution of rights and profits associated with temple management, I suggest that the Privy Council's engagement with the case served a larger ideological function. The petty squabble between the various sects of Brahmins functioned in the case as a metaphor for the decadent system of caste itself. Over the course of the chapter, I show how the very existence of the dispute became evidence of the dysfunction of Indian modes of social and temporal organization. Highlighting the political ramifications of narrative constructions, the Privy Council's judgment worked to render Indian history irremediably tainted, and Indian religion as riddled with superstition and irrationality. The case thus reveals the ambivalent interactions between Indian social and temporal organization and British concepts of historicity. Though the case deals explicitly with questions of religion, I suggest that the force of the legal opinion extends to secular temporalities and teleologies as well.

Chapter 4, "On Time: How Fiction Writes History in Wilkie Collins's *The Moonstone*," shows how the novel subtly reinforces the principles put forth in the judicial opinion. Written just five years after *Ramaswamy Aiyan* v. *Venkata Achari* was decided by the Privy Council, *The Moonstone* reflects many similar concerns with centering English modernity, especially by way of comparison with colonies such as India. Echoing the timeless quality assigned to Indian history evinced in *Ramaswamy*, the novel's Prologue notes that for "generation after generation, the successors of the three Brahmins watched their priceless Moonstone, night and day" over the ages "until the first years of the eighteenth Christian century saw the reign of Aurungzebe, Emperor of the Moguls," under whose "command havoc and rapine were let loose once more among the temples of the worship of Brahmah."[87] Drawing on Tzvetan Todorov's discussion of the mystery genre, I show how the novel invokes oppositional teleologies for India and Britain, often playing up sectarian tensions and Brahminism in the Indian context. Echoing the discussion of religion in Chapter 3, Collins's novel portrays the salutary effects of British solutions to Indian problems and shortcomings.

Chapter 5, "The Begum's Fortune: Adoption, Inheritance, and Private Property," examines eighteenth- and nineteenth-century inheritance laws and practices in India in order to analyze the intersections between state power, gender, and colonial policies of annexation. In particular, I focus on the case of *Troup* v. *East India Company* (1857), which involves the estate of Begum Sumroo, one of the wealthiest and most unconventional women in colonial India. Sumroo, who did not have biological heirs, sought to transfer her wealth to her son through adoption. In a case that revolved around the distinction between private and state property for native principalities, the colonial state declared that the Begum's property was subject to annexation. The annexation inaugurated a series of legal cases that unfolded over the unfortunate life of her adopted heir David Ochterlony Dyce Sombre. Taking the case of Begum Sumroo as my starting point, I explore the ways in which the normativization of Western notions of inheritance and property worked to undergird the expansion of Empire. I use the Begum's case to expose the mechanisms through which, in order for colonial rule to take effect, sexual normativity was heightened to secure the goals of territorial expansion, thus yoking the notion of private property to various controls over bodily and sexual privacy. Assertions of colonial sovereignty thus sought to disrupt unruly forms of sexual and social organization in order to more efficiently manage both affective relations and property ownership.

The final Chapter 6 continues this focus on the theme of adoption by considering the portrayal of adoption in the novels of George Eliot. At a time when, as the case of Begum Sumroo shows, questions of filial dependence or entitlements were being rigidly regulated in the colony, writers such as Charles Dickens, Charlotte and Emily Brontë, and George Eliot imbued adoptive relations with special sentimental and social value to expansively reform ideas of how family, home, and kinship were understood. So, for instance, this chapter shows how Eliot's *Silas Marner* (1861) champions the surrogate parental relation over wealth and property inheritance precisely when the Sumroo case legally restricts these ties in the Indian context. Yet, even for Eliot, when adoption raises the specter of racial or national difference as in *Daniel Deronda* (1876) – and even in *Romola* (1863), *The Spanish Gypsy* (1868), or *Felix Holt* (1866) – kinship remains ancestral, its hallmark being genealogical and not open to the caprice of nurture. At the same time, novels of adoption offer new ways of imagining the centrality of the individual in the family, and, by extension, within the nation. Expanding on earlier discussions about the rise of the individual in bildungsroman and mystery novels, I show that Eliot's realist novels both confirm the coherence between individualism and Englishness, and challenge the normative terms upon which such individualism is typically predicated. What this chapter thus clarifies is a contrapuntal relationship between law and literature around the question of adoption. Some of the most celebrated nineteenth-century English novels use adoption to break with the family romance plot, upending legal assumptions about rights and descent. However, a racial shadow persists, as even in the imaginative realm, adoption falters when tasked with miscegenation. Such shadows, as *Colonial Law in India and the Victorian Imagination* argues throughout, gain coherent form in colonial law.

PART I

Criminality

CHAPTER 1

"Power Able to Overawe Them All"

Criminality and the Uses of Fear

> Also, because there be some that, taking pleasure in contemplating their own power in the acts of conquest, which they pursue farther than their security requires, if others, that otherwise would be glad to be at ease within the modest bounds, should not by invasion increase their power, they would not be able long time, by standing only on their defence, to subsist . . . Again, men have no pleasure, but on the contrary a great deal of grief, in keeping company where there is no power able to overawe them all.[1]

> In the darkest region of the political field, the condemned man represents the symmetrical, inverted figure of the king.[2]

In the latter years of the nineteenth century, the government of India began publishing *The Gazetteer of the Bombay Presidency*, a multivolume encyclopedia of the history, geography, and culture of the presidency. Volume 14, on *Tha'na: Places of Interest*, highlights the semirural district in Maharashtra, which is "prettily placed on the west shore of the Sálsette creek, in wooded country, between the Yeur range of Sálsette hills on the west and the steep picturesque Persik peaks on the mainland to the south-east."[3] The entry catalogs idyllically situated fisher villages, a vegetable market, a Hindu temple, and "the Collector's house, a fine double-storied building with a large garden."[4] As we read on, we learn of the "public library" and the "new Maráthi school" and a "wide park-like esplanade crossed by broad tree-lined roads" that is surrounded by "well shaded European houses."[5] "This pleasant esplanade," the account tells us, "with the double-bridged creek and the wild Persik hills to the east, and wooded rice-lands and hill-sides to the west, forms a pretty scene, which especially during the winter rains, is in many points more like an English than an Indian view."[6] The "municipality was established in 1862," and aside from a few bouts of cholera and a persistent shortage of drinking water, life in the town seems fairly unremarkable.[7] After a short discussion of the pre-European history of a fort, and its conversion to a jail, we are told

"In 1844 the Judge, while visiting the jail with a few attendants, was seized by the prisoners. They passed a rope round his neck, and were on the point of hanging him when succour came."[8] Amid the otherwise unexceptional description, the scene of violence is jarring, both for its unexpectedness and its brevity. Immediately following the mention of this incident, the placid narrative resumes, with a discussion of renovations to the prison that began in 1869 and were completed in 1876. In fact, what is most remarkable about the relation of the event is how unremarkable it seems. At the same time, it is one of the few mentions of people in a narrative otherwise occupied almost exclusively with the landscape and scenery. "In the jail garden, laid as a pavement to a summer-house," for example, "are some inscribed Portuguese grave-stones, which were found in clearing away one of the fort buildings" and to "the west and south-west of the jail is the esplanade, which, in 1776, was formed by order of the Court of Directors by clearing away the houses."[9] A footnote meticulously directs us to the appropriate source if we are interested in learning more about the inscriptions on the Portuguese gravestones. No information is forthcoming about either the prisoners who attacked the judge, or the inhabitants of the homes that were cleared away to make room for the esplanade. In a narrative that makes little mention of the Indians living in the town, the inclusion of the encounter in the jail is all the more striking. The off-handed intrusion of violence into the quotidian scene of a judge's visit to a prison facility, though, is emblematic of more pervasive British fears of Indian criminality. Admittedly, we do not know what inspired the attack by the prisoners, or what, if any, punishment they received as a result of their attempt, but we do know that the eruption of fear and violence routinely punctuates the sight lines of colonial narratives. While in this instance the judge experienced the frightening episode, most often it was the prisoners who were afraid.

This chapter explores the uses of fear across a range of colonial situations, from the management of criminals to the exercise of sovereignty. In particular, I will examine the ways in which personal experiences of fear intersect with its political uses. Whether passively experienced, incited as a strategy, or used as tool for discipline and control, fear is an essential affect to colonialism. Over the course of the chapter, I show how fear functions in relation to the various positionalities of the subjects experiencing it. Within this context, my broad aim is to think through the relational positions, vis-à-vis fear, of subject, sovereign and colonial criminal. The Indian criminal's experience of fear sheds light on the exercise of colonial sovereignty across a range of economic and cultural spheres. Drawing on political philosophy and affect theory, I will bring broader questions of sovereignty to bear on a discussion of the intimate and quotidian experiences of fear in the context of the case of *The Queen* v. *Eduljee Byramjee* (1846).

My discussion of this landmark case that decided whether appeals against felony convictions could be made to the Judicial Committee of the Privy Council (JCPC) has three main threads. The first focuses on the affect of fear in the management of criminality in colonial India. Taking Hobbes's political philosophy and its later iterations through the nineteenth century, as a starting point, I show that the exercise of absolutism, and the principle of fear upon which it rests, is essential to both the administration of colonial criminal justice systems and the logic laid out by the Privy Counsellors in their review of *The Queen* v. *Eduljee Byramjee*. Because fear is oriented toward the future, it has the capacity to bring lived materialities into alignment with imaginative possibilities, both as a deterrent against criminality and as a vehicle for realizing certain forms of subjectivity under colonialism. The second thread relates colonial theories of fear to their practical application by examining the uses to which convicted criminals were put. Convict workers, for example, were economically profitable, while also serving the larger social function of instigating fear. As public examples of the perils of breaking the law, transported and executed criminals materially and ideologically shaped colonial subjectivity. Individual criminals became imaginative stand-ins for Indian society at large, thus expanding the reach of the disciplinary apparatus of the criminal justice system to the general population. Finally, the third strand of the chapter evaluates this slippage between the criminal and the colonial subject in order to examine the particular type of subjectivity that the JCPC relied upon to justify its decision. Despite the implicit differences between the rights of British citizens and colonial subjects, I show, the JCPC opinion depends upon equivalence between the two categories. What seems like a simple comparison of British and Indian rights and their associated legal processes, therefore, is more properly understood as a simile, in which two significantly different contexts are made to appear commensurate. Underscoring the rhetorical operation of the simile, in turn, brings the fictionality of equivalent rights into sharper relief. Ultimately, while the judicial opinion relates the justification for denying appeals in cases of felony conviction, the underlying narrative reveals the various subtle uses that the affect of fear serves in securing the rationale for the JCPC's legal judgment.

Representing the Defendants

The case *The Queen* v. *Eduljee Byramjee*, which exemplifies many of these nuances of colonial criminality, was heard before the Privy Council of Queen Victoria in 1846. Although the main issue to be decided was whether Indian subjects had a right to appeal in criminal cases, the arguments offered by both sides reveal the biopolitical stakes of claims to fear within the arena of criminal justice in colonial India. In order to fully consider the 1846 case, I begin by way of a discussion of the case that instigated that appeal, an 1844 trial in the Supreme Court of Judicature at Bombay.

In 1844, Eduljee Byramjee and seventeen other Parsis were brought to trial for the murder of another Parsi named Muncher-jee Hormusjee. Of the eighteen charged (one as the primary murderer and the other seventeen as accessories), a European jury returned a verdict of guilty against ten and acquitted the rest. The individual who was found to be primarily responsible for the killing was immediately put to death, and the rest of those convicted, including Eduljee Byramjee, were sent to Singapore where they would serve as convict workers for the remainder of their life sentences. In reading *The Queen* v. *Eduljee Byramjee*, I will consider the representations that emerge of the characters involved, as well as the broader representations of Indian criminality, as discussed earlier, that were circulating in the British public imagination in the nineteenth century.[10]

Eduljee Byramjee, on whose behalf the 1846 petition for appeal was filed, enters into the Privy Council legal proceedings as "a tent-maker, late of *Bombay*, but now a prisoner at *Singapore*, undergoing sentence of transportation."[11] The only other information about Eduljee Byramjee recorded in the case is that on the July 17, 1844, he "and sixteen others were charged as accessories to the murder" of Muncher-jee Hormusjee.[12] Eduljee Byramjee is introduced first by his proper name, second by his profession, third by his place of residence, and finally by his status as criminal. Of all the identifying characteristics, the most relevant to the documents that represent him is his status as criminal. Extrajudicial records reveal little else about Eduljee Byramjee or any of his codefendants.

From the outset, the verdict in the 1844 Bombay trial was controversial. A central issue was how many, and which, of the men charged with the crime actually carried out the murder. The convictions, secured through eyewitness testimony, were suspect from the start. While one witness claims to have seen the group of eighteen men carrying out the killing, many of the accused, including Eduljee Byramjee, were able to produce alibis.

Moreover, several of those who were acquitted obtained their release through offering the same alibi as others who were convicted. In short, it appears that the case against Eduljee Byramjee, and the cohort tried with him, was rife with faulty and contradictory claims. As documented in *A Detailed Report of the Proceedings on the Trial of the Eighteen Parsee Prisoners for Murder, Before the Supreme Court, Bombay, on Wednesday, July 17, 1844*, the testimony offered by dozens of witnesses was both confusing and inconsistent. The coroner's report from an examination of the victim's body suggested that, contrary to some witness testimony, a single killer, or at least a much smaller group, might have been responsible.[13] And almost as interesting as the question of the accuracy of the verdict itself are the claims by which it was challenged. In addition to the forensic evidence provided by the coroner's report, the ability of one of the convicts, Nasserwanjee Cowasjee, to have committed the murder was contested on the basis of his being "a man of unwieldy size and grievously afflicted with elephantiasis."[14]

What seems to be clear is that there were two parties within the Parsi community who had some sort of long-standing rivalry that was apparently aided, or at least acknowledged, by various governmental and non-governmental British residents in Bombay. At the start of the fray, in the *Chabook* newspaper office, an unemployed Englishman, Mr. McKenzie, hearing from the soon-to-be murder victim that he was in fear of his life, dispatched a memorandum to Mr. Weavers, the local constable.[15] McKenzie was friends with both Eduljee and Munchee, one of the accused killers and his alleged victim.[16] The police, though seemingly aware of the situation as it was unfolding, did not respond to the memorandum summoning them. When the constable was called to the witness stand to reveal the contents of the memorandum sent to him by McKenzie, the defense attorneys objected and the constable said it had only little relevance to the case at hand, so it was not entered into the record.[17] Since the contents of the memorandum are lost to history, we cannot discern what role, if any, the British played in the moments leading up to the confrontation. Based on the narrative constructed by the trial records, then, it seems that the conflict originated as a dispute among a group of otherwise unremarkable petty criminals.

Of the eighteen charged, Eduljee Byramjee and Nasserwanjee Cowasjee were the only two defendants who had their own attorneys representing them. The others either shared attorneys or went undefended.[18] In his opening statement, Mr. Cochrane, Eduljee Byramjee's lawyer, cites forensic evidence, questions the motivations of the witnesses who testified against his client, and offers an alternative version of events that places Eduljee Byramjee and Nasserwanjee Cowasjee at a garden house two miles away from the scene of the crime. He then proceeds to call a series of witnesses, including four Englishmen, to testify on behalf of the "good character" of Eduljee Byramjee.[19] Despite the attorneys' efforts, the 1844 jury found ten of the defendants guilty, including Eduljee Byramjee and Nasserwanjee Cowasjee, sentencing four to be hung and six to be transported to Singapore. Upon local appeal, three of the four sentences of hanging were converted to transport. One defendant, Burjorjee Jamsetjee, also known as China Budla, was hung.

After the trial, during the local appeals process, further statements were gathered, but these were as inscrutable as the ones offered in the courtroom. Though the statements offer little to clarify what actually happened, they reveal a colorful cast of characters whose personalities seem keen and vibrant. One, in particular, stands out. Manuckchund Damodhur, also a prisoner in the Bombay Gaol at the time China Budla and the other defendants were being held, gave a statement to Mr. Le Geyt, the senior magistrate of police. In the statement, Damodhur says that China Budla, who was ultimately hanged for the murder, confessed to him that he named the larger group of Parsis as accessories to secure legal representation on his own behalf: "'By these people being caught, my business will be done. I shall be released.' He then said, 'These people are retaining barristers, if they don't get a barrister for me I shall mention all their names . . . I have got no money.'"[20] Damodhur, the informant, goes on to say that China Budla later admitted that he acted alone in the stabbing, but that two others, Bomna and Lim Buckra, were with him. Summing up his statement, Damodhur comments, "I did not tell this to any one, why should I? No one asked me."[21] A pang of conscience seems to have struck Damodhur, since an addendum to the statement given to the Magistrate, signed in his own hand, reads,

> It was my intention to have told this, and I went into the court for that purpose, after I heard of the sentence on Friday evening. I was in court when the sentence was passed. I was going to the bar to tell what I knew – this was while the judge was speaking to the prisoners. One Nowloo, not Nowloo Hulkaroo, but one of his party, said to me, 'What, you have just come out of the gaol and want to go in again?' I had first said, 'I am going to tell something.' I said this loud and he heard me. I was afraid, and went down stairs, and sat in the sheriff's office.[22]

If Damodhur's statement is truthful, the import is that nine innocent men were transported to Singapore because Damodhur was afraid to tell the judge that China Budla confessed to him that he had acted alone. In particular, Damodhur was fearful of going back to prison himself if he tried to help someone else.

Following the verdict, one of the convicted defendants, who was not represented by counsel, wrote a letter to the editor of the English language newspaper, *The Bombay Courier*. In it he says:

> Mr. Editor, I am one of those unfortunates who were doomed to pass the remainder of their natural lives in the land of exile. I am 'No. 16 (undefended), Cowasjee Nowrojee, otherwise called Calloo;' a poor Parsee, following the employment of a cook, and was in the service of many respectable Parsee gentlemen; unjustly condemned, as will be subsequently shown."[23]

He goes on to say "I ask any rational mind, divested of all prejudice, to peruse and study that portion of the detailed evidence against me, printed in your paper, examine it with impartiality, lay his hand on his heart, and solemnly declare before his Maker, if 'justice has triumphed.' I defy him to do so."[24] In contrast to both the fearful and anxious voices of the witnesses, and the detached and lofty voices of the attorneys who represent their more affluent clients in the court proceedings, Calloo's "unrepresented" voice is clear in its call for justice and fairness. The solemnity of his claim calls out the prejudices of the colonial legal system and questions its rationality. But Calloo's letter is as much about fear as Damodhur's statement was.

Calloo's letter voices the very real fear that his only relationship to the justice system is through the mechanism of punishment. Yet, the type of fear gestured at by Calloo, the fear experienced by the defendants of an unjust system, is markedly absent from the official legal narrative of colonial criminality.

Imaginative Life and the Biopolitics of Fear

This absence is particularly notable because the record of the 1844 trial is riddled with other expressions of fear. The Parsi priest who was the opening witness for the prosecution, and on whose testimony the convictions seem to be largely based, admitted on the stand that he had given false information in his deposition. Citing the fear of retribution as his motivation for lying, in his testimony on the witness stand he claimed, "I got confused from having seen so much blood; I was afraid they would beat me if I told the whole truth, and because I was Munchee's friend; I was aware that Munchee was at war with this party; I did not mention their names for fear of being killed by them."[25] Several other witnesses as well mention fear as a motivating factor for their actions (such as not seeking help for the victim, or sending him warning of an imminent attack) and narratives (on the stand and at various interrogations). For example, one witness was "afraid they would beat me."[26] Someone else "got frightened."[27] Yet another was "very much alarmed."[28] And poor Damodhur, the erstwhile prisoner, "was afraid and went down stairs."[29] The multiple and repeated expressions of fear in the record merit a closer look.

Two things stand out about the representation of fear in the record: it is ubiquitous in the testimonies of the witnesses and it frequently hinders them from doing something that would have been the just thing to do. In other words, fear often prevents justice from being carried out. More precisely, according to the records, Indian fear prevents British justice from being carried out. Yet, even as the colonial record is replete with acknowledgements of each of the witnesses' fear of other members of the Parsi community, no acknowledgment is made of the defendants' very real fear of death at the hands of the colonial justice system. That aspect of fear is entirely elided from the colonial record, and yet it is precisely the prospect of execution that motivates the entirety of the trial.

These archives of the Eduljee case reveal that the emotion of fear is central to almost every action narrated by the Indian witnesses in the trial. But even from this vast historical remove, the witnesses' fear is represented as exaggerated and at times even comical. It reads as a sign of cowardice and incompetence, and a familiar portrait of the shifty and ineffectual Indian emerges in its trace. The fear – of death, grave injury, or imprisonment – especially within the context of colonial rule, is certainly not trivial. Yet within the record, the expressions of fear are offered as a reason for why justice was hampered.[30] It is this impression that Indian fear stood in the way of British justice that I want to examine more closely. What were the Indians so afraid of? Was it only the violence they suffered at the hands of each other, or were there larger, systemic reasons for their fear? It is significant that the Indians' fear of each other is amply documented in the archive, while the pronounced fear the eighteen prisoners must have experienced, several of whom were ultimately sentenced to death in the original verdict, is largely absent. With the exception of Calloo, who wrote about his fears in his letter to the newspaper, only Damodhur, who was recently released from prison, speaks about his fear of the justice system.

The testimony of Damodhur, who says he was afraid to speak before the judge for fear of being sent back to jail, offers some important insight. Ultimately, it was Damodhur's inability to speak that allowed the prosecution's narrative of events to go unchallenged. But Damodhur was caught in a classic double bind. In order to address the injustice the court was about to perpetrate, he had to risk further harm at the hands of the court himself. Self-interest intervened, and Damodhur remained silent. As Damodhur's example most clearly indicates, what appears as individual fear, or personal cowardice, often has larger political bases, namely in the fear of colonial law and policing.

Straddling the line between the personal and the political, Damodhur's fear gestures toward the larger unspoken fears propelling the narrative, namely those of the eighteen prisoners potentially awaiting the sentence of death. Yet, the prisoners' fear is overdetermined. If Damodhur's statement is accurate, China Budla's fear of appearing before the judge without legal representation is what drove him to implicate the rest of the defendants. Was this simply an act of malice, or a justified fear of a legal system that could, as Calloo suggests, convict and kill at will? While the defendants' fear of the colonial legal system is absent from the official record, reading in the interstices, another story begins to emerge. Examining the archive closely, we see that there are two types of fear, the personal and the political, that the narrative represents.

Writing about fear as a political idea, Corey Robin distinguishes between private fears, "like my fear of flying or your fear of spiders," which are "artifacts of our own psychologies and experiences and have little impact beyond ourselves," and political fears, which, unlike personal ones, "emanate from society or have consequences for society."[31] Yet the colonial archive runs together the innumerable fears of each of the individual witnesses, making it impossible to distinguish personal from political fears. Damodhur and China Budla's political fears are lost in the myriad other fears that surround them. Indeed, this blurring of personal and political fears serves a useful function within the colonial legal regime. The colonial records' emphasis on the fear Indians expressed of each other has the effect of justifying the need to step in and provide a system of justice and order to address these fears.

In a Marxian analysis of American slavery, Abdul JanMohamed makes a related argument about the strategic uses of fear. "[W]hile the master does not consider the slave's *life* to possess any use-value," JanMohamed writes, "the slave's *fear of death* does possess enormous use-value for the master and it is this fear that the master 'uses' to articulate the contract."[32] In JanMohamed's terms, fear is the central affect that carries forth the aneconomic terms of the master–slave contract.[33] Without the looming fear of death, the contract dissolves, as the enslaved person has nothing left to lose.

A similar point could be made in the context of the colonial criminal justice system as well. While the personal fears of the witnesses work to support the legal apparatus, the defendants' fears call into question the system's claims to justice. The only clue linking the two positionalities is Damodhur, the reluctant witness for the defense, who himself oscillates precariously between witness and defendant. At the crucial moment, though, Damodhur, like the death-bound subject, feels compelled to remain silent.

The affective value of fear, however, has yet another dimension. Against the muted fear of the prisoners awaiting their verdict is the backdrop of a very public British fear of the spectacle of Indian criminality epitomized, for example, in the campaign to suppress thuggee. Ultimately, both the official record of the witness testimonies in the 1844 case and the larger cultural/political narratives about thuggee collude to heighten fears of Indian criminality. In turn, the prosecution and punishment of criminals served vital colonial interests: public executions prompted greater obedience to British colonial power, and convict workers, like Eduljee Byramjee and his cohort of defendants, aided in further colonial expansion. In addition to its disciplinary value, fear served a vital purpose in the economic aspect of colonial criminality.

Capitalizing on Fear

The political and economic uses to which fear was put in nineteenth-century India, however, have a longer history in English political philosophy. In 1651 Thomas Hobbes published his political treatise *Leviathan* while in exile in France. As Britain strove to define and shape its own political sovereignty, across the globe, the East India Company was entering a period of rapid expansion. By 1647, the Company, having built twenty-three factories throughout India, was ushering in the era of British colonial dominance. With the English civil war raging at home and the early expansion of the British Empire afoot abroad, Hobbes's political philosophy usefully illuminates the coterminous origins of the modern European state form based in social contract theory, on the one hand, and the management of foreign dominions in the service of Empire on the other. Read in light of territorial acquisition in India and other colonies, *Leviathan* reveals that the motivating force of fear that impels national citizens to unite under a single sovereign also provides a justification for the expansion of national interests outward.

The figure of the sovereign, in Hobbes's words a "power able to overawe them all," is thus crucial to both the projects of nationalism and imperialism. While early forays into India were ostensibly mercantile, and conducted by the corporate entity of the East India Company, the sovereign was never wholly absent.[34] As early as 1617, trade between nominally private entities was mediated and secured by an agreement between King James I and Emperor Jahangir, who, in exchange for gifts offered by James, granted the English a "freedom answerable to their own desires."[35] State involvement in the colonial enterprise continued through the seventeenth and eighteenth centuries, and following the Sepoy Rebellion of 1857, the Crown officially supplanted the East India Company.

As discussed in the Introduction, the period of the rise of Empire was also the era during which the modern nation of Great Britain was coming into formation, first through an informal union between England and Scotland with the accession of James I in 1603, and then through the formal Acts of Union consolidating rule of the entire island in 1707. Many historians of the British Empire have drawn upon this shared history to show how more distant imperial pursuits in India and elsewhere provided a convenient backdrop against which to imagine a newly developing national identity. For example, Linda Colley suggests that "what most enabled Great Britain to emerge as an artificial nation, and to be superimposed onto older alignments and loyalties, was a series of massive wars between 1689 and 1815 that allowed its diverse inhabitants to focus on what they had in common, rather than on what divided them, and that forged an overseas empire from which all parts of Britain could secure real as well as psychic profits."[36] And, as Bernard Cohn observes, "The process of state building in Great Britain, seen as a cultural project, was closely linked with its emergence as an imperial power, and India was its largest and most important colony."

From the outset the rise of the modern British state was thus intimately tied to the acquisition of foreign territories. Yet, if the project in Britain was to secure the consent of the governed, colonialism relied on more overt claims to power. As Srinivas Aravamudan has shown, "Consent vocabulary dominated intra-European political philosophy even as conquest vocabulary was prevalent with imperial and colonial ventures that took place outside of Europe."[37] For Aravamudan, Hobbes's writings in *Leviathan* and elsewhere reflect this tension. Writing about Hobbes's characterization of the colonization of America, but equally applicable to the Indian context as well, Aravamudan observes that "Rather than imagining colonialism and imperialism as supplementary activities beyond the territory of the nation state, the Hobbesian framework considers state-formation and imperial activity in the early modern period as conjoint."[38] In other words, the model of state formation and sovereignty that Hobbes articulates can easily assimilate the goals of imperialism.

The "conjoint" nature of the processes of empire building and nation building is particularly evident in the economic realm. But the modern British political subject was also a direct product of the twin functions of colonialism and capitalism. Political shifts brought on by the economic effects of colonialism produced new frictions within the domestic sphere. Tying the acquisition of colonial territories explicitly to domestic economic reorganization, Saskia Sassen argues that colonialism bound together the wealth of the sovereign and the wealth of domestic manufacturers through a shared interest in the extraction of resources from foreign territories. Nuancing earlier more teleological theories of a world-system model of the rise of capitalism, Sassen attends to the local specificities within Europe that fostered different dynamics in various nations.[39] In the case of England, Sassen shows, the rise of capitalism produced three related effects. First, the link between capitalism and colonialism produced a "novel legal persona" in the form of the "national bourgeoisie" whose identity was derived from and dependent upon "foreign trade, global pillaging and colonization."[40] Second, "capitalism was dominant in the English economy at a time when it seemed kings and nobility were." And, lastly, "the political economy that was constructed as the bourgeoisie carved out a legal persona for itself, a rights-bearing subject that began as a legal non-persona striving against absolutism and the nobility."[41] Sassen locates the emergence of this rights-bearing bourgeoisie (as theorized in the political philosophy of John Locke) in the "growing power of Parliament," as well as in the rise of colonialism and its "exploitation of native or imported workers."[42] As Sassen argues, the origin of the rights-bearing subject, within the interwoven rise of parliamentary democracy and colonialism, speaks to the shared logic underwriting both, or all three, developments.

As colonialism increasingly influenced the political and economic contours of British sovereignty, novel forms of wealth and legal subjectivity came into existence. England's quest for colonies was especially significant because it occurred alongside domestic power shifts from the king to parliament, and correspondingly from feudalism to capitalism. At times symbiotic and at others contentious, the relationship between the nobility and the bourgeoisie was forged in colonialism, as during the eighteenth century "commerce quintupled and national income quadrupled."[43]

In this respect, Sassen shows, the rise of capitalism in England reflected a triangulation between the national bourgeoisie, the sovereign, and the colony, in which each figure both depended on and served to obscure the significance of the other. The competition for resources and political recognition was the motivating force of the relationship. But implicit in Sassen's model is the insecurity of each position, bourgeoisie and sovereign, within a triangulated and interdependent relationship that hinged upon global conquest. Viewed in this light, the dominant affective impulses that Sassen's model identifies, and that underlie Hobbes's political philosophy, are fear, threat, and insecurity. At its heart, then, the democratization of Britain that occurred over the course of the eighteenth and nineteenth centuries, cannot be separated from the more absolutist forms of power that colonialism invoked.[44]

Though Britain increasingly moved away from Hobbes's monarchism in the centuries that followed his writings, as my discussion of the uses of fear in managing Indian criminality in this chapter shows, his political principles were redirected rather than rejected outright. Hobbes's influence on political thinkers such as Jeremy Bentham, for example, is well documented, though as James Crimmins remarks, Bentham's indebtedness to Hobbes is felt rather than found explicitly in his writing. When read from the perspective of British domestic politics, it is possible to make the argument, as Crimmins does, that while "the individualism of Hobbes found its corollary in an absolutist theory of the state, the individualism of Bentham resulted, ultimately in democratic institutions."[45] Bentham's influence on legal codification in India, however, reveals a more absolutist imperative in the utilitarian's writings. While "both Hobbes and Bentham were legal positivists who expounded a command theory of law" that was faithful to "the intentions of the legally constituted sovereign," it was only in the colonies during the nineteenth century that this vision of the law materialized.[46] If Hobbes advocated for the power of a sovereign "able to overawe them all," nineteenth century codifiers, inspired by Bentham's failed advocacy for codification in Britain, sought to hold colonial populations under the thrall of the rule of law similarly able to "overawe them all." Within this context, the strategic use of the affect of fear, as Hobbes describes, was central to the law's efficacy in nineteenth-century India.

Affect and Effect

As Hobbes and later the utilitarians recognized, fear is an effective tool because it can motivate obedience. Exploring the uses of fear in Hobbes's

Leviathan, Roberto Esposito remarks that for Hobbes, within the realm of the state, fear carries both a "destructive" charge as well as a "constructive" one: "It doesn't only cause flight and isolation, but it also causes relation and union."[47] Distinguishing Hobbes's work from that of Montesquieu and Machiavelli, who recognized the despotic uses of fear but not its more ambivalent functions, Esposito characterizes fear as the basis for Hobbes's "entire political anthropology."[48] Articulating a kind of "homeopathic" logic of fear, Esposito notices that for Hobbes, and by extension for Bentham and the utilitarians in India, a certain amount of fear helps instigate the unity necessary to yield to the rule of a sovereign.[49] As Esposito shows, this fear serves an effective purpose in consolidating a notion of self against an enemy. Most useful to my argument here is Esposito's idea that "the community can survive the violence that traverses it only by shifting violence onto an enemy that is able to attract it."[50] For Esposito, as for Aravamudan, the deflection of internal fears outward helps resolve the paradox between "consent" and "conquest" in modern European state formation.

Additionally, Esposito identifies a sense of potentiality underlying the "homeopathic" uses of fear. In his work on the political uses of fear, Brian Massumi makes explicit this sense of potentiality by arguing that there is something uniquely generative about the affect of fear associated with a threat. For Massumi, the threat is both infinitely abstract, since by its nature it is never material, and always oriented toward the future. Thus the affect of fear associated with a threat is a "*felt quality*, independent of any particular instance of itself" because the threat can only be imagined as a future event.[51] Yet, because of its inescapable futurity, the "operative logic" of the threat is to seek "[i]ts own continuance" ultimately in the form of "preemptive power."[52] Of course not all fears and threats can harness state power, or violence of any sort, in order to be either enacted or countered. Nevertheless, the relationship to the future is the point on which I wish to focus. As Massumi suggests, fear centers around the relationship between one's imagination and the future. In particular, fear manipulates the relationship between past, present, and future. The threat, always a future event, is experienced in the present as a deferred fear. As Massumi notes, the past of the threat is actually the present, but the present is always marred by a future that promises to materialize the threat, even if the threat is never actually realized. In this sense, there is no true past, present, or future of the threat. Though the fear is felt in the present, its object is always the future. Explaining this complicated temporality, Massumi writes that the threat's "futurity doesn't stay in the past where its feeling emerged. It feeds forward through time. It runs an endless loop forward from its point of emergence in the past present, whose future it remains."[53] In this respect, the affect elicited by the threat "passes through linear time, but does not belong to it. It belongs to the non-linear circuit of the always will have been."[54] The slippery temporality of fear, and its ahistoricity, is an important component of its role in shaping the imaginative landscapes of colonizer and colonized alike, circumscribing futures and rewriting pasts. Most saliently, fear provided a rationale for, and was often used as a strategy by, colonial legal regimes. By holding the present in the thrall of the future, the threat reoriented the colonial subject's lived relationship to temporality.[55]

In the colonies, Hobbes's vision of a "power able to overawe them all" was reimagined by diagnosing a tendency toward barbarism and criminality that needed to be kept in check by the rule of law.[56] Along the lines of Massumi's argument, the fear that was incited through the specter of Indian criminality justified moral arguments in favor of Empire: Indian criminality served as an opposite against which British colonial benevolence could emerge. As an aside, this fear of the dangerous and ungovernable colonial subject was also beneficial in keeping otherwise potentially unruly English subjects loyal to the Crown.[57] And in contrast to the zealous prosecution of Indian criminality, European criminality was often effectively concealed. As Martin Weiner notes, "The hardening sense of racial solidarity increased the willingness of Anglo-Indian jurors to ignore prosecution evidence and even judicial directions, making the treatment of European violence against non-Europeans more lenient."[58] In an essay on the penal code, Thomas Macaulay expressed concern that Indian opinions of the English "national character" would be diminished "by the frequent exhibition of Englishmen of the worst description, placed in the most degrading situations, stigmatized by the courts of justice, and engaged in the ignominious labour of a gaol."[59] Arguing that "it is natural and inevitable that in the minds of a people accustomed to be governed by Englishmen, the idea of an Englishman should be associated with the idea of Government," Macaulay advocated for suspending prison sentences for European criminals and transporting them instead "to some British colony situated in a temperate climate."[60] With respect to both prosecution and punishment, European criminality was treated very differently from Indian criminality.[61]

While English criminality was perceived as a menace to colonial authorities, Indian criminality was seen as truly frightening. As Elizabeth Kolsky notes, "Perceptions of native deceit were so central to colonial understandings of Indian society that it would be impossible to comprehensively trace their emergence or diffusion."[62] As fears of Indian criminality permeated through colonial society, during the nineteenth century these fears were most acute around the figure of the thug.[63] In the 1830s W. H. Sleeman, a civil servant in India, began a highly publicized campaign to suppress thuggee. The thugs, it was believed, were a brutal band of hereditary criminals who robbed and strangled travelers in India as a form of worship of the Hindu goddess Kali. Although more current historians suggest that thuggee was at least in part a colonial fantasy, in the nineteenth century it played a powerful role in bolstering British systems of law and justice.[64] Countless travel journals and memoirs document British fears of Indian criminality, as these fears were yoked to the practical politics of strengthening British judicial reach. Like the campaign against sati, the fear of thuggee worked to prop up the narrative of the moral imperative of the British civilizing mission.

Interestingly, thugs did not attack European travelers, and as Radhika Singha observes, there was "no clamour from their Indian subjects for measures against thuggee."[65] So substantiating the existence of the cult, much less apprehending individual practitioners of thuggee, was rather challenging. Based on the historical record, Singha speculates that "there was a way of life in which criminality could form a part, sometimes a regular part, of a range of subsistence options, but it was not the criminality by 'birth and profession' projected by the Company's police and legal drives."[66] Equally importantly, as Parama Roy notes, thugs were seen "not as individual or collective subjects responding to socio economic transformations engendered by the sudden ascendancy of the East India Company or indeed to any other material circumstance, or even to chance, but as fulfilling a hereditary calling, if not a genetic predisposition."[67] The notion that thugs were motivated by biological and social reasons, rather than political ones, however, was central to British popular and legal representations.

As thuggee increasingly came to symbolize Indian criminality more broadly, fears about its spread inspired a series of judicial acts, including Act XXX of 1836, which suspended normal judicial procedures in the prosecution of thugs. Yet, as Singha observes, "the strangest feature of this enactment was the use of a cant term 'Thugs' without explaining what precisely the offence of 'Thuggee' was."[68] Lacking specific definitions of the crimes or perpetrators, colonial police and courts relied upon the testimony of "approvers," or witnesses, to capture thugs and bring them to trial. Thugs could then be convicted solely on the basis of these "approvers'" testimony and could be sentenced to life imprisonment with hard labor or transported to a penal colony. Over the course of the nineteenth century, the campaign against thuggee embodied the intensity of British fears of Indian criminality, as well as the lengths to which the colonial judiciary would go to assuage those fears.[69] "The targets of such measures," Singha writes, "were supposed to have placed themselves outside the pale of society, thereby forfeiting their claim to the protection of regular procedure."[70] Rules of evidence and due process, for example, were suspended if thuggee was suspected. The elevation of thuggee to a paradigmatic representation of Indian criminality thus had profound consequences for the prosecution and punishment of crime in the colonial territories.

In *Ramaseeana*, his exposé of thug life and culture, Sleeman explained that "India is emphatically the land of superstition and in this land the system of Thugee, the most extraordinary that has ever been recorded in the history of the human race, had found a congenial soil, and flourished with rank luxuriance for more than two centuries, till its roots had spread over almost every district within the limits of our dominions."[71] Sleeman's representation of thuggee as uniquely Indian and the biological metaphors that he used to identify the practice firmly with its geographical and cultural location speak to the extent to which thuggee came to exemplify the stakes of colonial difference. Echoing the necessarily unverifiable quality of the threat that Massumi identifies, Sleeman cautions against the idea "that the system has been suppressed in every part of India where it once prevailed (and I believe that it prevailed in more or less every part)." The complete eradication of thuggee, Sleeman warns, is "a proposition that neither ought nor can be affirmed *absolutely*."[72] Accordingly, the campaign to suppress thuggee brought new urgency, and could provide perpetual justification, for the expansion of colonial legal regimes.

If fear served a powerful function in spurring colonial conquest, however, the colonial subject, and in particular the colonial criminal, experienced a very different sense of fear. For criminals who were charged and prosecuted, threats of bodily harm, life imprisonment, and transport could be, and often were, materialized. Fear was instrumental in managing criminality in two important ways. First, the colonial criminal was a perceived source of fear and danger. Second, the figure of the criminal served as a spectral opposite against which British selfhood could be confirmed.[73] Yet even as the figure of the Indian criminal haunted the imaginative landscape of colonialism, by the nineteenth century, the literal body of the criminal served a series of practical uses in the quotidian administration of Empire, from building roads and bridges in remote outposts to instantiating the weight of colonial justice, and providing an impetus for codifying rules of law.[74]

"Terror and Example"

In England, the nineteenth century saw a movement away from execution, corporal punishment, and banishment as the primary modes of criminal justice, toward more humane forms of punishment and rehabilitation. Likewise, as detailed in Chapter 2, during the nineteenth century, prison reforms were implemented in England, with inmates' conditions improving and sentences, by then influenced by the American model of separation, shortening.[75] Also, while the transport of convicts to the remote realms of the Empire, first North America and then Australia, began in the English penal system in the seventeenth century, this lucrative use of criminal labor began to wane in the nineteenth century.[76] The practice of criminal transport, of course, provides a pivotal plot element within *Great Expectations*, but it is also featured in Dickens's other novels, in the characters of John Edmunds from *The Pickwick Papers* (1837), Mr Squeers from *Nicholas Nickelby* (1839), and Uriah Heep from *David Copperfield* (1850). During the first half of the nineteenth century, numerous novels, broadsides, and ballads painted a harsh portrait of the practice of transportation, and public sentiment rose against it. By 1868 criminal transport was officially abolished in Britain, but the practice had come to an end well before then. Within the colonies, during the same thirty-year period between 1830 and 1860, however, penal transport was becoming increasingly common.

Despite the obvious global reach of the project of Empire, as Anand A. Yang explains, "British discourse shied away from linking various modes of labor, including forced labor, for fear of diminishing the moral argument for empire."[77] Put into a broader context, as opposition to Australian transport began to mount in Britain in the 1830s, and paired with the abolition of slavery in 1833 (though slavery was not abolished in the East India Company until 1843), Indian convict workers were among the last ready supply of free labor to carry out the physical construction associated with Empire building.[78] In the nineteenth century, Indian convicts, along with indentured servants, were increasingly being used to mitigate this new labor shortage. According to Clare Anderson, "The comparative data reveals not just a shared chronology in the introduction of convict transportation from British India to southeast Asia, and from Britain and Ireland to the Australian colonies, but a dramatic global reversal in the mid-1810s, and again in the mid-1850s, when European flows went into decline at the same time that Asian flows increased."[79] Explicitly linking the rise of convict labor to the end of slavery, Anderson argues that the East India Company "used and supplied convicts *in preference to* and *to replace* slaves, on infrastructural and other kinds of working gang labour all over southeast Asia and in Mauritius."[80]

As Yang points out, especially given the local distaste for wage labor in Singapore, particularly at the rates the English were willing to pay, convict labor was indispensable to the expansion of Empire.[81] Between 1790 and 1860, fifteen thousand convict workers – comprising ordinary criminals and political prisoners – were transported to the Straits Settlement in contemporary Singapore.[82] Several thousand more were transported to other settlements throughout Southeast Asia.[83] These workers built roads and bridges, canals and railway lines, churches and government buildings. In fact, convict labor was in widespread use until the construction of the penal colony in the Andaman Islands following the game-changing Sepoy Rebellion of 1857, at which point it no longer seemed like a good idea to use political dissidents as loosely guarded workers in the vast construction project of Empire.

Especially in the Indian context, the affect of fear was central to the goals of penal transport. In addition to the financial value derived from convict labor, the architects of the colonial justice system also believed that transport was an especially effective method of deterring crime in India because of local fears of crossing the ocean.[84] Indeed, the 1838 *Report of the Committee on Prison Discipline* found transportation a good punishment because of the "horror" and "terror" it was reportedly able to incite.[85] And, previously, Regulation LIII of 1803 restricted the use of transportation to those prisoners receiving life sentences because colonial authorities did not want to diminish the "terror" of the punishment by allowing ex-convicts to return home.[86] Thus the colonial courts sought to use convicts like Eduljee Byramjee not only for their free labor but also to generate a powerful sentiment of fear, which they hoped would keep both criminality and political rebellion in check. During the years following the Sepoy Rebellion, penal transport to the Andaman Islands increased dramatically, with over 83,000 convicts transported between 1858 and 1939. "If intra-imperial penal transportation can be connected to the slave trade, slavery and indentured migration," Anderson argues, "it was also intertwined with the imperial management of subject populations, or colonial governmentality."[87] Penal transport served as a disciplinary threat against political dissidence.[88]

In addition to the question of transport, the case of *The Queen* v. *Eduljee Byramjee* also involved the threat (and use) of hanging. By the nineteenth century, capital punishment in Britain was becoming increasingly rare, and by the 1830s 97 percent of death sentences were pardoned. In India, however, public executions were very much a part of colonial governmentality. As Michael Mann notes, in 1772 Warren Hastings, the first governor general of Bengal, formalized the use of capital punishment for dacoits (bandits). Article 35 of Hastings' reform plan resolves that "every such Criminal on Conviction shall be carried to the Village to which he belongs and be there executed for a Terror and Example . . . and that the Family of the Criminal shall become the Slaves of the State, and be disposed of for the General Benefit of the Government."[89] The element of "Terror and Example" is critical for understanding the tactics of the colonial penal system. But no less importantly, the relationship between "Terror and Example" is fundamental to the corresponding link between the visual display of the carceral death-bound subject on the one hand and the capacity to shape living imaginations on the other hand.

Hastings's Article 35 is significant because it draws a concrete line between the capacity of the spectacle of public hanging to shape imaginative possibilities, and the role of the state in bringing that imaginative force to fruition through materializing the threat of bodily violence. The extension of the punishment so that "the Family of the Criminal shall become the Slaves of the State" ensures that the terror of the penal system is not experienced individually or subjectively, but rather works to draw in larger social configurations of family and community. In this respect, it serves explicitly to incite political terror in addition to personal fear.

This element of public terror and collective criminality is at odds with the shift in emphasis within the English criminal justice system toward individual culpability, which I discuss in the context of *The Moonstone* and detective fiction later in this volume. The focus on the social element of fear and discipline is also resonant with the construction of the figure of the thug, as demonstrated both in this chapter and the next. If Britain was moving toward recognizing more personal, individual, and psychological motivations for crime for its own citizens, within India, criminality and its punishment was still a spectacle. Underscoring the collective stakes of the 1846 appeal to the JCPC, the case consisted of two petitions, one on behalf of Eduljee and his codefendants, and the other which "was presented on the part of upwards of six thousand inhabitants of *Bombay*," who "after setting forth, in substance, the circumstances contained in the first-named Petition, prayed that Her Majesty would be pleased to exercise her prerogative of mercy, in favour of such of the convicts as she might deem entitled to remission of their sentences, and to grant them pardon."[90] While, as discussed later, the Queen's exercise of mercy was increasingly common in domestic capital cases, one of the key considerations of Eduljee's appeal to the Privy Council was whether colonial subjects could find similar reprieve.

"All Benefit to Be Expected from a Public Example"

After having exhausted the appeals process in India following the initial 1844 trial, Eduljee Byramjee and his eight codefendants pursued a final appeal to Queen Victoria's Privy Council. Aside from the question of mercy, which the defendants attempted to seek from the Queen, the appeal to the Privy Council was legally significant because it would set a precedent for whether felony cases could be appealed to the Crown. For the purposes of the original hearing, and for my own purposes here as well, the principal question of the appeal was whether, and to what extent, the British state would oversee the adjudication of criminal cases in the colonies. The potential for appeal in criminal cases is of central legal and political importance because it speaks to the access to rights through the courts. The types of redress available to the colonial criminal also had significant implications about what kinds of relationships to the state colonial subjects could imagine for themselves more broadly. In its most expansive sense, the question to be decided was what kind of subjectivity was available to colonized subjects. What kinds of rights did they have? How did the rights of colonial subjects relate to the rights of British citizens? What was the role of the courts in carving out rights attached to colonial subjectivity?

Attorneys for Eduljee Byramjee argued that the Charter of Justice of Bombay (1823) "gives a right of Appeal, in all indictments, informations, and criminal suits, and expressly reserves to the Crown the power to refuse or admit an Appeal from any Judgment or determination of the Supreme Court, upon such restrictions and regulations, as the Crown shall think fit to impose."[91] Given that the wording of the 1823 charter seemed to suggest that the final power of judgment in all legal matters pertaining to colonial justice rests with the Queen, one of the fundamental quandaries for the Privy Council to consider was how to limit the process of appeals without also implicitly limiting the power of the Queen.

After all, to rule that the colonial criminal had no right to appeal to the Queen was tantamount to saying that the Queen had no right to hear the appeal. In the words of Eduljee Byramjee's attorneys

> if there were no reservation in the Charter to admit Appeals, not otherwise provided for, the power of the Crown to admit Appeals would not have been parted with; for the Crown has no power to denude itself of any prerogative necessary to the administration of justice. It has no more right to weaken its power to give protection to the subject, than the subject has to diminish or qualify his allegiance. The rights of the sovereign and the rights of the subject are strictly correlative.[92]

The seeming tautology of the claim that the Queen has no power to limit her power is worth pausing on. The negative formulation of the Queen's power, where any attempt to "denude" her of it is to affirm her absolute right to it, is interesting. For the Queen, the impossibility of being outside of power is correlated to the subject's inability to diminish his allegiance. On its surface the argument suggests that the Queen has the power to hear the appeal, and this is a power she cannot abrogate. At first glance, as would be logical from the perspective of an attorney arguing on behalf of Eduljee, this argument would seem to extend the rights of the colonial subject, insofar as it would justify a right to criminal appeals. But the argument is considerably more complex.

If, indeed, the "rights of the sovereign and the rights of the subject are strictly correlative," positing the Queen outside her power opens the door to positing the subject outside his/her subordination. But, of course, the argument affirms that there is no outside to the Queen's power. Similarly, the nascent suggestion of the colonial subject being outside the sovereign's rule is quickly foreclosed. Therefore, despite calling for an extension of the rights of the colonial subject in the limited case of criminal appeals, the larger terms of even the defense argument extend the logic of colonial subordination.

The questions of sovereignty alongside those of subjectivity raised by the appeal are not incidental. Especially during the era prior to the Sepoy Rebellion of 1857, colonial rule was both uneven and varied depending upon context. Individuals who might have little interaction with the colonial government on a daily basis, might only feel the weight of colonial biopolitics in spaces like the courtroom, the hospital, or the prison.[93] In this respect, legal proceedings and any punishment that followed from them established the defendants *as* colonial subjects. Importantly, however, the Privy Council's holding, that "the Supreme Court has full and absolute power and authority to allow or deny that Appeal" worked to consolidate the colonial subject, in the era of Company rule, as a subject of the law rather than as a resident of Britain, to whom other rights would accrue.[94] Citing the normal process of criminal prosecution in England, the Privy Council ruled, "no right of Appeal in felonies has ever existed."[95] But the 1823 Judgement of Death Act passed by Parliament gave English judges the authority to immediately reduce death sentences for offences other than treason or murder, reducing the number of capital crimes to begin with.[96] For the relatively small number of British citizens convicted of these crimes on whose behalf the judges did not intervene, it is true that the only option was to appeal to the Crown for pardon, which is a plea for mercy rather than a form of judicial redress. However, between the 1820s and the 1840s, the number of executions carried out in Britain declined dramatically and capital punishment was "mitigated in practice by the exercise of the royal prerogative of mercy."[97]

Though Indian subjects could technically appeal to the sovereign as well, such appeals were not practical given the realities of geographical distance and the time they would require.[98] Moreover, Eduljee's appeal to the Queen's mercy is sidelined in the JCPC opinion by referencing the structural impediment to such a plea. The attorney general, on behalf of the government, points out that the role of the Privy Council is to advise the Queen on legal matters, not her royal prerogative, and therefore concludes that "it could never have been intended to refer to your Lordships, sitting as the Judicial Committee of the Privy Council, an application to Her Majesty to grant a free pardon."[99] Dr. Stephen Lushington, speaking on behalf of the JCPC, agrees with the attorney general, thus shelving the question of royal prerogative on the grounds that the request was misdirected. In practice, then, within the jurisdiction of the colonial courts, Indians were subject to the judicial laws of the government, but did not possess the rights of domestic English citizenship.

But the logic of the opinion relies on just such a direct comparison between English and Indian procedures. As the Privy Council noted in its opinion, "a power to grant an Appeal" is "for the purpose of ascertaining whether the 'Judgment or determination' of the Court was erroneous in point of law with reference to the indictment, or, in other words, whether there was an error upon the fact of the record, as in *England*. We do not think that by any construction the Crown can grant an appeal as to the verdict itself."[100] If, as Foucault suggests, the king's sovereignty is dispersed throughout his subjects in British modernity's movement toward parliamentary democracy, in colonial India, the condemned person is merely the receptacle of the king, or the law's, absolute sovereignty without recourse to the possibility of corresponding mercy.

In articulating the Privy Council's rationale, the Right Honorable Dr. Lushington noted that "the Supreme Court [of Bombay] was constituted a Court of Oyer and Terminer, and Gaol delivery, to administer Criminal Justice in such or the like manner, or form, or as nearly as the condition and circumstances of the place and person will admit, as our Courts of Oyer and Terminer, and Gaol delivery, may or do in *England*, due attention being had to the religion, manners, and usages of the native inhabitants."[101] Despite the claim to similarity between the two systems, however, the rights available in practice under the court's jurisdiction are fundamentally different. Because of this crucial distinction, the purpose served by the English and Indian courts is not, in fact, the same. Lushington's framing of the Indian court as functioning "in such or the like manner, or form, or as nearly as the condition and circumstances of the place and person will admit, as" their English counterparts should be read in this regard rhetorically as a simile rather than as a direct comparison. The trope of congruence makes clear the legal fiction of equivalent rights that sustains both Lushington's opinion and the broader rhetoric of the essential rationality and uniformity of colonial rule of law.

The convicted colonial criminal awaiting appeal occupies a liminal position that is both subject to the power of the law and outside the circuit of rights that typically attach to citizenship. For the carceral subject under colonialism, the law serves as the final arbiter of rights and privileges. Unlike the at least nominal claims to reciprocity between sovereign and citizen in Britain, in which appeals to the sovereign's mercy were not only practical but common, the law's force under colonialism is unilateral.

Like Hobbes's description of the sovereign that I cited earlier, the weight of the colonial justice system holds the colonized subject in the thrall of a "power able to overawe them all." Yet, unlike the sovereign whose power brings about the rights of state citizenship, the colonial condition is one of statelessness, as colonial subjects become, in Elizabeth Kolsky's terms, "aliens in their own lands."[102] If the English legal system was the measure of the normal operations of law and sovereignty, the tandem institution of the colonial courts was both inside and outside the logic of those normal operations. The courts were subject to the sovereign, while the Indian defendants were only subject to the courts.

Further, as the sole arbiter of justice, vested with the power to decide life or death, the colonial judiciary constituted a paradox, not only for those living under its rule, but also, as suggested earlier in the arguments presented by the attorneys for Eduljee Byramjee, for the Queen's exercise of sovereignty. The challenge for the Privy Council was how to secure the exceptional autonomy of the colonial judiciary without also calling into question the sovereignty of the Queen. In order for this to happen, the colonial criminal needed to be divested, in practice if not in theory, of any rights under the Crown.

Interestingly, resolving the paradox of colonial judicial sovereignty had the corresponding effect of bolstering the rise of Britain as a modern nation-state.[103] In delivering their opinion denying the right of criminal appeals to colonial subjects, the Privy Council argued the following:

> So we apprehend this Charter in India being granted in pursuance of an Act of Parliament here, if by the true construction of the Charter the prerogative of the Crown is in any way limited, it must be said to be limited, not by the Act of the Crown itself, but by the Act of the Crown acting under the authority of Parliament.
>
> It is for these reasons that their Lordships are of opinion (and perhaps other reasons might be given arising from a consideration of the peculiar circumstances of the case), that they must humbly advise Her Majesty, that the prayer of the Petition cannot be granted.[104]

Returning to the premise of the "correlative" nature of the relationship between sovereign and subject suggested by the attorneys for Eduljee Byramjee and the eight others before the Privy Council, we see that the ultimate decision was that, at least in the colonial context, the relationship is emphatically not "correlative." This opinion is notable for its imprecise comparison of the rights of domestic citizens and colonial subjects, and for its self-justification by heralding the authority of the modern parliamentary democracy. While the Council's rationale invokes rights "naturally" available to British citizens, these rights were, in practice, not available for colonial subjects.

The Spectacle of Violence

The discrepancy between the rights of British citizens and Indian subjects with regard to the question of capital punishment and criminal transport is an instance of the evolution of British modernity in opposition to the trajectory set out for colonial India. One crucial arena in which the ascension of British modernity developed inversely to the expansion of colonial rule is in the forms of punishment meted out by the respective penal systems.[105] As I discussed earlier, while medieval punishments like banishment and public torture and hangings were waning in England, these disciplinary modes were thriving in the colonies. In juxtaposing the two pathways to modernity, I will return to my earlier discussion of the function of the defendants' fear. In the context of the 1844 trial, I argued that the effect of keeping the defendants' fear absent from the record was to hyperbolize the prosecution witnesses' fear of the criminalized defendants. If, in that trial, it was useful to keep the threat posed by the accused criminal front and center, the logic of the uses of fear shifts in the transition from trial to punishment. In fact, the defendant's fear that was absent from the record of the colonial trial record returns at the moment of punishment as the pre-eminent logic for the prophylactic value of its visual display. The ways in which colonial subjects' experiences of fear were used and manipulated speaks to the biopolitical uses of fear.

In my discussion of the biopolitics of fear, I extend the classical Foucauldian notion of the physicality of species life to include larger Enlightenment ideas about the affective, or psychic, life of the human. For Foucault, bio-power is "the set of mechanisms through which the basic biological features of the human species became the object of a political strategy, of a general strategy of power, or, in other words, how, starting from the eighteenth century, modern Western societies took on board the fundamental biological fact that human beings are a species."[106] The notion of the biological centrality of species life, and its political uses, that Foucault discusses as the aftereffects of the Enlightenment in Europe, has a different history in the colonies.

In the Indian context, the management of species life evolved alongside a colonial politics that was very much still entrenched in notions of a pre-Enlightenment colonial subjectivity. And, even though colonial expansion occurred contemporaneously with the entry into European modernity, colonialism was itself in many ways more of a pre-Enlightenment project than a modern one.[107] As I discussed in the Introduction, British colonialism in India can be read as a protracted mourning for the loss of feudal power relations in Europe. As Europe renegotiated a more modern political bearing for itself, it relegated its imaginative past to the colonies. As a result, one of the great and lasting effects of colonialism was to yoke biopolitical strategies of management to affective ones. In this respect, the biopolitics of colonialism operated most efficiently on the threshold between the psychic and physical lives of its subjects.

It is in this threshold space that the logic of the Privy Council opinion cast its powerful effect. In denying the rights for colonial subjects to appeal criminal convictions, the Counsellors cited the "inevitable consequence" that would follow from the appeals process. If appeals were allowed, Privy

Counsellor Lushington mused, the practical impediments caused by distance and time would make swift executions impossible:

> To cause execution to be done, would be, in effect, to prevent the right of granting an Appeal vested in the Crown, and to take away from the prisoner convicted, the right of laying his case before his sovereign, and of obtaining a re-consideration of it ... Many very evil consequences must necessarily follow from this state of things. A long period must elapse before an application to the Crown could be made, and its decision could be known. And eventually, where the leave to Appeal was refused (and it must be presumed that this would generally be the case), execution would follow the sentence after so long an interval, that all benefit to be expected from a public example would be lost; and to this it might be added, that in a great majority of cases the convicts themselves would be kept in a state of miserable suspense, to suffer in the end the same ignominious death to which they were sentenced.[108]

In Lushington's logic, the "evil consequences" would be felt by society at large through the loss of the deterrent effect of the "public example," and by the criminal himself, who would be doomed to suffer in "miserable suspense." In other words, the JCPC ironically frames its refusal to grant appeals as an act of generosity to both the defendant and society at large. In both justifications, though, the logic rests principally on the political uses of terror, either that of the onlookers, or that of the defendants themselves.

Lushington's remarks on the "benefit to be expected from a public example" are all the more noteworthy in light of his strenuous advocacy for the abolition of capital punishment in England. In his analysis of the Privy Counsellor's long political and judicial career, Stephen Waddams notes "Lushington had been an active opponent of capital punishment from at least as early as 1813."[109] His activism, which included introducing an ultimately unsuccessful bill to Parliament in 1840 proposing the abolition of the death penalty, was steadfast throughout his career. "Though he conceded that capital punishment might have a deterrent effect in some cases," according to Waddams, "he considered that any advantage to the community on this account was greatly outweighed by other considerations."[110] Lushington lamented the irremediable nature of capital punishment, and in a session of Parliament in March 1832 argued that "it was a matter of history that the punishment of death had never proved effective for the prevention of crime."[111] The abolition of the death penalty was, for Lushington, a matter of modern progress, and he urged that since "general civilization had advanced, the Legislature must finally yield to the general feeling against the severity of punishment at present in force."

Lushington concluded "by observing that all he had stated was the result of the most deliberate consideration that he had ever given to any subject, from the year 1805 up to the present time."[112] Granted, Lushington was compelled to work within the framework of the laws as they existed in reaching his opinion in the Privy Council, but his advocacy on behalf of the abolition of capital punishment in England in contrast with the zealousness with which he pursued the swift and decisive implementation of capital punishment in the Indian context is indicative, if not of his personal hypocrisy, of a larger oppositional trajectory within English and colonial law, to which I have sought to draw attention. In India, it seems, the goals and the uses of punishment and fear were markedly different from those in England.

Returning to the discussion of Eduljee, if the strategy in the trial phase was to divide the defendants' fear from the witnesses', the strategy in the punishment phase was the opposite: to cathect a powerful sentiment of fear based on an identificatory impulse between the defendant being executed and the witnesses watching. The biopolitical turn operates in the seamless transition from the witness as allied with the colonial prosecution, to the witness as a disciplinary target. The threat invoked in the visual spectacle of the hanging is that anyone can slip from witness to defendant. In other words, the difference between witness and defendant that was heightened during the trial in order to secure a conviction disappears during punishment, when all colonial subjects are encouraged to identify with the fear of the defendant being executed or otherwise punished. The sleight of hand by which the subjectivity of the witness becomes indistinguishable from that of the defendant is a profound result of the biopolitics of fear under colonial law.

For Eduljee Byramjee and his cohort of defendants, the totalizing narrative of colonial criminality held fast. If the effect of colonial criminal punishment was, in the final gesture, to diminish the opposition between witness and defendant, colonial collaborator and enemy of the state, the punishment of transport, as well, furthers this goal. Like the hanging body of the publicly executed criminal, the bodies of the nine transported convict workers were neatly transformed into agents of Empire, toiling for the remainder of their lives in the construction of the new settlement of Singapore.

Another Eduljee

History, as it often does, provides the final plot twist in the narrative of criminal appeals. In 1903, a series of nighttime mutilations of livestock shocked the town of Great Wyrley in the British midlands. In addition to the animal slayings, the "Wyrley Ripper" was also suspected of authoring a series of menacing letters sent between 1892 and 1903. Many of the letters were addressed to the family of Shapurji Edalji, the local vicar, who had resided in Wyrley since 1875. The vicar, like his namesake Eduljee Byramjee, was of Parsi heritage but had converted to Christianity and married an Englishwoman with whom he had three children. An Indian vicar was anomalous in nineteenth-century England, however, and the family faced much hostility. George Edalji, the couple's eldest son, who was dark-skinned and myopic, was tormented and threatened with violence in the series of letters and hoaxes that targeted the family for a decade.[113] Despite this, the police in the town were suspicious of him, and in 1903 George, who was by then a twenty-seven-year-old solicitor, was arrested and convicted of the gruesome animal rippings, and sentenced to seven years' hard labor.[114] As in Eduljee's case sixty years earlier, the verdict attracted suspicion, this time throughout England, and ten thousand people, including several lawyers, signed a petition to the Home Office requesting a retrial.[115] After serving three years of his sentence, Edalji was released from prison, though he was permanently disgraced and his legal career was ruined. Because appeals were not permitted in criminal cases, George Edalji had little recourse in legally challenging what many believed to be his unfair conviction.

Among those persuaded of Edalji's innocence, however, was Arthur Conan Doyle, author of the immensely popular Sherlock Holmes mysteries. Convinced that Edalji was the victim of prejudice on account of his "bulge-eyed, staring appearance, which, when taken with his dark skin, must have made him seem a very queer man to the eyes of an English village," Conan Doyle embarked on a campaign to exonerate him.[116] Consumed by the case, Conan Doyle conducted his own investigation, uncovering ample evidence that cast doubt on the objectivity of the police work used to convict Edalji. Conan Doyle published his report in *The Daily Telegraph* without copyright, and the story was carried in newspapers across the globe. The publicity generated by Conan Doyle's report prompted the Home Office to reconsider Edalji's case, and he was ultimately pardoned and restored to the bar. Despite receiving a pardon, however, Edalji was not compensated for his imprisonment. Strangely, the Home Office believed he was responsible for having written the threatening letters, though he was never formally accused of this offence. The racially charged case was a flashpoint in the effort to implement a process of criminal appeals in Britain that would enable judicial remedies for faulty legal verdicts. Shortly after Edalji's pardon was issued, the Criminal Appeals Act of 1907 resulted in the creation of the Court of Criminal Appeals. The creation of this new venue, ironically what Eduljee Byramjee sought in his failed appeal to the Privy Council, ushered Britain out of the Victorian era into more modern forms of criminal justice that would account for the possibility of mutable judgments and differing perspectives. This discrepant trajectory into modernity for the criminal in Britain and India forms the basis for Chapter 2. Mirroring the legal context of this chapter, in literature as well, we see that as Britain moved toward greater checks on the univocal punishment of criminals, the treatment of the criminal in India would become increasingly absolutist.

CHAPTER 2

The Social Life of Crime
Charles Dickens's Great Expectations and Philip Meadows Taylor's Confessions of a Thug

At its heart, as I suggest in Chapter 1, the question of whether to consider criminal appeals hinges on the possibility of retelling a story and coming to a different conclusion. Consistent with nineteenth-century English investments in narrative certainty, especially within the realm of the law, the Judicial Committee of the Privy Council (JCPC) in *The Queen v. Eduljee Byramjee* held that criminal appeals should not be entertained. But the question before the Privy Council was not only one of narrative, as the "petitions did not allege that any error appeared on the face of the record."[1] Instead, the appellants "complained of the direction of the Judge, the evidence and the verdict."[2] What Eduljee disputed was not the narrative itself, but the interpretation that the narrative engendered. What he asked for was a different conclusion from the one arrived at in his trial in Bombay. In many ways, the George Edalji case sixty years later can be read as just the kind of alternative ending that Eduljee sought. With this in mind, the institution of the Criminal Court of Appeals in response to the miscarriage of justice in 1907 provided a corrective to the narrative of judicial certainty that underwrote the JCPC opinion in 1846.

Opening up a criminal verdict to reconsideration necessarily admits the fallibility of legal judgments and processes. By contrast, refusing the possibility of appeals has the effect of solidifying a teleological narrative in which the narrative logic is intrinsically tied to the narrative outcome. A story, in other words, arrives at its sole rational and predictable conclusion. In this model, time only heads in one direction, tracking along with a singular narrative of progress. Such a relationship between the unfolding of a narrative and a corresponding linear development is fundamental, as well, to the genre of the bildungsroman that this chapter examines. In this context, Joseph Slaughter draws our attention to the "ideological confluence between the technologies of the novel and the law" that invoke "a common vocabulary and transitive grammar" in order to uphold the concept of development across the two arenas.[3]

The bildungsroman transforms the univocal teleology of the law into a narrative of personal development. Franco Moretti treats the popular genre's obsession with youth and the development into adulthood as symptomatic of Europe's stumbling entry into modernity. In the wake of the eighteenth-century revolutions, Europe sought "order and meaning" by organizing historical events into narrative certainty, such that "reality's meaning is now to be grasped solely in its historico-diachronic dimension."[4] With its emphasis on development and progress, the bildungsroman becomes, unsurprisingly, the iconic genre of the nineteenth-century novel, or the "symbolic form of modernity."[5] Within the "classical bildungsroman," Moretti observes,

> narrative transformations have meaning in so far as they lead to a particularly marked ending: one that establishes a classification different from the initial one, but nonetheless perfectly clear and stable – definitive, in both senses this term has in English. This teleological rhetoric – the meaning of events lies in their *finality* – is the narrative equivalent of Hegelian thought, with which it shares a strong *normative* vocation: events acquire meaning when they led to *one* ending, and one only.[6]

In Moretti's characterization of it, the bildungsroman shares the same teleological impulse toward a single, final ending that I identify in the JCPC opinion of Chapter 1, as well as in the genre of the judicial opinion more broadly. For both the bildungsroman and the narrative logic of the JCPC, "a story is more meaningful the more it truly manages to *suppress itself as a story*."[7] In other words, the meaning of the story does not unfold exclusively on the level of plot, but rather the underlying principles and logic of the narrative should make a particular conclusion (both in terms of plot and interpretation) inevitable. A consideration of this suppressed story and its relationship to the more overt narrative of the plot also motivates my reading of the two novels that I consider in this chapter.

Both *Confessions of a Thug* and *Great Expectations*, each in its different way, are premised upon a suppressed narrative of racialized criminality that also underlies the legal judgment in *The Queen* v. *Eduljee Byramjee*. Notions of criminality that become apparent in the literary context of the novel reveal the cultural assumptions that structure the logic of the JCPC opinion. At the same time, the overt narrative of the opinion, and its stated goal of inciting terror for the purpose of "public example," makes evident the structuring logic that drives the contrast between representations of English and Indian criminality in the two novels.[8]

Both Philip Meadows Taylor's *Confessions of a Thug* and Charles Dickens's *Great Expectations* offer portraits of nineteenth-century criminality. Focusing on India and England, respectively, the suppressed subtexts that make certain outcomes inevitable for the main characters within each novel reveal the divergent attitudes toward criminal punishment and rehabilitation in the two contexts. *Great Expectations* is a classic bildungsroman in which the physical development of Pip, the novel's protagonist, parallels the moral development of the convict Magwitch, with whom he is implicitly aligned. Magwitch, who we later learn is Pip's benefactor, assumes the role of a father figure for the orphaned Pip and the convict's redemption over the course of the novel occurs in tandem with his assumption of fatherly care for Pip. In this manner, Magwitch's hardened criminality is slowly transformed into what was, for Victorian readers, a more readily sympathetic paternalistic masculinity. Recast in this fashion, Magwitch's development emblematizes the potential for the criminal's rehabilitation and assimilation into the ideological, if not the physical, social community.

Magwitch's ascent within the social imaginary becomes especially evident when contrasted with the irremediable stasis of Ameer Ali, the villainous antihero of *Confessions of a Thug*. If Magwitch's narrative is metonymically associated with the potential for English criminal rehabilitation, Ameer Ali's incapacity for reform resonates with broader ideas of Indian stagnation as well, as discussed in Chapters 3 and 4.

The potential for development, individual and national, is implicitly connected in both of these novels to the possibility of reform for the wayward criminal. Over the course of this chapter, I explore the contrasting visions of British and Indian criminality, especially with regard to questions of development and futurity. In particular, I compare Magwitch's conversion into a fatherly figure with Ameer Ali's toxic fatherhood, embodied in his repeated incapacity to intervene in the killing of small boys, and his failure to parent his own children. Taken together, the representations of Magwitch and Ameer Ali, I argue, map contrasting ideas of English and Indian masculinity onto the possibilities for criminal rehabilitation. In turn, the social response deemed appropriate to each instance of criminality implies a different conception of futurity available to both the criminal and the broader society he reflects.

Thug Lives

According to Weld Taylor, Philip Meadows Taylor's brother, Dickens had read "*Confessions of a Thug* with a great deal of interest" and the two later became acquainted.[9] Taylor contributed to Dickens's periodical *Household Words*, and his already popular *Confessions of a Thug* was reissued in 1858, during the period of the Sepoy Rebellion, and just before Dickens began work on *Great Expectations*. Taylor's novel presents a fictional account largely based on the work of W. H. Sleeman, whose campaign against thuggee I discuss at length in Chapter 1. As one of the main sources of information on thuggee available to British readers, Sleeman's *Ramaseeana: Or a Vocabulary of the Peculiar Language Used by the Thugs* purported to be a study of the secret language of thugs.[10] It aimed to provide an introduction to the history and practice of thuggee based on several narratives related to Sleeman by "approvers," or informants to the British. Both Sleeman and Taylor characterize thuggee as a form of hereditary criminality that was so widespread as to be emblematic of Indian society and culture at large.

Beyond serving as the inspiration for Taylor's novel, Sleeman's work was foundational to fostering the equivalence between the colonial subject and the criminal that was becoming increasingly prevalent in the early nineteenth century. As the commissioner for the suppression of thuggee and dacoity, Sleeman played a central role in apprehending and prosecuting thugs. Equally importantly, his writings were instrumental in creating a portrait of Indian criminality. In his Introduction to the *Ramaseeana*, Sleeman describes the thug as simultaneously ordinary and exceptional, a kind of Indian everyman much like Magwitch is, in his own way, iconically English. Sleeman begins with speculation about the origins of thuggee, which he variously traces to ancient times referenced by Herodotus, and "parties of vagrant Mahommuduns who infested the roads about the ancient capital of India" in the sixteenth century.[11] Whatever its origin, Sleeman avers that there are "seven clans of Mahommudan Thugs," whom "all Thugs throughout India, whether Hindoos or Mahommuduns, are admitted to be the most ancient, and the great original trunk upon which all the others have at different times and in different places been grafted."[12] The common genealogy shared by all thugs marks both a hereditary basis for their criminality and forms a solid connection across the diverse group.

In addition to a shared genealogy, Sleeman also depicts all thugs as united in their service of the Hindu goddess Kali. Melding Hindu and Muslim religious beliefs, Sleeman claims that

> there is not among them one who doubts *the divine origin of the system of Thuggee* – not one who doubts, that he and all who have followed the trade of murder with the prescribed rites and observances, were acting under the immediate orders and auspices of the Goddess Devee, Durga, Kalee or Bhawanee, as she is indifferently called, and consequently there is not one

> who feels the slightest remorse for the murders which he may, in the course of his vocation, have perpetrated or assisted in perpetrating.[13]

According to Sleeman, various gangs of thugs across India might have had minor differences, but for the most part they are indistinguishable from one another. They share common practices and a uniformity of custom, despite local variations, and despite adhering to different religious faiths.

In addition, Sleeman claimed, the system was so widespread, and thugs were so completely integrated into Indian society, that they were a universal feature across the subcontinent. Yet, according to Sleeman, because thugs were a secretive cult, many Indians did not even know of their existence. In fact, "to men who do not know them, the principal members of these associations will always appear to be among the most amiable, most respectable, and most intelligent members of the lower, and sometimes the middle and higher classes of native society."[14] In short, thugs could be found anywhere, and virtually anyone could be a thug. Interestingly, from their shared genealogy, common religious beliefs, and uniform secret language, the thugs, in Sleeman's portrait of them, represented a sense of unification across the subcontinent that was much more consistent with British ambitions than Indian realities. While the British sought to expand their jurisdiction across the subcontinent (in which project the campaign to suppress thuggee played a central role), India had never been a unified nation.

For Sleeman, however, thuggee was emblematically, even biologically, Indian, and this is reflected in the metaphors that he employs to describe the practice. In the instance above, Sleeman refers to the "great original trunk" that is "grafted" onto different times and places. Merging the land with its inhabitants and culture, Sleeman writes of "the congenial soil" that India provided to thuggee:

> But India is emphatically the land of superstition and in this land the system of Thuggee, the most extraordinary that has ever been recorded in the history of the human race, had found a congenial soil, and flourished with rank luxuriance for more than two centuries, till its roots had penetrated and spread over almost every district within the limits of our dominions, when the present plan of operations for its suppression was adopted in 1830 by then Governor General Lord William Bentinck.[15]

In this passage, Sleeman naturalizes the relationship between the territory and the acts that it inspires and supports. Not only is thuggee represented as essentially Indian, but India is also characterized as naturally fertile to thugs. The biological metaphor repeats throughout the text, for example, in the assertion that it is impossible to "affirm absolutely that it has been suppressed while any seeds of the system remain to germinate and spread again over the land . . . for there is in it a 'principle of vitality' which can be found hardly in any other."[16] Moreover, thuggee's hold over the land is so thorough that no attempt to suppress it, however systematic, could ever be "affirmed *absolutely.*"[17]

In Sleeman's representation, thuggee's association with India is at once cultural, spatial, biological, and temporal. In addition to being everywhere, endemic in the very land, and involving potentially everyone, thuggee's indeterminate origins fold India's past into its present, highlighting the popular perception of India as intrinsically atemporal.[18] Sleeman claims that a "thug considers the persons murdered precisely in the light of victims offered up to the Goddess; and he remembers them, as a Priest of Jupiter remembered the oxen, and a Priest of Saturn the children sacrificed upon their altars."[19] The indecipherability of thuggee's historical origins, coupled with the comparison to ancient Roman mythology, has the effect of both collapsing Indian temporality onto itself, and mapping India's present onto Europe's past. Unlike the teleology of the bildungsroman, the narrative of thuggee is ahistorical and nondevelopmental. S. Shankar addresses this point when he suggests that the "geographical extensiveness and historical length of the phenomenon of thuggee . . . allows colonialist accounts reciprocally to elaborate colonial power along the two axes of space and time." In order to be most effective, Shankar argues, "[n]ot only must such power colonize the land, the territory, the geography – the 'space' – but it must also colonize the chronicles, the tradition, the history – the 'time' – of the society that it wishes to conquer."[20] While I will take up the point of temporality more fully in Chapters 3 and 4, here I simply wish to stress that one of the main purposes of the campaign against thuggee was to create a portrait of Indian criminality, and teach Indians to recognize it as part of their past, present, and, if not forcefully suppressed, their future. By the time of the passage of the Criminal Tribes Act of 1871, and throughout its expansion over the late nineteenth and early twentieth centuries, vast swathes of the Indian population, irrespective of religion, came to be classified as criminal castes and tribes.

"And Strike Terror into the English Government"

As discussed in Chapter 1, more recent historians – including Stewart Gordon, Radhika Singha, Parama Roy, Sandria Frietag, David Arnold, and others – have cast doubt on Sleeman's narrative, suggesting that thuggee was in large measure a product of the colonial imagination. While the veracity of Sleeman's claims about thuggee has been debated by scholars, however, two things are undeniably true: (1) Sleeman's work shaped the scope and nature of criminal prosecution in India, and (2) it profoundly influenced literary and cultural representations of India in Britain. Accounts of thuggee constituted a popular element in British depictions of colonial life, and the publishing success of Philip Meadows Taylor's *Confessions of a Thug* testifies to the genre's appeal. As Máire ní Fhlathúin notes, "What purport to be wholly factual narratives of the discovery and eradication of a long-established association of religiously-motivated murderers . . . are, in the course of the nineteenth century, incorporated into most of the genres of fiction, as well as popular sermons."[21] So indistinct was the line between fact and fiction that T. D. Landon's nineteenth-century travelogue "includes the account of a visit to the 'Thug Institute' in Jabalpur, in 1851, where he claims to have found Ameer Ali, 'chief of thugs'; the reader is referred to Taylor's *Confessions* for his story."[22] The pervasive conflation of fact and fiction in depictions of the figure of the thug in turn has had an abiding influence on representations of Indian criminality, and racialized criminality more broadly, as nondevelopmental and therefore not open to rehabilitation.

Confessions of a Thug tells the story of Ameer Ali, a self-professed thug, as narrated by an unnamed British official in the service of the Nizam of Hyderabad. Over the course of the novel, Ameer Ali relates his ascent within the world of thuggee as he becomes one of the most prolific thugs in Hindostan, killing a staggering 719 people. He is finally captured by the British, and, in order to avoid hanging, becomes an approver to aid in the campaign against thuggee. The narrative opens with Ameer Ali recounting how he entered the world of thuggee. We learn that Ameer Ali was five years old and traveling with his family when he met an older man, posing as a fellow traveler, who offered him sweets. Tempted by the treat, he befriends the man, who then introduces himself to the boy's family. He tells them that he is one of a group of soldiers traveling in the same direction as the family and suggests they all travel together. The family readily agrees, and they set off the next day. It soon becomes clear, however, that the man's group is actually a band of thugs, and the family is robbed and strangled. The young Ameer Ali alone is spared, and adopted by Ismail, a thug leader, who brings him home and provides him with a happy childhood. If, as we see later, the humanization of Magwitch unfolds around his development of fatherly care for Pip, the portrait of the thug is riddled with instances of toxic fatherhood. At the age of nine, Ameer Ali's adoptive mother dies, and he spends the rest of his childhood under the tutelage of a local mullah, who teaches him to read and write Persian. Several years later, Ameer Ali overhears his father speaking in a mysterious language with a group of men who visit the house regularly. Eventually Ismail reveals that he is "a Thug, a member of that glorious profession which has been transmitted from the remotest periods," in which "the Hindoo and the Moslim both unite as brothers."[23] Ameer Ali is initiated into the cult of thuggee, and becomes one of its most successful practitioners. The long, and at times tedious, novel details Ameer Ali's numerous thug exploits, as he comes to dominate his profession. Along the way, he marries and has a daughter and a son who dies at a young age. At several points in the narrative, Ameer Ali tries to spare one young boy after another from among his victims to bring home and adopt, but his efforts are repeatedly thwarted and the children are killed, either by himself or one of his associates. Eventually Ameer Ali falls under British surveillance and is apprehended by the Company's army. His wife, who never suspected that Ameer Ali was a thug, dies shortly after his capture, and the kindly mullah who schooled him takes in his daughter and sees to her marriage. In captivity, Ameer Ali learns that one of his victims was his biological sister, whom he killed in order to steal an amulet that was said to have protective powers. We learn that the amulet received its reputation because the girl had stayed behind when the rest of her family went on a journey and never returned. The novel ends with Ameer Ali, in "fear of the horrible death of hanging, the dread of the Kala Panee," choosing to cooperate with the British in exposing his former associates.[24]

Before Ameer Ali begins his story, the Introduction asserts that the events of the narrative are "almost all true" and that, where it exists, the element of fiction "has been supplied only to connect the events, and make the adventures of Ameer Ali as interesting as the nature of his horrible profession would permit me." In the Introduction, the narrator marvels at how "the system of Thuggee could have become so prevalent," yet remain "unknown to, and unsuspected by, the people of India, among whom the professors of it were living in constant association."[25] Borrowing heavily from Sleeman, Taylor attributes this paradox to "the peculiar construction of Oriental society" in which "in every part of India many of the hereditary landholders and the chief officers of the villages have had private connections with Thugs for generations."[26] The landholders and thugs are depicted as having formed a mutually beneficial relationship wherein the landholders would permit the thugs' "atrocious acts to pass with impunity" in exchange for a "portion of their gains" or "a tax upon their houses, which the Thugs cheerfully paid."[27] Likewise, they were aided by "hermits, fakeers, and religious mendicants" who "afforded the Thugs places of rendezvous or concealment, while the fakeers, under their sanctimonious garb, have enticed travelers to their gardens by the apparently disinterested offers of shade and good water."[28] Mirroring Sleeman's *Ramaseeana*, *Confessions of a Thug* represents thugs as wholly incorporated within the fabric of society.

To this end, rather than forming a peripheral or parallel society, thugs comprise the central social group within the novel. By inverting the typical proportion of criminals to noncriminals, the novel creates the sense that thugs are a representative element of Indian society. In the opening sentence of the novel, Ameer Ali invites his interlocutor to listen to his story, which he says "will be understood" by him because he is familiar with "the peculiar habits of my countrymen."[29] Later, the narrator muses about the remorseless nature of the thug, and wonders how "Hindoo and Moslem, of every sect and denomination, should join with one accord in the superstition from which this horrible trade has arisen." "In the Hindoo perhaps it is not to be wondered at," he speculates, "as the goddess who protects him is one whom all castes regard with reverence . . . but as for the Moslem . . . [h]is Koran denounces murderers."[30] Defying divisions of all varieties, thuggee is depicted as a point of unity across the subcontinent. In fact, according to Ameer Ali, thuggee is as Indian as a good hunt is English: "How many of you English are passionately devoted to sporting? Your days and months are passed in its excitement. A tiger, a panther, a buffalo, or a hog, rouses your uttermost energies for its destruction – you even risk your lives in its pursuit. How much higher game is a Thug's!"[31] Only after his capture by the British, in fear for his life, does Ameer Ali agree to cooperate in telling his tale: "Life, sahib, is dear to everyone; to preserve mine, which was forfeited to your laws, I have bound myself to your service, by the fearful tenure of denouncing all my old confederates, and you well know how that service is performed by me."[32] Importantly, the narrative runs together "your laws" and "your service" highlighting the extent to which English individuals were seen by both colonizers and colonized alike as emblems of the law. Appearing more sociopathic than sympathetic, Ameer Ali describes his killings in gruesome detail.[33] Only rarely does he express any revulsion at his acts, as he narrates his role in countless murders, bloody sword fights, and the piling of victims into mass graves.

As a representation of Indian criminality, one of the most interesting aspects of the novel is Taylor's depiction of interpersonal relationships, and especially fatherhood, within the thug community. Early in the novel, Ameer Ali paints an intimate portrait of affection between himself and his adoptive father:

> I continued to be the object of his greatest care, and I reciprocated his affection, for indeed I was more kindly treated by him than I ever had been by my father, who was a proud and ill-tempered man. My new mother, too, never gave me reason to be displeased with her, for having no child of her own, I was her pet, and she lavished on me all the means in her power. I was always well dressed, and had every indulgence that a child could wish for.[34]

Despite the violent circumstances under which Ameer Ali came to be adopted, he develops a closer bond to his adoptive father than he shared with his biological one. After the death of his wife, Ameer Ali's mother, Ismail says to his son, "You are the only solace to a life which has now no enjoyment but what is produced by the development of your thoughts and actions."[35] On the occasion of his first killing, Ameer Ali's father praises his son fondly: "'You have done well,' he said in a low and kind voice, 'you will receive the reward of this soon.'"[36] And as he continues to excel at his monstrous profession, Ameer Ali reports that his father "was overpowered with joy, and every new feat that I performed seemed to render me more dear to him. He caressed me as though I had still been a child."[37] And finally, at the end of the novel, when Ismail turns to Ameer Ali and says "Thou art not my son, but I have loved thee as one," the revelation of his adoption makes little difference to the affection shared between the two men.[38]

Though in a narrative written twenty years earlier, in many ways Ismail is a mirror of the criminal Magwitch in *Great Expectations*. While Magwitch dreams of making Pip a gentleman, Ismail's fatherly care leads Ameer Ali into a life of crime and murder. If, as I claim below, Magwitch's affection for Pip serves a primary function in humanizing the convict, quite the opposite is true in *Confessions of a Thug*. While the affection between the two men is represented as genuine, it is also undoubtedly perverse, as Ameer Ali earns his father's praise and respect through a murderous pact. "I am yours to death," Ameer Ali tells his father upon his initiation into thuggee, "and I only pray that an opportunity may soon be afforded me to prove to you my devotion."[39] Ironically, while Ameer Ali initially had "wished to become a soldier, and to enter one of the bands in the service of Scindia to fight against the unbelieving Feringhees," he admits, "this too has passed away, and now I desire nothing but to become a Thug, and follow you, my father, through the world."[40] Within the moral economy of the novel, fighting the British is only marginally preferable to becoming a thug, so Ameer Ali was destined for dishonor one way or another. In short, rather than uplifting him, Ismail's adoption of Ameer Ali ensures his degeneracy.

Within the global narrative of development, colonial Britain envisioned itself as a parental figure to the childlike East. But the emphasis on paternity was more than simply ideological. During his tenure, Governor General Dalhousie aggressively pursued his doctrine of lapse, which gave the East India Company the right to annex the territories of Indian sovereigns who died without a male biological heir. The policy monetized genealogical kinship and reproduction insofar as it became a requirement for retaining sovereign control of independent territories. Adoption, in the novel and in the doctrine of lapse, was not an acceptable substitute for biological kinship[41]. Though the policy reached its apex during Dalhousie's rule, it was widely practiced between the 1820s and the 1850s, during the time Taylor was writing *Confessions of a Thug*. Ameer Ali's failure as a father, then, can also be read as a sign of the Indian incapacity for self-rule and regenerative sovereignty. Within the novel, the recurrent theme of the injurious effects of Indian fatherhood amplifies the ideological subtext of the policy of annexation, as generation after generation of men prove incapable of fatherly care.

Like the system of thuggee itself, toxic fatherhood repeats generationally in the novel. After the death of Ameer Ali's only son, he repeatedly fails in his own attempts to adopt a child from among his victims. On one of their travels, Ameer Ali sees a young boy among the group's intended victims. Feeling the loss of his own son, Ameer Ali muses, "He is a pretty boy, and I have no son to bless me; he will never know the difference between me and his father after a few days."[42] Later, during an entertainment session the thugs hold to entice their prey, Ameer Ali looks admiringly at the boy: "How I shall love that boy! Said I, inwardly, as I looked on his fair beautiful features and expressive eyes; he came to me readily, and I fondled him, and displayed to his admiring eyes my beautiful sword and dagger."[43] Nevertheless, shortly after, the boy and his mother stumble upon the scene of murder: "I shall never forget her – never; I shall never forget her wild look and her screams. I tore the boy from her arms and left her in the midst of the Thugs."[44] As Ameer Ali struggles with his nemesis Ganesha to spare the child, he laments that Ganesha "rudely snatched the child from my arms" and "hurled him into the pit" along with the rest of the bodies, where "the poor boy lay senseless and dead at the bottom."[45]

On another occasion, Ameer Ali describes saving a child "from the general slaughter," whom he "determined to adopt . . . as my own, and to bring him up in the holy faith I professed myself."[46] Yet "when his mother died," Ameer Ali "could not force him away from the body, he clung to it, young as he was, with a frantic force."[47] Unable to calm the boy, Ameer Ali describes how he drew his sword "and threatened him, but he was insensible to his danger."[48] After the boy bit his ear, Ameer Ali admits that he "killed him: but oh, how did I do it! It was the devil's work, not mine."[49] Ameer Ali's rage at the boy's inability to reciprocate his affection leads him to kill the child. Here, the narrator intervenes to beg "him to refrain from reciting the dreadful particulars."[50] Repeatedly, though Ameer Ali expresses grief over the deaths of various young boys, his affections for the children are never enough to save their lives. In his first expedition, Ameer Ali expressed concern for a fair, fine boy" whom he hoped would be spared. Instead, Ameer Ali watched "with intense agony" as the scene of destruction unfolded:

> There sat the old man; beside him his noble-looking boy; behind them their destroyers, only awaiting the signal; and the old man looked so unconscious of danger, was so entirely put off his guard and led into conversation by the mild, bland manners of my father, that what could he have suspected? That he was in the hands of those from whom he was to meet his death? Ah, no! And as I gazed and gazed, how I longed to scream out to him to fly![51]

Ameer Ali overcomes his desire to aid the boy and his father, and a moment later "the Thug had thrown his handkerchief round the neck of the old man, another one his round that of the son, and in an instant they were on their backs struggling in the agonies of death. Not a sound escaped them but an indistinct gurgling in their throats."[52] Ameer Ali's capacity to sanction and aid in the child's death confirms his own entry into the community of thugs.

Over and over in the novel, thug masculinity is defined by an ability to countenance the death of a child. In one notable instance, Peer Khan, one of Ameer Ali's closest friends, brings his young son along on an expedition. When the boy unexpectedly witnesses a scene of murder, he recoils in terror, and falls from his horse: "His eyes became fixed, and were wide open, his tongue cleaved to the roof of his mouth, he uttered no sound, but clasped his hands in agony; and before I could dismount, or even Peer Khan, who was superintending the work, he had fallen from his pony insensible."[53] Later, when the boy dies from his terror and the injuries it provoked, Peer Khan finds himself unable to tolerate his son's death, and unable to continue as a thug. Ameer Ali attempts to console his friend, but Peer Khan cannot be persuaded. "I am broken in spirit," he insists, "and am no longer fit for my profession."[54] Shortly after leaving the band of thugs and returning home "to make the remainder of [his] life acceptable to Alla," Peer Khan dies from his grief.[55]

The depth of Peer Khan's mourning is contrasted with Ameer Ali's capacity to move past his own son's death. While he professes sorrow at the loss of his son, Ameer Ali frames his love for his family in chilling terms: "I loved them, sahib, with a love as intense as were the other passions of my nature."[56] Over the course of the narrative, despite multiple attempts, Ameer Ali remains unable to nurture a child. On the final page of the novel, he speaks fondly, but fleetingly, about his daughter: "I used often to think on my daughter, but her too I have almost forgotten; yet I should not say forgotten, for I love her with a parent's affection, which will last to the latest moment of my existence. But she is happy, and why should she know of me?"[57]

Interestingly, Ameer Ali's descriptions of the death of a child are often followed by asides from the narrator. For example, after the death of Ameer Ali's son, the narrator opines that "the mind would ordinarily reject sympathy with the joys or sorrows of a murderer like Ameer Ali, one so deeply stained with crime of the most revolting nature, yet for the moment I was moved to see . . . the simple mention of the death of his favourite child could so much affect him, even to tears, and they were genuine."[58] While ostensibly commenting about his sympathy for the thug, such interjections serve to humanize the narrator more than to elicit sympathy for Ameer Ali.[59] The narrator's sympathy in the face of the thug's "rank guilt" is far more remarkable than Ameer Ali's expression of grief for his lost child. And, indeed, the novel seems unusually preoccupied with relating the deaths of children, inciting sympathy from English readers, while painting a portrait of Indian brutality. In the middle of the novel, spanning a hundred and fifty pages or so, four young boys are killed.

The novel's recurrent, even insistent, theme of failed, or toxic, paternity has larger implications not only about the failure of the thug to develop within the traditional terms of the bildungsroman, but also about the cultural and political representation of India more broadly. If, as in Robert Filmer's model, the figure of the father is analogous to that of the sovereign, *Confessions of a Thug* implicitly casts doubt on Indian capacity for self-rule. From the despotic act of killing a disobedient child to the inability to protect an innocent one, Taylor depicts Indian fatherhood as profoundly ineffectual. While it might seem unwarranted to extrapolate larger cultural analyses from the portrait of a thug community, the novel offers little evidence of Indian society outside of that environment. As Javed Majeed points out, in *Confessions of a Thug*, "Cultist aspects of *Thagi* merge into mainstream religious aspects of Indian society; as a result, there is a tendency for Indian society as a whole to stand condemned."[60] In particular, Majeed frames Taylor's representation of thuggee in relation to larger ideological questions of Indian self-rule. Amid the vast heterogeneity of the subcontinent, thuggee was portrayed as one of the few indigenous unifying "systems." "The author's implication," Majeed writes, "is that this grotesque cult is the only way anything approaching a cultural unity in India can be achieved among Indians themselves, which underlines the importance of the civilising and unifying role of the British themselves in India."[61] On the one hand, Indian heterogeneity was seen as a structural impediment to self-rule, and on the other hand, the only viable method of fostering unity was through the expansion of British hegemony and criminal law.[62]

As "one of the first novels to display many of the themes which seem to typify the later Anglo-Indian novel as a whole," *Confessions of a Thug* set the stage for British representations of India.[63] Because specific references to India were surprisingly rare in British fiction, Taylor's immensely popular novel has had a disproportionate effect on successive generations of British and European cultural production.[64] From novels such as Wilkie Collins's *The Moonstone*, Charles Dickens's *Edwin Drood*, Jules Verne's *Around the World in Eighty Days*, Arthur Conan Doyle's *The Sign of Four*, films like *Indiana Jones and the Temple of Doom* and *The Deceivers*, and countless nineteenth-century historical texts and travel narratives, to more modern novels and histories such as M. J. Carter's *The Strangler Vine*, Mike Dash's *Thug: The True Story of India's Murderous Cult*, and Kevin Rushby's *Children of Kali: Through India in Search of Bandits*, the work of Sleeman and Taylor has shaped the discourse and perception of Indian criminality as well as Indian society and sociality.

During the nineteenth century, thuggee, like other flashpoint issues such as sati and caste, was seen as evidence of India's essential degeneracy. As I discuss in detail in Chapter 3, British colonialism justified itself in large part by a belief that India was constitutively incapable of generating a viable futurity. In *Confessions of a Thug*, the string of dead children that occupies the middle section of the novel resonates symbolically with the conception of India as a land with no future. In his elegant and compelling critique of "the child as the privileged ensign of the future," Lee Edelman exposes the emotional and political heft attached to the figure of the child.[65] If, as Edelman suggests, the ideal of the child serves a coercive function in perpetuating a normative futurity, within the context of *Confession of a Thug*, the failure to ensure life for the child symbolizes not only the failure of Indian masculinity but also an absolute failure to secure futurity itself. This symbolic lack of a future is made clear especially when *Confessions of a Thug* is read in comparison to *Great Expectations*, in which Pip's future emerges as the promise held by mercantile colonialism.

If, in Taylor's text, the children's deaths foreclose the future, Ameer Ali stubbornly lives on. The thug's depravity cannot be extinguished, as evidenced in his intractable hold on life.[66] Unlike the noble and self-sacrificial Magwitch, Ameer Ali is shown to be cowardly, but alive, suspended in a perpetual present. And also in contrast to Magwitch, Ameer Ali cannot be rehabilitated; he can only confess. With his associates caught, and his trial impending, Ameer Ali thus chooses life: "It was clearly the crisis of my fate, and, I must confess it, the fear of the horrible death of hanging, the dread of the Kala Panee, and the advice of the Moonshee caused my resolutions of dying with the rest to give way to a desire of life."[67] While the narrative of the text undermines any sense of a viable futurity, it consigns the thug, and by extension India as a whole, to immortalizing and endlessly reliving a decadent and destructive past in the form of a confession.

But, of course, the figure of the thug does have a future well beyond nineteenth-century India. In contemporary American and Anglophone popular culture, the word thug continues to signify racialized criminality. And in spite of its movement across space and time, the term resonates powerfully with its historical precursor, resurrecting every major trope, including an insatiable taste for luxury, a propensity for violence, and toxic masculinity and fatherhood. If novels such as *Great Expectations* play a role in the genealogy of criminal rehabilitation in England, *Confessions of a Thug* continues to haunt the imaginative landscape of the present in a starkly material fashion.[68] In the final pages of Philip Meadows Taylor's fictional account, Ameer Ali chooses to "confess" and cooperate with his captors in order to avoid his own fate of hanging. In doing so, within the novel, he secures his life and fulfills the disciplinary desires of the colonial state's legal and political campaign. But, through this "confession," the thug has taken on an afterlife well beyond the scope of even Taylor's capacious imagination.

Crime and Its Punishment

If *Confessions of a Thug* secures the portrait of Indian criminality as a consequence of the paradigmatic failure of Indian masculinity and paternity, *Great Expectations* performs the opposite function, humanizing the criminal as an agent of fatherly care. Charles Dickens published *Great Expectations* in his weekly periodical *All the Year Round* between December 1860 and August 1861, before it appeared as a three-volume novel in October 1861. In its treatment of the relationship between the young protagonist Pip and the convict Abel Magwitch, the novel represents a significant literary contribution to the evolving views on criminality and punishment in nineteenth-century England.

Dickens was known to be interested in the penal system, and often incorporated a critique of the harsh courts and prisons into his works of fiction.[69] Having spent a brief period at the age of twelve working in a blacking factory while his father served time at a debtor's prison, Dickens was well-acquainted with the dehumanizing conditions of early nineteenth-century prisons. He was also keenly interested in penal reform, which was one of the signal social movements of the nineteenth century. During his travels to America in 1842, Dickens visited Eastern State Penitentiary in Philadelphia, where he recoiled at the effects of solitary confinement, and the abysmal Tombs in New York City, which, according to Sean Grass, he found "to be far less brutal than the years upon years of isolation within individual cells" that the solitary system imposed.[70] Dickens weighed in on the debate between solitary confinement and silent work prisons in his travel narrative *American Notes*, in which he argued forcefully against isolation for prisoners.

But Dickens's most important, even if more indirect, contribution to the conversation on penal reform was through his fiction, in which he was able to craft characters and narratives in order to shape readers' thoughts and feelings. When Dickens's *Great Expectations* was serialized in *All the Year Round*, "the magazine was selling approximately one thousand copies a week," and, as Jan Alber notes, "the installments of Dickens' novels must have shaped the popular understanding of the prison in a significant way."[71] In *Great Expectations*, written toward the end of his career, Dickens guides readers to identify with Pip as he moves from fear of the criminal Abel Magwitch to genuine affection for him.[72] The story unfolds around two main threads featuring Miss Havisham, a wealthy but embittered woman whom Pip believes to be his benefactor, and Magwitch, who we later learn is his benefactor.

Phillip Collins writes of Magwitch that "Dickens is interested in him, and wants us to share – indeed, to anticipate – Pip's later affection for him, after the terror and revulsion he had excited earlier."[73] In many ways, Pip's journey from terror to acceptance and affection mirrored the larger trajectory of criminal justice reform, moving away from strictly punitive measures and toward rehabilitation. As discussed in the previous chapter, between 1832 and 1841 the number of offences punishable by death dramatically decreased, and capital punishment became increasingly rare. By the time Dickens wrote *Great Expectations*, for example, returning illegally from transportation, as Magwitch did, was no longer a capital offence.[74] Setting *Great Expectations* in the semi-recent past therefore has the effect of affectively reconstructing the logic for criminal rehabilitation.

Though the novel was published in 1861, the majority of the action takes place between the 1820s and the 1840s. In England, this was the era in which the penal system was reformed and transportation became increasingly rare. In India, the period coincided with the campaign to suppress Thuggee and the increased transportation of convicts, including Eduljee Byramjee, who was sent to Singapore in 1844. Reading *Great Expectations* alongside Philip Meadows Taylor's *Confessions of a Thug* thus makes evident how the specter of the monstrous Indian served as a useful, and perhaps necessary, backdrop for the humanization of the English criminal. Placing both of these novels in the relation to the JCPC opinion shows the material consequences of the logic of Indian punishment that underwrote the possibility of English rehabilitation.

"The Terror of Childhood"

Dickens's novel opens with a young Pip sitting by his parents' graves, while the narrator (the adult Pip) muses about his name and identity. We learn that Pip's name is derived from his "father's family name being Pirrip," and his "Christian name Philip." Pip describes how his "infant tongue could make of both names nothing longer or more explicit than Pip." "So, I called myself Pip," he relates, "and came to be called Pip."[75] Reflecting what Moretti identifies as a central tension inherent in the bildungsroman between "the ideal of *self-determination* and the equally imperious demands of *socialization*," Pip's identity is at once social and individual, patrilineal and self-made. One of the guiding questions from the outset of the novel, then, is to what extent is Pip (or the convict he is about to meet) an individual, and to what extent is he a product of the various social forces that shape him? The answer to this question is to be found as much in the generic qualities of the bildungsroman as it is in the plot of the novel. Moretti, in fact, identifies this structuring tension as fundamental to the genre of the bildungsroman. "How can the tendency towards *individuality*, which is the necessary fruit of a culture of self-determination," Moretti asks, "be made to coexist with the opposing tendency to *normality*, the offspring, equally inevitable, of the mechanism of socialization?"[76] Moretti proposes that the vision of development the bildungsroman offers, and instantiates, relies upon the illusion of self-determination in order to make complete the ultimate acquiescence to the social norm: "It is not sufficient for modern bourgeois society to simply subdue the drives that oppose the standards of 'normality'. It is also necessary that, as a 'free individual,' not as a fearful subject but as a convinced citizen, one perceives the social norms as *one's own*."[77] As Moretti's observations about the bildungsroman reveal, the development of the modern liberal subject is neither individual nor purely social. Instead, the liberal subject, or the protagonist of the bildungsroman, must come to believe that their desires are their own. They must take responsibility for whichever way their desires lead them, and they must accept that any departure from the rightness of the law is a defect of character rather than a fault of society. Despite the social forces that produce criminality, in order to be open to rehabilitation, the individual criminal must accept their guilt as though it were exclusively a product of their own will. This is in contrast to the portrait of Indian criminality painted by Sleeman and Taylor, in which both criminality and culpability are extended across the social arena rather than limited to the individual. Unlike Magwitch, and despite his "confession," Ameer Ali never rises above his crime, or develops as a sympathetic character.

As a representation of English subject formation, the project of the bildungsroman, therefore, is to transact this movement between individuality and socialization by securing consent to the normal that is masked under the illusion of individual desire. As Foucault, Althusser, H. L. A. Hart, and others have explained, this tension is also of course a defining characteristic of legal subjectivity in European modernity. Within *Great Expectations*, Pip, and by extension Magwitch, must both take responsibility for their own actions, including crimes, and believe that they are motivated by their own desires. By highlighting the element of fear in Pip's development, while also consigning it to the realm of childhood, the novel marshals strategies of social coercion into a narrative of consent.

A few lines after the opening scene described earlier, Pip is startled out of his thoughts by a "terrible voice," as Magwitch, the escaped convict, takes him by the shoulders and leans over him. The "fearful man" inspires "terror" in Pip, as "his eyes looked most powerfully down into mine, and mine looked most helplessly up into his."[78] Before releasing him, Magwitch extracts a promise from Pip, upon penalty of death, to bring him a file and some food the following morning. Pip feels a "sense of helplessness and danger," but as he watches the convict limp away across the cold and damp marsh, we sense that Pip's terror begins to mingle with pity. Pip provides the convict with the rations he requests, including some drink and savories prepared for the upcoming Christmas holiday. Almost from the first moments of their encounter, Pip is placed in the position of being able to extend aid to Magwitch. But the risk of helping the convict comes with a risk for Pip, too, thus joining their fortunes.

Even at his young age, Pip is aware that helping Magwitch is the right thing to do, even if it involves breaking the law. Opening up a space between justice and the law, the text enables the reader to follow Pip's lead in sympathizing with the hungry convict. Initially, of course, Pip sneaks into the pantry and steals food for Magwitch because he is frightened of him:

> I have often thought that few people know what secrecy there is in the young, under terror. No matter how unreasonable the terror, so that it be terror. I was in mortal terror of the young man who wanted my heart and liver; I was in mortal terror of my interlocutor with the ironed leg; I was in mortal terror of myself, from whom an awful promise had been extracted; I had no hope of deliverance through my all-powerful sister, who repulsed me at every turn; I am afraid to think of what I might have done, on requirement, in the secrecy of my terror.[79]

But over the course of the narrative, Pip's "terror" becomes more complicated, as he begins to feel sympathy for Magwitch. The "secrecy" of Pip's "terror" and the moral dilemma that it inspires are represented as intensely personal. Within the economy of the novel, Pip's pity is individual, while his sense of fear is instigated by social interactions. By conjoining the sentiments of terror and sympathy, and building both into the developmental plot of the novel, however, Dickens brings pity and sympathy for the criminal into the realm of the social. The personal identification that Pip feels with Magwitch parallels the attachment that we as readers feel for Pip, drawing us, as well, into sympathy with Magwitch. The secondary narrative of sympathy for Magwitch, however, is thoroughly interwoven with the primary one of Pip's development. What we learn over the course of the novel, in fact, is that Pip's own development is conditional upon his allowing his identification with Magwitch to percolate to the surface.

From the outset a strong identification exists between Pip and Magwitch. Pip's terror of Magwitch, for example, is matched by his terror of himself, "from whom an awful promise had been extracted." Pip worries about "what [he] might have done," suggesting that under the right circumstances, anyone has the capacity to become a criminal. And following his encounter with Magwitch, Pip asks Joe what it means to be a convict:

> While Mrs. Joe sat with her head bending over her needlework, I put my mouth into the forms of saying to Joe, 'What's a convict?' Joe put *his* mouth into the forms of returning such a highly elaborate answer, that I could make out nothing of it but the single word 'Pip.'[80]

Although he remains terrified of Magwitch as an individual, within his imagination, Pip replaces the definition of a convict with his own name.[81] Similarly, after a fight with "the pale young gentleman," Pip fears "that the Law would avenge it" and he "devised incredible ways of accounting for that damnatory circumstance when [he] should be haled before the Judges."[82] Pip's concerns about his own criminality, in turn, serve to humanize the figure of the criminal. If a child can imagine himself a criminal, the novel suggests, so can anyone else. And at its heart, the bildungsroman is about the imagination and production of identities, bringing those identities into alignment with social norms.

As Jeremy Tambling remarks, "*Great Expectations* certainly recognizes itself to be about the creation of identities, imposed from higher to lower, from oppressor to oppressed."[83] But as the opening lines of the novel suggest, social identities, as well as personal ones, are both externally-imposed and self-made.[84] The mirroring and intermingling of Pip's ascent with Magwitch's criminality hints at the complexity of how identities in the novel are formed and shaped. Lacking biological parents, Pip is brought up "by hand" by his abusive sister and kindly brother-in-law. Pip also gains parental figures in Miss Havisham and Magwitch. In many respects, the absence of the nuclear family unmoors Pip from the normative space of ideological subject formation, and frees him to craft his own identity. It also enables unruly affective relationships, including the one between Pip and Magwitch.

Unlike Ameer Ali's failed attempts at fatherhood, Magwitch's role as a secret father figure to Pip is crucial to the novel's capacity to humanize the convict. Importantly, Magwitch's status as a convict becomes the occasion for him to receive Pip's aid as well as to extend kindness of his own. Hunted and starving, Magwitch is arguably as vulnerable as Pip when the two first meet. The convict is in this sense akin to the child. When the police catch up to Magwitch, his punishment becomes the means by which he repays his debt to both Pip and society at large. After Pip helps him, Magwitch uses the money he earns while on transport in Australia to make Pip a "gentleman." Though transported for life, Magwitch risks everything, ultimately including his life, to return to England and see Pip as an adult. The unfolding of the mystery around Pip's true benefactor helps consolidate sympathy for Magwitch as we begin to suspect that the convict is the source of Pip's "great expectations." Magwitch's rehabilitation thus mirrors Pip's growth into adulthood. Occupying in turns both the position of the child and the father, Magwitch emerges as fully human and deserving of sympathy by the end of the novel.

Though the novel does not ultimately validate Magwitch's dream of destabilizing class hierarchies by making Pip a gentleman, it does elicit compassion for the convict. In fact, the moral economy of the novel rests as much on Magwitch's attempt to make Pip a gentleman as it does on his failure to accomplish that goal. As a suspense novel, the narrative strategy of *Great Expectations* is to create a sense of ambiguity about assumptions typically taken to be factual, or even natural. Yet this element of suspense is framed within the larger teleology of the bildungsroman so that the plot and the genre of the novel move toward two different conclusions. While the plot makes it increasingly clear that Pip's material success, and ultimately his spiritual growth as well, is the product of his early interactions with Magwitch, the genre of the novel works to perpetuate the notion, or at least illusion, that Pip's development is the product of individual will. As we move through the novel, individualism and socialization come together as Magwitch grows into a parental role, while Pip becomes complicit with a paternalistic colonialism, consolidating plot and genre. Just as it is impossible to disentangle Pip's development from its social production on the level of genre, it is similarly impossible to isolate Magwitch's criminality from its social causes on the level of plot.

By unsettling conventions about social and individual responsibility for crime, the novel compels a rethinking of criminality more broadly. Narrating an experience from his childhood, Magwitch relates how he "got the name of being hardened":

> 'This is a terrible hardened one,' they says to prison wisitors, picking out me. 'May be said to live in jails, this boy.' Then they looked at me, and I looked at them, and they measured my head, some on 'em, – they had better a measured my stomach, – and others on 'em giv me tracts what I couldn't read, and made me speeches what I couldn't understand.

> They always went on agen me about the Devil. But what the Devil was I to do? I must put something into my stomach, mustn't I? – Howsomever, I'm a getting low, and I know what's due. Dear boy and Pip's comrade, don't you be afeerd of me being low.[85]

In this scene, the identification of the child Pip with the figure of the criminal at the beginning of the novel comes full circle, as the criminal Magwitch is identified with the figure of the child.

Harking back to the initial feelings of "terror" that Pip experienced when he first encountered Magwitch on the marshes, Magwitch implores Pip's friend Herbert not to "be afeerd of me being low."[86] The scene challenges Victorian stereotypes and attempts to paint a more complex portrait of the relationship between poverty and criminality. In addition, Magwitch references the nineteenth-century pseudoscientific practice of phrenology, which attributed behavioral qualities, such as criminality, to physical variations in head size and shape. By asserting claims to science and rationality, phrenologists sought to provide a biological, and hyper-individualized explanation for social ills. Yet, the novel works against this logic. "By implication," as Grace Moore suggests, "it is in fact the body politic, the state, which manifests these traits through its criminal negligence of its citizens."[87] Magwitch's narrative both renders the criminal human and condemns the social prejudices that invariably associate poverty with criminality. Of course, the kind of biological basis for criminality that is readily dismissed in *Great Expectations* was wholeheartedly endorsed in the representation of thuggee.[88] In the Indian instance, it is not that social inequities result in individual instances of criminality, but rather that criminality is a widespread and endemic condition that necessitates the intervention of the law.

Yet, despite its critique of processes of criminalization and the ways in which criminals are treated by society, the novel largely preserves a host of social norms. In the end, the individual criminal is thwarted, as ultimately Magwitch is arrested and sentenced to death for disobeying the rules of his transportation. Although the narrative intervenes in the legal judgment and allows him to die naturally, Pip does not become the wealthy gentleman that Magwitch had hoped to make him. While the novel redeems the criminal morally, it only goes so far to upend class norms. In the end, Joe pays Pip's debts as hard work and perseverance are celebrated over meteoric ascent.

Similarly, though the novel seems to feature formidable women characters, it ultimately falls back on popular Victorian stereotypes of gender and sexuality. Miss Havisham, for example, appears full of vengeful self-determination, but by the end of the novel we realize her identity is developed entirely in response to the various men who shape it (her brother and Compeyson, for example). To the extent that she is agentive at all, she is dependent upon Jaggers to execute her wishes. And Miss Havisham's narrative ends in a dramatic sati-like immolation, which finally frees Pip from her icy grip on his emotions. Mrs. Joe suffers a long-drawn illness and painful death, likewise freeing Joe to marry a much younger Biddy. Finally, Estella marries Pip's nemesis Bentley Drummle, and at the close of the novel is age-worn and unhappy. And while the novel seems replete with alternatives to the nuclear family, in the end, all prove unsuccessful: Miss Havisham's adoption of Estella is disastrous and Magwitch's attempt to bequeath a fortune to Pip fails. At the same time, normative family ties are reaffirmed as the Aged Parent and Wemmick share a happy bond, Herbert and Clara marry, and Joe and Biddy produce a new young Pip, who will grow up in a proper nuclear family. Ultimately falling back on the inescapable teleology of the bildungsroman, the text places various norms in abeyance only to restore, and thus naturalize, them at the conclusion. In a novel that otherwise reconciles all manner of social norms to their predictable order, then, its treatment of criminality stands out.

Reforming the Criminal

Importantly, *Great Expectations* was not unique in its nuanced and compassionate representation of criminality. Newgate novels, which featured criminals from Newgate Prison as main characters, were immensely popular during the first half of the nineteenth century.[89] Walking by Newgate prison in *Great Expectations*, Pip is accosted by a "partially drunk minister of justice" who offered to "show me where the gallows was kept, and also where people were publicly whipped, and then he showed me the Debtors' Door, out of which culprits came to be hanged."[90] While controversial for their capacity to incite interest in and sympathy for criminal elements, these novels were instrumental to, as well as symptomatic of, changing attitudes toward crime and punishment. Novels such as Edward Bulwer's *Paul Clifford*, Harrison Ainsworth's *Jack Sheppard*, and Dickens's *Oliver Twist* crafted detailed and complex portraits of the circumstances and motivations for criminality.[91]

In his comprehensive study of the Newgate novel, Michael Hollingsworth writes, "During the critical decade of the eighteen-twenties, when reform of the parliament and reform of the criminal law were equally overdue, the Newgate theme was everywhere, and it occurred in a few novels without drawing particular notice to itself. Between 1830 and 1847, however, a series of novels having criminals as prominent characters aroused widespread attention."[92] As social attitudes and legal policies toward corporal and capital punishment shifted, the novels reflected a heightened interest in psychologizing the figure of the criminal.[93]

Prior to the advent of the Newgate novel, lower and working-class readers were entertained with execution broadsides, or cheap pamphlets produced for popular consumption. The broadsides detailed scandalous crimes and offered equally sensational scenes of punishment and execution. Heather Worthington notes that in these broadsides "the demonstration of sovereign or state power was encapsulated in pictures and prose and the spectacle of public execution reached a wider audience than would have been possible in reality."[94] But over the course of the nineteenth century, the disciplinary goals of public executions were increasingly supplanted by a growing police force, as focus shifted to policing the living rather than executing the condemned. In 1829 Home Secretary Robert Peel set up the Metropolitan Police in London and a detective force was started in 1842. By the 1850s policing was widespread throughout Britain. In addition, a series of reform acts were passed between the 1820s and 1840s, and by the middle of the nineteenth century, as Hollingsworth notes, "in most instances, the offender was not to be stricken by death from membership in the human race."[95] As a result, the Newgate novelists "examined the criminal as one who, however perverted, must be recognized as belonging to the human family."[96]

The Name of the Father

Hollingsworth's metaphor of the "human family" speaks to the significance of kinship ties as a foundation for "membership in the human race."[97] The connection between the family and the race or nation has a long history in English political philosophy, perhaps most prominently in the work of Robert Filmer. In his defense of the monarchy in the seventeenth century, Filmer argued that fatherhood is analogous to kingship insofar as both are sovereign over their respective domains:

> If we compare the natural duties of a father with those of a king, we find them to be all one, without any difference at all but only in the latitude or extent of them. As the father over one family, so the king, as father over many families, extends his care to preserve, feed, clothe, instruct and defend the whole commonwealth. His wars, his peace, his courts of justice, and all

> his acts of sovereignty, tend only to preserve and distribute to every subordinate and inferior father, and to their children, their rights and privileges, so that all the duties of a king are summed up in an universal fatherly care of his people.[98]

The role that Filmer ascribes to the father to "preserve, feed, clothe, instruct and defend" his child is mirrored in Magwitch's desire to create a gentleman out of Pip.[99] And it is Ameer Ali's incapacity to fulfill this role that marks him as fundamentally alien, both as a racialized criminal and ultimately outside the fold of humanity itself. By contrast, as I have suggested, it is arguably Magwitch's extension of fatherly care toward Pip that most clearly humanizes him within the text.

If Magwitch's surrogate fatherhood of Pip is the justification for his return to England, the text also suggests that it was Magwitch's own lack of parental care that precipitated his descent into criminality. Again, this is in contrast to Ameer Ali's adoptive father, who affirmatively indoctrinates him into a life of crime.[100] In the scene cited earlier, in which Magwitch recounts his earliest childhood memory, he says, "Summun had run away from me – a man – a tinker – and he'd took the fire with him, and left me wery cold."[101] Alone and poor, the child Magwitch was judged a criminal before he became one by the jailers and phrenologists who "measured my head" and "giv me tracts what I couldn't read."[102] James E. Marlow reads this scene as a "rare satire on the procedures of phrenology" in which "Dickens shows how society uses phrenology to blind itself to the true causes, which would necessarily reveal its own contribution."[103] While Marlow sees a more robust critique of "political reactionism" in Dickens's text than I do, it is clear that the phrenologists sought to identify Magwitch as an outsider and a criminal based on visible, biological, and hereditary traits.[104] According to Marlow, "Magwitch proves that this version of human nature is wrong. Magwitch in fact proves the capacity of man to transcend the jungle mentality, to avoid the cannibal disposition inculcated by English society."[105] Marlow's choice of metaphors in describing the "jungle mentality" of hereditary criminality is suggestive of the racial undertones of phrenology. It also points to the racialization of the very concept of hereditary criminality.

In *Culture and Imperialism*, Edward Said characterizes *Great Expectations* as "both more inclusive and more dynamic" than interpretations that "situate it squarely within the metropolitan history of British fiction" would suggest. Despite the fact that Pip accepts Magwitch "as his surrogate father, not as someone to be denied or rejected," Said observes that within English society Magwitch "is in fact unacceptable, being from

Australia, a penal colony designed for the rehabilitation but not the repatriation of transported English criminals."[106] By implicitly condoning Magwitch's return, therefore, the novel unsettles the neat division between the metropolitan space and the colonies. Said reads Magwitch's exile and subsequent return as "not only penal but imperial" and argues that "Magwitch's delinquency is expiated" when "Pip takes on a new career with his boyhood friend Herbert Pocket, this time not as an idle gentleman but as a hardworking trader in the East, where Britain's other colonies offer a sort of normality that Australia never could."[107] In this manner, "Dickens settles the difficulty with Australia" by redirecting the colonial impulse to Egypt and mercantilism.[108] In Said's reading, the colonies are peripheral within the novel, but importantly structure its action, both by providing the scene of Magwitch's exile and the destination for Pip to realize his "great expectations."[109] Despite his association with Australia by virtue of his transport, however, within the novel Magwitch's exile seems to have less to do with colonialism than criminality.[110] And though the narrative clearly critiques the transport of criminals to Australia, it does not reject colonialism itself. Rather, to the extent that *Great Expectations* deconstructs the relationship between criminality and Empire at all, it seems to do so by championing mercantile colonialism as an alternative, or even an antidote, to criminality.

When Pip loses Magwitch's funds, he journeys with his friend Herbert to Egypt, to embark on a life of his own. Just as colonialism rounds out the narrative of Pip's *Bildung* by providing him a socially legitimized means to achieve his goal of becoming a gentleman, it also informs the novel's treatment of the criminal. Pip realizes his great expectations by going to the colonies, while Magwitch redeems his criminality by returning to England and reaffirming his ties within the nation. Pip's journey to Egypt affirms his English colonial aspirations, while Magwitch's return from Australia affirms his Englishness. Magwitch's loyalty to both Pip and the English nation is in turn rewarded with the reader's sympathy.

Indeed, as noted earlier, the novel's compassion for Magwitch seems largely based on the fact that English society, or the state, failed in its duty, in Filmer's words, to "preserve, feed, clothe, instruct and defend" him when he was a child.[111] Dickens's censure of the criminal justice system thus hinges upon the implication that the state bears responsibility for creating an environment that fosters opportunity and respectability and discourages criminality. To this end, certain assumptions about what the colonies are and are not suitable for are implicit in Dickens's representation. While the colonies serve a positive function in providing an opportunity for Pip to realize his expectations, the novel discourages their use as a dumping ground for English criminals.

Moreover, the novel condemns the use of the penal colony to alienate the convict from the community of the nation. In fact, while Pip's standard English speech and time spent in London signify a certain cosmopolitanism, Abel Magwitch is decidedly English.[112] According to Robert McColl Millar, Joe Gargery "speaks in Kentish dialect throughout the novel," and this "undoubtedly contributes to our perception of him as pure-hearted" (66). Similarly, Magwitch's working-class dialect and hard-scrabble life identify him as iconically English, in the company of characters from other Dickens novels such as *David Copperfield* and *Oliver Twist*. Despite his exile in Australia, Magwitch is, of course, ethnically English and racially white. Dickens's sympathetic representation of Magwitch is, therefore, very specifically a portrait of English criminality.[113]

The iconic Englishness of both Pip and Magwitch is not incidental. Folding Magwitch's development into Pip's, the bildungsroman treats Magwitch's criminality as a stage to be overcome in the larger movement toward respectable masculinity. The fact that this masculinity is realized through Pip's colonial ambitions allies the protagonist's individual development with England's position within the world. The process of becoming an individual on the level of plot rests upon the foundational narrative of nation-formation that underlies the genre of the bildungsroman. As Moretti reminds us, the bildungsroman is a genre reserved for the development of citizens, not of subjects: the protagonist must arrive at the endpoint of development "not as a fearful subject but as a convinced citizen."[114] Moretti's choice of adjectives to describe the distinction between the "convinced citizen" and "fearful subject" reveals the terms by which these categories are made real. The archetypal protagonist of the bildungsroman, the citizen, must be convinced of the terms of normativity that structure recognition. But importantly, the "convinced citizen" emerges in opposition to the "fearful subject," rather than to the "unconvinced citizen." The implicitly coercive worlding of the bildungsroman sidelines internal opposition, and instead invokes the external figure of the "fearful subject" as a model of inadequacy, and as a foil to the fully developed citizen.[115] Essentially following Hobbes's logic in which fear motivates unity, the bildungsroman relies on the specter of the "fearful subject" in order to constitute the "convinced citizen."

In the context of *The Queen* v. *Eduljee Byramjee*, the Privy Council noted that the fearful subject served a strategic purpose in disciplining both the individual criminal and Indian society at large. With this in mind, comparing Dickens's *Great Expectations* to Philip Meadows Taylor's *Confessions of a Thug* helps us decipher how the logic of the law provides a subtext for these two very different literary representations of criminality. The JCPC opinion rejected the possibility of felony appeals, thus effectively foreclosing the development of the Indian criminal into a reformed citizen. In particular, the opinion invoked a false analogy between the rights of the citizen and the subject, ensuring the continued distinction between the two categories. While the British citizen could appeal to the Queen for mercy, this was not practicable for the Indian subject. Thus the Indian criminal could neither assert a plea for mercy, nor could he exercise the more fundamental rights of citizenship by making the plea at all.

The inability of the Indian to develop into the citizen is evident in both the legal and literary instances. Reading *The Queen* v. *Eduljee Byramjee* alongside the two novels makes clear that the broader narrative of English penal reform, in fact, depends upon drawing a distinction between the irredeemable Indian criminal and his more humanized English counterpart. In this respect, *The Queen* v. *Eduljee Byramjee* and *Great Expectations* implicitly depend upon the foil of the "fearful subject" in order to assert the possibility of English criminal rehabilitation. More specifically, the *Bildungsheld* and the rehabilitated English criminal emerge into full-fledged humanity in opposition to the undeveloped "fearful subject."

As the contrast between the examples of Ameer Ali and Magwitch shows, one of the primary ways through which humanity is registered in the bildungsroman is through the development of the father figure. As Joseph Slaughter observes in the context of Goethe's *Wilhelm Meister's Apprenticeship*, "socially responsible fatherhood supplies the novel's model of civic virtue," and the "cultivation of 'the feeling of a father' toward minors and of a brother toward others marks the symbolic promotion of the subject to citizen – to a person before the law."[116] Slaughter's observation is more broadly applicable to the nineteenth century political aesthetic that drives the competing portrayals of subjecthood and citizenship in *Confessions of a Thug* and *Great Expectations.* The God-King-Father paradigm endows the father figure with a measure of sovereignty that makes fatherhood central to a particular vision of full-fledged citizenship. As we have seen in the case of Ameer Ali and India more generally, the failure to inhabit the role of father is central to the corresponding failure to rise to the level of human, and by extension, citizen of a viable nation.

Exploring the relationship between the bildungsroman and human rights law, Slaughter "elaborates the conceptual vocabulary, deep narrative grammar, and humanist social vision that human rights law shares with the bildungsroman in their cooperative efforts to imagine, normalize, and realize what the Universal Declaration and early theorists of the novel call 'the free and full development of the human personality.'"[117] The teleology at work in the bildungsroman, Slaughter shows, underlies the conditions of the human subject's emergence as the bearer of rights as well.

In particular, Slaughter examines the tension between claims to universalism that human rights law aspires to, and its more accurate reliance on locational specificity that the bildungsroman often reveals. While both human rights law and the bildungsroman participate in "abstract universalism," they, in fact, "posit the nation-state as the highest form of expression of human sociality and the citizen as the highest form of expression of human personality."[118] For Slaughter, while "the 'state/citizen bind'" is "posited as the ultimate horizon of human personality development, the nation-state consistently emerges as a problem for the abstract universalism under which both human rights and Bildung are theorized."[119] Drawing on the work of Hannah Arendt and Giorgio Agamben, Slaughter examines the stakes, within both human rights law and the bildungsroman, of isolating the citizen within the broader category of the human.

While the development of the individual into the human by virtue of citizenship is characteristic of mainstream works within the genre, as I discuss earlier, the bildungsroman also fundamentally demarcates the citizen from what Moretti identifies as the "fearful subject." The oppositional rather than partial quality of the noncitizen is significant because it highlights the extent to which, as for Hobbes and the line of thinkers who follow him, the presence of an external threat is instrumental to the very terms of citizenship that the bildungsroman envisions. The "fearful subject" is emphatically not imagined as part of the human community, and stands no chance of developing into the "convinced citizen." This oppositional condition that is counterproductive to the development of either the citizen or the individual is the disciplinary target of representations of Indian criminality.

By contrast, the developmental narrative of *Great Expectations*, and the notions of English criminality and rehabilitation that it represents, depend upon an autonomous individuality that emerges from the grips of social influence. Society might have contributed to Magwitch's criminality, for example, but his capacity to accept individual responsibility for his actions and make amends is a necessary condition of his rehabilitation. As I discuss in Chapter 4, notions of individual responsibility, cultivated in the bildungsroman, feed into the possibility of individual guilt, a requisite for the mystery novel.

If individuality is a defining characteristic of English criminality in particular, and citizenship more generally, Indian criminality was accorded a more collective, or universal, aspect within Victorian representations. The Thuggee and Dacoity Suppression Acts of 1836–1848, the response to the Rebellion of 1857, and the Criminal Tribes Act of 1871 all sought to address what was perceived as the widespread lawlessness endemic to India. Though *Great Expectations* does not explicitly address the question of India, as Hyungji Park observes, when Dickens began writing *Great Expectations* in 1860, "the Indian Rebellion of 1857–59 would have been a powerful and recent memory."[120] Priti Joshi, in tracing the influence of the rebellion on Dickens's *A Tale of Two Cities*, observes that "his sentiments, as so often, echoed those of the majority of his compatriots as well as guided them: his 1857 Christmas story, about innocent Britons encountering 'hostile attack' in a 'strange wild place' mirrored the general understanding in Britain of the 'Mutiny.'"[121] Dickens's well-known rage at the rebellion is evident in a letter to a friend dated October 4, 1857, in which he related his fantasy of being "Commander in Chief in India" so that he may "strike that Oriental race with amazement" and "blot it out of mankind and raze it off the face of the Earth."[122] Dickens's aspiration to "exterminate the Race upon whom the stain of the late cruelties rested" is characteristic of Victorian representations of Indians as inherently criminal. Further, his view of "the colonial and the criminal coexisting and corroborating each other," which Park identifies, is consistent with a broader cultural association between the colonial subject and the figure of the criminal as evidenced in *Confessions of a Thug*.

Reframing the Thug

In 2018, Yash Raj films produced Vijay Krishna Acharya's blockbuster epic *Thugs of Hindostan*. Based loosely on *Confessions of a Thug*, and featuring Bollywood superstars Amitabh Bhachchan, Katrina Kaif, and Aamir Khan, the film contests the historical narrative crafted by W. H. Sleeman and Philip Meadows Taylor. Drawing on contemporary revisions of colonial narratives, the film represents the thugs as political insurgents fighting against the British. The elderly leader of the thugs, Azaad, whose name signifies freedom or liberation, seeks to avenge the East Indian Company's annexation of an Indian kingdom in whose army he was a general. After the British slaughter the king, Azaad adopts Zafira, the young princess, and trains her as a fierce and skilled warrior. As a surrogate father to Zafira, the sagely and stalwart Azaad amends Taylor's portrait of toxic fatherhood, while also fostering her feminist sense of independence. Meanwhile, he also takes under his tutelage a young man called Firangi, who shares a name with a main informant Feringeea in Sleeman's text. Unlike Sleeman's character, however, the charming Firangi, whom the movie suggests is part English, moves fluidly between British and Indian circles, baffling both, before making his true loyalty to Azaad known. Along the way, Firangi falls in love with the beautiful Zafira, and participates in a plan to free Azaad, who has been captured by the British. The romance, however, is short lived, and the film ends with Zafira restored to the throne, and Firangi on a ship "heading straight to 'Inglanstaan.' Also known as England."[123] In the final scene, Firangi declares "white folk have robbed a lot from us, it's our turn now."[124] As a revisionist reading of colonial characterizations of Indian criminality, *Thugs of Hindustan* is one among many contemporary Bollywood films that promote nationalist alternatives to nineteenth-century narratives.[125] In challenging the archive, these films, though not necessarily any more historically accurate than their colonial counterparts, intervene in the narrative of Indian degeneracy and stagnation that novels such as *Confessions of a Thug* perpetuate. Often, however, they work to narratively fold anti-colonial movements into contemporary Hindu nationalism, thus implicitly perpetuating an anti-Muslim subtext. In this respect, despite their interventionist aims, the films betray their colonial influence by restaging the enduring history of sectarian prejudice and strategies of division that I discuss in Chapter 4.

As we see in Chapters 3 and 4, the question of historicity is central to both legal and fictional narratives. If the genre of the bildungsroman sets the model for fictionalized narratives of development, this ideal is readily mapped onto narratives of national development as well. Historian Lynn Hunt relates the production of Western modernity in the seventeenth and eighteenth centuries to a "sense of rupture" with the past. Hunt comments on how this "temporal break" corresponds to a spatial register, as Enlightenment philosophers "took the fateful step that led toward European and eventually a more general Western superiority, in which the developmental schema is, as it were, spatialized."[126] As Hunt and others such as Arjun Appadurai and Johannes Fabian have observed, nineteenth-century advancements in the natural sciences were often fueled by, and reaffirmed, a developmental model of history in which the primitive past of Europe was understood as the non-European present.[127] The inevitable, though varied, nature of human development thus forms the subtext of scientific, historical, fictional and legal narratives of the nineteenth century. The bildungsroman foregrounds the development of the individual subject within a normative teleology, while, as I show in Chapter 3, the JCPC opinion in *Ramaswamy Aiyan* v. *Venkata Achari* reoriented Indian legal precedents around Western historical time. The reordering of legal time affected what kinds of identities, and their associated narratives, were made legible by the law, while others were deemed backward or made irrelevant. If the bildungsroman depicts the normative development of the English citizen, *Ramaswamy Aiyan* v. *Venkata Achari* reveals the cultural logic at work in the JCPC's efforts to wrench Indian temporality into alignment with Western historicity.

PART II

Temporality

CHAPTER 3

Injurious Pasts
The Temporality of Caste

> And so Kant's forecast was fulfilled in this manner, when he posed the question: "How is history *a priori* possible? Answer: when the soothsayer himself shapes and forms the events that he had predicted in advance."[1]

In the early years of the nineteenth century, James Mill began writing his multivolume *History of British India*, a sourcebook that would shape generations of British attitudes toward India. Echoing the developmentalism of the bildungsroman as discussed in Chapter 2, Mill's history is built upon a subtext of Indian stagnation as compared to Western progress. As I show in this chapter and Chapter 4, Mill's representation of Indian history coincides with legal and fictional narratives that lead inescapably to a predictable end. Framing religion as the preeminent organizing principle of Indian society and history, Mill's narrative reaches a conclusion that is foregone before the narrative even begins. While appearing to document the past, the *History of British India* thus diagnoses the inescapable condition of the future. This paradox of the open-ended teleology is a consistent feature in colonial representations of India, in both legal and fictional narratives.

As was common in the Romantic literature with which the *History of British India* was contemporaneous, for Mill, the exotic was readily conflated with the ancient.[2] As a ready signifier of India's ancient past, the importance of religion is amplified in Mill's analysis, which revolves disproportionately around a discussion of Hinduism, exaggerating the centrality of religion as such, and privileging a monolithic version of Hinduism on a subcontinent that was religiously quite diverse. As I show with regard to both *Ramaswamy Aiyan* v. *Venkata Achari* (1863) and *The Moonstone*, this inflated attention to religion had the effect of casting Indians as guided by superstition and belief rather than rational principles. The notion of the Indian's unique susceptibility to the whims of religion was also a key element of the rhetoric of thuggee, as we saw in the preceding chapters.

The same tendencies toward Hindu fanaticism, in other words, which in the case of thuggee extended even to Muslims, were seen as contributing to both the unremitting criminality and the innate backwardness of Indian society.

Religion was not only perceived as the source of Indian criminality, but for Mill, it was also the source of Indian law. "No where among mankind," Mill writes, "have the laws and ordinances been more exclusively referred to the Divinity, than by those who instituted the theocracy of Hindustan. The plan of society and government, the rights of persons and things, even the customs, arrangements, and manners, of private and domestic life; every thing, in short, is established by divine prescription."[3] In turn, Mill conflates the religious origins of the law with an ancient or primitive quality. In support of the primitivism he ascribes to Indian law, as well as to Indian society at large, Mill notes the "leading institutions of the Hindus bear evidence that they were devised at a very remote period, when society yet retained its rudest and simplest form."[4] As Hindus were "lingering" in the "pastoral state," he writes, "there arose among them one of those superior men, who . . . clothing himself with a Divine character, established as a positive law, under the sanction of Heaven, the classification of the people and the distribution of occupations."[5] But, according to Mill, because the "human race is not destined to make many steps in improvement at once," this visionary of social progress made a fatal mistake in the form of the caste system: "Ignorant that professions, when once separated, were in no danger of being confounded, he established a law, which the circumstances of the time very naturally suggested, but which erected a barrier against further progress; that the children of those who were assigned to each of the classes, into which he distributed the people, should invariably follow the occupation of their father through all generations."[6] In this respect, caste bears an important correspondence with the legal concept of precedents, which I discuss in detail below. Like the legal precedent, caste draws a firm continuity between past and future, consolidating identity by virtue of its immutability. Using his understanding of the "law" of caste as evidence, Mill observed that the esteem in which Brahmins, or priests, were held, indicated the essential primitivity of Hindu society, both at its inception and in Mill's own time, as the "priesthood is generally found to usurp the greatest authority, in the lowest state of society."[7] "It is only in rude and ignorant times," according to Mill, "that men are so overwhelmed with the power of superstition as to pay unbounded veneration and obedience to those who artfully clothe themselves with the terrors of religion."[8] In framing Indian history as a failed developmental narrative, texts such as Mill's confirm an inevitable narrative of unfulfilled progress. As with the bildungsroman, the conclusion of Mill's history is predetermined at the outset.

I begin by rehearsing Mill's implicit argument because it is useful in setting up the relationship I draw over the course of this chapter between ordering time and producing meaning. In the epigraph above, Reinhart Kosellek observes that "*a priori* history" is possible when the "soothsayer himself shapes and forms the events that he had predicted in advance."[9] Historians such as Mill, by framing the narrative course at the outset as one of inevitable stasis, predict and affirm the inevitability of a particular future, which they arrive at by narrating a specific version of the past.

When allied with state power, narrating the past is deeply related to predicting and determining the future. In England's distant past, for example, religion and superstition guided the soothsayers and narrators of the future. This changed, however, as the state became more centralized and absolutist. "The genesis of the absolutist state," Kosellek observes, "is accompanied by a sporadic struggle against all manner of religious and political predictions. The state enforced a monopoly on the control of the future by suppressing apocalyptic and astrological readings of the future. In doing so, it assumed a function of the old Church for anti-Church objectives. Henry VIII, Edward VI, and Elizabeth I all proscribed in strong terms any prediction of this nature."[10] In England, the movement toward state, rather than church, control over the narrative of the future accompanied the rise of absolutism.

My argument in this chapter is that a similar pattern can be observed in the colonial state as well. I show, throughout this volume, that the paths to modernity in the British and colonial contexts were often divergent, and the instance of the colonial legal system's use of history and temporality is no exception. Just as the English monarchs prized control away from the church, colonial law and history both painted Indians as inexorably wedded to religion, while also attempting to displace religious law with their own absolutist government and judiciary. Moreover, what Mill identifies as the Indian's extreme religiosity implicitly aligns India's present with England's past, supplying a rationale for the project of bringing Indian temporality into the fold of Western modernity.

When read in light of nineteenth-century Western philosophies of history, the case of *Ramaswamy Aiyan* v. *Venkata Achari*, which I examine in this chapter, provides insight into how colonial law worked to reshape Indian temporality and history. While the case was explicitly about apportioning rights to priests at a temple in the Madras Presidency, the underlying issues touch on the organization of legal historical time and its relationship to making certain identities visible within the terms of modernity. As we see both in this chapter and Chapter 4 on Wilkie Collins's *The Moonstone*, questions of history are deeply entwined with notions of individuality and subjectivity. Constraining Indian narratives within Western ideas of time and modernity had the corresponding effect, I argue, of naturalizing British history and the conclusions to which it inevitably led. As Kant's riddle demonstrates, and *Ramaswamy Aiyan* v. *Venkata Achari* bears out, within a teleological model, controlling the narrative of history is tantamount to predicting the future.

To be clear, my argument is not that British colonialism was coherently organized around enunciated ideological goals, much less a deliberate teleology, or that it functioned with an efficiency and self-awareness that allowed it to obtain a totalizing hold on Indian society or history. In fact, as I show, upper-caste Hindus often colluded with the colonial state to augment their social and financial capital. I also do not claim that the identities made possible or recognized within the terms of Hindu religious time are preferable to those allowed by Western modernity. Rather, my interest is in tracing the relationship between the colonial government's overt attempt to streamline the unwieldy pre-colonial legal system and the kinds of sovereignty and subjectivities that this project enabled.

Ordering the Courts

In 1772, Warren Hastings, the East India Company's newly appointed Governor of Bengal, sought to reform the practice of colonial law so that "in all suits regarding inheritance, marriage, caste and all other religious usages and institutions, the laws of the Koran with respect to the Mohamedans and those of the Shaster with respect to the Gentoos shall invariably be adhered to." Under Hastings's plan, which was adopted as law in 1780, British and colonial judges would adjudicate legal disputes using principles taken from Hindu and Muslim religious texts. Based on the advice of Orientalist scholars and translators, such as Sir William Jones and Henry Thomas Colebrooke, "Anglo-Hindu law relied exclusively on Dharmaśāstra as the source for practical Hindu law in British courts, essentially meaning that the translations provided by the Orientalists became a uniform basis for positive law among Hindus throughout the British-dominated regions of India."[11] By casting these religious texts as the source of Indian law, the colonial legal system implicitly conferred upon them a stable and firmly grounded sense of authority. Yet, Siraj

Ahmed has made the point that while "the East India Company proclaimed that its legal codes alone articulated Islam and Hinduism's authentic laws," in fact, "religious authority had never been principally textual in precolonial India."[12] Instead, religious traditions were fluid and contextually driven, as "radically heterogeneous instances of language in use where both the form of language and its conceptual relationship to reality varied from one tradition to another."[13] In this respect, religious practices were reoriented around a set of texts that were made to function as legal doctrine.

In addition to foregrounding religion as the primary governing logic for Indian personal law, the system also divided and categorized various religions across the subcontinent. Hindu law "applied to persons from the Indian subcontinent who were not Muslim, Christian, Jewish, or Parsi. Thus, in addition to those denominated 'Hindu,' Hindu law applied also to Sikhs, Jains, and Buddhists."[14] Hastings thus laid the foundations for the colonial adjudication of legal cases in India from the local courts in the presidencies to the Judicial Committee of the Privy Council in London.

From the outset, Hastings was met with opposition, as British jurists worried about the practicality of administering a form of law (whether Hindu or Muslim) that was completely foreign to their training. One of the more obvious challenges associated with using the religious texts stemmed from the fact that most British judges were unfamiliar with both the texts themselves as well as the languages in which they were written. In order to aid British legal practitioners, in 1776 Hastings "commissioned a digest of Hindu law that appeared as the *Code of Gentoo Laws*, a curious work that consisted of Nathaniel Halhed's English translation of a Persian rendering from an oral Bengali paraphrase of a Sanskrit original compiled by twelve pandits employed by Hastings" (Hinduism and Law 25). British judges were also aided by Indian pandits and maulvis, religious scholars who acted as consultants to clarify matters of religion to the courts. These "court officers," as Lauren Benton and others have noted, "were distrusted from the start" and "a disproportionate effort of English legal experts in India in the late eighteenth century was devoted to translating Hindu legal texts so that judges would not have to take the word of court officials."[15] By 1864, suspicion of the pandits and maulvis led to their removal altogether from the courts, as British jurists came to rely exclusively on English translations of religious texts. This reliance on poorly translated texts led to the "reification, and rampant misinterpretation, of Hindu and Muslim law, and over time the effect was to allow English law and the common law practice of referring to precedents to alter indigenous law to make it more English."[16]

One effect of the turn to religious texts was to cement the ancient character attributed to Indian legal traditions, while forming precedents out of the English legal interventions that were generated by the ostensible attempts to adhere to them.[17] The translated texts that were used as sourcebooks for Hindu law were from the outset highly mediated. As such, they were representative neither of tradition nor of lived modernity. In describing eighteenth-century efforts to codify Hindu law, Tirthankar Roy and Anand V. Swamy note that the "legal regime that Hastings had set in motion … tried to be traditional in molding law after religious codes; it tried to be modern in creating a single procedure valid for all."[18] The attempt to resurrect doctrine of the ancient past as a means of adjudicating cases in the colonial era, however, served to collapse the distinction between the ancient and the contemporary, thus rendering Indian law both atemporal and implicitly undeveloped.[19]

According to Rosane Rocher, and confirmed as well in Mill's history, the adoption of Hindu law was initially palatable to British lawmakers because "the Hindu tradition rhetorically presented itself as derivative from the pronouncements of hallowed sages."[20] As a result, the implementation of Hindu law "reinforced widely shared, Western, eighteenth-century notions, that a once glorious Hindu Indian civilization had decayed, and that its essence had to be retrieved from foundational texts."[21] Indian history was perceived as following an inverse trajectory of progress, a kind of *Bildung* in reverse. Rocher explains, however, that it was this respect for the "glorious" past that led to the seeming contradiction wherein "a British jurist, who, in England, would of course have sought to enforce the latest legislation, did not appear to find it odd to vest the authenticity of Hindu law in its most ancient recoverable sources."[22] In this manner, the "Dharmaśāstra became completely enmeshed within the colonial state and its traditional standing in the realm of civil society was translated into British legal discourse and ossified through it."[23] Within the legal sphere in precolonial India, however, the Dharmaśāstra had never functioned as the positive law it came to embody in the eighteenth century. Rather, in the spirit of Kant's riddle of history a priori, the colonial judiciary invented the tradition of Hindu law with one stroke, and predicted (accurately) the backwardness it would signify for the Indian future with another.

Reflecting a faith in the benevolence of British rule, for the most part, the consensus among nineteenth and twentieth-century legal scholars was that the effort to revitalize and apply religious law in colonial courts was a benign, if misguided, attempt by the British to respect and assimilate the ancient traditions of the subcontinent.[24] Richard Lariviere, for example, characterizes "the creation and development of modern Hindu law" as "predicated on well-intentioned misunderstanding and innocent irony."[25] Lariviere dismisses any suggestion that the colonial policy was a "calculated attempt . . . to subvert the traditions and oppress the peoples of India" suggesting that such readings "give these early British more credit than they deserve as political schemers and less credit than their explicit statements about their motives indicate."[26] Likewise, J. Duncan Derrett remarks admiringly that "British judges and their Hindu and Muslim colleagues handled the Hindu law with ultra-sensitive care. The diffidence of the Privy Council in contexts which had a connexion with what western jurists meant by 'religion' is remarkable."[27] And Ludo Rocher aims to "show how and why, despite the best intentions to remain faithful to the law of the śāstras, the British could not avoid departing from the original intent and meaning of the sacred texts when it came to applying them in the courts of law."[28] While historicizing the practice, however, Rosane Rocher identifies some of the problems with the evolution of Anglo-Hindu law, which she describes as a plan "hatched in profound ignorance of the complexity of the śāstras on which the administration of justice to Hindus was ordained to be based."[29] Rocher also notes that the question has arisen "of whether dividing law along religious lines, Hindu and Muslim, was part of a conscious policy of 'divide and rule.'" Ibid. p. 79.

More recently, legal historians have taken an increasingly neutral, if not overtly negative, stance about both the motives and the outcomes of the colonial legal system's reliance on religion. Benton, for example, nuances the "confusion" engendered by British attempts to administer Hindu and Muslim law, focusing in particular on the chaotic conditions that such efforts created. At times, Benton shows, the chaos afforded savvy Indian litigants opportunities for forum shopping and enabled the destabilization of colonialist goals. Highlighting the "doubled movement of integration into the state and distinction from it," Rachel Sturman argues that the colonial state promulgated "a Hindu law that both implicitly and explicitly grappled with the ethics of reinforcing difference and inequality, in ways that resonated with the paradoxes of egalitarianism within liberal political thought."[30] For example, cases involving caste, such as the one I examine in this chapter, represented a challenge to the principles of liberalism that the colonial courts at least nominally strove to uphold. In Sturman's reading, the colonial turn to Hindu law was less about religion *per se*, but, as I discuss in Chapter 5, was acutely focused on codifying property rights within the domestic and family sphere. The desire to find, or invent, an ancient Indian logic to what were essentially colonial legal principles resulted in a "bifurcated system of civil law, in which British law would form the basis for most matters of law – territorial law, as well as an edifice of procedural or adjectival law" while in matters of "personal law" Indians would be "governed by their own religious laws." Ultimately, the "system of personal law construed Indians as essentially defined by religion and as divided into two religious categories: Hindu and Muslim."[31] In this respect, as I discuss earlier, colonial legal interventions augmented popular ideas of Indians as essentially guided by religion and ancient strictures.[32]

The Indian reception of these legal interventions was more equivocal. Citing "textbooks prepared by Indian jurists such as S. V. Gupte, D. F. Mulla, G. D. Banerjee, R. Sarvadhikari, and others," Ludo Rocher asserts that "there are no major differences between treatises written by Western authors" in discussions of "the relative value of the manifold sources of Hindu law."[33] According to Rocher, Indians during the colonial era not only accepted English interpretations of Hindu scripture, but also sought to represent the interpretations as essentially Indian. Yet the attempt to channel a diverse and often abstract tradition of religious law into a uniform positive law was at best a fraught enterprise. As Roy and Swamy note, the courts applied expert testimony unevenly: "The lower-court judges, who were mainly Indians, were repeatedly instructed that they were not to apply anything other than Hindu and Islamic law in matters of property, whereas in the appeals courts and in legislation, the judges and jurists often departed from a strict interpretation of religious codes."[34] While Indian judges were encouraged to apply religious law, English judges were given more liberty to decide cases based on principles of justice, equity, and good conscience.[35] Because on any given topic the "opinion of the pundits was far from unanimous . . . judges seem to have accepted the version of religious law that suited their own sensibility."[36] In this manner, regardless of intentions, the consultation of "religious texts" largely became a pretext for the application of English law.

Brahminism and the Law

One undeniable effect of the turn to religion in the colonial legal sphere is that it cemented the association between Brahminical knowledge and state power. Both during the era of court pandits in the eighteenth century and in the nationalist movement of the nineteenth and early twentieth centuries, existing social hierarchies were mapped onto Indian interactions with the English. Despite the challenges to caste privilege espoused by the Bramho movement in Bengal, for example, the intelligentsia was largely composed of upper-class and upper-caste Hindus.[37] In South India, as well, the Hindu elite often looked to the colonial government, including the courts, in order to reinforce local caste and class privileges. As the primary Indian interlocutors with the English and the colonial state, the intelligentsia were instrumental in developing the notion of the Indian legal subject. As Anindita Mukhopadhyay argues, it was during the eighteenth and early nineteenth centuries that the Indian elite came to embrace "the reorientation of ideas regarding the constitution of themselves as legal subjects, prodded on by alien laws that had reorganized their social and cultural spaces."[38] For "the middleclass elite, the ideal of maintenance of law and order followed their perception of the natural order of the social hierarchy, based on a rational state organization which would, ironically, be spearheaded by British rule."[39] The paradox of constructing a native elite, including the notion of legal subjecthood, by virtue of accepting subordination to the English is a familiar topic of postcolonial criticism.[40] As the subaltern studies scholars and others have shown, the Indian elite was a central force in aligning caste privilege with colonial legal subjecthood.

As with many personal law cases in the colonial courts, the case I examine in this chapter deals with matters of caste and religious privileges. *Ramaswamy Aiyan* v. *Venkata Achari*, heard before Queen Victoria's Privy Council in 1863, attempts to resolve an extended conflict between two groups of Brahmin priests competing for the right to perform *purohitam* (priestly services) for pilgrims visiting a temple at Rameswaram in South India.[41] The litigation, which spanned more than a century, focused on the "*mirassi*," or funds associated with these religious rites, and the rents and fees required for the maintenance of various "*Gurukals*" (religious schools).[42] Of the roughly forty-page case summary, the first twenty pages establish the evolution of the case dating back to the initial dispute in the 1700s. While the monetary stakes are fairly insignificant, the case is representative of what Roy and Swamy describe as a "rare but fascinating category of disputes related to the right to worship in temples."[43]

The basic details of the case are as follows. In 1835, a group of Arya Brahmins, filed a suit in the Mathura *Zillah* (Municipal) Court claiming that their sect enjoyed full rights of *purohitam* at Rameswaram, and that they were due rents and fees from a competing group of Telugu and Tatwadi Brahmins dating back to 1725. The suit alleged that the ancestors of the Aryas had contracted with a group of Telugu and Tatwadi Brahmins, who, for a fee, would be allowed to administer *purohitam* to certain groups of pilgrims. The Arya Brahmins charged that over the intervening years, the Telugu and Tatwadi Brahmins ceased paying the fees and rents. The *Zillah* Court, on the basis of the analysis offered by the court pandits, decided in favor of the Aryas. The Mathura District Court in an 1849 appeal upheld this ruling. In a second appeal by the Telugu and Tatwadis, the case was heard at the Mathura Subordinate Court in 1853, and in 1854 the judge once again decided in favor of the Arya Brahmins, citing scriptural and testimonial evidence that was presented by the Aryas as proof of the strength of their claims.

On June 29, 1857, the Telugu and Tatwadi Brahmins filed yet another appeal at the Civil Court at Mathura in which the judgment reversed all previous decisions, finding that the evidence submitted by the Arya Brahmins was unreliable, that both classes of Brahmins had "rights," and also introducing the "rights" of the pilgrims, who, the court believed, should be free to decide which group of Brahmins they would choose to hire. In 1857, the Arya Brahmins appealed the Civil Court ruling to the *Sadr Diwani Adalat* (the Supreme Court of Revenue). In this iteration, the Telugu and Tatwadi Brahmins took a different approach, claiming that the argument was irrelevant in any case, since the statute of limitations had expired on any claims the Arya Brahmins might have had to past due rents or fees. The *Sadr Diwani* court, on the basis of the statute of limitations, dismissed the case. Finally, in 1863, the Arya Brahmins filed an appeal with the Privy Council (*Ramaswamy Aiyan* v. *Venkata Achari*). The Privy Council, affirming the 1857 Civil Court decision, ruled against the Arya Brahmins' monopoly on rights and profits associated with the administering of *purohitam* at Rameswaram. However, the Privy Council importantly based its ruling not on the statute of limitations but on larger issues of "rights" and "proof."

After three successive decisions between 1835 and 1854, what happened in 1857 to begin the process of unraveling the logic affirming the historical narrative supplied by the Arya Brahmins? Thinking through this question involves examining the rationale of the JCPC's opinion as well as the history of the period in which it occurred. While it is impossible to attribute the shift in legal reasoning to any specific historical event, the timing of the *Sadr Diwani* appeal suggests that the larger sociopolitical context that led to the Sepoy Rebellion of 1857 would have influenced the legal sphere as well.

The Biopolitics of Bureaucracy

In the wake of the rebellion, as the Crown consolidated its jurisdiction over the subcontinent, efficient modes of organizing and categorizing the population became increasingly necessary and caste was a preexisting system of classification that the British could shape to suit their needs. While publicly they maintained a moral distaste for the very premise of caste, it nevertheless proved institutionally useful for British bureaucratic purposes. Moreover, as I discuss later, caste and religion at times served as a cypher for larger arguments about history and temporality more broadly. In my reading of *Ramaswamy Aiyan* v. *Venkata Achari*, I argue that the performative effect of the judicial outcome was to restructure the temporal terms within which caste was understood, relegating the origins of caste conflicts and injustices to the ancient Hindu past, while locating their resolutions in the modernity of rational British justice. In this regard, the case of *Ramaswamy Aiyan* v. *Venkata Achari* is as much about questions of temporality as it is about caste, or rights. Ultimately, the transition in legal reasoning, from acknowledging and affirming divisions between intra-caste sects to homogenizing across broad caste groups, is related to larger discursive interventions in Indian temporalities.

In his foundational work on colonial strategies of knowledge production, Bernard Cohn notes, "The idea that India had been ruled by 'despots' was revalorized in the nineteenth and twentieth centuries as one of several ruling paradigms that formed the ideological infrastructure of British rule in India."[44] In contrast to what was constructed as the leaden despotism of the Indian past, as exemplified in the caste system, the imperial government sought to represent itself as a benevolent and modernizing force grounded in justice and the rule of law.[45]

Contemporary scholarship has shown, however, that caste became increasingly systematized in the nineteenth century under British imperial rule. In particular, caste emerged at the forefront of Indian politics at the moment of transition from the more diffuse rule of the East India Company to the centralized authority of the Crown. As Mithi Mukherjee remarks, it was "the Queen's Proclamation of 1858 that set the stage for justice as the discourse of governance." It was also during this period, however, that "the British legal and administrative policy came to be based on actively foregrounding the caste system."[46] The inherent divisiveness of the caste system, Mukherjee suggests, was useful for the British, both in terms of encouraging local animosities, and in providing a structure for categorization and governance. In particular, she identifies "the deployment of the discourse of justice as equity as a strategy to fragment Indian civil society," which became "most evident in the colonial administration's use of the category of caste in the post-1857 period."[47] Explicitly linking the rise of the use of caste with the consolidation of imperial rule in the wake of the rebellion, Mukherjee suggests that caste was invoked for the purpose of dividing (affectively and statistically), in order to rule.[48]

Scholars such as Arjun Appadurai, Nicholas Dirks, Uma Chakravarti, Bernard Cohn, Susan Bayly, and others have also demonstrated that the caste system served a practical bureaucratic function for British rule. The system of classification created a method by which to order, and ultimately govern, a vast and diverse population. In her extensive study, *Caste, Society and Politics in India from the Eighteenth Century to the Modern Age*, for example, Bayly remarks that "the increasingly powerful and intrusive colonial regime that came into being after the 1857 Mutiny-Rebellion found more and more reasons to count and classify the sub-continent's peoples, and to call on Indians to report themselves as members of specific social, economic and occupational categories, each supposedly possessing its own 'essences' and qualities."[49] Highlighting the centrality of the 1857 Sepoy Rebellion and the 1871 Census, Bayly discusses how the imperial government sought to gather information to more effectively manage the population.

The evolution of British attitudes toward caste, from tolerance of the system within the realm of personal law to more overt government uses of it in projects such as the census, is also relevant to the case of *Ramaswamy Aiyan* v. *Venkata Achari*. As Arjun Appadurai argues, the census in India served a critically different function from the one it served in England. While in England, the census was "overwhelmingly territorial and occupational," in India the census was concerned with classifying and exoticizing on the basis of religion and caste.[50] The British census operated "within a framework of commonsense classifications shared by officialdom with ordinary people," and as a result, it "did not have the refractive and generative effects that it did in India."[51] Prior to the second half of the nineteenth century, the colonial enumeration of Indian populations was geared toward the largely pragmatic purpose of aiding in taxation. After 1858, however, counting people became intrinsically tied to questions of caste, tying Indian identities to religion and tradition, as much as to land holdings and financial matters. This shift from economics to religion is central as well to my reading of *The Moonstone* in Chapter 4.

In the context of *Ramaswamy Aiyan* v. *Venkata Achari*, as I discuss later, foregrounding religion within the legal sphere had the larger effect of consigning Indian political, economic, and legal traditions to the more obscure realms of belief and superstition, while allying the British system with order, law, and justice. In my reading of the case, I argue that locating the temporality of the dispute in the ancient or mythic past serves the correlative function of establishing the modernity of colonial legal ameliorations.

Through colonial initiatives highlighting social issues such as caste, sati, and thuggee, as discussed in Chapters 1 and 2, a particular notion of an Indian past emerged into representation. And, importantly, this was a past that was incommensurate with enabling a viable present. Through recourse to its rhetoric of equity and justice, the imperial regime, and in particular its legal system, cast itself as a remedy to India's injurious past. As we saw with regard to the failed development of Ameer Ali in Chapter 2, the British narrative of progress relied on the justificatory force of a damaging past that needed to be supplanted and overcome through the implementation of modern scientific and legal rationality.

The courtroom was an important arena in which religious conflicts, including those related to caste, and their colonial resolutions played out. As Pamela G. Price notes, litigation became increasingly popular in the nineteenth century in South India. Socially elite litigants such Ramaswamy Aiyan and Venkata Achari often used the court system to both establish their own status and also to avail themselves of "officially recognized arenas for confrontation and competition."[52] While litigants frequently turned to the courts to adjudicate matters of "caste membership and caste usage," in these instances the courts "tended to evaluate statements according to fixed frameworks – objectified visions – of social and political relationships."[53] Stabilizing caste identities and the rights associated with them "was necessary for the universal application of rules in a centralized system of dispute management." With a mind toward creating precedents linking the past to any future litigation, the courts' "processes of and calculation either established or denied the authority of written statements as representations of a stable and absolute reality, not one of transformable and relative statuses and identities."[54] What Price identifies is a fundamental tension between the courts' goal of universalizability on the one hand, and fluid social identities and relationships on the other.[55] Caste fixity therefore was a prerequisite of the application of the rational and consistent rule of law that the colonial courts sought to represent. The trajectory of the decisions along the appeals process in *Ramaswamy Aiyan* v. *Venkata*

Achari reflected an understanding of caste that was consistent with these new goals of social categorization.

Litigating Time

The Privy Council's headnote summary of *Ramaswamy Aiyan* v. *Venkata Achari* announces it as a case that will evaluate the Arya Brahmins' claim to a "hereditary right" of *purohitam* by way of the "documentary proof of its origin" or "by proof of such long and uninterrupted usage as, in the absence of documentary proof, would suffice to establish a prescriptive right."[56] From the outset, the case is framed in terms of "rights" and the "proof" used to establish those rights. While the litigants on both sides refer to the ancient hereditary origins of their rights, the Privy Council reframes the debate in terms of "documentary proof" established over a recorded length of modern history. The various notions of temporality at play in the case, however, are related to the issue of rights, and, in particular, which kinds of rights are represented as alienable and which are deemed inalienable.

In an essay on law and temporality Renisa Mawani makes the claim that "law is fundamentally about time."[57] For Mawani, law does not simply operate within a neutral temporal field, but rather creates the framework through which time becomes meaningful and derives its authority. "Law draws its meanings and gains its authorizing force," Mawani argues, "through specifications and limits on time (minimum/maximum sentences or statute of limitations, for example) and through the temporalities it inhabits and brings into being."[58] The law's engagement with time structures the past, present, and future, making certain legal outcomes and lived realities possible while foreclosing others. The early colonial turn to religious texts in dealing with matters of personal law in India, for example, framed Indian legal subjects' imaginative relationship to their past while also making available a particular notion of the future. Colonialism, Mawani argues, harnessed temporality as part of its governing strategy:

> Colonial futures figured crucially as sites of governance, potential transformation, and, ultimately, annihilation. The future of the colonies was to be distinct from the past, a new time to be captured via observation and prediction and to be refashioned and improved through persuasion, coercion, and brute force.[59]

In Mawani's reading, the law plays a crucial role not only in reflecting temporalities but also in predicting and creating them. In turn, the law's temporality shapes broader imaginative and lived possibilities.

Though, as Mawani notes, competing temporalities often produced unevenness and uncertainty, instituting a teleological notion of Western, secular time as the dominant temporality of colonial law had a profound effect on local cultures and societies:

> In India, for example, record-keeping practices introduced by the East India Company and expanded by the British crown, instantiated Western time as the legitimate temporal register. The use of calendric dates and chronological times in public life introduced new discourses of time while diminishing the significance of Hindu, Muslim, and other chronologies.[60]

Even as early colonial courts turned to the Dharmaśāstra for guidance in matters of personal law, the legal interventions they made reaffirmed the dominant temporality of Western law. Often, as is the case in *Ramaswamy Aiyan* v. *Venkata Achari*, the law explicitly sidelined competing chronologies in favor of its own "single, Western, secular, and overarching time."[61]

Therefore, mapping out the competing temporalities is crucial to reading the history and outcome of the case. The Privy Council opinion begins with a catalog of the original dispute, which claims to traverse a history of Brahminical rights originating "under a grant from *Mavalivana Rajah* dated about 1,000 years previously."[62] The complaint, which consists of ten parts, is presented in the law report in extensive detail. The fifth part of the complaint, for example, alleges that

> the father of the first Defendant, and others, brought an action in the District *Moonsiff's* Court of *Paramagoody*, asserting, among other allegations, that they were the proprietors of the *Mirassi* of administering *Purohitam* to twenty-four classes of pilgrims, including also the six classes; that *Annasami Vadhiyar* and three others, having, in the year *Parthiva* (1826), administered *Purohitam* to *Sengendi Parishie*, one of the twenty-four classes of pilgrims, appropriated to themselves the incomes derived therefrom.[63]

In addition to the "twenty-four classes of pilgrims" and the various persons and sects named in the suit, there are also multiple temporalities: *Parthiva* is a year in the cyclical Hindu calendar that repeats indefinitely every sixty years. The reference to the Hindu calendar introduces two competing temporalities into the narrative of the case: the cyclical time of Hinduism and the secular linear time of the law.

The different temporalities in *Ramaswamy Aiyan* v. *Venkata Achari* must, in turn, be read in light of a larger conversation about temporality and its relationship to colonialism. Ankur Barua usefully historicizes the nineteenth-century European "notion that individuals in ancient Indic civilization were in thrall to immensely vast and endlessly repeated cosmological cycles and were therefore devoid of a linear consciousness of time."[64] In particular, Barua takes issue with the "'straight line versus eternal cycle' dichotomy that has often formed the backbone" of Western understandings of Indian "temporal consciousness."[65] For Barua, the pervasive focus on the cyclicality of Indian time "seeks to connect the absence of a historical sense with specific characteristics of Sanskritic culture, which are held to have obliterated it or at least impeded its growth."[66] The cyclicality of Indian time, Barua argues, has been conflated with stagnancy, and used to produce spurious cultural assessments such as the familiar trope of India as a land without history that was popularized not only by theorists such as Marx and Hegel but also by novelists such as Wilkie Collins, as I discuss in Chapter 4. *Ramaswamy Aiyan* v. *Venkata Achari* represents the process of replacing the religious cyclicality that characterized Indian time with the secular linearity of Western time. Moreover, the bifurcation along religious and secular lines also reflected a corresponding division between the ancient and modern, where Indian law was relegated to ancient religious time while British law ushered in modern secular time.

For the Privy Counsellors in England, the multiple temporalities would undoubtedly have caused confusion. As a result, the Privy Council report reflects the logic that sorting out the conflicts of the various groups and individuals necessitates reordering Indian temporalities to bring them into alignment with secular English time. There is, for example, an attractive simplicity in the analysis of Judge A. W. Phillips, acting judge of the Subordinate Court:

> The proceedings and documents connected with this case are most voluminous, and much that is introduced is totally foreign to the subject, which, divested of all extraneous matter, consists, after all, of only two points to be decided on, first, as to whom the proprietary rights of administering certain rites belongs. Secondly, whether the six classes were rented by the Plaintiffs' ancestors to those of the Defendants, or not.[67]

Leaving aside the contextual details, Judge Phillips isolates the dispute to questions of rights and heredity. While the Subordinate Court judge began the process of requesting and evaluating historical proof to assess the litigants' claims to rights, in 1854 the court was willing to accept a variety of evidence based in local values, beliefs, and temporalities.

In affirming the rights of the Arya Brahmins in 1854, Judge Phillips of the Subordinate Court framed his decision as follows:

> The hereditary right of the Plaintiffs has been not only acknowledged, but proclaimed by the individual recognized by all classes of Hindoos (Brahmins included) as their head and High Priest. It has also been acknowledged by Brahmins, not parties to or interested in any way in this suit. The *Zemindar* of *Ramnad*, as appears from other documents, acknowledges the same, and directs the *Aryas* to perform the ceremonies with regard to himself . . . Other proofs, too numerous to detail, are produced, all showing, in the plainest possible manner, that the right of the Plaintiffs was generally acknowledged.[68]

Following the early colonial practice of integrating British legal methods and local traditions, the Subordinate Court's decision of 1854 accepted a mode of history, and historical privilege, that was ultimately alien to normative British history and temporality. It is therefore curious how evidence that in 1854 established rights "in the plainest possible manner" such that the "Court feels no hesitation in declaring its opinion, that the Plaintiffs have fully and satisfactorily proved their proprietary right to the whole *Mirassi*" came to be dismissed as irrelevant in 1857, and once again by the Privy Council in 1863.

Beyond Memory and History

The Madura Civil Court heard the Telugu and Tatwadi Brahmins' appeal on June 29, 1857, just under two months before the Sepoy Rebellion began. Though we cannot know the extent to which larger historical events influenced the case, the Civil Court judge's ruling reflects a marked shift in the terms of the debate. While the stakes of the early suits were recognized as primarily monetary (who has a right to the "*mirassi*" and rents), in the later iterations, the terms became decidedly more focused on recorded history as a means to determining those rights. In contrast to Judge Phillips, of the Subordinate Court in 1854, Judge Baynes of the Civil Court in 1857 found the evidence presented by the Arya Brahmins entirely unconvincing. His judgment turns on what kinds of claims to history, and the rights associated with them, can be submitted as "proof":

> The *Aryas* found on a grant by *Stree Rama*, which certainly is not proved; the *Parishais* on a grant by *Mavalivana Rajah*, which is equally destitute of proof. In short, there is nothing on which to rest a judgment, save the apparent and notorious facts of the case, undeniable by either party, namely, that there is a Holy shrine at *Rameswaram*, to which pilgrims resort. *Aryas*, *Parishai Bhattars*, and *Gurukals* have been worshipping at it, and dwelling in its vicinity from times not only beyond all memory, but all history.[69]

In a critical departure from the previous practice of adhering to religious testimony, the 1857 Civil Court judgment explicitly frames the value of "proof" within the terms of "memory" and "history," decisively ruling that local and religious histories and narratives would not be considered as evidence by the court.

From this point forward, the opinions in the case were concertedly focused on authorizing certain modes of history over others. If the earlier decisions attempted to resolve the minutiae of caste conflicts, and their associated profits, the later ones shifted the discursive stakes to the larger issue of the role of history itself in legal decisions. In particular, Western secular temporality emerged as the dominant temporality of the law, as Indian temporalities became increasingly relegated to the domain of religion.

The intervening appeal to the *Sadr Diwani Adalat*, filed in 1857, provides an important indication of the shifting valuation of history and temporality and its relationship to broader questions of cultural, social, and political rights. The appeal to the *Sadr Diwani Adalat* resulted in a judgment delivered on October 30, 1858, exactly four months and ten days after the end of the rebellion. This decision, in favor of the Telugu and Tatwadis, dismissed the case based on the "[r]egulations of limitation." Avoiding the question altogether of which histories and their associated evidence may be deemed legitimate, the court shifted its emphasis to modern legal time, the passage of which became the sole basis for the evaluation of rights. Reframing the narrative in terms of the expiry of the statute of limitations placed the law in control of the relationship between the organization of time and the distribution of rights. Sidestepping the question of whose narrative counts as "proof," the decision served to establish British legal time as the only relevant temporality to the question of rights. In this sense, the *Sadr Diwani* decision was significant to the law reconfiguring Indian social and political life around normative British temporality.

The Temporality of the Law

By 1863, the year that the Privy Council in England heard the case of *Ramaswamy Aiyan* v. *Venkata Achari*, Queen Victoria had been proclaimed Empress of India, and the Sepoy Rebellion, while formally suppressed, had spawned the beginnings of a nationalist independence movement. Along with the greater stability of state control, therefore, came a more anxious imperial regime. More than ever, broad public acceptance of British norms and standards was imperative to the continuing existence of the Empire. One important arena in this respect was the standardization of time. In *Rule by Numbers: Governmentality in Colonial India*, U. Kalpagam discusses the ways in which "colonial state practices in India reconstituted temporalities, and thereby ushered in new modes of temporal discourse" for political uses.[70] As U. Kalpagam shows, "temporalities hitherto perceived and experienced as cyclical, non-secular, subjective and local were now seen to be either transformed, subordinated or made to coexist with linear, secular, objective and universal time."[71] From eighteenth-century Orientalist attempts to comprehend Hindu chronology to nineteenth-century efforts by James Mill and others to write Indian history by "constructing a chronology in the new temporal framework," bringing about a shift in temporal norms constituted a key element of colonial rule. While "at the beginning of the colonial period there were 13 calendric systems in what was then identified as the Indian subcontinent," by the nineteenth century standardizing time and temporality became important for the quotidian administration of life.[72] Prisons, factories, transportation, communications, schools, and hospitals, increasingly came into alignment with Western time.[73] Linking the standardization of time to the explicit ideological goals of the colonial state, Kalpagam argues that the "conception of a uniform and objectified time arises out of the necessity to identify repetitions and patterns in events that were to be progressively brought under control."[74] Ultimately, "a new experience of temporality was ushered in through the bureaucratic practices of the colonial state, and this new experience enabled both a rational history and the idea of 'progress' to take hold of the colonial imagination."[75]

The Privy Council's decision in *Ramaswamy Aiyan* v. *Venkata Achari* is an example of how the courts served to bring Indian conceptions of temporality into commensurability with British ones by privileging the normative terms of Western historicity. By allying Indian temporalities with religion, in a case involving caste and temple rituals, the Privy Council implicitly validated the dominant temporality of British legality, which it represented as invested in questions of rights and access.

From the outset, the Privy Council's opinion, delivered by the Lord Justice Knight Bruce, was framed as an attempt to ascertain the existence of the rights of *purohitam* through evaluating the litigants' "proof" by way of documents recorded in modern historical time. In his summary of the appellants' case, for example, Justice Knight Bruce is concerned with establishing a legally validated timeline of the dispute. Having remarked that the Arya Brahmins assert their rights based on "an event which they ascribe to a very remote age," he proceeds to revalue the historical record, making reference to twenty-one dates from 1714 to 1841.[76] Locating the history of the conflict entirely within the realm of verifiable dates reframed the notion of "proof" that could be made visible to the court: modern historical dates took precedence over ancient religious ones.

The Privy Council's reliance on documentary evidence dating back to 1714 cast the litigants as subjects of written records and legal time, rather than as religious subjects under mythic time. Having established a historical narrative of the conflict, thereby dismissing religious proof on the basis that it lacks historical verifiability, Justice Knight Bruce offers the following evaluation of the evidence submitted by the Arya Brahmins on behalf of their plaint:

> The earliest in date consists of extracts from one of the *Puranas*. These, like the statements in the pleadings of the Appellants' case, carry us far beyond the bounds of legal or historical evidence. But it is argued, and fairly and properly argued, that these ancient books may legitimately be used as evidence that a certain state of facts, or a certain state of opinion, existed at the date of their compilation. That date is sufficiently uncertain; for we are not told when this particular *Purana* is supposed to have been written; and it appears from the writings of eminent Orientalists, that the period during which the eighteen recognized *Puranas* were composed is a very wide one, extending probably from the eighth to the sixteenth century.[77]

In explaining the Privy Council's rejection of the evidence proffered by the Aryas, Justice Knight Bruce explicitly equates the veracity of the proof with the verifiability of its historical date.[78] Though it could be "fairly and properly argued" that the ancient books served as evidence of prevailing beliefs and sentiment, they could not be taken as historical proof. The texts, in other words, were useful as indexes of beliefs, but not facts. The statement indicates the Privy Council's foundational methodology insofar as it provides the grounds to dismiss alternative logics that do not conform to Western modernity. The temporality of Western modernity, then, provides the organizing principle by which individuals, events, practices, and ultimately, rights, could be recognized by the imperial courts.

At the same time, the alternative temporality that the appellants invoked is not at all a subalternized history. *Ramaswamy Aiyan* v. *Venkata Achari*, like many nineteenth-century Indian legal disputes, involved upper-caste Indians who sought to use the colonial courts to improve their own social positions. The debate between the two groups of Brahmins was in turn leveraged by the British courts to reframe the unwieldy narrative of caste complexities and temple rights into the governable terms of British legality and temporality. Cementing Indian temporalities to religion had a broader influence on economic, social, legal, and political relations as well.

For example, the case touched on the social organization of money. While the narrative framework of the debate provided an entry point that was religious, the stakes of the debate from the litigants' perspective at least were also, perhaps even primarily, monetary. In this sense, a significant question to be decided was whose narrative terms would control the right to collect money? Justice Knight Bruce sidelines the religious framework of *purohitam*, secularizing the question of monetary gains: "The privilege of exercising these functions, when alienable for money, ceases to be the subject of religious sentiment, and becomes a mere proprietary right; and every long-continued enjoyment of the privilege by others is of course capable of being ascribed to a presumed grant or alienation of which the direct evidence is lost."[79] Dismissing the religious logic of these financial transactions therefore also had the effect of installing British legality and temporality as the principal logic of monetary exchange.

The process of adjudicating the alienability of rights in the case is also significant. By framing the Indian logic of rights as mythic or irretrievably ancient, tied inextricably to the privileges of caste, the British court placed the monetary value of priestly services provided at temples under the governing authority of British legality. By constructing an opposition between religious rights and those alienable for money, the Privy Council's decision restricted the religious sphere from providing a viable marketplace of monetary exchange.

But for the court as well as for the litigants, the most important question to be decided was access to rights and privileges. The previous decision delivered by the Civil Court in Mathura invoked not only the equal access to the rights of *purohitam* to be enjoyed by various sects of Brahmins but also mentioned the rights of preference for those using the Brahmins' services. In ruling that "both *Aryas* and *Parishai Bhattars* have a clear prescriptive right, and are both competent to act as ministering guides, or *Purohithars*, to any pilgrims who may choose to employ them as such," the court explicitly declared its refusal to infringe "on the rights and liberties of third parties, who have hitherto apparently received little consideration in this case, namely, the pilgrims."[80] But drawing attention to the pilgrims as the "third parties" obscures the interests of the other "third parties" to the case, the British themselves. In the final portion of this chapter, I will return to the legal maneuvers by which the colonial courts inserted themselves into the conflict while appearing only to resolve it.

As the lengthy history of *Ramaswamy Aiyan* v. *Venkata Achari* makes clear, the progression of opinions did more to restructure the caste system than to eliminate it. Framing its decision as a refusal to "parcel out the Hindoo community as a flock of sheep between these rival shearers" and "consign the flock to their mercy," the Civil Court in the wake of the rebellion began the process of smoothing out the complexities and irregularities of the caste system in order to bring it under the jurisdiction of codifiable British legality.[81] The Privy Council's opinion deals with broad categories of priests and pilgrims, diminishing the differences between the various sects of Brahmins. If, as I discuss in Chapter 5, marriage and normative reproductivity provided ease of governance, caste served a similar function as well. The ready categorization of the population of India undoubtedly made for easier governability.

Establishing Precedents

Streamlining both temporality and caste thus furthered the goal of management. Within the legal sphere, establishing universal linear time was conducive to the system of legal precedents of British law. As Rosane Rocher notes, the courts developed a new emphasis on historical continuity through precedents. "The quest for consistency morphed into a quest for replicability," Rocher writes, "shifting from as faithful an application of original textual and customary sources as seemed feasible, to foregrounding precedents."[82] By establishing case law through precedents, the colonial courts gradually came to manufacture Hindu tradition as well as to regulate and govern it. Rocher continues to outline how the "courts became an increasingly self-referencing, professional enterprise, prepared not only to apply Hindu law, but to shape it."[83] Francis Workman Macnaghten, a Supreme Court judge in the Bengal Presidency, for example, "prefaced his *Considerations on the Hindoo Law, as It Is Current in Bengal* with the unambiguous statement, 'It is our duty to select such parts of the code, as may be most beneficial to the people . . . We may hope, in time, to cleanse the system of its exaggerated corruptions, and to defecate the impurity of the ages.'"[84] Mcnaghten's graphic scatological metaphor suggests eliminating the "impurity of the ages" entails reforming the temporality of the law as well as its governing ideological structures.

Rocher's discussion of the shift away from religious texts and toward precedents shows how the colonial legal system reshaped the imaginative contours of Indian legal history through altering the social value of Indian temporalities. As Rocher notes, "A system of case law came about, a conception of law that was a hallmark of British common law, but which was alien to Hindu law."[85] Shifting emphasis away from tradition and local history, and instead building a new history based on judgments pronounced by British and imperial courts essentially rendered Indian conceptions of the past irrelevant, while also ensuring that the future would continue to be shaped by the logic of British legal decisions.[86]

The precedent set by *Ramaswamy Aiyan* v. *Venkata Achari*, for example, would affect not only the history of Indian law but also the history of caste, granting it a rigid immutability. Weighing the historical evidence as though its only alternative is a narrative of caste and religion, the Privy Council concluded that "their Lordships may dismiss the oral testimony with the observation that it is almost necessarily inconclusive. The question is one on which the Hindoo community has for many years been divided."[87] Because the conflict had existed for years, the justices reasoned, there was no cause to assume that either group had a claim to different rights than the other. In other words, the existence of the conflict, rather than confirming the differences between the two sects, was used as a reason to homogenize the parties as Brahmins who have been disputing for centuries.

Starting the historical record in 1714, with the first written document of "proof," limited the dispute to the history of the dispute itself, thus undermining the value of oral and religious histories that might otherwise have provided a context for the broader terms of the debate. On the one hand, then, the Privy Council's opinion put in place a precedent for evaluating Indian caste conflicts within the teleology of Western historicity. On the other hand, it perpetuated larger cultural representations of the flawed nature of Indian history and its capacity to enter into modernity. Indian history was shown as producing conflicts but it was dismissed as incapable of resolving the conflicts it gave rise to. In the logic of the opinion, Indian history (oral and religious) could only explain the existence of the conflict, whereas a British teleology based in documentary evidence and legal precedents was necessary to resolve it.

Demonstrating the law's capacity to produce history and predict the future, legal precedents serve to shape a linear history on the basis of past judgments. Alerting us to the role of precedent in constructing a common social identity, Ayelet Ben-Yishai argues that in Victorian England "precedential reasoning" served to create a common identity by assimilating past narratives into the present and future. "The form of precedent" she writes, "is thus not simply a vehicle for transferring legal content and meaning from the past into the present. Rather, the meaning of precedent lies in its form, in the complicated process of bringing the past into the present for the sake of a future."[88] In this respect, precedents secured the future by creating a narrative about the past that would continually generate a predictable outcome. For Ben-Yishai, the common law's capacity to survive the utilitarian advocacy of positive law lies in the precedent's hold on the social imaginary: "The idea of a smooth and uninterrupted temporal flow, where change is invisible if not nonexistent, is, after all, central to the common law's vision of itself, and by extension to the Englishman's view of his past and his identity."[89] The congruency between "precedential reasoning" in the law and in Victorian realist fiction forms the basis for Ben-Yishai's innovative analysis.

The stakes of a common identity that precedents helped foster are equally relevant in the colonial sphere. As I discuss in the afterword, legal precedents extend beyond British rule and into the postcolonial era. And, as Rocher observes, "[p]rior dispositions of cases were, of course, not always found to have been right, but precedents they tended to remain, due to principles that were tellingly expressed in Latin, not in Sanskrit . . . In such cases, Anglo-Hindu law amounted to an Anglo disposition of Hindu law."[90] If, as I have suggested, colonial logic constructed caste as operating within a similar, if competing, kind of "precedential reasoning," or the principle of stare decisis to which Rocher refers, such representations served to highlight Indian religiosity in contrast to colonial legality. Taken alongside the universalization of Western temporality, the shift toward precedents impacted Indian history itself and its relationship to the future. *Ramaswamy Aiyan* v. *Venkata Achari*, for example, established a precedent whereby British courts could rewrite the history of local customary practices in order to bring them into alignment with imperial legal temporality, thus also consolidating the notion of a decadent and outmoded Indian past. In broad terms, the administration of law organized around British teleology would have a significant impact on the imaginative and discursive relationship to modernity in the colony and into the post colony.[91]

Finally, then, the effects of the JCPC's opinion were threefold: (1) it served to consolidate dominant Western conceptions of a despotic Indian past, (2) it cemented the modern temporality of British legal historicity, and (3) it validated a streamlined version of the caste system that was more rigid, and, as a result, better suited to the uses of imperial management. Perhaps most importantly, it accomplished all of this under the guise of equalizing the access to rights by various groups of Indians. In reality, however, the opinion sidelined the complex architecture of caste irregularities in order to reframe the system into a more rigidly hierarchical and normativized state. Thus, while appearing to bring the disputing Brahmins into the fold of the secular humanist ideal of equal rights, the decision, in fact, moved toward consolidating the four-tier system of caste we know today.

An important consequence of the systematization of caste is that it reaffirmed already well-established ideas of the collective nature of Indian society as opposed to the individual subjectivity of Western modernity. If the bildungsroman is the genre that represents the nineteenth-century tendency to obscure the role of society in crafting the illusion of free will, the mystery or detective novel, as we see in Chapter 4, makes the stakes of the individual apparent. The bildungsroman, as a narrative of progress, hinges upon history marching toward a predictable end, namely the fully developed individual. As I show in Chapter 4, however, the detective novel, through a process of shedding the burden of history, allows consciousness, and culpability, to emerge as fully individual.

CHAPTER 4

On Time
How Fiction Writes History in Wilkie Collins's The Moonstone

Judicial opinions share an interesting generic trait with the detective novel. As Tzvetan Todorov observes, the detective novel "contains not one, but two stories: the story of the crime and the story of the investigation."[1] Though the second story reveals the logic of the first, the "characters of this second story, the story of the investigation, do not act, they learn. Nothing can happen to them: a rule of the genre postulates the detective's immunity." In this respect, the teleology of the detective novel inevitably works to ensure that the detective and the society affected by the crime remain above the fray. Likewise, the judicial acts I discuss in this volume occupy a similar position of immunity. As I outlined in Chapter 3, for instance, the opinion in *Ramaswamy Aiyan* v. *Venkata Achari* recast the original events into a narrative decipherable within the terms of British history and temporality. The "second story" of the judicial opinion thus illuminates the "first story" and confers "immunity" on the judiciary, who, by all appearances, "do not act, they learn." My reading of *Ramaswamy Aiyan* v. *Venkata Achari* questioned the law's passive reception of the narrative, arguing that the Privy Counsellors and the colonial judiciary played a more active role in crafting both the narrative and its underlying assumptions. By ordering Indian history within a teleological narrative, the legal opinion conceals its own historical foundations and imaginative license. This concealment of history is likewise, for Franco Moretti, central to the detective novel. As a genre that establishes its alignment with modern law by focusing on the agent and not the action of the crime, "detective fiction detaches prose narration from historiography and relates it to the world of Law."[2] The disengagement from history, in turn, performs a rejection of the typical model of *Bildung*. In detective novels characters "do not grow." Instead, "*Bildung*, expelled from within the narrative, is then evaporated by its relationship with the reader," who "reads only with the purpose of remaining as one already is: innocent."[3] In this chapter, I use the work of Todorov and Moretti, among others, to explore the intersections between the detective novel's teleology and its role in the production of social innocence. In this respect, I see the detective novel as a paradigmatic genre for Victorian ideals of rationality that sought to explain and order the chaotic mystery of the colonial world, while affirming the innocence and benign goodwill of the imperial project. By reading *The Moonstone* alongside *Ramaswamy Aiyan* v. *Venkata Achari*, we see how the mystery genre inaugurates a philosophy of history that privileges individual guilt by way of directing attention away from more social or collective forms of culpability.

In 1868, Wilkie Collins published *The Moonstone*, a novel about the disappearance of, and mystery surrounding, a valuable Indian diamond gifted to a young English woman on the occasion of her eighteenth birthday. Appearing serially in his friend Charles Dickens's *All the Year Round*, the story was an immediate commercial success. Since then, the novel has become iconic of the mystery genre, prompting T. S. Eliot famously to dub it "the first, the longest and the best of modern English detective novels."[4] While contemporary readers of *The Moonstone* may not think of it as "modern" any longer, notions of temporality and progress are central to the novel's representation of Victorian England. Written just five years after *Ramaswamy Aiyan* v. *Venkata Achari* was settled by the Privy Council, *The Moonstone* reflects many similar concerns with underscoring English modernity, especially by way of comparison with colonies such as India. As a detective novel that revolves around uncovering a singular criminal agent, the novel demonstrates the importance of individuality to English notions of criminality, as discussed in Chapters 1 and 2. Moreover, as I show, like the Privy Council opinion in *Ramaswamy Aiyan* v. *Venkata Achari*, the genre of the detective novel evolves out of, and instantiates, a theory of history that places evidence and individual agency at the center of understanding and narrating events within the flow of time.

More specifically, the process of detecting guilt searches for individual agency at the expense of social, cultural, or historical explanations for criminal acts. Within this logic, for reasons explained in the preceding chapters, the criminal in Collins's novel is predictably English. As I show, however, the essential Englishness of the culprit does not result in a corresponding critique of English imperialism, as the focus on individual guilt sidelines national histories. Instead, the innocence of the close-knit rural English community is highlighted in contrast to a singular guilty criminal from whom it stands apart. By reintroducing history into the literary narrative, I aim to detect the complex networks of evidence and truth-claims that the novel proffers often by distorting and distracting from the actual historical record. Returning our attention to real events and histories makes evident the colonial crimes that have been assiduously covered up, especially through the genre's persistent recourse to individual guilt.

I supplement my literary reading of the novel with the historical narrative not only, or even primarily, as a means of remedying the inauthenticity of the history that forms the basis for the fictional narrative in *The Moonstone*, but rather to complicate the congruency between the resolution of the mystery and its reliance on underlying fact claims. The novel purports to begin with a reference to a historical event, the defeat of Tipu Sultan of Mysore. This event gives rise to the action of the novel by providing the explanation for how the diamond was acquired. But while the obvious historical reference for the gemstone is the famous Koh-i-noor diamond, it never belonged to Tipu Sultan, but was taken from the child prince Duleep Singh, during the British annexation of the independent territory of Punjab. Similarly, the fictional narrative traces the diamond to the temple of Somanatha, to where it is restored at the end of the novel. Historically, however, Somanatha was famous in the nineteenth century for its lost temple doors, whose attempted restoration by Lord Ellenborough resonates with Collins's fictional account of the diamond. These two historical references, of the Koh-i-noor diamond and the temple doors, haunt the novel, providing it with an alternative subtext. By substituting the narrative of Duleep Singh in place of the novel's choice of Tipu Sultan, I show how a different set of facts makes possible the discovery of a different resolution to the mystery. If Collins's narrative looks generously upon the restoration of the diamond to the moon god of Somanatha (contrasting British benevolence with the overt violence of Tipu Sultan), the supplementary narrative of how the stone was appropriated from Duleep Singh reveals that the mystery cannot be so easily resolved. The Koh-i-noor diamond was not returned in secret to its rightful owner, but rather was openly and ostentatiously displayed in the Queen's crown jewels. The mystery of *The Moonstone* unfolds and is able to be resolved precisely by suppressing and indeed crafting a fiction about the historical narrative within which it arises. If the mystery of *The Moonstone* turns on the secret (of both the theft and the return), the reality of British colonial power depends upon hypervisibility and the spectacle of display. As I show, the genre of the detective novel allows the crime to be individualized while power is made more diffuse, both in colonial and domestic contexts.

In his groundbreaking reading of *The Moonstone*, D. A. Miller observes that the work of detection is surprisingly not performed by the visiting police detective but is instead carried out by members of the community in their quotidian interactions with one another. "The exercise of policing power," Miller writes, "inheres in the logic of the world, but only as a discreet 'accident' of normative social practices and models of conduct. The community does not mobilize in a concerted scheme of police action, and yet things turn out as though it did."[5] The community's unwitting cooperation with the goals of police surveillance and detection, for Miller, confirms the Foucauldian diffusion of state power:

> That none of these characters *intends* to assist the work of detection is irrelevant to the fact of their practical collaboration, without which the mystery would never be solved. In effect, the work of detection is carried forward by the novel's entire cast of characters, shifted not just from professional to amateur, but from an outsider to a whole community. Thus, the move to discard the *role of the detective* is at the same time a move to disperse the *function of detection*.[6]

In addition to rendering the external detective unnecessary, shifting the burden of detection to the community as a whole confers upon the community the capacity to police both its boundaries and its norms without articulating any explicit legal rationale to which it can be held.

But it is Miller's related point that the community's participation in catching the thief implicitly works to affirm collective innocence that interests me here. Within this reading, the detective novel is as interested in producing public innocence as it is in identifying singular criminal aberrations. In fact, the notion of individual guilt relies on a more universal civic innocence in contrast to which it can be readily discerned. As "the universality of suspicion gives way to a highly specific guilt," the genre becomes "[e]ngaged in producing social innocence."[7] Combined with the detective novel's tendency to relegate history to the margins of the narrative, the genre's affirmation of public innocence makes it an apt vehicle for conveying the ideology of imperialism. Following the Sepoy Rebellion of 1857, as the legal and political administration of India was transferred from the Company to the Crown, shared underlying assumptions prevailed in both the mystery novel and the general mood of the English nation. The imagination of an innocent public community that was divested of the burdens of history made it easier to turn a blind eye to colonial violence and exploitation.

Setting the Stage

Read in this light, *The Moonstone* begins with a red herring in the form of a prologue that draws on a dehistoricized narrative of conquest and plunder. The prologue, which claims to be "Extracted from a Family

Paper," details the backstory of the fated diamond.[8] According to the letter, John Herncastle, a soldier in the East India Company's army, acquired the gem during the storming of Seringapatam. The historical event to which the letter refers marked the defeat of Tipu Sultan in 1799, and helped consolidate British rule over the subcontinent. The letter, written by a relative who was reproachful of John Herncastle's actions, explains how the diamond came into his possession. Melding fact and fiction, the prologue traces the origins of the diamond to the "earliest known traditions," which "describe the stone as having been set in the forehead of the four-handed Indian god who typifies the Moon."[9] Through the letter, we learn that the "adventures of the Yellow Diamond begin with the eleventh century of the Christian era" when "the Mohammedan conqueror, Mahmoud of Ghizni, crossed India; seized on the holy city of Somnauth; and stripped of its treasures the famous temple, which had stood for centuries – the shrine of Hindoo pilgrimage, and the wonder of the Eastern world."[10] Despite "the rapacity of the conquering Mohammedans," the letter reveals, "the inviolate deity, bearing the Yellow Diamond in its forehead" was removed by "three Brahmins" during the night "to the second of the sacred cities of India – the city of Benares."[11] Appearing before the three Brahmins in a dream, the "deity commanded that the Moonstone should be watched, from that time forth, by three priests in turn, night and day, to the end of the generations of men."[12] To further protect the sacred stone, the deity attached a curse to whoever might attempt to steal it.

Echoing the atemporality of Indian history evinced in *Ramaswamy*, the prologue notes that for "generation after generation, the successors of the three Brahmins watched their priceless Moonstone, night and day" over the ages "until the first years of the eighteenth Christian century saw the reign of Aurungzebe, Emperor of the Moguls," under whose "command havoc and rapine were let loose once more among the temples of the worship of Brahmah."[13] Also as in the Privy Council opinion, the novel translates ancient mythic times and narratives into legible events within an English historical narrative. During the Mughal era the letter claims, the "shrine of the four-handed god was polluted by the slaughter of sacred animals; the images of the deities were broken in pieces; and the Moonstone was seized by an officer of rank in the army of Aurungzebe."[14] Miserable and powerless, the three Brahmin guardians watched as "the Moonstone passed (carrying its curse with it) from one lawless Mohammedan hand to another" until finally it "fell into the possession of Tippoo, Sultan of Seringapatam," who had the stone mounted in his dagger.[15] It was in the battle for Seringapatam that the fictional John Herncastle and his cousin, the author of the letter, encountered the diamond.

The letter details how in the aftermath of the siege "the soldiers found their way, by a guarded door, into the treasury of the Palace, and loaded themselves with gold and jewels."[16] Among the "deplorable excesses" that the letter describes is a scene in which John Herncastle, having slain an Indian in Tipu's army, turns to face his cousin, holding Tipu's diamond dagger dripping with blood. The Indian's final words, that "The Moonstone will have its vengeance yet on you and yours!" inaugurate the action of the novel, and set the stage for the cursed diamond's entry into the idyllic setting of the English country house.[17] The prologue closes with the cousin's condemnation of Herncastle's actions, and his belief that Herncastle "will live to regret it, if he keeps the Diamond; and that others will live to regret taking it from him, if he gives the Diamond away."[18] The origin story of the yellow diamond presented in the prologue invokes both the "fantastic" qualities of Hindu mythology as well as the historical analog of the famed Koh-i-noor diamond.[19]

The three time periods of the prologue – the ancient Hindu period, the eleventh- to fifteenth-century waves of Muslim conquest, and eighteenth-century English colonial – lay the historical groundwork for the eventual resolution of the diamond's fate in nineteenth-century England and India. Though written in the 1860s, well after the Indian Rebellion and the Queen's Proclamation, the action of the novel takes place between 1848 and 1850, during the waning period of Company rule. The plot unfolds in a series of installments told by eleven different narrators, beginning with Gabriel Betteredge, the trusted household servant. In his testimony, Betteredge establishes the oppositionality between these earlier historical periods outlined in the prologue and the "age of progress" that characterizes the timeframe of the novel.[20] Repeatedly invoking the reader's "cultivated modern taste" and "the modern way of looking at it," Betteredge stakes out his narrative's claim to modernity and draws a direct contrast with the ethos of the past.[21] Moreover, the novel as a whole echoes Betteredge's investment in confirming the modernity of Victorian England, especially in relation to other places, charting a grid of time and place in which certain geographical spaces are necessarily linked to corresponding temporalities.[22]

While the prologue and epilogue of *The Moonstone* focus largely on the diamond, the lengthy plot of the novel is centered almost exclusively on a wealthy English family. The drama unfolds after Rachel Verinder "put the Indian diamond in the Indian cabinet, for the purpose of permitting two beautiful native productions to admire each other."[23] On the same night, the gem is stolen from her bedroom. Initially, suspicion falls on three

Indian jugglers who mysteriously appear at the Yorkshire country estate on the night of the birthday party. Despite their arrest and detention for the theft, however, it is soon established that the "poor ill-used Indians" are "as innocent as the babe unborn." Over the course of the narrative, suspicion is cast on Rosanna Spearman, a shy servant with a criminal past who commits suicide by drowning herself in quicksand, Rachel Verinder herself, whom the renowned Detective Cuff suspects of stealing the diamond to cover her debts; Godfrey Ablewhite, another cousin who is hypocritically involved in Christian evangelism and desires a romantic connection with Rachel for his own financial gain; and Franklin Blake, Rachel's true love and the cousin who delivers the diamond to her. With the help of Ezra Jennings, a biracial, terminally ill opium addict who "was born, and partly brought up, in one of our colonies," we learn that Franklin Blake removed the diamond from Rachel Verinder's room under the influence of opium administered to him without his knowledge or permission.[24] Blake gives the diamond to Godfrey Ablewhite for safekeeping, but he instead steals the gem and attempts to take it to Amsterdam where he can have it recut and sold to pay off his debts.[25] Godfrey, who tries to leave London disguised in blackface, is ultimately tracked down and clandestinely murdered by the Indians, who reclaim the diamond.[26]

In the novel's epilogue, Mr. Murthwaite, a traveler in India who was also a guest at Rachel's birthday party, reports seeing the diamond restored to the deity at the "sacred city" of Somanatha.[27] Disguising himself and joining a group of Hindu pilgrims, Murthwaite recognizes the three Indians from the night of Rachel's party at the country estate, who by traveling to England and killing Godfrey Ablewhite "had forfeited their caste in the service of the god."[28] At the end of the ceremony in which the diamond is revealed, the three Brahmins embark separately on their "purification by pilgrimage."[29] The novel closes with a nod to the cyclicality of Indian time, as "after the lapse of eight centuries, the Moonstone looks forth once more, over the walls of the sacred city in which its story first began."[30] "So the years pass, and repeat each other; so the same events revolve in the cycles of time," Murthwaite remarks, and asks, "What will be the next adventures of the Moonstone? Who can tell?"[31] As the narrative of the mystery moves forward, reflecting the inevitability of British progress, the temporality of India remains stubbornly stagnant. Finally, folding the present into the past, the gem, the deity, and the devotees end up exactly where they began, oblivious to the linear narrative of history and impervious to the forward movement of time. As I argue in this chapter, the novel's mystery genre works to naturalize a teleological narrative of history that solidifies the relationship between the restorative British present and the stalled Indian past. As the mystery unfolds, it becomes increasingly clear that the temporality of the novel is intimately related to the teleology of an imperialist vision of history.

As numerous critics – including Christopher GoGwilt, Jaya Mehta, Melissa Free, John Reed, Ashish Roy, Krishna Manavalli, Upamanyu Mukherjee, Lauren Goodlad, and others – have shown, the novel's mystery plot is inseparable from its imperial underpinnings. For decades, critics have debated whether *The Moonstone* is critical of, or complicit with English colonialism. Nineteenth-century reviewer Geraldine Jewsbury found the novel sympathetic to the Brahmins and remarked that "few will read the final destiny of The Moonstone without feeling the tears rise in their eyes as they catch a glimpse of the three men, who have sacrificed their cast[e] in the service of their God."[32] In the 1970s, John Reed inaugurated a line of criticism that saw Collins's novel as a "broad indictment of an entire way of life" that blithely profited from imperial exploitation.[33] In a similar vein, Lillian Nayder argues that while "many of the narrators in *The Moonstone* subscribe to the imperial ideology of their day, Collins is himself performing an act of ideology critique in his novel."[34]

Postcolonial critics of *The Moonstone* are largely split into two camps: those who view the novel as critical of the imperial project, and those who view it as upholding colonial logic, if not making a direct case for English imperialism. Melissa Free, Jaya Mehta, and Yumna Siddiqi have, to varying degrees taken the novel as evidence of Collins's anti-imperialism. Others, such as Upamanyu Mukherjee, however, wonder if the novel can be truly subversive "if its 'anti-imperialism' consists of using stereotypical representations of the colony, to criticize not so much British aggression abroad, but the authority's failings at home?"[35] Mukherjee sees the novel as employing a familiar strategy whereby the colony becomes a vehicle for self-examination, rather than an object of analysis in its own right. Most specifically, Ashish Roy expresses overt skepticism about the novel's anti-imperialism:

> Poised at the threshold separating history from fiction, the parallel between the Koh-i-Noor and the sacred Moonstone does not however comprise an anti-imperialist sentiment. Rather, it tactfully programs its 'important particulars' in a 'foundational' intersection of two histories so that empire becomes the object of strong recuperative concern.[36]

As evidence of Collins's imperialist logic, Roy cites the novel's treatment of history as "the diamond fabricates the arrival of modernity out of two native pre-texts of temporality."[37] For Roy, eight hundred years of Indian conflict sets the stage for Collins to laud the emergence of British progress, converting cyclical Indian temporalities into a coherent linear modernity. The production of a celebratory linear narrative of the return of the gem also underlies the liberties the novel takes with historical facts and figures.

To my mind, the key to deciphering *The Moonstone's* colonial politics lies in a series of historical substitutions and elisions. As I discuss later, the mystery genre suppresses collective history in the service of identifying individual guilt. But this substitution of the individual for the collective turns on a series of corresponding substitutions that resurface the relevance of history. In order to uncover the logic by which Collins's novel and the mystery genre operate, we must examine the interplay between Collins's fiction and the history that it invokes.

Sectarianism and Subjection

Collins's fantastical mystery plot draws on, and reframes, a variety of historical events. While specific incidents within the narrative have some basis in history, Collins's representation adds both sensational and moralistic details. For example, Collins attaches the myth of the sacred diamond to the historical temple of Soma, the moon god, for which Somanatha, or the novel's Somnauth, was famous. Collins's invocation of the historical elements, including the raid on the temple by Mahmud of Ghazni in 1026, is noteworthy. Since the nineteenth century, Somanatha has become emblematic of larger sectarian tensions between Hindus and Muslims in Gujarat and beyond. The narrative of religious conflict provides the subtext for both the framing device of the prologue and epilogue in *The Moonstone*, and for the colonial strategy of "divide and rule." Instantiating the tendency to ascribe a central role to religion that I discuss with regard to the law in Chapter 3, Collins's narrative reinforces the notion that religion is the primary interpretive framework through which Indians view the world. And despite the explicit secularism of the constitution, contemporary Indian society continues to reflect the legacy of divisions fostered during the colonial era. In her study of Somanatha, historian Romila Thapar offers "an attempt to explore the interpretation of one event that has been projected in the last two centuries as central to the relations between two communities in South Asia, the Hindu and the Muslim."[38] In Thapar's account, the fact of Mahmud of Ghazni's raid is indisputable, but what is contested is the historical significance attributed to the event as a catalyst for, and symbol of, centuries of religious animosity between Hindus and Muslims on the subcontinent.

Thapar argues that colonial historians such as James Mill cast the event as symptomatic of Muslim violence and Hindu trauma and humiliation. This, in turn, fed the "popular European myth from the time of the Crusades that Islam was a religion of barbarism as compared to the civilizing qualities of Christianity."[39] Drawing exclusively from Turko-Persian sources, Mill and others perpetuated a "theory of a permanent confrontation between Hindu and Muslim, which became the perspective through which events such as the raid on Somanatha were viewed."[40] Such narratives not only justified British colonialism as a salve to Muslim plunder but also enabled the "construction of a collective memory" that would later be deployed by nineteenth-century Hindu nationalists as well as Hindutvas of the contemporary moment to justify violence against Muslims.[41] "Mill's periodization of Indian history into Hindu and Muslim civilizations and, finally, the British presence, superior to both," set the stage for both fictional narratives such as *The Moonstone*, as well as real historical interventions to avenge the "trauma" of "Muslim rule."[42]

One such instance was Lord Ellenborough's effort to reclaim the temple doors of Somanatha from Afghanistan, where Mahmud of Ghazni was believed to have taken them. As governor general of India from 1842 to 1844, Ellenborough issued "what came to be called 'The Proclamation of the Gates' in 1842."[43] In a scandal that ultimately led to his downfall, however, Ellenborough's attempts to restore the temple gates by virtue of the colonial army's success in Afghanistan fell fantastically flat. From the start, there was British resistance to the governor general's plans. Influential opponents such as Thomas Macaulay accused Ellenborough of "defending" a "religion encouraging idolatry, superstition, human sacrifice, *suttee* and *thugee*."[44] Nevertheless, Ellenborough's motion in the House of Commons was successful, and the "restoration of the gates of Somanatha" became crucial to solidifying the narrative that the British were aiding "not merely the bringing back of a trophy of success from Afghanistan," but were "restoring to its original position" the treasure taken eight hundred years ago "by the now conquered enemy."[45] The gates were transported from Afghanistan to Agra, where they "were found not to be of Indian workmanship." In the end, the "attempt became the butt of jokes," but its influence in disseminating the narrative of Hindu trauma and British benevolence was profound.

In addition to carving Indian history into eras of religious rule, colonial historiographers and administrators thus also cast Hindus as victims and Muslims as oppressors within a dichotomy that obscured the motivations of British interventions.[46] Despite Ellenborough's failure, the effort generated valuable propaganda. In the literary realm, the event is an important historical referent for the narrative of cultural and religious restoration with which Collins's novel closes. As Thapar notes, "the notoriety of the gates had made Somanatha into an item of popular interest in Britain," and the idol features as an "undercurrent in one of the most widely read mystery novels of the nineteenth century."[47] According to Thapar, "Wilkie Collins read the history of India by Talboys Wheeler and corresponded with a civil servant posted in Kathiawar for information on the story."[48] Echoing Ellenborough's theme of cultural restoration, Collins's final narrator, Mr. Murthwaite, the English traveler in India, relates the thrall of the Hindu pilgrims who witness the unveiling of the yellow diamond returned to the deity's forehead: "After the lapse of eight centuries, the Moonstone looks forth once more, over the walls of the sacred city in which its story first began."[49] While Murthwaite cannot explain how the stone "has found its way back to its wild native land – by what accident, or by what crime, the Indians regained possession of their sacred gem," the plot of the novel leading up to this point solves exactly that mystery.[50] Viewed in conjunction with historical efforts such as the Proclamation of the Gates, *The Moonstone* can be read as a vehicle for reframing efforts to reclaim the treasures of an ancient Hindu past.

Collins's narrative of the stone's restoration was written twenty years after Ellenborough's tenure as governor general, but it is set only five years after the incident of the doors. Collins's fictional depiction of the analogous event is, however, ambivalent. While the broad arc of the novel affirms the narrative of British benevolence, it also nuances British interventions. Importantly, within the novel it is the three Brahmins who "regained possession of their sacred gem" (466). In *The Moonstone* the British are not only unhelpful in restoring the stone but also actively responsible for the theft to begin with. In Collins's tale, then, the British colonizers can also be seen as conquering invaders, implicitly allied with colonial history's representation of "Muslim rule."[51]

Yet the novel functions on two levels: that of the mystery and that of the overarching narrative that explains the mystery. In other words, while the plot of the novel vilifies Herncastle, the narrative frame reserves judgment on the actions taken by the three Brahmins to reclaim the diamond, and romanticizes the religious ceremony that ends the story. If on the level of plot the British act as the conquerors, Collins's narrative as a whole conveys some support for the conquered. The double valence of the plot and narrative is emblematic of both the novel's mystery genre and the colonialist framing of Indian history. While certain details of the plot are sympathetic to the three Brahmins, however, the narrative voice (both of the novel and of the eleven narrators) is unambiguously British, and the overarching plot validates British benevolence. Moreover, Collins's representation of the stalwart Brahmins is also rooted in orientalist representations of Hinduism, and Indian society more broadly.

According to Krishna Manavalli, Collins's portrayal of the Brahmins serves to represent "the Indian tradition in predominantly Brahminical terms" and "Indian society as religious and caste-ridden."[52] As a result, "India becomes fixed in a primordial past, one that is opposed to and distanced from European modernity, even as Collins's own attitude towards the prevalent nineteenth-century notions of progress remain ambivalent throughout the novel."[53] Invoking what she terms the "Brahmin sublime," Manavalli argues that Collins fuses "the idea of the Gothic sublime" with "the problematic of caste" to create a "dark and ancient prehistoric India as a sublime 'Brahminical' land of beauty and terror."[54] The focus on Brahminism thus solidifies both the ancient temporality of India, and, by contrast, the modernity of England. In solving the mystery of the diamond, therefore, Collins's narrative provides the key through which an ancient Indian past can be made legible to modern English audiences. Much like nineteenth-century colonialist historiography, it does so by inaugurating two narrative temporalities in which the modern is used to explain and translate the ancient.[55] The two narrative temporalities are also germane to the novel's mystery genre.

Opposing Temporalities

In "The Typology of Detective Fiction" Tzvetan Todorov writes about the temporality of the whodunit novel. For Todorov the detective novel has two stories: one that relates the crime and the other that reveals who committed the crime. These narratives develop simultaneously, but unfold in oppositional temporalities. While the narrative of the crime moves forward in time, the narrative of detection moves backward. Describing the "duality" of detective fiction, Todorov observes that the "novel contains not one but two stories: the story of the crime and the story of the investigation. In their purest form, these two stories have no point in common."[56] One story is of the past, while the other is of the present, and the two never meet.[57]

Implicitly, the temporality of the detective novel works to explain the mystery of a past event from the vantage point of the present. But, no less importantly, it undoes the uncertainty of the past by teleologically reconstructing the present. The two temporalities are distinct, even as one provides the narrative context for the other. In differentiating between "these two stories," Todorov notes "that the first – the story of the crime – tells 'what really happened,' whereas the second – the story of the investigation – explains 'how the reader (or the narrator) has come to know about it.'"[58] The story of the investigation, and even more so the explanatory voice of the overarching narrative, provides the epistemological framework within which the mystery can ultimately be decoded.[59]

Mark Currie extends Todorov's premise with the claim that all fictional representations of time essentially follow the same model.[60] For Currie, "the whodunit acts as a kind of typological model for much fiction beyond the genre" and can be applied to "any narrative which involves an interplay between narrated time and the time of the narrative, where the time of the narrative functions as the site of self-conscious reflection both on past events and on the nature of writing about them."[61] Currie further likens the narrative form of the novel to that of writing history. Both the novel and history share a similar underlying relationship between past and present:

> narrative explanation, as many historiographers have observed, is always an account of the present, and an attempt to dominate the past by understanding it from the point of view of the present, as if progress is a continuous improvement of that understanding.[62]

In this respect, the "detective and the historian share this structure of moving forwards by knowing the past." Currie also compares the novel's treatment of time to philosophical theories on the topic. The two differ, he argues, in that the novel, unlike philosophy, has "at its disposal all the temporal resources of narrative fiction as a complement to the resources of reasoned argument."[63] As a result, for Currie, "narrative fiction is fundamentally capable of being constative and performative at the same time."[64] The novel does not simply represent a particular version of history or a truth claim about it, but it also performs it. In order to make sense of the plot, the reader must accept the narrative temporality, and enter into its logic. In particular, each event in the novel must be seen as conditional upon the event that precedes it in order for the plot to make sense. And in order to rationally comprehend the plot, the reader must accede to the forward movement of time both within the plot and in the lived experience of reading. For this reason, especially when reading a novel, "the irreversibility of time is inseparable from rationality itself."[65] More specifically, certain representations of temporalities structure, and are dependent upon, corresponding rationalities.

Fictional Historicism

In *The Moonstone*, the temporality of the prologue moves from the eleventh century through 1799, while the main story takes place in the late 1840s. The novel was written and most popularly read, however, in 1868. In the intervening years between when the novel is set and when it was published, the momentous Sepoy Rebellion occurred and, as a result, the Crown formally took over administration of the colony. The narrative temporality of the novel is thus crucial to understanding the particular decoding of events it puts forth. Interestingly, despite its historical significance, the novel makes no mention of the rebellion, instead foregrounding the siege of Seringapatam and the slaying of Tipu Sultan. Jaya Mehta argues that in substituting Seringapatam for the rebellion, Collins chooses "an event more distant, more equivocal, and hence more susceptible to revisionism than the more recent event."[66] For Mehta, the substitution "inverts moral and political sympathies" thus "allowing the reader to read the illegitimacy of empire into the antecedents of the unmentioned Mutiny."[67] By staging the acquisition of the diamond as a consequence of the siege of Seringapatam, Mehta argues, the novel displaces the antipathy toward Indians felt in England in the wake of the Sepoy Rebellion.

As Mehta also notes, however, "Tipu was a popular villain of cult status back in England," so his invocation served to merge, and perpetuate, British and Hindu fears of the predatory Muslim.[68] In addition to being a worthy adversary on the battlefield, and stoking English animosity through his political alliances with the French, Tipu harbored a well-known hatred of the English. He famously commissioned an almost life size wooden automaton of a tiger mauling a British soldier that, when a crank was turned, emitted frightful screams from an organ hidden inside the belly of the tiger. After the siege, the giant toy became a symbol of English triumph, and was brought to London, where it is still on display in the Victoria and Albert Museum. Therefore, even as Collins mutes the reaction to the mutiny, his substitution of Tipu is not entirely neutral. Instead, it once again reinforces the commonplace colonial trope of the rapacious Muslim invader.

Moreover, although it sets the stage of conflict in Seringapatam and perhaps even draws an oblique parallel between Tipu and Herncastle, the novel stops short of a clear condemnation of imperialism. Rather, as Ashish Roy argues, "*The Moonstone* produces a *mythos* entirely consonant with arguments for empire."[69] While the internal mystery uncovers Herncastle's guilt and hints at a broader British culpability, the external authorial narrative redeems British imperialism by revealing the truth and restoring the gem to its rightful place in the temple's deity. Even if the temporality of the narrative highlights the continuity of Tipu Sultan and John Herncastle, the temporality of the novel draws an implicit distinction between the excesses of the East India Company and the rule of law after the Queen's Proclamation. Arguably, the novel's acknowledgement of the East India Company's corruption feeds into the popular narrative of the ameliorative effects of the state's assumption of control.

Equally importantly, in addition to comparing Herncastle to the "lawless Mohameddans," *The Moonstone* also constructs a historical continuum between Mahmud of Ghazni, Aurangzeb, and Tipu Sultan. While the novel serves to linearly connect various Muslim rulers, it simultaneously muddies the narrative of British expansionism. As noted earlier, in the prologue we learn that the stone eluded "Mahmoud of Ghazni" only to be captured in "the first years of the eighteenth Christian century" by "an officer of rank in the army of Aurungzebe."[70] Over the years, the stone "passed (carrying its curse with it) from one lawless Mohammedan hand to another," until it "fell into the possession of Tippoo, Sultan of Seringapatam, who caused it to be placed as an ornament in the handle of a dagger, and who commanded it to be kept among the choicest treasures of his armoury."[71] As the precious gem folds generations of otherwise unconnected Muslim rulers into its narrative, a clear teleology emerges of the historically continuous, yet morally stagnant, "lawless Mohammedans."[72] And across the years, "the successors of the three guardian priests kept their watch," marking the Hindus' unwavering passivity. By stringing together temporally and geographically distinct eras, cultures, and locations, Collins creates a monologic narrative of Muslim conquest and Hindu victimization that corroborates a broader imperialist narrative as discussed earlier.[73]

By contrast, however, the novel makes little mention of British colonial expansion during the same period. Instead, the prologue casts John Herncastle as the only named villain amid the scene of plunder following the siege of Seringapatam. The narrative acknowledges the corruption of the British soldiers but it individualizes the specific theft of the diamond and frames it within a fractured family history in which one cousin exposes the transgressions of another. This, of course, sets the stage for the final resolution of the mystery fifty years later in which Godfrey Ablewhite is revealed to be the thief of the diamond, while his cousin Franklin Blake is vindicated, criminally and romantically. In this manner, the novel casts widespread reports of plunder after the fall of Tipu as secondary to the narrative of family strife and the triumph of individual honor over individual guilt.

Interestingly, however, Collins's depiction of the raid on Tipu's treasury is one of the more historically accurate elements of the story. An anonymous letter written by one of the soldiers present at the siege remarks that it is "not perfectly known who had the honor of exterminating the scourge of the East" and admits that "it is supposed some jewels found which he constantly wore and were inestimable have occasioned this silence," though he feels that "they were certainly fair plunder."[74] The soldier further notes that Tipu's body was found late in the evening, under a pile of "others thrown over it during the slaughter." The body was returned to "the survivors of his family," though the soldier felt "it ought rather to have been hung by the heels on a Gibbet as a memorable example to mankind" as punishment for Tipu's "unrelenting, unmanly, unprecedented cruelty of mind which vented itself for the most part in a rooted antipathy and inveterate hatred to Europeans."[75] Collins's narrative, in which "General Baird himself had found the dead body of Tippoo under a heap of the slain" as "the soldiers found their way, by a guarded door, into the treasury of the Palace, and loaded themselves with gold and jewels," closely echoes the soldier's letter.[76]

The Law of Time

By incorporating a pastiche of historical details into his fictional representation, Collins's narrative seems to imbue the Indian elements of the story with historical accuracy.[77] In this respect, the novel coats the Indian plot with a veneer of facticity, invoking the Victorian aspiration to empiricism and rationality reflected in such areas as the law, the natural sciences, and medicine. As Yumna Siddiqi explains, in "fiction of intrigue," especially during the late nineteenth century, "imperial domination, premised upon power over and knowledge of the Other, is expressed in a discourse of law and order."[78] "Running through these stories," she argues, "is a concern with the rule of law: the stories are located squarely within the domain of the legal."[79] If, as Siddiqi suggests, the mystery novel is an archetypal vehicle for working through cultural anxieties about the dual forces of modernity and imperialism, the turn toward the law, which she sees as intrinsic to the mystery genre represents a "concerted attempt to make sense of – that is, to impose cognitive order upon – a seemingly inexplicable, uncertain, and dangerous world."[80] In *The Moonstone*, a preoccupation with law and modernity is not only embodied in the individual narrative of Inspector Cuff, the esteemed detective brought in to work on the case, but is at the heart of the novel itself. Most obviously, the solution of the mystery of who stole the diamond restores order to the violated space of the English country house.

While many critics read the exposure of Godfrey Ablewhite as the criminal as evidence of Collins's critique of imperialism, I argue that the relationship between law, history, and fiction within the text points to a more complicated stance on Empire. More specifically, as I have shown, I see the imposition of historicity on the Indian narrative as complicit with a pervasive teleological fiction about Indian, and specifically Hindu, subjection. The novel shows how zealous Hindus have kept watch over a sacred gem, and how generations of Muslim invaders have plundered and destroyed temples as the Hindus stood passively by. Such a narrative affirms the salutary effects of British colonialism in bringing law and order to a land overrun by greed and lawlessness. It also perpetuates stereotypes about both Hindus and Muslims, and fosters divisions between the two most populous religions on the subcontinent. Grafting the narrative of the diamond onto a history of sectarian strife in Somanatha further infuses the narrative with a sense of religious significance. It is thus ironic that the principal historical referent, as I discuss later, is a young Sikh king who is left entirely out of the narrative.

Despite its demonization of Muslims, the novel's largely negative representation of its Hindu characters makes it clear that they are neither the heroes nor the victims of the story. While their villainy may be matched by their religiosity, the fact remains that within the narrative, the Brahmins manipulate a small English boy to their advantage, break into residences and offices, rob and murder Godfrey Ablewhite, and smuggle the diamond to India. In an unsettling scene narrated by Gabriel Betteredge toward the beginning of the novel, the "jugglers" hypnotize and interrogate a "little delicate-looking light-haired English boy" whom they have recruited to assist them.[81] The disguised Brahmin asks the boy to put out his hand for his "catechism," and when the boy recoils in fear, his captor asks "him (not at all unkindly), whether he would like to be sent back to London, and left where they had found him, sleeping in an empty basket in a market – a hungry, ragged, and forsaken little boy."[82] Betteredge's characterization of the request as one made "not at all unkindly" only serves to heighten the sinister undertones of the interaction. Emotionally drained after the hypnotic experience, the boy finally reaches his limit, and is unable to answer any more of the Indian's questions: "I am tired. The mist rises in my head, and puzzles me. I can see no more to-day."[83] We learn later that the Indians superstitiously believe the boy's clairvoyance will guide them in their quest for the precious diamond. The exploitation of the child, however, has an interesting historical analog.

As I have discussed, Collins traces the fictional diamond's acquisition to Tipu Sultan and the siege of Seringapatam, but the famous Koh-i-noor diamond, upon which the story's gem is largely based, was actually taken from a child king. Not only does the novel imagine a continuity of Muslim plunder, it also dehistoricizes the British acquisition of the precious stone. If, as suggested earlier, shifting the scene to Seringapatam perhaps mutes British panic over the rebellion, then, it also defers the blame for taking a gem, and a kingdom, from a young boy. To return to Mark Currie's terms, changing the temporality of the narrative also changes the teleology and the rationality that corresponds to it. Situating the stone as a spoil of the raid on Tipu makes possible the narrative of individual greed and adrenaline-fueled revenge. The history of the Koh-i-noor, however, paints a grimmer portrait of manipulation and psychological torture. In 1849, one year before the theft of the fictional diamond from the eighteen-year-old Rachel Verinder in Collins's novel, the real Koh-i-noor was taken by treaty from Duleep Singh, the young Maharaja of Punjab.

The Mystery of History

In 1799, the same year that the British defeated Tipu Sultan in Mysore, Ranjit Singh, the last great ruler of the Sikhs, captured the important Punjabi city of Lahore. As Khushwant Singh notes in his biography of the famous Sikh chieftain, the "possession of the city made him the most powerful chieftain in northern India" and solidified his rule over the rest of Punjab.[84] Under Ranjit Singh, the Sikh empire comprised a vast and fertile territory in the northwest of the subcontinent, spanning from Tibet to Afghanistan. In addition to expanding his territory, Ranjit Singh also had his sights on the Koh-i-noor diamond, which he eventually acquired as a reward for securing the protection of the fallen Afghan ruler Shah Shuja Durrani. Interestingly, Ranjit Singh also sought to reclaim the temple doors of Somanatha, bringing Collins's constellation of events together, but in a very different context.[85] Though the British kept a close eye on his empire, the sovereign territory of Punjab eluded their capture during Ranjit Singh's lifetime.

In the years following Maharaja Ranjit Singh's death in 1839, however, Punjab descended into turmoil, and the East India Company sought to gain control over the territory. In their history of the Koh-i-noor diamond, William Dalrymple and Anita Anand outline how the British came to possess the territory and the famed diamond, which, like the fictional Moonstone, was said to be haunted by a powerful curse.

The gem, which some Hindus believed to be the mythical Syamantaka diamond of the *Bhagavad Purana*, was a prized treasure of several kingdoms throughout the subcontinent before it came into the possession of Ranjit Singh. Like the fictional gem that was followed around by the three Brahmins, at the time of his death the Koh-i-noor was coveted by Ranjit Singh's Brahmin advisors, who wished to have the stone donated to the temple of Jagannath in Puri.[86] Singh's heirs and political advisors, however, had other plans, insisting that the diamond was not the personal property of Ranjit but rather belonged to the Sikh state.[87] As though spurred on by the diamond's famous curse, in "the four years following Ranjit Singh's death, Punjab had lost three maharajas, two crown princes, one dowager queen and numerous aristocrats."[88] At the end of the line was "a tiny doe-eyed child by the name of Duleep Singh," and "[d]esperate for a symbol of unity, the entire durbar united behind Ranjit Singh's five year old son."[89] But the young king was vulnerable, both to betrayal from within his own kingdom and to manipulation by the British on the sidelines.

The boy's brief reign coincided with Lord Dalhousie's ascension in the East India Company. Dalhousie, who favored a policy of colonial expansion and annexation, saw an opportunity to seize the important territory and set about accomplishing the task. Following the First Anglo-Sikh War in 1846, the East India Company negotiated a treaty with Punjab ensuring that Duleep Singh would claim his sovereignty when he came of age at sixteen, with the British remaining as regents in the meantime.[90] A couple of years later, however, under the pretext of squashing a small-scale rebellion in which a group of Sikhs murdered two English soldiers, the East India Company started the Second Anglo-Sikh War.[91] This time, the now ten-year-old maharaja was forced to relinquish his sovereignty, while his mother was banished from the territory.[92] Alone and terrified, they boy had little power to resist Dalhousie's directives.

Dalhousie's aggressive plans to annex the Punjab and claim the Koh-i-noor diamond finally came to fruition, though they were not universally popular even among the British. In a defiant and almost taunting letter to Sir John Hobhouse, president of the Board of Control, justifying the annexation, Dalhousie challenged his colleagues to reverse his actions if they disagreed with his policy:

> Disallow my act, reverse my policy, you will disgrace me, of course, but do not let that stand in your way. I shall submit quietly to the consequences

> now: well satisfied that the disgrace will be but temporary; that time and events will right me; and that a very few years only will pass before the course of affairs in the Punjab will prove the correctness of my view and will *compel* you to the adoption of the policy I have set up.[93]

Whatever objections there might have been to his perceived arrogance, Dalhousie's actions ultimately went unchallenged. Dalhousie was so eager to claim the diamond that he had its forfeiture written specifically into the Treaty of Lahore by which the British gained control of the territory in 1849.[94] As a sign of his fidelity, Dalhousie arranged for the Koh-i-noor to be delivered directly to Queen Victoria.

Having separated the boy from both his mother and his inheritance, Dalhousie next sought to ship Duleep Singh away from his homeland.[95] "I am sorry for him, poor little fellow," Dalhousie wrote to Hobhouse, but nevertheless, he resolved, "The Maharaja is allowed to remain this year, as the hot weather is on. Next year he must go."[96] Dalhousie arranged Duleep Singh's adoption to "a Scottish doctor by the name of John Spencer Login and his wife Lena," who "would look after the young maharaja until he became a man."[97] Duleep Singh grew up with the Logins, eventually converting to Christianity and traveling to London, where he became a favorite in Queen Victoria's court and settled into a life among the aristocracy.[98] The maharaja was granted an annual stipend of four lakh rupees (£40,000), but "the full allowance was never paid, and he received no compensation for the loss of his jewels."[99] As he grew into adulthood, Duleep increasingly desired a reunion with his mother. The two exchanged emotional letters, and in 1861 Duleep Singh obtained permission from the British government to travel to India and bring his mother back to live in London.[100] Two years later, however, Rani Jindan died, leaving her son with a growing awareness of the injustice perpetrated against him in his youth (260).

The maharaja married and had three children, as he sought in vain to regain his fortune. In pleading letters, Duleep Singh wrote to government officials and aristocratic friends, arguing much like David Dyce Sombre, whom I discuss in Chapter 5, that portions of the land and jewelry seized from him was private, not state, property.[101] Duleep reasoned that the government, under whose care and guardianship he was placed, must only have acted in his best interest, and hence must now return the private portion of his estate (valued in the amount of £3,000,000). He hired attorneys to catalog his wealth and tried desperately to reclaim it from his "guardian," the government. The British, however, were unrelenting and Duleep grew increasingly embittered as he lost more of his fortune and was even forced to relinquish his country estate upon his death. He was especially angry that his children would be left without a significant inheritance.

Toward the end of his life, Duleep converted back to Sikhism and began to dream of returning to India and leading a Sikh army in an uprising against the British. He even entertained a plot with the Russians to reclaim his territory in Punjab, going so far as to attempt a journey to India. The British, however, held him under surveillance and arrested him in Aden. Embittered and isolated, the disgraced maharaja wrote to his friend Sir Robert Montgomery saying, "I neither respect such a tyrannical and unjust administration, nor am I any longer loyal to the British Crown (having offered my services to Russia)."[102] He closed the telegram with the wish that "God may before I die enable me to have my revenge on the India administration and humiliate that Government, and to cause the expenditure of many more millions of poor John Bull's money than the £3,000,000 I should have asked for for the loss of my private property, out of which I have been so piously swindled by the Christian British nation." In 1893, at the age of fifty-three, "Duleep Singh died penniless and alone in a shabby Parisian hotel."[103] His eldest daughter and last heir, the beautiful Bamba Sutherland, repatriated to Lahore, where she died in 1957, forever haunted by the fortune and title that was stolen from her family.[104]

"The Influence of Character"

Though Collins, writing in 1868, could not have known the full tragedy that the loss of his kingdom and the Koh-i-noor would entail for Duleep Singh, he could not have been unaware of the true means by which the British came to possess the famed diamond. In his preface to the novel, Collins acknowledges that the "story of the Diamond, as here set forth ... is founded, in some important particulars, on the stories of two of the royal diamonds of Europe."[105] He states that his sources are the "magnificent stone which adorns the top of the Russian Imperial Sceptre" which "was once the eye of an Indian idol" and the "famous Koh-i-Noor," which "is also supposed to have been one of the sacred gems of India; and more than this, to have been the subject of a prediction, which prophesied certain misfortune to the person who should divert it from its ancient uses."[106] Of the two, Collins would have been far more familiar with the Koh-i-noor, since its arrival and display in London was the subject of much fanfare in the British press. In any event, neither stone has a history that corresponds to the details laid out in *The Moonstone*, which of course are largely manufactured by Collins himself. The significant point, however, is not that Collins manufactures the history, but rather, in Currie's terms, what the narrative performs. In Collins's hands the colonial government's exploitation of the child king that haunts the true narrative of the Koh-i-noor is reframed as an adventure story of individual greed in which the evil Tipu Sultan is robbed of a jewel by a wayward soldier in the East India Company army. John Herncastle's greed and guilt in turn sets the stage for, and mirrors, the resolution of the mystery and the identification of Godfrey Ablewhite as the gem's thief.

But if Collins selectively revises the history of the Koh-i-noor in the prologue, his stated aim in crafting the story of intrigue is to "trace the influence of character on circumstances," or, in other words, to delve into the psychological motivations of his characters. Collins distinguishes between his approach in *The Moonstone* and his earlier works in which "the object proposed has been to trace the influence of circumstances upon character."[107] Though he uses circumstance to frame the narrative, Collins's turn to the psychological begins, at least for his English characters, in the prologue. Faced with the same circumstances, for example, Herncastle and his cousin choose very different paths. This narrative of free will and self-determination sets the stage for how characters respond to the array of conflicts and challenges that unfold over the course of the novel.[108]

But how does the aura of historicity attached to the diamond in the prologue intersect with the psychological exploration of the main story? Within the novel, which stories are open to psychoanalysis and which can only be explained through recourse to history, however fictitious the details may be? And, relatedly, what does the mystery genre have to do with the relationship between history and fiction? In his influential essay "Clues," Franco Moretti refers to detective fiction as a "hymn to culture's coercive abilities," which, he says, "prove more effective than pure and simple institutional repression."[109] The detective novel serves a disciplinary function by inducing its readers to identify a singular criminal and rally around their exposure and capture.[110] By participating in the detection of guilt, readers police not only the subject under investigation, but themselves as well. Relatedly, for Moretti, the detective novel serves a unique social function in positing a crime and identifying guilt with a singular individual, thereby absolving the rest of society from any shared culpability. "Because the crime is presented in the form of a mystery," Moretti reasons, "society is absolved from the start: the solution of the mystery proves its innocence."[111] The mystery novel individualizes guilt by constructing a singular agent with the psychological motivation to commit the crime. When we identify the criminal, we correspondingly render ourselves innocent.

In turn, the focus on individual guilt and the intentionality of the criminal reflects a "new relationship to legal punishment," namely in terms of a shift "in the middle of the nineteenth century" from execution to trial.[112] Centralizing the rise of the novel within this shift, Jonathan Grossman argues "that the novel, in becoming the ascendant literary genre of the nineteenth century, played an active role in a process through which a reinvented criminal trial supplanted the spectacle of the gallows as the culmination of justice."[113] Though Collins's novel does not deal with the question of punishment, its attention to narrative and subjectivity are in line with the shift that Moretti observes. The various narrators in *The Moonstone* function like witnesses in a trial, as the reader sorts through the testimony to assign guilt by the end of the novel. For Moretti, the interest in the individuality of the criminal is indicative of a deeper change in the law from an emphasis on the crime to an emphasis on the criminal. If execution serves to make a spectacle of the crime, the aim of the trial is to put the criminal on display, visibly and discursively.[114] For this reason, according to Moretti, it is crucial within modern criminal justice that the "criminal is the person who always acts *consciously*."[115] Detective fiction reflects this turn toward consciousness and narrativity, as it "detaches prose narration from historiography and relates it to the world of Law."[116] Citing Max Weber, Moretti distinguishes between the law's interest in subjective guilt and history's inquiry into "the 'objective' grounds of concrete events and the consequences of concrete 'actions.'"[117] Unlike the law, history "does not seek to pass judgement on the agent."[118] In Moretti's view, for the law, as well as for the detective novel, "history assumes importance only as *violation* and as such, must be ultimately repressed."[119] The explanatory context of history in these arenas is not only extraneous, it actively undermines the emphasis on individual subjectivity and consciousness in the establishment of guilt. For Moretti, this repression of history marks detective fiction's capacity to enforce social normativity, and ultimately explains its affinity with bourgeois liberalism and the "sui generis totalitarianism of contemporary capitalism."[120] Individual guilt requires individual self-policing.

Moretti's observation about the detective novel's repression of history is particularly interesting when paired with Todorov's comments on the genre's temporality.[121] As Neil Sargent notes, Todorov's analysis "implies a particular philosophy of history at work in the text, in which the relationship between past and present is understood in strictly teleological terms."[122] Though Todorov draws attention to the genre's temporality, however, his analysis of the genre's "philosophy of history" has less to do with history per se than it does with teleology. For Moretti, the genre must actively disengage from history in order to psychologize the actions of the criminal outside of the social forces of history and reality. On the one hand, then, the mystery novel must reject history in order to privilege the development of individual subjectivity, but on the other hand it relies upon a clear teleology in order to establish a timeline of the crime.

In addition to providing the foundations for individual consciousness, the idea of a teleology detached from history also enables a particular notion of progress. A teleology that is grounded in individuality rather than history suggests a sense of progress that allies the forward movement of time with self-determination and free will. This emphasis on individual agency is, in turn, the cornerstone of nineteenth-century English legal philosophy's criteria for establishing culpability.

What is the effect, then, of the Indian historical references that, in Moretti's terms, "violate" the narrative of Godfrey Ablewhite's subjective motivations? Do they call into question the very notion of individual agency that is pure of historical influence? Or do they center the primacy of English individual agency, and by extension national progress, by virtue of its contrast with the historically laden colonial subject? A related consideration is whether the act of murder committed by the three Brahmins can be extricated from its historical motivations. To what extent are the three Brahmins subjectively culpable within the terms of modern methods of establishing guilt? While it may be impossible to answer these questions with only Collins's novel in mind, when the novel is placed in relation to *Ramaswamy Aiyan* v. *Venkata Achari*, it becomes part of a narrative pattern that works to standardize English notions of temporality and progress by way of comparison with Indian backwardness. *The Moonstone* relies on many of the same characterizations of the cyclicality of Indian history and the stagnancy of the Hindu past as the legal case. And, as in my discussion of the JCPC's opinion, in *The Moonstone*, as well, Indian history is persistently invoked as the framing device within which the narrative of English free will and progress emerges.

In this context, *The Moonstone* is interesting for both its "repression" of history, and its obsession with modernity. For all of Gabriel Betteredge's insistence on "time and the progress of modern enlightenment," with the exception of the specific dates given in the narratives and a few mentions of trains and contemporary newspapers such as *The Guardian*, there is very little historical detail in the main section of the novel.[123] The English plot, unlike the Indian one that bookends the novel, is governed by imagination rather than history. As such, the characters are free to inhabit subject positions unconstrained by the burden of history or reality. Through first-person narrations extricated from history, each English character embodies the possibilities of free will and self-determination.

Of course, Collins's intentions in structuring his novel this way remain lost to history. We can, however, look at the performative effects of the historical details that erupt into the narrative fold of the English mystery. The main narrative of *The Moonstone* is focused on English characters at a "quiet English house suddenly invaded by a devilish Indian Diamond."[124] These characters are purely fictional, and for all practical purposes are, in Moretti's terms, represented as outside history. They are all individually named, and are self-narrating subjects. While this portion of the narrative embodies a teleology outside of history, historical details provide the context for its emergence. The substitution of Tipu Sultan for Duleep Singh, as I have shown, is particularly noteworthy in terms of a teleology divorced from history. If, from the English viewpoint, the siege of Seringapatam toppled a tyrant to avenge a past of "lawless Mohammedan" plunder, Dalhousie's annexation of Punjab was not so readily justifiable. In taking Punjab, and the Koh-i-noor, the English effectively stole Duleep Singh's future. Such a theft would be difficult to incorporate into a narrative of progress and Pax Britannica. It is therefore significant that Collins chose to incorporate the anodyne history of Tipu in place of the more controversial annexation of Punjab from Duleep Singh. This is especially significant given the fact that Duleep Singh's affairs were unfolding across the present time of both the novel's writing and its temporal setting. If, as Neil Sargent suggests, the "operative principle behind the detective's method is that the past is complete and exists in an already defined relation to the present," altering the events of the past has the corresponding capacity to unsettle the verdict on the present.[125] By shielding readers from the true story of Duleep Singh and the Koh-i-noor diamond, Collins renders a very different verdict on the present than what history would seem to justify.

PART III

Adoption and Inheritance

CHAPTER 5

The Begum's Fortune
Adoption, Inheritance, and Private Property

In the preceding chapters, I have explored the relationship between teleological history and the production of a correspondingly normative individual subject. Building upon my argument in Chapter 4, in which the individual arises through a shedding of collective history, while society emerges into shared innocence, I will turn now to the relationship between individualism and sovereignty. Using Begum Sumroo, one of the most significant women in colonial India, as my primary example, I discuss the ways in which Mughal theories of sovereignty and filial relations intersected with those of the British Raj. In particular, I show how networks of sovereignty that functioned through loyalty and filiation in the Mughal era gave way to the more rigid singularity of the law under British rule, affecting not only territorial sovereignty but also the organization of private property and family. As modes of sovereignty were streamlined into top-down legal frameworks under British rule, the law increasingly determined how and to whom legitimacy, or even rationality, was accorded. As we will see, Begum Sumroo and her adopted son David Ochterlony Dyce Sombre were casualties of British expansionism and its quest to supplant Mughal sovereignty. My argument in this chapter is that, like the agency attributed to the individual criminal in the detective novel, British colonial sovereignty rested on claims to rational intentionality that derived from the singular authority of the law insofar as it functioned as a metaphor for the Crown. For Franco Moretti, the emphasis on singular guilt serves a normativizing function, impelling the innocent to band together in order to detect the criminal. Likewise, the singular intentionality of the law serves a similarly disciplinary purpose, regulating affection and inheritance in order to separate the rational from the improper or lunatic. Because questions about the Begum's sovereignty were intimately related to questions of kinship and affection, I will begin by examining the practice and concept of adoption in the Mughal court more broadly. Ultimately, as I show, the British Raj worked to undermine forms of sovereignty that were not exclusively individual, and forms of kinship and affection that were more collective and less centered on biological reproduction. In the following chapter, I show how adoption narratives function differently in the English context, as individualism affirms Englishness within George Eliot's realist novels.

In his work on Mughal sovereignty, Azfar Moin describes the evolution of political models from "discipleship" to "kinship." His exhaustive analysis, which begins with the Timurids and ends at the height of the Mughal era in the seventeenth century, shows how Safavid and Mughal sovereigns from Iran and India drew on religion and cosmology in authorizing what he terms "sacred kingships." For example, "at the turn of the Islamic millennium" in the sixteenth century, the great Mughal emperor Akbar "fashioned his imperial self, in effect, in the mold of the awaited messiah. In doing so, he had embraced a powerful and pervasive myth of sovereignty," namely the expected arrival at the millennium of a "holy savior" who "would manifest himself" in order to "usher in a new earthly order and cycle of time – perhaps the last historical era before the end of the world."[1] Akbar "was neither the first nor the only one" to make such messianic claims to sovereignty, as he "had competed for the millennial prize with many others."[2] As David Gilmartin observes, the "very 'spirit of the age' that gave credibility to Mughal sovereignty provided fertile ground also for myriad, competing claims."[3] As a result, Mughal sovereignty can be understood both in terms of the singularity of messianic status as well as the multiplicity of competing claims. Alongside the vertical claim of "a genealogically transmitted 'divine light'" there existed as well a horizontal field of competitors to the same status. In addition to the horizontal competition in claims to sacred sovereignty, Mughal rule also functioned through horizontal networks of loyalty and filiation.

Moin relates the ways in which Akbar's grandson, the emperor Shah Jahan, in his reformation of the perceived decadence of the Mughal empire, "abandoned the controversial practice of accepting noblemen and gentlemen officers as disciples and instead revived the custom of incorporating them as 'sons of the emperor's household,'" thus "transforming the Mughal imperial paradigm from one of Sufi devotion (*muridi*) to that of adoptive kinship (*khanazadgi*)."[4] Under Shah Jahan, the "household" became a model of imperial political organization, in which the "imperial city functioned, in an ideal sense, as a vast extended family tied together by client-patron relationships extending outward from the emperor, who appeared as 'the pivot of a hierarchical, nested series of realms.'"[5] This movement from loyalty to kinship as an organizing principle for political communities may perhaps be viewed as a sign of increasing Islamicization, but as I discuss in Chapter 3, the Mughal Empire, like the subcontinent as a whole, was never religiously homogenous.[6] My interest here, in any event, is not in the religious motivations in the shift, but rather in the cultural and political uses to which it was put. As we see in the case of Begum Sumroo, models of kinship and adoption often work against the normative impulse of British colonial law, which was in contest with Mughal social and political frameworks. Moin argues that "a strong case can be made that under Shah Jahan the Mughal empire completed a major symbolic and institutional shift, in which sovereign charisma came to be formally dispersed in a graded and mediated fashion in which the idiom of kinship superseded the practice of discipleship" upon which previous generations of sovereignty were based.[7] While, as Moin notes, "[l]ittle scholarship exists on the question of how courtiers and officers were incorporated as 'sons' into the imperial household," it is clear that what Moin terms the "filial idiom" of adoption emerged during the seventeenth century as a paradigm of political kinship within Mughal sovereignty.[8] Though Begum Sumroo did not descend from the dynastic traditions that Moin describes, she was part of the broader network of Mughal sovereignty and aspects of her rule resonate with his analysis. In particular, I will focus on the Begum's invocation of filial ties, both in forming treaties and relationships with the British, and through adopting David Ochterlony Dyce Sombre as her son and heir.

In the eighteenth and early nineteenth centuries, the British East India Company was in the process of consolidating its market interests and expanding its territorial holdings in South Asia. A complex struggle for land and power was afoot, with competing interests at stake between various local Hindu sovereigns, the waning Mughal Empire, and the increasingly influential British East India Company. As much in dispute as the land itself were the ideological grounds upon which claims to ownership and sovereignty could be made. Some of the most important legal maneuvers aimed to establish a set of norms by which authority could be secured and continually justified. On the one hand, then, eighteenth-century India was characterized by a marked lack of uniformly hegemonic structures.[9] As I discuss in detail in Chapter 3, until 1864 the East India Company courts were implementing an amalgamation of Hindu, Muslim, and English law. On the other hand, as Gilmartin notes, the British "had already begun by the late eighteenth century to move, amid much contestation, to a rhetoric of sovereign legitimation associated with what had increasingly come to be called the 'rule of law.'"[10]

This period of social and cultural flux formed the historical milieu of the woman who would become Begum Sumroo. Aside from the fact that she was born in the middle of the eighteenth century, little is known with certainty about her early life.[11] Some biographical sketches of the Begum describe her as a Kashmiri nautch girl (courtesan), while others claim she was a Sayidda (direct descendent of the Prophet Mohammed), whose father's death forced the family into poverty. What seems certain is that Farzana, as the Begum was known in her youth, was a young teenager when Walter Reinhardt, who was in his forties, met her in Delhi. Reinhardt, who took the name Sombre (known locally as Sumroo), was a soldier from Europe.[12] While many narratives refer to Sombre as the Begum's husband, there is no evidence that the two were legally or religiously married.

For his part, Walter Sombre's military alliance with the emperor Shah Alam II led to his acquiring significant power as the sovereign of the principality of Sardhana, near Meerut in what is now Uttar Pradesh. Like much of the history surrounding the Begum, the details of Sombre's acquisition of Sardhana are also murky. Sombre seems to have made use of his untraceable roots to form strategic alliances with whoever might be beneficial to him at any given time. In the words of one nineteenth-century British historian, "Sumroo sold his sword first to one party and then to another, as interest might dictate," for example by carrying out the execution of British captives at Patna.[13] The Begum governed alongside Sombre and even participated in military excursions with their army. By all accounts, she was politically astute and was well regarded by British and Indians alike.

Though the Begum had no children, Sombre fathered a son with another Indian woman.[14] Following Sombre's death in 1778, this other woman, who reputedly suffered from mental illness, and her son continued to live under the Begum's care. The son, known as both Zafaryab and Louis, was variously described as an alcoholic and of "weak mind." Consequently, after Sombre's death his territory and private property were granted to the Begum instead of Sombre's son.[15] Thus the Begum, at the age of around twenty-five, gained possession of Sombre's fortune and became the ruler of Sardhana.[16] The young Begum retained control over the estate, while providing Zafaryab with a generous maintenance allowance. Zafaryab soon died, however, leaving behind a daughter named Julianne who married George Alexander Dyce, a colonel in the Indian army. The couple had two daughters (Mary Ann and Georgiana Dyce) and a son (David Ochterlony Dyce), all of whom were eventually adopted by the Begum as her children.[17] In the end then, the Begum adopted the great-grandchildren of Walter Sombre. In the years after his death, the Begum took on Sombre's faith, converting to Catholicism and by all appearances practicing it with great zeal for the remainder of her life.[18] The Begum ruled Sardhana successfully, developing it into one of the more prosperous territories in the region.

As was common in Mughal India, however, the Begum did not own her territory privately but held it by grant under the emperor. As the East India Company made incursions into the Mughal Empire, these land grants that were held, often generationally by local sovereigns of independent territories, ceded to the British. When the Begum died in 1836, the Company seized all the lands under her dominion. The Begum, however, had clearly designated David Dyce Sombre, her adopted son, as the heir to her *altumgha jaghir*, or the portion of her lands that formed a private hereditable estate. Despite this, the Company asserted its claim to her entire estate and, immediately following her funeral, took possession of the territory. The conflict between Sumroo's estate and the Company can thus be seen as a contest over different forms of sovereignty, as much as over land, as the Begum sought to preserve Mughal practices of inheritance while the British moved to institute, in Gilmartin's words, the "modal value" of "legalism."[19] While they successfully annexed the bulk of his inheritance, Dyce Sombre was still enormously wealthy, inheriting around £500,000 from the Begum in cash and moveable property. To regain his territory, Dyce Sombre filed numerous complaints with the Company and the government, but was ultimately unsuccessful. Having lost his lands, after a brief sojourn in Calcutta, David Dyce Sombre left India for England, where for a time, he mingled with the upper classes and married Mary Anne Jervis, a popular socialite. Their relationship was turbulent, and in British legal proceedings three years later she had him declared a "lunatic" and gained control of his fortune. Dyce Sombre spent the rest of his life trying to overturn this judgment and reclaim his funds. In my reading below, I show how the judgment of David's "lunacy" can be read in light of the larger discourse of race and rationality in colonial-era law. Over the course of this chapter, I will show how questions of rationality central to the story of Dyce Sombre relate to those of legal subjectivity and recognition at work in the Begum's dealings with the East India Company.

For several decades after her death, the Begum's property was the subject of a series of prominent legal cases, including *Troup* v. *East India Company* (1857), *Forester and Others* v. *The Secretary of State for India* (1872), *Prinsep and East India Company* v. *Dyce Sombre* (1856), and *Reiner*

v. *Marquis of Salisbury* (1876). Taken together, the Sumroo cases detail the complexities of property ownership and inheritance within colonial law. The annexation of the Begum's lands by the British resulted in protracted legal proceedings that revealed the racial, sexual, and societal fault lines of colonial life. The legalism underlying British forms of sovereignty, as Gilmartin explains, "rested preeminently on a civilizational claim to superior reason, and one capable of delivering the material, technological, and military power (and 'progress') to serve as a practical seal on sovereign authority. And perhaps most important, nothing embodied this claim to superior reason more clearly than the theoretical supremacy of law."[20] If, as I have suggested in the previous chapters, modernity became the watchword of the colonial era, in this chapter I demonstrate how the normative terms of modernity came to legally, as well as socially, regulate spheres from sexuality, reproduction, and kinship, to the idea of rationality itself. Yet, as I also show, the complex affective ties inaugurated by the Begum, and compounded by her heirs, were often inscrutable to the rationality of the law.

The Begum's story, like that of her adopted son, David Ochterlony Dyce Sombre, fascinates for its mythic quality and its political intrigue. The controversy surrounding the inheritance and its annexation inspires myriad questions that are both inescapable and largely unanswerable. What motivated the Begum to acquire her territory and then give it to Dyce Sombre? Was her cunning matched by her kindness? Did she act out of desire or greed? Was Dyce Sombre really "of unsound mind"? Or was Mary Anne Jervis cruel and manipulative? Did Dyce Sombre stifle and abuse his wife, or did she capitalize on prevailing racial prejudices to defraud him of his money? Are any of their motivations readable, or do they ultimately remain subordinated to the various ideological frames that we might use to decode them? The records that exist of the Begum Sumroo, at best, read her as a shrewd political figure, subsuming her affective choices within rhetoric of strategy and profit. Against this, I keep open the possibility that generosity and affection motivated the Begum in ways that are difficult to decipher within the legal frameworks that I explore in this chapter.[21]

Family Politics

While Begum Sumroo features prominently, and almost obligatorily, in the chronicles of various British travelers to India, these narratives offer notably conflicting and speculative accounts of her life, based largely in gossip and rumor.[22] Thus, her history is remarkable both for what is revealed, as well as for what has been concealed, as a result of her deeply ambivalent position within, and in relation to, the burgeoning British Empire. Regarding the Begum's personal history, the various narratives are rife with controversies and contradictions. The narratives concur, however, in their persistent, almost obsessive, characterization of the Begum as simultaneously hypersexual and masculine, both of which were the subject of curiosity within nineteenth-century British accounts.

W. H. Sleeman, for example, who rose to prominence as a result of his campaign to suppress thuggee as discussed in Chapter 2, was uncharacteristically admiring of the Begum.[23] In *Rambles and Recollections of an Indian Official*, he remarked that the Begum "bore the character of a kind-hearted, benevolent, and good woman," and attributed to her an "uncommon sagacity and a masculine resolution."[24] More in keeping with Sleeman's fascination with the macabre, he also recounts a narrative of her cruelty in which two enslaved girls belonging to the Begum set fire to some houses on her property and fled. When the girls were captured and brought back, "their guilt being proved to the satisfaction of all present, she had them flogged till they were senseless, and then thrown into a pit dug in front of her tent for the purpose, and buried alive."[25] Despite the seeming ruthlessness of this episode, Sleeman muses that "among natives there is no particular mode of execution prescribed for those who are condemned to die" and, in any case, "perhaps the punishment was not much greater than the crime deserved and the occasion demanded." The Begum seems to have earned Sleeman's esteem in part because of her willingness to adopt "European modes of social intercourse," such as "appearing in public on an elephant, in a carriage, and occasionally on horseback with her hat and veil, and dining at table with gentlemen." He affirms that the Begum was respected not only by "the thousands who were supported by her bounty," but also by Lord William Bentinck, who "was an excellent judge of character."[26]

A similar narrative appears in a range of Victorian travelogues. Reginald Heber in *Narrative of a Journey through the Upper Provinces of India from Calcutta to Bombay, 1824–1825*, describes her as "a very little, queer-looking old woman, with brilliant, but wicked eyes, and the remains of beauty in her features," and George Hewett in *Private Record of the Life of General Sir George Hewett* refers to her as a "woman of masculine disposition and extraordinary achievements."[27] Her reputation for typically masculine pursuits, such as her military prowess, prompted even Dyce

Sombre to praise his mother as a "remarkably talented person" who "had a masculine spirit of her own."[28]

The persistent attention to gender ambiguity in descriptions of the Begum suggests the extent to which she unsettled fixed, if often conflicting, gender stereotypes. Indeed, the paradox of violability and debauchery that characterized Western notions of the feminized Orient has been amply theorized as providing a justification for the masculinized civilizing mission of colonialism.[29] The figure of the ambivalently gendered Begum no doubt circulates within these constitutive gender assumptions. Most explicitly merging the Begum's gendered and sexual transgressiveness, Emma Roberts writes the following in *Scenes and Characteristics of Hindostan, With Sketches of Anglo-Indian Society*:

> She has long since abandoned the restrictions imposed by Asiatic prejudice, and sits at table with large parties of gentlemen without scruple. She formerly attended to the Mohammedan precepts as far as they related to the preparation of food; but once passed the rubicon, she refused to return to her trammels again, not even following the example of the English ladies, when they retired from table, but preferring to remain with the gentlemen, on the plea that she made it a point never to leave her 'pipe half-smoked.'
>
> The dress of the Begum differs in some degree from that of other Hindostanee ladies, her highness choosing to substitute a turban for the veil invariably worn by the females of her country; a circumstance which, though apparently trifling, shews that she entertains little or no regard for native opinions and prejudices, the turban being only assumed by dancing-girls during some performances which are considered highly indecorous, and are not exhibited before ladies.[30]

Not surprisingly, it is from the position of English femininity, in which the norms of race, gender, and sex are most rigorously policed, that the disciplinary judgment is also most clear.[31] Roberts represents the Begum's transgression as both gendered, in her refusal to display feminine social behavior, and sexualized, in her preference for the turban, which is read as "indecorous."

Yet, the implications of the Begum's performance exceed any interpretation offered by Roberts. In Roberts's reading, the Begum's behavior is masculine and her clothing is "indecorous," suggesting that she is at once both too manly and too womanly.[32] But the real threat posed by the Begum is the extent to which the stereotypes used to understand her fail to capture the entirety of her persona.[33] The Begum's preference "to remain with the [English] gentlemen" represents the possibility of sexual encounters not accounted for by the charge of masculinity. At the same time, her turban signifies masculinity as much as it does the "indecorous" female sexuality of the "dancing-girl," or courtesan, with which Roberts associates it. The anxiety produced by the Begum's practices, then, is not simply that she challenges gendered and sexual norms but also that she unhinges the terms by which the norms themselves are understood, defined, and fixed. Roberts also distinguishes between transgressions against "Mohammedan" or "Asiatic" codes of behavior and those against English ones, which seem to rise to a greater degree of offense. Within Roberts's English vision of sexuality and civility, overcoming "native opinions and prejudices" is acceptable, perhaps even desirable, whereas refusing to abide by English norms seems to meet with stricter censure. That the Begum was "not even following the example of the English ladies" is especially remarkable to Roberts.

"By unsettling gender and cultural identities," Durba Ghosh observes, "Begum Samru created a sense of cultural confusion for her European guests, while simultaneously affirming that her status as a political ruler of some importance afforded her the privilege of eccentricity."[34] The Begum's performance, then, can be read as challenging the hierarchies of gender and sex, and also of race. In so doing, the Begum retained a sense of privacy and autonomy in both her sexuality and public dealings that remained inscrutable to British norms and sensibilities.[35]

Love Beyond Kinship: An Unfamiliar Bequest

The challenges to normativity implicit within the Begum's persona and performance extended as well to her relations with others in terms of constructing social, familial, and political affiliations. Refusing to adhere to the privilege granted to certain affective bonds with regard to the transfer of property, the Begum engineered her own lines of kinship and succession that were often matrilineal, sometimes through adoption, and sometimes through treaties of friendship and community.[36] To ensure that her possessions legally transferred to her adopted heir Dyce Sombre, in December 1831 the Begum drafted a will "in the English language" witnessed by members of the British military and civil service. [37] Here she clarified that she wished to bequeath all the property over which she served as sovereign, along with her "Havaleee" (bungalow) and lands in Delhi, to Dyce Sombre:

> And as to and in respect of all and singular lands, tenements and heredit-aments situate at Agra, Delhi, Bhurtpoor, Meerut and Sirdhana or any

> place, and all that the province called Badshahpoor Jhaursah and all and singular other my lands, messuages, tenements . . . whatsoever and wheresoever the same may happen to be situated . . . I give and devise the same unto the said David Ochterlony Dyce.[38]

Later in the same will, the Begum identifies "the said D. Ochterlony Dyce, his heirs, executors and assignees for ever" as beneficiaries of not only all her lands, but also of her homes, jewels, household items, cattle, armories and weapons, cash monies, bonds, bills, and other securities.[39] In other words, the Begum's will unequivocally bequeaths her estate to her adopted son.[40]

Additionally, the Begum sought to explain and reinforce her relationship to her heir in strategic ways. For instance, her will transfers her name to David Dyce as a sign of her adoption of him. "It is my particular wish," she affirms in this legal record, "and I here request that the said David Ochterlony Dyce may assume the name of David Ochterlony Dyce Sombre."[41] Presumably, by formally linking her name (derived from Dyce's great grandfather and the Begum's lover, Walter) to David in her will, the Begum attempted to foreclose legal challenges to their kinship.

The Begum nevertheless remained suspicious that her will would be contested. In anticipation of such difficulties, she also formalized a "Deed of Gift" in 1834, which she "prepared in the Persian language, which was familiar to her" because she "did not think the Will, which was in the English language sufficient."[42] If the Company refused to recognize Dyce Sombre as her legitimate heir, the deed of gift would grant him the property outright. Abdicating her sovereignty in favor of Dyce Sombre during her lifetime would eliminate questions about the legitimacy of her will. Also, because the British pledged to respect her sovereignty during her lifetime, the Begum perhaps reasoned that abdication would be seen as a legitimate expression of sovereignty that should be covered by the agreement. The fact that the deed is in Persian is also significant. It makes the Begum's "familiarity" with this language the sign of an alternative affective economy whose terms of intimacy may be unrecognizable under British colonial law.[43] Moreover, it gestures toward an alternative sovereignty in which adoption and filiation are understood as a sustaining political practice.

Despite the Begum's multiple attempts to secure her property for Dyce Sombre, however, the East India Company annexed her lands immediately following her death. Six months later, the Legislative Council of India passed Act No. XVII of 1836 extending legal jurisdiction over the Begum's territory. The act stated that when the "territories which were lately held by the *Begum* Sumroo, and which lapsed to the East India Company on the 27th of *January*, 1836, should be annexed to any District under the Government of the Company, all Laws and Regulations then in force within such District should be in force in the territories so annexed to such District."[44] In bringing Sardhana into the legal fold of the colonial courts, the act also invalidated any civil or criminal matters that may have arisen prior to the annexation of the territory.[45] At the same time, the act supplanted Mughal sovereignty with a legal framework that erased the inheritance arrangements the Begum sought to make.

In the end, while the British were willing to grant Dyce Sombre his substantial cash inheritance, they divested him of his control over the Begum's lands. As a result, as was common under the Raj, Dyce Sombre retained great personal wealth but had to forsake any rights to govern the territory as its sovereign. As Michael Fisher notes in his brief biography of the Begum, "under British rule, she ultimately created a personal but not a ruling family for herself, well beyond the customary definitions of a family" (112). Almost immediately after the annexation, Dyce Sombre began legal proceedings to reclaim his lands. The legal challenges, which eventually generated three appeals to the Privy Council, and the complex familial networks they invoked, would continue to confound English society for decades after the deaths of both the Begum and Dyce Sombre.

"A Faithful Friend of the Company"[46]

During her lifetime, however, the Begum drew on the notions of kinship and loyalty that were hallmarks of Mughal sovereignty in order to engineer a mutually profitable relationship with the British. In 1803 Marquess Wellesley, governor general of India, wrote to the Begum expressing his desire to establish a treaty of "friendship between you and the honourable English Company's Government," and asked the Begum to "direct your endeavors in such a manner as may be beneficial to both parties."[47] As this and other communications reveal, in exchange for the Begum's military aid, the Company pledged to recognize her "rights and privileges" over her dominions. A dossier compiled by Dyce Sombre to substantiate his case against the East India Company, for example, contains a letter dated August 5, 1805, to the Begum from Marquess Cornwallis, who was "in charge of the affairs of the Honorable Company and in the command of the King's and Company's forces in India." In it Cornwallis praises the

Begum for her constant "duties of fidelity," including her "prompt and successful exertions in rescuing [the collector of Saharanpur] . . . from a situation of imminent danger by the aid of [her] troops."[48] He goes on to say: "I have resolved to leave you in the unmolested possession of your Jaghir, with all the rights and privileges which you have hitherto enjoyed."[49] Despite the tacit implication in the statement of the Company's power to "molest" the Begum and dispossess her of her territories, the official intent is to affirm the quid pro quo relationship through which the Begum secured her sovereignty. Following this, an agreement ratified between the corporation and the Begum confirms her legal claims over her lands in exchange for particular favors. Her lands, this treaty establishes, "shall remain to her as before from the Company as long as she may live" so long as "the troops of the Begum shall, according to custom, be always ready in the service of the East India Company."[50] Under the treaty, the Begum's territory held as a *jaghir*, or land grant for the duration of the recipient's life, would cede to the East India Company, the paramount power at the time, upon her death.

The dispute initiated by Dyce Sombre against the East India Company, however, contests the terms under which the Begum held a portion of her lands. While the East India Company claimed that her sovereignty was conditional and limited to her lifetime, Dyce Sombre and his heirs sought to prove that a portion of her estate was held in *altumgha*. Under Mughal rule an *altumgha jaghir* was "a royal grant, which the British Government have declared to convey a title to a rent-free tenure in perpetuity."[51] The controversy over the nature of the Begum's ownership, and thus the legitimacy of her adopted heir's inheritance, resonated with the broader legal grounds by which British terms of sovereignty sought to supplant Mughal ones. If treaties the Begum made with the British during her lifetime affirm the Mughal value of "fidelity," a greater emphasis on legalism prevails after her death. Within this context, adoption plays a crucial role, not only as a displaced paradigm within Mughal sovereignty but also as a means of delegitimizing Indian territories upon the sovereigns' deaths. The strategies of colonial expansion employed against Begum Sumroo are emblematic of, and anticipate, later nineteenth-century legal maneuvers used during the transition from the East India Company to more overt British state imperialism. Governor General Dalhousie's doctrine of lapse, for example, refused to recognize adopted heirs, thus justifying the annexation of any territory in which the sovereign died without a biological male heir. Dalhousie's doctrine, which conjoined the territorial expansion of the empire with the normativization of reproduction and inheritance, was in force from 1848 until 1857, when the Crown assumed control of the colony.

Though Dyce Sombre appealed directly to the East India Company immediately following the annexation, even writing to Queen Victoria to intervene on his behalf, it was not until 1848 that the case was brought to court.[52] By 1843, Dyce Sombre had already been declared a lunatic in the court of Chancery in England (the commencement of his lunacy was backdated to October 1842), and John Pascal Larkins had been appointed administrator of his estate. In August 1848 a suit was filed in Delhi on behalf of Dyce Sombre, which "prayed that the Plaintiff, *Dyce Sombre*, might be declared entitled in perpetuity to the *Altumgha Jaghire* of *Badshapore Jharsa*, and to the *maal* and *sayer*, and other privileges and profits appertaining thereto."[53] The suit further sought to recuperate "the mesne profits and revenues arising from the *Altumgha Jaghire*, and the *maal* and *sayer* and privileges aforesaid, which have accrued due and been received by them, from and after the date of the resumption thereof, together with interest."[54] The East India Company, invoking strategies of modern legal time discussed in Chapter 3 of this book, responded that according to the Bengal Regulation of 1803, the statute of limitations for civil suits expired in February 1848, seven months before the suit was filed. In a similar pattern to the one we see in *Ramaswamy Aiyan* v. *Venkata Achari*, the court also ruled in favor of the East India Company's assertion that the statute of limitations had expired. The following year, in July 1851, David Dyce Sombre died, making his widow Mary Anne Dyce Sombre one of the wealthiest women in England, and instigating another round of legal battles.[55]

In 1857, six years after her husband's death, Mary Anne Dyce Sombre, along with David Dyce Sombre's sisters Mary Ann Troup, Georgiana Solaroli, and their respective husbands, appealed the *Sadr Diwani* decision to the Privy Council in England. *Troup* v. *East India Company* sought, successfully, to overturn the lower court's ruling on the statute of limitations. In 1862, Mary Anne Dyce Sombre married George Cecil Weld-Forester, 3rd Baron Forester, a prominent Conservative politician in England, who, in 1865 filed a suit in Delhi to reclaim Badshapore (the contested portion of the Begum's territory) and the value of the arms that were seized in 1836 when the East India Company annexed her territory. In 1872, *G. C. W. Forester and Others* v. *The Secretary of State for India in Council* reached the Privy Council.

The value of the property under dispute was significant, and the claim was assessed at "a little short of a quarter of a million sterling."[56] At the heart of the suit was the question of whether the East India Company had a legitimate right to seize Badshapore Jharsa along with the rest of the territory of Sardhana. Citing evidence amassed by David Dyce Sombre, the plaintiffs once again sought to prove that Badshapore was granted to the Begum by emperor Shah Alam II as an *altumgha jaghir*, or an inheritable estate. During his lifetime, David collected substantial evidence consisting of records of the original grant, affirmations of the grant from successive Indian rulers, and letters from various East India Company officials (including William Bentinck) attesting to their intent to allow the Begum to keep her property under the terms by which she had always held it. In response, the Company challenged the plaintiff's historical narrative, and additionally claimed to have acquired Badshapore Jharsa by default when they conquered the surrounding territory. Because, they argued, the Begum was "an independent, or quasi-independent sovereign" and therefore by definition not a private owner, the annexation was a political act and therefore not subject to the jurisdiction of the municipal courts.[57] The Privy Council decided against the Company on their claim about jurisdiction. They also ruled that the arms had been seized illegally but refused to award specific damages and remitted the case to India to settle the details.

The question of the history and terms of the land grant, however, was more complicated, and here the Privy Council ultimately held in favor of the Company. Because the appellants were not able to produce the original copies of the deed, the Counsellors reasoned that "there is no evidence that anybody ever saw it" and, further, that it might not exist.[58] Nevertheless, because the lower courts had accepted the copies as evidence, the Counsellors treated it as such as well. Despite the Begum's deed being confirmed by the Maharaja of Scindia, who followed Shah Alam II, and records of multiple correspondences with the Company affirming the Begum's claim to her *altumgha jaghir* during her lifetime, the Privy Counsellors returned to the original deed to rule that it could not have been granted by Shah Alam II in 1789 as the appellants claimed. According to Company, the original date of the thirtieth year of Shah Alam's rule, or year 1203 in the Islamic calendar, would correspond to 1788 in the Western calendar during which time Shah Alam was captured, blinded, and held prisoner by a neighboring ruler: "the months of Shawul and Zilhij of the thirtieth year of *Shah Allum*, fall within autumn 1788, when he was a helpless prisoner in the hands of *Gholam Khadir*, the Rohilla who put out his eyes."[59] Based on this, the Counsellors believed that Shah Alam would not have been in a position to make a land grant to the Begum. The appellants, however, claimed that the date corresponded to the autumn months of 1789, when Shah Alam was freed and restored to the throne under the protection of the Maharaja of Scindia. The Counsellors conceded that the appellants' date "perhaps may be capable of being reconciled with the date of *Shah Allum's* accession by some peculiar mode of calculating the Jalus year," in which case "their Lordships would be sorry to make their decision turn in any way upon a disputed point of Indian chronology."[60] Nevertheless they decided in favor of the Company's accounting of events, finding that "even if the dates in question are taken to fall within the year 1789, there is reason to doubt whether *Shah Allum* was at that time in a condition effectually to alienate any part of the revenues of the territories within which *Badshapore* is situated."[61] Based on this, the Privy Counsellors reached "the conclusion that the Appellants have not given evidence which can be accepted as sufficient proof of a grant, of which the original is neither forthcoming nor accounted for, unless the presumption of its existence can be assisted by the other evidence in the case." Focusing on questions of historical accuracy enabled the Council to, at least in appearance, reframe the debate around facts rather than cultural practices, such as the conventional terms of hereditary grants. Yet as the debate over the dates indicates, the objectivity of historical time cannot be taken for granted. As I remarked with regard to *Ramaswamy Aiyan* v. *Venkata Aiyan*, the Privy Council in this case as well, affirmed Western historical time as a remedy to the confusion and implicit unreliability of Indian temporalities.

The Counsellors also discredited further evidence in the case. In several letters over the course of her lifetime the Begum "contended that the tenure was altumgha" and she "sometimes appealed to the Government to continue it after her death as a matter of favour" and sometimes "attempted to raise a claim as of right."[62] In each instance, however, the Counsellors found that the *altumgha* right belonged to Reinhardt's son Zafaryab, rather than to the Begum. In the end, the Judicial Committee of the Privy Council held that the East India Company had acted within its rights, and dismissed Dyce Sombre's heirs' appeal to reclaim Badshapore Jharsa. Interestingly, the judges "regretted that the Government did not, in some way or another, investigate the title of Mr. *Dyce Sombre*, in 1836, as a question of right, instead of dealing with it by an act of power" and further that in 1849 "they did not fairly try the question of title, instead of meeting it by a plea of the *Statute of Limitations*."[63] In closing, the Counsellors speculated that the Begum's "persistent statement of there having been some grant to *Zuffur Yuab Khan* was not without foundation," but they saw no proof of the Begum's further contentions that she, and later her heir David Dyce Sombre, were entitled to it in perpetuity.[64] The Counsellors further inferred that the Begum "had in some way usurped his interest when she got undisputed command of the troops; and that the British power found her in the enjoyment of the estate, and left her so during her life."[65] What they did not see evidence of, or could not imagine, was the Begum's affection for Walter Reinhardt and his heirs that might have motivated her actions.

Privacy and Property

As the Sumroo cases show, the legal positions that justified large-scale colonial land grabs often worked in concert with more local and often less visible encroachments upon intimate and domestic spaces. If early colonial expansion made use of miscegenation and informal kinship relations, the British state had more of a vested interest in making recalcitrant populations more readily governable.[66] Along with an increased focus on legalism and rationality, the transition to the Raj involved greater scrutiny of and restrictions on sexual relationships between British and Indians. According to William Dalrymple, "in the 1780s, more than one-third of the British men in India were leaving all their possessions to one or more Indian wives, or to Anglo-Indian children."[67] Such bequests, however, become increasingly rare as the British presence came under the sway of both Christian evangelism and rational legalism: "Between 1805 and 1810, *bibis* (Indian wife or partner) appear in only one in four wills; by 1830 it is one in six; by the middle of the century they have all but disappeared."[68] The movement toward greater racial and sexual normativity reflected both shifting mores in Victorian England as well as the expanding legal jurisdiction of the imperial state.

In the legal cases dealing with the Begum's property, the privacy of her personal affairs intersects with questions of both private property and sovereignty.[69] During the early nineteenth century, local principalities still hampered the East India Company's acquisition of land. One of the Company's strategies in challenging David Dyce Sombre's inheritance was to undermine the scope of the Begum's sovereignty. In the court records, the Begum's sovereignty relates to the terms of her rule over specific territories. The Begum's territorial sovereignty, however, was not unrelated to the broader social context within which her autonomy was recognized. Repeatedly, in the historical records, the Begum's "masculine disposition"[70] is invoked to explain her political astuteness. At the same time, her sovereignty is always hemmed in by the suggestion of her feminine vulnerability. While she was deemed sovereign enough to extend the services of her army to the Company, she also required the patronage and protection of the Company to maintain her sovereignty. The relationship between gender and sovereignty thus raises important questions about privacy, in terms of both private property and bodily privacy.

Discourses of sovereignty, both historically and at present, are often implicitly masculinized, just as privacy is regularly invoked to protect the rights and bodies of women. For example, the concept of privacy appears twice in the Indian Penal Code, in sections 354 and 509. In both instances, the law seeks to protect the privacy of women from such things as voyeurism and insults to their "modesty." While intruding upon a woman's privacy is punishable by law, often, such legal protections for women fail to correspond to any sort of broader autonomy. In the Begum's instance, the "delegated sovereignty" that she exercised over her territory is at least implicitly related to the juxtaposition of masculine and feminine traits commonly ascribed to her. Descriptions of the Begum's femininity often appear at odds with more masculine displays of sovereignty, and English representations of her convey a general sense of eccentricity rather than authority. Accordingly, her clothing and hospitality are often the focus of English narratives, while her military expertise is invoked as evidence of her gender incongruity and cultural oddity. As Michael Fisher remarks, to her British observers, "she was exceptional, defying the social-class, religious, moral, and gendered stereotypes of the modern age, including what they expected of Indians."[71] But the various descriptions of the Begum's gender nonconformity come at the expense of serious discussions of her sovereignty. The persistent sense of surprise evinced in English narratives of the Begum's gender fluidity, as discussed earlier, bring together questions of sovereignty and privacy by showing how gendered notions of privacy have shaped the recognition of sovereignty. In this respect, discursive constructions of the Begum provide the subtext for the legal recognition of her sovereignty.

In her groundbreaking essay on the rani of Sirmur, Gayatri Chakravorty Spivak explores the role of language and narrative in the production of the rani within the colonial archive. The rani and the Begum were contemporaries, and their stories are populated with many of the same characters. Spivak describes David Ochterlony, the namesake of David Ochterlony Dyce Sombre, for example, as "the kind of person one imagines in the first flush of enthusiasm against Imperialism."[72] Like Sumroo, the rani "emerges in the archives because of the commercial/territorial interests of the East India Company."[73] In their quest to conquer the lower Himalayan territory in which Sirmur was situated, the British deposed her husband and made the rani custodian of her young son, the prince who was heir to the throne. The rani, who for Spivak is emblematic of the narrativity of the archive, becomes a trope to provide the justification for the eventual annexation of Sirmur.[74] Spivak observes that the representation of the rani in the archives is the "construction of a fiction whose task was to produce a whole collection of 'effects of the real.'"[75] Letters between various Company figures cast the rani as in danger of committing sati (though her husband was alive) and in need of British assistance to preserve the nominal sovereignty of her son, the heir. The fiction of the rani's impending sati, from which she needed to be rescued, provided the reason for taking control of the rani's affairs in order to ultimately seize her kingdom. For Spivak, any trace of the rani's real motivations and desires are impossible to decipher, as she is persistently caught "between patriarchy and imperialism."[76] Remarking on the discursive construction of the rani, Spivak argues that the archive reveals the ways in which fictions about the rani were promulgated in order to provide a narrative foundation for material events and interventions. The colonial state thus made fictions crafted from sweeping ideological narratives real. In Spivak's reading, the archives "show the soldiers and administrators of the East India Company constructing the object of representations that becomes the reality of India."[77] Outlining the political consequences of these narratives more broadly, Spivak argues that the "'misreading' of this 'fiction' produced the proper name 'India.'" The emergence of the political state of India was thus made real through the questionable interpretation of fictions about individuals and groups of people.

Extending Spivak's analysis of the fictional element within the archive, Betty Joseph discusses the similar case of Rani Bhishnukumari of Burdwan. The rani was a young widow and guardian of her eight-year-old son who was heir to the family's zamindari, or landholding grant. During the Mughal era, zamindars, who were not landlords in their own right, administered territories and collected taxes on behalf of the local sovereign. Zamindaris were, in practice, hereditary estates and during the ascendancy of Company rule in the 1770s "women managed three of the largest zamindaris" in Bengal.[78] Joseph explores the complicated political and economic questions that frame both the Company's reform of the zamindari system, and women's places within it. "At this time, having just defeated Bengal's local rulers and having acquired the right to Bengal's revenues," Joseph observes, the East India Company was "confronted with a choice: should the acquired territory be remade in a normative metropolitan agrarian capitalist image or should it be shuttled back into feudalism, a system already under attack back home by bourgeois radicalism?"[79] Joseph's discussion of the Company's decision by which "the landscape of Bengal was transformed into a venue of English feudalism" shows how the broader discourse on Indian women shaped Company policy. One important area of change was from the "relative indifference to gender the Mughal state had shown in its award of zamindari leases" to the Company's "preservation of private property through male inheritance and primogeniture."[80] The movement toward private property thus accompanied a sidelining of women from the administration of territories.

Discursively, however, the representation of the confined and oppressed Indian woman circulated in opposition to the putatively more liberated English woman. As the Company took legal steps to remove female zamindars and replace the zamindari system with private property and primogeniture, it cultivated a narrative of native misogyny from which Indian women needed to be saved. Joseph further demonstrates that the "rani of Burdwan's was not a singular case," but instead the Company removed "many ranis who were a source of grief to the Company." Among these was Rani Bhabhani of Rajshahi, who in 1771 "foiled an attempt by the Company to sell her *dewry* farms (traditional holdings kept exclusively for the support of women in zamindari households) by publicizing it as an effort to rob her of her 'Honour.'"[81] Marshaling narratives of feminine propriety, and allying them with the inviolability of private property, the rani managed to turn the tables on the Company and forestall its effort to seize her land. In other instances, however, Joseph argues that the English employed a "theoretical fiction" to reconcile their ideals of gender and femininity with the forcible removal of a host of female rulers. Ultimately, the narrative of the "secluded woman" was invoked as both the cause and evidence of women's incapacity for successful rule. "The idea that the female ruler was incapable," Joseph claims, "was an argument made on the ground of essence and shows that the theoretical fiction of the secluded woman ... was now replacing real historical referents like the ranis of Rajshahi and Burdwan, who had satisfactorily met Company revenue projections for many years."[82] The imagined concept that Indian women were unable to govern took root in cultural and legal narratives and with time, the fiction of female incapacity came to overshadow the real women who successfully governed and administered their territories.[83]

Though history may not provide an accurate representation of the characters formed and occluded by the colonial imagination, it does provide a sense of the fraught discursive context in which these characters were made real. The ranis and Begum Sumroo were emblematic of the substantial political role women played in the late eighteenth and early nineteenth centuries. As Durba Ghosh observes, the Begum's involvement in political affairs was "not unusual for the time in the context of northern India," but what was uncommon was "that she became successor to Samru's lands and armies, rather than being the custodian on behalf of a favored son," as was the case with the ranis of Sirmur and Burdwan.[84] Similarly, Urvashi Dalal outlines the history of several women who played important roles in territories formally ruled by men, usually their husbands or sons. She also, however, details the many instances of women who, like the Begum, independently ruled territories in eighteenth and nineteenth-century India, including Ahilyabai of Indore, Mamola Bai of Bhopal, Laria Begam of Orccha, and, most famously, Laxmi Bai of Jhansi.[85] While, as Rosalind O'Hanlon shows, the Mughal court prized manliness as a virtue of sovereignty, in practice masculinity was an ideal open to being emulated by women as well as men.

In the transition from the Mughal Empire to the British Raj, complicated traditions of gender, kinship, inheritance, and sovereignty often presented barriers to instituting legal norms, particularly in the arena of private property. Nevertheless, as I show throughout this book, the imposition of the "rule of law," including its underlying discourses of rationalism and civilizational progress, stood at the heart of the colonial project. In what Spivak describes as "an alien legal system masquerading as law as such," the law was used to regulate social relations, including sexual and affective ones, and, relatedly, to regulate the rights and distribution of property. [86] As Indrani Chatterjee has suggested, prior to the institution of colonial law, social and intimate relations were better understood as a series of "practices" that were varied and diverse. "Thinking of practices," Chatterjee explains, "in turn, helps to focus attention on both formulations of, and contests within, local societies in the eighteenth and nineteenth centuries – around simultaneously large concepts (like blood, descent) as well as small scale actions that rendered these concepts meaningful."[87] Reshaping the social "practices" of precolonial India into the formalized terms of the law afforded greater ease of governance, particularly in the complex terrain of familial and property relations.

As British rule was consolidated across the subcontinent, property ownership and transmission increasingly became the focus of colonial courts and administrators. Still, as Mytheli Sreenivas explains, "a vast diversity of family and property forms existed that bore little relationship to the legal norms" that the colonial courts sought to establish.[88] Despite legal efforts to create a narrative of appropriate kinship and inheritance, the "universalizing impulse of the law did not eliminate such diversity" and often "the interaction between the law and indigenous social practice depended on already existing ideologies and structures of gender, kinship, and economic relations among various social groups."[89] The particular instance of Begum Sumroo's conflict with the East India Company cannot be entirely separated from these larger currents in property ownership, gender, inheritance, and adoption. The "'masculinization' of the colonial economy overall" that Sreenivas and Joseph identify shaped the Company's interactions with local sovereigns as property models shifted from royal grants to private ownership.[90] Likewise, broader policies on adoption, private property, and gendered inheritance provide the context for the Company's interactions with the Begum.[91] If Begum Sumroo's sovereignty originated in the complex affective and political alliances she created, the Company's annexation of her territory undermined her own brand of Mughal sovereignty as much as the social configurations on which it was based.

The Last Word

The story does not end, however, with the loss of the Begum's lands. One of the more interesting aspects of the narrative unfolds after the death of David Dyce Sombre. This is also where fiction and imagination most clearly collide with fact, shaping the material outcomes of legal actions. Narratives of Indian degeneracy and weak-mindedness that proliferated in the nineteenth century combined with fictions of Oriental sexuality and licentiousness to provide the backdrop for the legal resolutions of David's estate.

Having lost his lands to the Company, David embarked on a tour of China and Europe, eventually arriving in London, where he took up residence. In London, however, he was largely a misfit. Michael Fisher's fascinating biography of David Dyce Sombre paints a tragic portrait of the Begum's heir struggling to find his bearing in a city that was almost uniformly hostile to him. While his wealth afforded him entry into elite circles, his race and ethnicity barred him from truly finding acceptance. In 1841 David was elected to parliament to represent the district of Sudbury, but he was soon removed from office because he was found to have bribed his constituents to secure their votes. Likewise, his marriage to Mary Anne Jervis was similarly unsuccessful. Mary Anne was known in London's aristocratic circles for her singing and her flirtations with influential elderly men. Though her father was a viscount, their fortune was meager compared to David's astronomic wealth. Perhaps David's inheritance helped lessen the influence of concerns expressed by Mary Anne's friends and family about David's race. In any event, though their courtship was often contentious and their engagement was long, in 1840 David and Mary Anne were married. In 1843, after three years of a rocky relationship, however, Mary Anne and her family succeeded in legally declaring David a lunatic. Mary Anne's father had prior experience with lunacy commissions, as several years earlier he had employed one to effectively disinherit his elder son.

Without taking an explicit stand on the veracity of David's "lunacy," Fisher provides a rich history of the context and events of the Chancery trial. One of the main grounds for Mary Anne's charge against David seems to have been that he routinely questioned her fidelity, even accusing her of having had an incestuous relationship with her father, a charge that he later withdrew. Such accusations, predictably, drew public critique. It is impossible, however, to extricate the censure David faced for his criticism of Mary Anne from the broader environment of Victorian racial and sexual mores. Of explicit consideration in the trial, for example, was the question of whether David's Indian blood and upbringing might mitigate or explain his purported lunacy. Former colonial officials were consulted and many offered their opinions on whether David's behavior was insane or just Indian. Perhaps the Begum's own unconventional demeanor and behavior, which was tolerated as merely eccentric under Company rule, would have been deemed "lunatic" under the more rigidly normative standards of the Raj. Charles Trevelyan, a former administrator with the East India Company, worried that finding David a lunatic would offend the masses of India, most of who evinced the same beliefs and behaviors as David. David's jealousy, his inappropriate requests for duels, and his belief in the supernatural, all of which were taken as signs of his lunacy in England, Trevelyan argued, were perfectly normal in India.[92] Indeed, while many of David's comments and actions concerning his wife and others seem tasteless, offensive, or even illegal (such as urinating on a lamppost), it is difficult to see how they rise to the level of "lunacy." Nevertheless, on the basis of medical exams, some of which were conducted by doctors with no expertise in mental illness, and testimony supplied by the couple's various acquaintances, the jury declared David a "lunatic," backdating the origins of his ailment to October 1842. Following the trial, his funds were sequestered and placed under conservatorship, and David was confined in "the elegant Hanover Lodge, a two-storied, Doric-pillared, nine-bedroom villa in Regent's Park," which David referred to as the "Imperial Gaol."[93] Five months into his confinement, while on a tour of England, David escaped from Liverpool and fled to France, where he endeavored to clear his name and regain control of his finances.[94]

Over the remainder of David's life, he visited several of the most prominent physicians in England, continental Europe, and Russia. These doctors, he asserted, examined him and found him sane. Despite repeated appeals to the Lord Chancellor, however, he was unable to reverse the commission's ruling. In his first appeal, David's lawyer proffered the argument that his actions were "but the result of his Indian birth and upbringing."[95] In another attempt, the Lord Chancellor dismissed the testimony of "five of the most eminent physicians in London" because it was "informally and irregularly introduced to the knowledge of the Lord Chancellor by means of a document signed by certain noblemen and gentlemen."[96] While David failed to overturn the finding of "lunacy," in 1847 the Lord Chancellor decided that "the whole residue of his income, after the payment of £4000 per annum to Mrs. Dyce Sombre, was left to his sole disposal."[97] With his funds in his possession, David was able to travel throughout Europe, Russia, and the Middle East.

In 1844, when David returned to England for one of his appeals, he had a chance encounter with the "retired East India Company official Henry Thoby Prinsep, whom Dyce Sombre had known well in Calcutta."[98] In the socially hostile environment of London, perhaps David was relieved to be reacquainted with someone familiar to him. The two men seem to have become friendly, and in his *Refutation* David presents letters indicating that Prinsep attended hearings and sought to assist in clearing David's name. Whether because this new friendship reminded him of his ties to India and to his adopted mother, or out of spite for Mary Anne, David decided to write a will in 1849 giving substantial gifts to several East India Company officials, including Prinsep. More significantly, the will "left most of his wealth to create and endow 'Sumroo's College . . . for higher classes of natives of India, without any distinction of Religion, to qualify them for holding public and other situations of trust.'"[99] In the first version of this will, David included bequests to Mary Anne and his sisters Mary Ann and Georgiana. In a codicil, however, he disinherited all of them and left generous amounts (totaling £48,500 plus pensions) to various Company officials in order "to ensure that even his enemies on the East India Company's Court of Directors would fight vigorously in support of this will."[100] Arguments over this last will form the basis of *Prinsep* v. *Dyce Sombre*, the final case I will examine in this chapter.[101]

The suit, in which Thoby Prinsep pursued his claim against Mary Anne Dyce Sombre, was heard by the Privy Council in 1856, five years after David's death in London at the age of forty-two.[102] The central issue in the case was the question of whether David was of sound mind when he wrote his will. This question was complicated by the fact that in 1847 the Lord Chancellor returned control of his finances to David, while in 1849, just after the will was written, he refused to supersede the Lunacy Commission. One obvious inconsistency raised was if David was sane enough to administer his finances, how could he be unfit to live freely and independently? The Privy Counsellors resolved this tension by observing that "the fact of his being a lunatic was no reason why he should not have every comfort and enjoyment his fortune would afford, and he was capable of having."[103] "The disposition by Will of the whole fund," they reasoned, however, "was manifestly a totally different matter; a power of testation requiring the exercise of sound judgment, which none but a man of sound mind could possess."[104] In their evaluation of whether the will was enforceable, the Counsellors revisited the original evidence by which David was judged a "lunatic."

Importantly, the basis on which the Counsellors assessed David's sanity rested almost exclusively on his accusations against Mary Anne. The Counsellors also judged David's "personal conduct," which they believed "may be described in one sentence – the most unrestrained sensual indulgence of every kind."[105] In particular, the Counsellors sought to evaluate the extent to which David's "conduct and character" were "affected by birth, and the blood that flows in his veins."[106] Reflecting the imperial sensibility of their time, the Counsellors acknowledged that "Asiatic blood did, and probably to a considerable extent, flow in the veins of Dyce Sombre," and they vowed to "endeavour to give this circumstance its proper weight."[107] On this matter, the Counsellors determined that they "may safely conclude that the Asiatic origin and habits of the deceased would probably render him more prone to jealousy and suspicion than would be the case with respect to Englishmen."[108] Narratives about the misogyny of Indian men that justified the annexation of territory from Indian women, as discussed earlier, were ultimately not unrelated to those deployed against David to justify his "lunacy."

From the outset, David's sanity was weighed against Mary Anne's chastity. The Privy Council's report is openly salacious, and David's own licentiousness and the hyperbole of his accusations form the default basis for affirming Mary Anne's fidelity. For example, the Counsellors admit that "what Dyce Sombre stated to have occurred is not beyond the range of possibility," but they nevertheless conclude that they "cannot doubt that all those statements are false," and "that it is utterly contrary to all probability that a man of sound mind could have believed that which Dyce Sombre stated to be true." Therefore "the belief of the deceased must have sprung from insane delusion."[109] While Mary Anne is portrayed as "a lady, admitted on all hands to have been most irreproachable in her conduct, respecting whom her husband had made the foulest charges," no amount of evidence presented by some of the most eminent physicians in the world could convince the Counsellors of David's sanity.[110] Regarding the medical opinions, the Privy Council asserts it is "more proper to draw its conclusions from facts rather than from the inferences of others, however skilled in cases of insanity."[111] Having downplayed the medical expertise, the Counsellors conclude that "it has been our duty to trace the history of the deceased, more especially from his marriage."[112] But while the adjudication of the validity of David's will on the basis of his marital relations may seem questionable to twenty-first-century readers, Mary Anne's fidelity was quite literally monetized by the Privy Council. The British courts, like the colonial ones in his mother's case, overturned David's wishes as expressed in his will.

Through the Privy Council's decision, Mary Anne succeeded in preserving her reputation and her rights to David's fortune. The fact that she needed to secure one in order to maintain the other should not escape notice. David's race no doubt aided Mary Anne's cause, as she likely was able to leverage one form of privilege in order to gain access to another. If the Begum drew on Mughal frameworks of both "fidelity" and adoptive kinship to secure her fortune, Mary Anne affirmed marital fidelity under British law to preserve hers. As for David, most representations depict him as something of a bumbling fool, if not malevolent. Perhaps, however, like his mother, he simply wanted to maintain control over his body and his property, living as he wished and giving his inheritance to whomever he chose.[113]

Ironically, in the end, Mary Anne employed much the same strategy against her husband as the Begum Sumroo did against Walter Reinhardt's son and consort. Though perhaps the Begum could not have anticipated the tactics employed by her daughter-in-law, the resonances between the two instances are striking. Following David's death, Mary Anne "evoked his exotic appeal by appearing occasionally in English high social circles wearing Indian-style clothes, graciously accepting the epithet 'The

Begum.'"[114] Whether motivated by guilt or affection, Mary Anne donated a significant amount of money to charitable projects in Sardhana, ultimately fulfilling, at least in part, David's wishes. At the end of her life, Mary Anne divided her £570,000 between charities and her second husband's family.[115] In 1893 Mary Anne, like the Begum Sumroo before her, died without any biological heirs.

Narratives of Adoption

As we have seen, under colonial law, dates and events, rather than affective relationships, came to form the primary means of deciding the value of truth claims. If *Ramaswamy Aiyan* v. *Venkata Achari* reveals the turn toward the primacy of Western historical time and its associated record-keeping in order to establish legally validated narratives, the Sumroo cases reveal the normative patterns of kinship and filiality that authorize inheritance and lines of succession. These two issues of temporality and kinship come together in a handwritten government correspondence in the India Office Records at the British Library. Dated February 7, 1838, the document details the "decease of the Begum Sombre, or Sumroo, the lapse of her possessions to the British government, and the various proceedings consequent thereupon."[116] It briefly mentions a "claim which was preferred thereto Mr. by David Ochterlony Dyce Sombre" regarding the portion of the Begum's will concerning the "Pergunnah of Badshapore and other landed possessions which he alleged the Begum to have held under a different tenure from the Jaidad of Sirdhana." The correspondence, which describes Dyce Sombre only as the Begum's "residuary legatee," primarily attempts to resolve the question of whether the government should honor the Begum's request to provide pensions for troops in her service during her lifetime. By referring to a series of interactions with the Begum, the document establishes a historical record of the government's rationale for rejecting the bulk of the Begum's requests to secure the pensions, thus validating the legal narrative of events over the affective one of the Begum's desire to compensate her troops for their loyalty. As discussed earlier, the Company's recourse to the rule of law replaced models of fealty and affection upon which Mughal sovereignty was often based. The passing reference to Dyce Sombre as the residuary legatee, however, is important. In legal as well as common parlance, an heir is someone who inherits property because of a legal or biological relationship to the deceased. By contrast, a legatee, who may be unrelated to the deceased, inherits property as a result of a bequest in a will. The narrative of the will, in other words, takes the place of biological kinship, which necessitates no explanation. By identifying Dyce Sombre as the Begum's legatee rather than heir, the correspondence implicitly reframes the adoptive relationship between parent and child as a legal one between deceased and residuary legatee. At the same time, the government's decision to refuse Dyce Sombre's claim simultaneously refuses to entertain the possibility of individual choice that might have motivated the Begum's bequest.

This move to prioritize legal relationships over affective ones, as I have argued, also has a direct bearing on forms and practices of sovereignty and personhood, both in terms of public politics and intimate family relationships. Within the Indian context, as Dalhousie's doctrine of lapse makes clear, there was a strategic political value to undermining adoptive relations. Disrupting the transmission of territory and sovereignty to adoptive heirs ensured the expansion of British rule. The Begum's case, and the more widespread application of Dalhousie's doctrine, reveals how colonial law leveraged formations of kinship in order to enable the Company to amass territorial sovereignty. As the Begum's relationship with Dyce Sombre demonstrates, however, adoptive kinship is not purely, or even primarily, a political relationship. In Chapter 6, I read George Eliot's adoption novels against the background of the Sumroo cases in order to show that the public uses to which the prohibition of adoptive relations was put in India was reimagined in England. In Eliot's novels, we see adoption emerge as a narrative of individual choice that is crucial to the modern imagining of the English nation and family.

CHAPTER 6

Foundlings and Adoptees
Filiality in the Novels of George Eliot

> But I've a claim on you, Eppie – the strongest of all claims. It's my duty, Marner, to own Eppie as my child, and provide for her. She's my own child: her mother was my wife. I've a natural claim on her that must stand before every other.[1]

In the exchange above, Godfrey Cass, the son of the village squire, enters the rustic home of the humble weaver Silas Marner and stakes his "natural claim" to seventeen-year-old Eppie, Silas's adopted daughter. This moment crystallizes ideas about familial relations in George Eliot's celebrated Victorian novel *Silas Marner.* Godfrey's self-assurance in asserting his parental rights is bolstered by several convergent factors: his superior social status, his confidence in the primacy of the blood tie, his ability to conjure the heteronormal family, and his legal claim. Indeed, as his wife Nancy tells Eppie moments later, Godfrey's entitlement is a "lawful" one to which Eppie must capitulate. When Eppie affirms Silas as her only "father," without whom she "can't think o' no happiness" and determines to "cleave to him as long as he lives," Nancy insists, "What you say is natural, my dear child – it's natural you should cling to those who've brought you up . . . but there's a duty you owe to your lawful father."[2] Splintering the "natural" from the "lawful" in this climactic scene of the novel, George Eliot confronts conventional assumptions about the rights of kinship, and about legal and affective bonds, that Eppie's chance arrival in Silas's life have raised.

If Godfrey's belated claim on Eppie is conditioned on an argument of "natural" kinship firmly linked to marital status and blood relation, Nancy's retort reframes natural human relations to include the circumstances of nurture. Nancy deems it "natural" that Eppie "should cling to those who've brought [her] up." Reflecting this attention to care and feeling, some of Eliot's "adoption novels," as Marianne Novy argues, "emphasize nurturance rather than genetics" (122).[3] At a time in

England when adoption was still legally unregulated, it was in many ways easier to undertake. At the same time, informal adoption also lacked legal sanction and safeguards.

Eliot's sympathetic portrait of Eppie's attachments to Silas provides a counter-narrative to the series of legal justifications for the law's downplaying of adoptive ties in the Sumroo cases as discussed in Chapter 5. As Eliot and other popular Victorian novelists in England were grappling with the emotional depths of adoptive relations, Begum Sumroo's own adoption narrative reached its tragic end.[4] But against the Begum's failures, *Silas Marner*, as Novy argues, becomes another kind of "dramatized child custody case," one that allows us to at least imagine that "adoptive parenthood is the crucial parenthood."[5] As this chapter will show, the literary text supplements the courts' treatment of Begum Sumroo and David Dyce Sombre by acknowledging the deep structures of feeling associated with such relationships.

In her reading of *Silas Marner* and adoption laws in nineteenth-century England, Sarah Abramowicz shows how adoption is allied with literature while biological kinship is associated with the law. Adoption, she explains, is based on narrative claims to family, in which individual choice provides the motivating force for kinship. If, as I have suggested in previous chapters, the individualism that was fostered in the bildungsroman and consolidated in the mystery novel, can be read as a defining characteristic of English identity, Eliot's realist novels carry this project forward. Adoption, in this regard, can be seen as associated not only with individualism, as Abramowicz elegantly demonstrates, but also with Englishness. By contrast, as Chapter 5 shows, biological kinship is relegated to more collective forms of identity, and more explicitly subject to the rule of law. In short, the individualism upon which adoptive kinship has been narratively predicated was not available to subjects of Indian colonial law, such as Begum Sumroo. As the debates over Dalhousie's controversial interventions were playing out on the subcontinent, the affective dimension of adoption was garnering interest in the realist novels of such authors as Charles Dickens, Emily and Charlotte Brontë, and George Eliot. In this chapter, I will read George Eliot's adoption novels, in particular *Silas Marner* and *Daniel Deronda*, as contesting and contextualizing the limitations placed on adoptive kinship under colonial law.

I will also explore the unevenness of literary affirmations of the adoptive parental relation within these novels. Despite Eliot's sympathetic portrait of the affection between Eppie and Silas, in her novels that deal with interracial or international adoption, kinship remains genealogical and not open to the individualism of nurture. This is evident, for example, in *Daniel Deronda* (1876) and *Felix Holt* (1866), and characterizes the nineteenth-century English novel more generally. This chapter will thus demonstrate how claims based on blood and national origin haunt writers even as open to, and affirming of, adoptive affections as Eliot.[6]

In contrast to the consolidation of English identity and individualism that Eppie's relationship with Silas affirms, Daniel Deronda's adoption is not so easily assimilated to narratives of national belonging. As a result, it must be anchored instead within the Jewish community. These racial and religious categories of difference, I argue, prompt Eliot to think that Eppie's love for Silas matters, while Daniel Deronda's bonds with his adopted father, Sir Hugo, remain doubtful.[7] Likewise, suggestions of innate difference, represented by an inalienable sense of Jewishness, seems to be what draws Daniel to his own birth mother, as well as to the novel's other Jewish characters Mordecai and Mirah. In these instances, Eliot's broad support for adoptive affections seems tempered by an unwitting recourse to biological explanations.

Substantial criticism already exists on the figure of the orphan child in Victorian literature and culture.[8] In most of these accounts, the ubiquity of the orphan in nineteenth-century fiction is closely tied to "the central role which the family played at this time."[9] Moreover, as Laura Peters shows, "[t]he family and all it came to represent – legitimacy, race and national belonging – was in crisis: it was at best an unsustainable ideal" that redeemed itself by "scapegoating" the orphan.[10] This chapter begins with the premise that the figure of the orphan child in Victorian literature symbolizes vital social shifts within the family form. Further, I consider how adoption becomes the instrument through which writers such as George Eliot negotiate questions of kinship, inheritance, and gender identity that attach to familial identity. While the figure of the orphan may be read as a "scapegoat," the orphan was also central to bringing narratives of the family into alignment with the broader emphasis on individualism.

Literary depictions are rife with concerns over the family in crisis. Using the example of Heathcliff in *Wuthering Heights*, Tess O'Toole observes that the "particular importance of adoption to the Victorian novel lies in adoption's relationship to the antithetical impulses that the Victorian family plot displays." In particular, the novel's "drive to preserve and defend the family and to safeguard its integrity is balanced by the need to revitalize the family, the need for blood regeneration."[11] Within this context, adoption signifies a specific remediation that allows for the continuity of familial affection in the face of quotidian tragedies such as the death of a parent or the birth of an unwanted child. Adoption, at least in its literary guise, thus challenges commonplace assumptions about biological ties and allows for unanticipated forms of attachment. In so doing, it also poses a threat, especially in the psychosocial sense, to normative notions of familial life.

Reading Eliot's novels within the broader legal context of adoption in the nineteenth century reveals tensions between law and literature, as well as within literary texts themselves. Because the social practice of adopting children was far from formalized, legal solutions to adoptive relations evolved alongside literary ones.[12] As Penny Martin has observed, during this time "[a]nybody could give or sell a child to somebody else and anybody could take on a child – without it acquiring any legal rights within a new family" (135).[13] The informality of adoptive relations thus made them particularly adaptable to uncommon social arrangements. Some of the most celebrated English novels of the time use adoption to break with the family romance plot, upending legal assumptions about rights and descent. However even in the midst of new social and familial possibilities envisioned through adoption, race continued to shape the imaginative realm. In cases of miscegenation, for example, adoption often failed to offer a viable alternative to the terms of normative genealogy and inheritance.

By Right of Blood

In *Silas Marner*, as in the Sumroo cases, inheritance is central to the promises of filiation. Joseph Wiesenfarth connects adoption and economic concerns in his observation that "[t]he two most important events in *Silas Marner* are the theft of the gold and the coming of the child."[14] In the novel "the coming of the child," which is to say Eppie's unannounced arrival on Silas's hearth one snowy winter evening, is deliberately romanticized. Eliot announces such a romance with the figure of the child in the epigraph itself, quoting from Wordsworth, "A child, more than all other gifts/ ... Brings hope with it, and forward-looking thoughts."[15] As we soon find, however, the romance of the child, its very promise of a futurity, is also entangled in other things, namely the problem of wealth.[16] The future of the child is inescapably tied to the future of wealth through inheritance, of both actual and social capital.

The child's ability to secure an inheritance and thereby a future is, as Eliot shows, conditioned by various measures of social legitimacy. The child is able to inherit wealth only if claims to family privilege and descent made on her behalf are socially and legally recognized. In contrast to adoptive relations, Godfrey Cass's claim on Eppie articulates the symmetry between genealogical ties and social inheritance. Godfrey's possessive pronouncement, "[I] . . . own Eppie as my child," simultaneously avows her as his daughter and bestows on her the capacity to become the heiress to his wealth.[17] That is, through Godfrey's disclosure Eliot shows how inheritance and blood ties are mutually conditional. Despite having disavowed her all these years of her life, in restoring ties of blood, he also restores her potential to inherit his wealth. In a strange but revealing moment, that gestures toward the connection between adoption and individualism, Godfrey first tries to utilize the force of his social status alone to make a case for himself as an adoptive father to Eppie. In Godfrey's view, if Eppie were to consent to occupy "the place of a daughter" to Nancy and him, she would benefit by a radical change in her social position. Indeed, before he fully reveals himself as Eppie's birth father, Godfrey attempts to convince Silas to relinquish Eppie to him because of the change of "fortune" it would entail for her. To Silas, Godfrey says:

> You'd like to see her taken care of by those who can leave her well off, and make a lady of her . . . And we should like to have somebody in the place of a daughter to us – we should like to have Eppie, and treat her in every way as our own child . . . It'ud be a great comfort to you in your old age, I hope, to see her fortune made in that way.[18]

At this point in the story, Godfrey, who is still hesitant about revealing the secret of his biological ties to Eppie, makes the liberal case for adoption as a means to a better life for the disadvantaged or poor child.[19] He is proposing the substitution of one adoptive paternal relation with another. But in so doing he devalues the emotional singularity of every adoptive relation, highlighting the individual choice of the parent at the expense of the individual identity of the child. By suggesting that parental figures can be infinitely substituted, Godfrey recognizes the materialist logic of adoption, while undermining the affective experience of it. Eppie rejects his offer of fatherhood and its accompanying inheritance, defiantly announcing, "I don't want to be a lady – thank you all the same . . . I couldn't give up the folks I've been used to."[20] By staging Eppie's refusal, Eliot, at least in this instance, rejects a purely economic logic for adoptions.

Following Eppie's rejection, Godfrey is forced to reveal his long-kept secret, clarifying once and for all the fact that he is not simply an "unfamiliar father" to Eppie but rather a biological one, who wishes to "provide for [her] as [his] only child."[21] Interestingly, this invocation of blood ties becomes a substitute for the adoptive relation Godfrey first proposed. Having failed to secure a bond of affection, Godfrey resorts to asserting bloodline ties, insisting that Eppie return to him if for no other reason than to claim the privileges of her birth. Godfrey warns Silas of impeding such a return: "You're putting yourself in the way of her welfare; and though I'm sorry to hurt you after what you've done, and what I've left undone, I feel now it's my duty to insist on taking care of my own daughter"[22] (170). His wife Nancy, as before, legitimizes Godfrey's right over Eppie, asserting her view that "Marner was not justifiable in his wish to retain Eppie, after her real father had avowed himself."[23] "[H]er code," Eliot writes, "allowed no question that a father by blood must have claim above that of any foster-father."[24] Eliot's portrait of Godfrey and Nancy Cass reveals how the intertwined rights of class and blood work to legitimate social ties of kinship. Yet, in this case, Eppie's refusal privileges individualism and upends social conventions when she declares, "I can't feel as I got any father but one . . . I can't think o' no other home. I wasn't brought up to be a lady, and I can't turn my mind to it. I like the working-folks, and their victuals, and their ways."[25] For Wiesenfarth, Eppie's disavowal of economic privilege in favor of affection for her true or "long-loved" father and the "working-folks" affirms George Eliot's "rejection [of] a Cinderella-pattern" in favor of a very different "happily-ever-after world" for the adopted child.[26]

The "happily-ever-after world" that Eppie aspires to is one of emotional riches rather than material wealth. In restoring Eppie to Silas rather than Godfrey, the novel reinvents the narrative of return, validating chosen communities over biologically scripted ones. Eppie's response, I argue, is a powerful and unwavering endorsement of forms of recognition and affection that develop by chance between adoptive relations, feelings that cannot be readily scripted into existing social institutions. Rather, they can only be recognized in the individual choices that adoption both makes possible and demands. The "lawful" claim made on the figure of the child may have to relinquish its primacy, Eliot suggests, to unanticipated but formidable reservoirs of feeling that lie outside legally sanctioned consanguineous relationships. As *Silas Marner* shows, love fostered between strangers is a formative aspect of human nature that can and does confound the unity of the blood tie. Eppie's defense of her love for Silas is based on feelings developed by sharing life experiences and giving and receiving care.[27] Through her portrait of Eppie, George Eliot offers what Ian Watt affirms as a "characteristic of the novel" itself. For Watt, "literary traditionalism was first and most fully challenged by the novel, whose primary criterion was truth to individual experience – individual experience which is always unique and therefore new."[28] In Abramowicz's words, Eppie's preference for Silas reveals the novel's sympathy with more individual narratives that validate "the child's own narrative of who she is and who her parent is, a narrative grounded in her memory of her early experience."[29] If the novel is aligned with individualism, the law, in regulating public matters such as property and name, functions in the realm of the social. Building on discussions in the previous chapters, the emphasis on individualism marks adoptive narratives as paradigmatically English, while Indian narratives, such as the Begum Sumroo's, are consigned to the collective and governed by the rule of law. In refusing the public recognition that the law affords, therefore, Eppie implicitly lays claim to a markedly English individualism.

Eppie's defense of her foster father thus offers a new and pointed refusal of blood and property, the very things that legally derived kinship claims are founded upon. Familiarity, not family, is newly valorized as Eppie decides that her feelings are stirred only for those whose care and ways she is "used to."[30] Silas echoes the affective weight of Eppie's sentiments, saying to Godfrey: "Your coming now and saying 'I'm her father' doesn't alter the feelings inside us. It's me she's been calling her father ever since she could say the word."[31] This emphasis on the word "father" radically transforms the expected terms of kinship, confirming narrative, over blood and law, as the primary defining feature of kinship. The vertical promises of ancestral inheritance are cast aside, as are commonplace legal and social ideas about blood bonds. In their place, Eliot valorizes adoption as a vital form of kinship that prioritizes care over genealogical and economic claims.

The Coming of the Child

In *Silas Marner*, adoption holds the possibility of altering economic, familial, and social relations, not only for Eppie but for Silas as well. As Brian Swann observes, before Silas becomes a "father," he is a "mystic" and "fetishist."[32] Silas's occult powers, along with his cataleptic fascination with gold, at first ally him squarely with capitalist accumulation. Over the course of the narrative, Silas's enthrallment with gold is replaced with the human affection he feels for Eppie. His adoption of Eppie, in other words, has the capacity to alter the course of Silas's life, endowing it with the "beatific sense" that Swann associates with his character.[33] Within the novel, adoption serves to "awaken" Silas from a deadened existence.[34] Eppie's arrival in Silas's life engenders new possibilities for him so that on the strength of her presence alone Silas is able to find a sense of belonging in Raveloe, a community from which he had until then been alienated. Swann's assessment that "[t]he subject of *Silas Marner* is mystic creation" resonates in new light if we consider how the novel elevates the stranger's capacity to care for an unknown child. The experience of adopting itself becomes restorative for Silas's "wounded spirit" as "contact with another human being awakens him."[35] Silas is transformed, as if by alchemy, through Eppie's arrival.

Moreover, Eppie's arrival alters aspects of Silas's life seemingly unconnected to his adoption of her. Importantly, while the narrative justification of the adoptive bond is grounded in individualism, the act of adoption draws Silas into the fold of the community. Prior to this moment, Silas the miser is in every way an outcast in Raveloe. He lives under the "Lethean influence of exile," having been betrayed by his faith, his friend, and his fiancée.[36] Driven out of Lantern Yard, his birthplace, Silas seeks "refuge" as a stranger in a distant village[37] (16). When we first encounter him, Silas is a "wanderer," belonging to the class of "pallid" and "alien looking men" who are part of the "remnants of a disinherited race."[38] Silas, the "emigrant," is regarded with suspicion for his "alien" background by his new neighbors. He is judged a lonely eccentric and even his benign talents at effectively using medicinal herbs to ease villagers' afflictions are associated with "the old demon-worship."[39] The first impression the novel paints of Silas is of a social recluse totally shunned by the community in which he lives and works.

In this alienated state, Silas's relationship to futurity is routed exclusively through money. His sense that "the future was all dark," for example, is relieved by money alone: "for twenty years, mysterious money had stood to him as the symbol of earthly good, and the immediate object of toil."[40] In a classically Marxian sense, Silas's disaffections from community are sublimated into his labor and the accumulation of money that results from it. Silas's relationship with money thus takes the place of his relations with humans:

> So, year after year, Silas Marner had lived in this solitude, his guineas rising in the iron pot, and his life narrowing and hardening itself more and more into a mere pulsation of desire and satisfaction that had no relation to any other being. His life had reduced itself to the functions of weaving and hoarding, without any contemplation of an end towards which the functions tended.[41]

Such descriptions of Silas cast him as the perfectly atomized subject of capital, motivated only toward the production of value. As Silas's "life" is "reduced" to his labor, he clings "with all the force of his nature to his work and his money" so that they "fashion him into correspondence with themselves."[42] In other words, before Eppie arrives Silas is shown as isomorphic with the commodity chain to which he belongs.

Whatever imaginative life Silas possesses at this stage is condensed into what Jeff Nunokawa identifies as a kind of perverse "money love" that becomes his sole fixation.[43] The "fetishistic revelry" that Silas engages in each night provides the structuring logic for Silas's sense of futurity, notably through the metaphor of "unborn children":

> But at night came his revelry; at night he closed his shutters, and made fast his doors, and drew forth his gold ... How the guineas shone as they came pouring out of the dark leather mouths! ... He loved the guineas best ... the crowns and half-crowns that were his own earnings ... he loved them all. He spread them out in heaps and bathed his hands in them; then he counted them and set them up in regular piles, and felt their rounded outline between his thumb and fingers, and thought fondly of the guineas that were only half earned by the work in his loom, as if they were unborn children – thought of the guineas that were coming slowly through the years, through all his life, which spread far away before him, the end quite hidden by countless days of weaving.[44]

Importantly Eliot describes Silas's captivation with his gold in psychic and libidinal terms. Silas's affections are clearly stirred by the sight of his treasures, and his "love" of them is decidedly tactile as he caresses and grasps the gold in order to derive enjoyment from it. The gold seems generative for him because he invests it with a unique possibility of renewal. In other words, the gold, by becoming part of what Swann describes as "a fertility rite," accumulates great symbolic value.[45] At the same time, the money takes the place of the "unborn children" he might otherwise expect in the future.[46] Despite the novel's largely sympathetic portrait of Silas, there is no doubt that it is critical of his nightly ritual of resurrecting the buried gold to gratify unfilled desires. "It had been," Eliot explains, "a clinging life, and though the object around which its fibres had clung was a dead disrupted thing, it satisfied the need for clinging."[47]

Silas's worship of gold, his complete identification with it, has predictably attracted considerable critical attention. Scholars have read it as evidence of the novel's mythological, theological, psychological, and historical investments. For instance, Brian Swann identifies a kind of primitive fetishism in Eliot's representation of the "superstitious" stage of human development when "dead objects" were "invested with psychic energy."[48] In his discussion of how Eliot's prose upholds conventions of social propriety and prohibitions, Nunokawa reads the "illicit atmosphere" of Silas's nightly congress with his gold as "a condensed catalogue of sexual deviance."[49] Ultimately, Nunokawa goes on to argue, Eliot reproduces the social prohibitions and propriety of her times by rehabilitating Silas to society. Swann makes the further point that Silas's rehabilitation, through which he forsakes his interest in gold to form deeper connections with people, is a sign of Eliot's "move from theology to psychology."[50] This rehabilitation into society can also, however, be read as a metaphor for his renewed inclusion, by virtue of his fatherhood, into the fold of society. In forsaking his "primitive" attachment to gold, Silas develops into the modernity of English individualism.

Yet only a few critics have considered Silas's evolution through the lens of adoption. Among them, Robert Dunham makes the valuable point that reading Eppie's arrival in Silas's life as an allegory of the "angelic" misses the weight of "the agency of the child" that drives the narrative.[51] Dunham notes that most "readers recognize that something 'magical' happens to Silas Marner as a result of his daily association with the child."[52] By linking Silas's "regeneration of spirit" specifically to the figure of the Wordsworthian child, Dunham discerns one kind of romantic resolution to the "condition of crisis," reflected in Silas's alienation and greed, that characterizes his life prior to the child's arrival.[53] Drawing loosely on this framing, I suggest that the "magical" transformation Eppie incites both works to reform conceptions of family in the English novel and reflects broader changes unfolding in Victorian England. More specifically, as Abramowicz suggests, the organizing principle of English families was increasingly moving toward narratives of individualism and choice, in an opposite trajectory to the increased emphasis on biological kinship and normative patterns of inheritance developing under colonial law.

A Family Conjured from Gold

Highlighting the element of individualism detached from the social structure of capital, the notion of family that Eliot develops rejects monetary as well as biological or theological conceptions of human social relations. Instead, the novel privileges a purely affective attachment as the grounds for the new sociality into which Silas is incorporated. Eppie initially mirrors and then displaces Silas's monomaniacal attachment to his gold. When she first arrives into Silas's home, Eppie is mistaken for the very gold that has fascinated Silas up to this point. Her mother having died, the toddler Eppie crawls into Silas's cottage seeking warmth at his hearth. But Silas, distracted and mourning the theft of his gold, misrecognizes her:

> to his blurred vision it seemed as if there were gold on the floor in front of the hearth. Gold! – his own gold – brought back to him as mysteriously as it had been taken away . . . The heap of gold seemed to glow and get larger beneath his agitated gaze. He leaned forward at last, and stretched forth his hand; but instead of the hard coin with the familiar resisting outline, his fingers encountered soft curls. In utter amazement, Silas fell on his knees and bent his head low to examine the marvel: it was a sleeping child – a round, fair thing, with soft yellow rings all over its head.[54]

In numerous passages such as this one when Silas contemplates how Eppie both resembles and replaces his gold, Eliot's logic of substitution of the child for gold becomes evident.[55] Silas's preoccupation with his gold – that "dead disrupted thing" to which he has clung – transforms into love and admiration for another human life. The figure of the "sleeping child," at first mistaken for gold, comes to totally eclipse the spectral lure of his coins. "[T]he gold," Eliot writes, "had turned into the child" in Silas's mind.[56] Henceforth, Eppie reigns supreme in Silas's life, reconfiguring it in every sense.

Not all critics, however, see Eppie's entry into Silas's life in purely positive terms. Writing of the aftermath of Eppie's intrusion into Silas's solitary life, Jeff Nunokawa argues that Silas's rehabilitation also serves a disciplinary function. Nunokawa reads representations of queerness in Silas's life before Eppie, thereby recognizing her arrival as a normativizing influence. Critiquing Eliot's valorization of the child, Nunokawa calls out Eliot's "frank efforts to propagate a preference for family ties, or, more to our point here, her efforts to propagate an aversion for other kinds of congress."[57] However, while Silas's socialization as a father to Eppie certainly marks a qualitative shift in his life, the conclusion that Eppie's arrival simply reflects Eliot's "support for family values" seems too simple.[58]

Even if we accept that in *Silas Marner* "a faith in the family . . . is urged, and urged again, as conspicuous doctrine," it is necessary to recognize that the uniqueness of the relation between foundling and found father, in fact, recalibrates how the family or kin relation itself is understood.[59] Christopher Flint has claimed that there is an affinity between narrative and genealogy in which narrative arrangements reflect a "peculiar correspondence between the creation of families and texts."[60] Within this framework, Eliot's endorsement of "the tender and peculiar love" between

Silas and his charge suggests a willful rearrangement of the customary narrative about how normal families come into existence and endure.[61] Families, like texts, are constructed out of narratives as much as they are out of biological facts of birth. Silas's ties with Eppie fall squarely outside the zone of the heteronormal family constituted through marriage and biological reproduction. Indeed Nunokawa misses just this point by identifying Eppie as Silas's "stepdaughter" rather than his adopted daughter.[62] Without overstating the point, the story of Silas and Eppie queers the traditional family narrative.[63]

Eppie's exceptional status in Silas's life is easy to observe in the way that she compels the articulation of a new set of rights in *Silas Marner*. When faced with the prospect of relinquishing the child soon after she enters his life, Silas refuses to "let go," saying, "No-no-I can't part with it, I can't let it go . . . It's come to me – I've a right to keep it."[64] This assertion of a right to "hold on" forms the basis of a new and spontaneous declaration about ties that comprise human relations.[65] Despite previously having "no distinct intention about the child," Eliot describes Silas's claim over the presumptive orphan as an affirmative speech act: "his speech, uttered under a strong sudden impulse was almost like a revelation to himself"[66] (115). At a time when the social status of orphans was precarious, Silas's desire to claim the child confers unique value upon her. As Laura Peters notes, orphans in Victorian society most often occupied a "scapegoat status."[67] As a reminder of tragedy, the orphan was seen as a "threat" to the sanctity of the family. Peters explains that "the orphan, as one who embodied the loss of the family, came to represent a dangerous threat; the family reaffirmed itself through the expulsion of this threatening difference."[68] By his embrace of the putative orphan, Silas and thus George Eliot, counter entrenched social prejudices against the orphan as a figure to be reviled.

Eppie's effect on Silas's life is profound. Silas's fearless declaration that he will keep the child "[t]ill anybody shows they've a right to take her away from me" undoes the primacy of the blood tie as the basis of family.[69] At a time when there was no scientific way to prove lineage, Silas effectively neutralizes the claim of the natural family by insisting that the affection of an "old bachelor" for a foundling child is just as vital. This vitality of their familial relationship is elaborated in the novel through the processes of everyday care: "But I want to do things for it myself," Silas says, "else it may get fond of somebody else, and not fond o' me . . . I can learn, I can learn."[70] Not unlike Begum Sumroo in Chapter 5 then, Eliot weaves a picture of intimacy between adoptive parent and child that is affective, first and foremost. While initially Silas "trembles at an emotion mysterious to himself" when he holds Eppie, this feeling is quite soon changed to that of fondness and even of "perfect love."[71] Peters has described not only how Victorian orphans were seen as "outsiders" or "foreigners" but also how their unfamiliarity kept them from properly entering the domestic fold.[72] The orphan figure, Peters notes, inspired "fear, anxiety, guilt, and inadequacy," conjuring a set of emotions and feelings precisely antithetical to the ones Silas expresses for Eppie.[73] In *Silas Marner*, the orphan's very status of being unclaimed produces innovative familial bonds, transforming other social relations as well:

> The child created fresh and fresh links between his life and the lives from which he had hitherto shrunk continually into narrower isolation . . . there was no repulsion around him now, either for young or old; for the little child had come to link him once more with the whole world. There was love between him and the child that blent them into one, and there was love between the child and the world.[74]

By recoding the terms by which the family is recognized and granted social status, Eliot's narrative intervenes in the primacy of the normative family.

Adoption as Social Stigma

Several scholars have written about what Nina Auerbach terms the "orphan archetype" of the nineteenth-century English novel. With Jane in Charlotte Brontë's *Jane Eyre*; Oliver in Charles Dickens's *Oliver Twist*, Esther in *Bleak House*, Pip in *Great Expectations*; Heathcliff in Emily Bronte's *Wuthering Heights*; and Jude Fawley in Thomas Hardy's *Jude the Obscure*, among others, there is no dearth of orphans in the English literary imagination.[75] The harrowing and hardscrabble lives of these orphans suggest the extent to which they were maligned and left on the fringes of society. Coupling Peters's insights with Auerbach's, we see that "the figure of the wandering orphan, searching through an alien world for his home" was emblematic in the nineteenth century of both threat and dispossession.[76] In her valuable study *Reading Adoption*, however, Marianne Novy makes the case that the task of the nineteenth-century adoption novel was to refute the stigma imposed upon orphan children. Remarking that "disturbed genealogies and displaced children are common in the eighteenth- and nineteenth-century British novel," Novy identifies in the novel "an attack on stigma."[77] "Many eighteenth- and nineteenth-century novels," she notes, "dramatize the adoptee's struggle against stigma, most often the stigma of illegitimacy but sometimes simply the stigma of being a poor dependent, not a birth child of the family."[78]

Silas Marner doesn't simply dramatize Eppie's adoption as a point of plot, though. In this work Eliot uses the act of adoption to contend directly with, and dispel, the various kinds of stigma that orphans inspire. For instance, Silas's adoption of the child is shown to be free of the kinds of secrecy and shame that usually haunt orphans with questionable or illegitimate origins. "For it would have been impossible for him to hide from Eppie that she was not his child," Eliot writes, describing the open adoption Silas favors so that there is no "complete shrouding of the past which would have made a painful barrier between their minds."[79] And while Eppie occasionally wonders about her mother, she never pauses to consider who her birth father might be. Eliot shows that this nonchalance is the result of her feeling that she already had "a father very close to her, who loved her better than any real fathers in the village seemed to love their daughters."[80] Adoptive love is valorized in this instance as a formative aspect of Eppie's character, its expression encompassing not only this particular individual relation but also transcending the everyday ones that are already known socially in the village. Eschewing concealment and gossip in favor of pride and disclosure, Eliot celebrates this father-daughter relationship as deservedly inspiring societal admiration: the weaver, we are told, was henceforth "regarded as an exceptional person" for having "done what Silas has done by an orphan child."[81] This general regard that adoption confers on Silas, rehabilitating him in the process as a figure previously viewed with great suspicion in Raveloe, also confirms the way that this uncustomary arrangement is seen as inaugurating a broader transformation in the world at large. The adoption of the orphan, in other words, propels the narrative in *Silas Marner* while also becoming in itself the social mission of the novel.

In the novel it is Nancy Cass, Godfrey's wife, who expresses the prejudices against adoption most intractably, invoking Victorian religious convictions about providential design. Wondering whether she was right to defy her husband's desire to "adopt a child," Nancy muses:

> To adopt a child, because children of your own had been denied you, was to try and choose your lot in spite of providence: the adopted child, she was convinced, would never turn out well, and would be a curse to those who had willfully and rebelliously sought what was clear that, for some high reason, they were better without.[82]

Through Nancy's aversion to adoption, Eliot channels common Victorian fears that adoption sullies some divinely conceived, and socially recognized, patterns of heredity. Nancy is not only worried that adopting a child would be a deliberate defiance of God's destined plans for her, but she is also convinced that doing so would incur God's wrath in the form of a corrupted child. "It will be wrong," Nancy insists in the face of Godfrey's protests, "I feel sure it will."[83] The adoptee in Nancy's way of thinking would be the very sign of unfaithfulness. Eliot, reinforcing how common such assumptions were, notes that "adoption was more remote from the ideas and habits of that time than of our own," implying already a change in collective feeling towards this practice, and emphasizing its alliance with modernity.[84] In her aversion to adoption, Nancy represents increasingly outdated ideas about external laws, rather than individual desires governing the formation of families. As England moved away from such conceptions of the family, however, colonial law worked to impose a socially governed and regulated vision of the family in India. Between 1848 and 1857, when Dalhousie's doctrine of lapse was in effect, biological kinship was an explicit condition for the public recognition of sovereignty and the inheritance of title and property.

The gradual social acceptance of adoption is reflected first and foremost by the overt exaltation of the ties between Eppie and Silas and the celebration of this relationship by Silas's neighbors. However, a more subtle confirmation of it comes from the fact that even those scared of adoption evince a shift in their reactions. Nancy's initial aversion to orphan adoptions is shrouded in rumor and fear. Recalling a story once told to her by an acquaintance, she is convinced that adopted children are inherently criminal, given to being "transported."[85] Yet, Godfrey challenges Nancy's convictions. In asking, "But why do you think the child would turn out ill?" Godfrey, despite his duplicity, advances the ethics of adoption in the novel.[86] Godfrey's defense of adoption results from a cover up; he wishes his biological fatherhood to remain hidden. Obscuring his identity as father, however, means that he relinquishes his "natural" claim on Eppie, thereby making natural parentage less consequential. When he does reveal his deception, affirming, "Eppie is my child," it is with regret, as he "oughtn't to have left the child unowned."[87]

Godfrey's revelation at this late point in the story is relevant beyond the fact that it allows him to reassert his natural claims. It is significant because it persuades Nancy that the affective ties of kinship arise from something other than biological ties. Nancy, so scared of the stigma of adoption until this moment, suddenly opens herself to being a surrogate parent:

> Do you think I'd have refused to take her in, if I'd known she was yours? . . . 'O, Godfrey – if we'd had her from the first, if you'd taken her

> as you ought, she'd have loved me for her mother – and you'd have been happier with me . . . our life might have been more like what we used to think it 'ud be.'[88]

This is a curious moment. Nancy's previous stigmatization of adoptees transforms once she realizes that the child has a biological tie to her husband. She suddenly imagines herself as Eppie's adoptive mother. It would appear that in holding fast to the naturalness of Godfrey's relation to Eppie enables her to envision herself as a surrogate. For Nancy, the primacy of the marital bond enables her to overcome her fear of adoption. She is thus able to articulate a softer, more accepting view. Encapsulated in this new vision, despite its reliance on the marital norm, is the idea that an intimacy that comes from nurture is what conditions maternal love. Time, not blood, is offered as the relevant condition for the ideal cultivation of feelings of love and kinship. Nancy, having rejected adoption before, becomes increasingly open to its possibilities. Her rueful sense that "[i]t'll be different coming to us, now she's grown up" (164) marks the lag in her delayed recognition of the relational possibilities adoption brings.[89] Nancy's conversion from skeptic to potential adoptive parent marks a subtle transformation in the novel so that by its end Eliot represents not only an idealized romance of adoption but also a general shift in the cultural mood of those who resist it.

This kind of generalized acceptance of adoption is also seen in *Felix Holt, The Radical* (1866), George Eliot's novel about tumultuous social reforms in Treby, a fictitious English mining town in the Midlands.[90] Although tangential to the class conflicts between the landed gentry and the working class, *Felix Holt* reproduces the dynamic of gentleness and care between adoptive father and daughter shown in *Silas*. Like Silas and Eppie, the Reverend Rufus's adoption of Esther is depicted in terms of a permanent and deep relation. The novel often marks Esther as somehow apart from the society in which she is raised. Possessing a refined air, Esther's fashion sensibilities as well as her mannerisms are clearly derived from her French birth mother, Annette Ledru. Esther, it seems, carries in her person a remainder of Annette's bearing, a biological resemblance that endures even though her mother dies when Esther is a child.

In *Felix Holt* this mark of alterity becomes a sign of Esther's foreignness. Where Silas's difference was *within* national culture, Esther's is clearly framed by her transnational ties. Silas's migrant difference as he moved from one township to another was assimilated through adoption because it confirmed the new sense of family and individual choice that was at the heart of English self-conceptions and could be readily extended to both father and adoptive daughter. Esther's difference from the English people around her, however, concerns her maternal origins outside England. She is separated from others in Treby who understand her manners as alien. The suggestion is that Esther's comportment and interests indicate a Frenchness that is regarded with skepticism in the novel, not only by Felix but also by Rufus's parishioners when years earlier he shelters Annette, the lost and wandering Frenchwoman who is Esther's birth mother. Specifically, Felix deplores Esther's pretensions – her love of romantic poetry and aesthetic self-fashioning – as signs of class conceit. This is the foreign quotient that in Esther's case is ultimately sublimated into her identity in terms of class.

Nevertheless, the adoptive relation is still elevated in this novel, too. Reverend Rufus's love of his daughter is constant. The magnitude of his romantic love for Annette transforms into a permanent magnanimity towards the child she has left in his care. In sheltering Annette, an unwed mother, and then adopting Esther, her illicit child, Rufus's morality runs counter to the tenets of Victorian Christianity. For this reason he has to give up his priestly duties, a sacrifice he makes and one that the novel characterizes as the higher moral choice. By sacrificing his pastoral credentials in favor of a pastoral care for the stranger, Rufus enacts a lasting ethics of adoption as care that Silas previously displays. Even when, through the discovery of her paternal biological ties, Esther is elevated from orphan to heiress of the Transome estate, the love she and her adoptive father share is not diminished. Esther's discovery of her true parentage simply serves to domesticate her alien transnationality into English aristocracy. Indeed, in the end when Esther relinquishes her ties to the Transomes in favor of a future with the much poorer Felix, she in effect refuses both class and nation as adequate markers of her separation from those around her.

"I Am Not My Father's Son"[91]

George Eliot's last novel *Daniel Deronda* (1876), however, poses the problem of adoption in a far more ambivalent way than her earlier work. The novel, which focuses on questions of religion, gender, racialization, and ethnicity, is as path breaking as it is controversial. Critical appraisals of the novel routinely note the "double plot" of *Daniel Deronda* that distinguishes the "English" story from the "Jewish" one. As Sarah Gates has observed, F. R. Leavis's proposal that the Jewish part of the novel be excised from the plot so that we focus only on Gwendolen Harleth's fate has produced a flood of counter arguments.[92] Scholars concerned with the form and genre of the work assert that the social realism of Gwendolen's story cannot be understood without the allegorical romance of Deronda's discovery of his Semitic roots.[93] The question this debate raises is about the extent to which the English novel itself should be concerned with the national bounds of England and a provincial idea of Englishness. By championing Deronda's Jewishness – described as the novel's "epic recovery of Judaic roots" – Eliot counterintuitively emphasizes a syncretic aspect to Englishness.[94] Daniel's appearing to be both English and Jewish makes Englishness itself hybrid.[95] Such a syncretism derives its plot from a narrative of transnational adoption. At the same time, Deronda's ultimate avowal of his Jewish roots and his leaving England seem to validate a nativist ideal that privileges an ethnically demarcated birth identity.

The ambivalence of Deronda's position is captured most eloquently by Aamir Mufti:

> This linking of Jewishness with the social and psychic effects of illegitimate birth makes crystal clear the relationship of the Jews to the language of national belonging, to nation-thinking, as I have called it here, with its ideological reliance on the family, inheritance, and organic reproduction: the Jews constitute a scandal in national life, surrounded by rumors, suspicions, and crises of (communal) regeneration and of legitimate authority but at the same time, in the very persistence of their communal identification, they represent a kind of hope for a fractured and atomized humanity.[96]

In Eliot's double gesture, Mufti sees "not the cultural and moral separatism of 'alienism' of the Jews, but rather the artificiality, atomism, and moral indifference of society itself."[97] While Mufti offers an important intervention into more claustrophobic readings such as those put forth by Susan Meyer and Edward Said, it also frames a vision of belonging, and the adoption through which it is shaped, as indefinitely open, and perhaps never secure.

In light of this chapter's exploration of adoption, the uncertainty in *Daniel Deronda's* portrayal of adoptive bonds is important. As I show later, the book's repudiation of natural motherhood goes against the grain of its seeming confirmation of ethnic and religious identity based in biology. Daniel discovers his mother only to be forcefully rejected by her. Yet, it is only through this discovery that he can be certain of his Jewishness. Thus Eliot casts Daniel's search for his roots simultaneously in terms of a blood betrayal and a blood bond. The oscillation between these narratives where the disclosure of the natural mother leads to a profound disappointment, as well as to a resolute racial allegiance, shows the limit of Eliot's openness to adoptive relations. What is significant is that across her oeuvre, George Eliot's novels are only concerned with paternal adoptions. In *Silas Marner* and in *Daniel Deronda*, the adoptive parent is thus always the benevolent father and not a mother. The case of Begum Sumroo discussed in Chapter 5 presents, in this respect, an alternative to Eliot's gendered mold.

Daniel Deronda's preoccupation with what constitutes nurture and belonging for children is apparent from the very beginning of the novel. What is surprising is Eliot's recourse to a "sweet habit of the blood" to describe the child's developing awareness of their own kin and home. Eliot writes:

> A human life, I think, should be well rooted in some spot of a native land, where it may get the love of tender kinship for the face of earth, for the labors men go forth to, for the sounds and accents that haunt it, for whatever will give that early home a familiar unmistakable difference amid the future widening of knowledge: a spot where the definiteness of early memories may be inwrought with affection, and – kindly acquaintance with all neighbors, even to the dogs and donkeys, may spread not by sentimental effort and reflection, but as a sweet habit of the blood.[98]

Whereas *Silas* and *Felix* thwart blood claims, *Daniel Deronda* seems to take being "rooted in some spot" and surrounded by familiar "sounds and accents" as potent forms of kinship. Rather than circumventing the claims of organic and biological forms of kinship, *Deronda* begins by validating their primacy. However, if we read *Deronda* carefully, we see that what actually unfolds in this work is an unresolved and uneasy tension between various forms of kinship, of blood and race, as well as of friendship and fraternity.

The prospect of being defined by the "sweet of habit of blood" is both borne out in the case of Daniel Deronda and challenged. In this work, as opposed to others, Eliot seems to suggest that the familial tie is ultimately enigmatic, vacillating between some primal identification and other more accidental ones. The fact of Daniel's adoption by Sir Hugo Mallinger compromises the sense of primacy that Eliot otherwise accords to forms of natural kinship in this novel. There are two aspects of Sir Hugo's relationship with Daniel worth pausing on. The first is the closed nature of the adoptive relation itself. While Silas openly avows Eppie from the first moment of her coming, Sir Hugo's adoption of Daniel is shrouded in secrecy and rumor. He is never directly named as Daniel's father, his paternal influence marked only loosely in avuncular terms: "He had always called Sir Hugo Mallinger his uncle, and when it once occurred to him to ask about his father and mother, the baronet had answered, "'You lost your father and mother when you were quite a little one; that is why I take care of you.'"[99] In this moment, the adoptive relation is reframed as one that compensates for a fundamental loss but can never approximate the absence of the parental tie. Still, we learn that this lack does not reduce Daniel's affection for him as, at least initially, "he was too fond of Sir Hugo to be sorry for the loss of unknown parents."[100] The closeness that the two share spawns rumors that Daniel is actually Sir Hugo's illegitimate son. When Gwendolen inquires about Daniel's family, Mrs. Davilow gossips that, "Well – every one says he is the son of Sir Hugo Mallinger, who brought him up; though he passes for a ward."[101] She also speculates that "[o]ne would guess, without being told, that there was foreign blood in his veins."[102] In this way, the novel shows how socially precarious Daniel's adoptive position makes him. The moment when Sir Hugo finally discloses the summons Daniel receives from his mother, revealing the fact that Daniel is not tied to him biologically, highlights the secrecy that is intrinsic to their relationship. "I have never prepared you for it," Sir Hugo tells Daniel, adding too that "I have never told you anything about your parentage" and that "secrecy was her wish."[103] Daniel, we learn, immediately recognizes this moment of confession as "a sacramental moment."[104]

The narrative of Daniel's adoption by Sir Hugo highlights the element of secrecy. Sir Hugo's silence nuances the narrative differently from Silas's frankness, precluding *Daniel Deronda* from celebrating the adoptive tie. The hidden nature of Daniel's ties to Sir Hugo infects the relationship and diminishes trust between the two. Sir Hugo senses the barrier when he confesses that perhaps he was "wrong" to undertake the secret venture and asks his son's forgiveness.[105] Daniel, too, realizes the enormous stakes of such reticence when he reflects on "the resolved concealment" on Sir Hugo's part, a point that makes any "interference" between them "untrustworthy."[106] The second point of note in Eliot's representation of this relation is the question of Daniel's name. "[T]he very name he bore might be a false one," Daniel muses, both reckoning with his inability to name Sir Hugo as his father and anticipating his conversion.[107] Ironically, as Eliot later reveals, Sir Hugo is the one responsible for Daniel's alterity because he asked Leonora to choose a "foreign" name for him. Leonora later tells Daniel that when "Sir Hugo said, 'Let it be a foreign name,' I thought of Deronda."[108]

The absence of a paternal name is symbolic of a larger lack in Daniel's case. Sir Hugo's compassionate adoption of Leonora's son fails to overcome the sense of an absence that haunts Daniel from childhood. The novel repeatedly shows Daniel brooding about his difference from the Baronet, suggesting those separations of caste and origin that the discovery of his Jewishness will later illuminate. For example, the young Daniel displays an agonizing ambivalence about his absent father. "Would it ever be mentioned to him?" Daniel wondered, "Would the time come when his uncle would tell him everything? He shrank from the prospect: in his imagination he preferred ignorance."[109] Rather than reassuring him, Sir Hugo's presence only amplifies Daniel's doubts about his birth father's absence. Being adopted in this case augments rather than dispels the existential uncertainty that haunts Daniel. He constantly wonders about his father – who he was, whether he "had been wicked" – while shrinking from the discovery of the truth.[110] Daniel's adoption, in other words, commences a prolonged psychological injury, one that is never quite resolved in the book. In contrast to her endorsement in *Silas Marner*, Eliot depicts the adoptive relation in *Daniel Deronda* in contradictory terms, as an incomplete kind of reprieve that continually crushes its protagonist even as it saves him.

Despite the doubts that plague their relationship, however, Eliot confirms the sentiments of love and friendship between Sir Hugo and Daniel. "Whatever else changes for you, it can't change my being the oldest friend you have known, and the one who has all along felt the most for you. I couldn't have loved you better if you'd been my own," Sir Hugo tells Daniel. Sir Hugo's words poignantly testify to his deep affection for Daniel. At the same moment, by giving Daniel his mother's letter, Sir Hugo eclipses his own claims in favor of another symbolic order altogether. Because the adoptive relation faltered from the beginning in declaring its primacy, it is easily overshadowed by the summons from the Princess Eberstein invoking a biological bond.

"Not Quite a Human Mother"

Daniel's meeting with his "unknown mother," the Princess Leonora Halm Eberstein, is pivotal to the novel in many ways.[111] It joins the English plot of Daniel's upbringing to his Jewish future by retroactively inventing a coherent historical past for him. As Margaret Homans has suggested, for Daniel, the princess's appearance "grants him that desired past, complete with birth mother and neatly boxed birth culture."[112] The lack of biographical history that characterized Daniel's orphan status is suddenly supplemented, and he is given a genealogical narrative that subsumes, from this point forward, the narrative of his adoptive life. His conviction that his destiny is bound up with the creation of a Jewish future is formed when his birth mother suddenly reveals the name of his real father to him. In doing so, she bequeaths to Daniel a heritage whose reality he could previously only conjure but never confirm. However, the princess's coming forth as Daniel's birth mother also curiously denatures the sacrosanct place of the natural mother, thereby keeping open the question of filiation beyond blood ties.

From the moment he learns of her existence, Daniel is seized by the suspicion that the flesh and blood Leonora would not live up to the image he had formed of his ideal mother. Eliot's descriptions heighten this distinction between the fantasy mother and the real one. Receiving the letter that makes his mother a "living reality," Daniel finds himself becoming "remote" from her, yearning instead for the "image of a mother" that has "long been secretly present with him."[113] Daniel thinks of Leonora as a "veiled figure" in contrast with "that image which, in spite of uncertainly, his clinging thought had ... made the possessor of his tenderness and duteous longing."[114] His emotions increasingly withdrawn, Daniel admits to being in "a state of comparative neutrality towards" the princess.[115] In his imagination, Daniel "lived through so many ideal meetings with his mother, and they had seemed more real than this!"[116] The gap between Daniel's fantasy and the reality of Leonora's presence is magnified in Eliot's subsequent portrait of the princess.

The Princess Halm Eberstein forcefully denatures motherhood in her interactions with her son. Looking at her face, Daniel intuits her "aloofness," described by Eliot as his realization of his mother's "strangeness." It was, Eliot writes, "as if she were not quite a human mother, but a Melusina, who had ties with some world which is independent of ours."[117] A fiercely feminist figure, the princess deliberately escapes the patriarchal constraints of femininity and motherhood. Her interactions with Daniel articulate a chain of refusals – of motherly love, marital ties, her heritage, and ultimately of her child – that characterize, in Daniel's view, her "inhuman" mothering.[118] A burst of declarations captures the princess's absolute recalcitrance to conventions of maternal feeling: "I had not much affection to give you. I did not want affection. I had been stifled with it. I wanted to live out the life that was in me, and not to be hampered by other lives."[119] The princess resents forms of affection that seek to hem her in, and stridently avows the primacy of her own desires. "I was living a myriad lives in one," she asserts, and "I did not want a child. I did not want to marry."[120] She is frank in her claim to freedom: "I had a right to be free. I have a right to seek my freedom from a bondage I hated."[121] Disavowing the fantasy of maternal reunion, Leonora declares, "I did not wish you to be born. I parted with you willingly."[122]

Repudiating all expectations of conventional motherhood, the princess articulates a recalcitrant femininity. She is undoubtedly Daniel's biological mother, but her maternity nonetheless abjures the requirement to love her natural born child, to submit to marital bonds, or to accept her communal ones.[123] The princess's vehemence against these codes stirs in Daniel, as it likely did for many readers of the time, "the sort of commotion that might have been excited if he had seen her going through some strange rite of a religion which gave a sacredness to crime."[124] The confusion of feeling that Eliot describes in Daniel is a delicate one. It both validates the princess's volitional life choices as real and even sacred but still shows how Daniel experiences them as akin to a "crime."

By unmooring femininity from its equivalence with maternity, the princess, like Begum Sumroo in Chapter 5, enables broader interventions in the rigidity of gender norms. In many ways, the princess is a kind of inverse double of the Begum. Like the Begum, she displays an uncommon independence, living by her own sovereign desires. Yet, unlike Sumroo, who does everything in her power to secure a child and adoptive heir, Leonora desires freedom from the confines of motherhood. Unlike many women of their time, both the Begum and Leonora attempt to autonomously decide whether or not to raise a child, as well as what to bequeath them.

Through her portrait of the princess, however, Eliot ultimately presents dissident feminine difference as the limit point to conventional notions of kinship. "I am not a monster," the princess says, "but I have not felt exactly what other women feel – or say they feel, for fear of being thought unlike others." Leonora explicitly calls attention to the social aspect of disciplinary demands on women:

> When you reproach me in your heart for sending you away from me, you mean that I ought to say I felt about you as other women say they feel about their children. I did *not* feel that. I was glad to be free from you . . . I will not pretend to love where I have no love.[125]

In blunt terms the princess clarifies how her freedoms are invariably at odds with an affirmation of Deronda's familial ties. Deliberately given up by his mother, Deronda cannot now lay claim to some kind of "tender kinship" on the basis of their blood tie. Instead, the princess's words reveal a careful enunciation of feminist motives. The gap between what women truly feel and what they "say they feel" signals the broader coerciveness of the social nature of motherhood. Women, Eliot suggests, often profess a natural maternal feeling because they feel compelled to do so. In this respect, Eliot's depiction of the unruly princess also probes the limit point of the social acceptance of individualism when it takes the form of feminism. The princess ruptures these societal dictates and fervently defends an autonomous femininity at odds with dominant gender conventions. Her defiant refusal of motherly feelings, though, also lends credence to the adoption narrative in the novel. However insignificant and insecure Daniel feels about his place in Sir Hugo's household, there is no doubt he can find no bond with Leonora. "I am your mother. But you can secure no love for me," she says to him adamantly.

The princess's representation of feminist resistance in *Daniel Deronda* has received substantial critical attention. For Susan Meyer, Leonora's "passionate rage" and "resistance to the subordinate position of women" are emblematic of the novel's attempt to reconcile unruly feminine desires with the problem of the unloved child.[126] The princess's critique of gender norms is explicit, as she attempts to explain to Daniel the impossibility of her position: "[Y]ou can never imagine what it is to have a man's force of genius in you, and to suffer the slavery of being a girl."[127] The princess's platform in *Daniel Deronda* problematizes the compulsory valorization of blood ties over adoptive ones. Through the princess's feminism, the novel, even if obliquely, undoes the assumption that giving birth obligates affection and extended dependency between mother and child. It is thus possible to read in *Daniel Deronda* an argument for how adoption cultivates non-genealogically derived feelings that serve the goals of feminism.

Adopting the Faith

When Leonora frees Daniel from any bonds with her, she envisions also releasing him from the Jewish faith of his birth. But just as a critique of gender normativity underlies the novel's tentative support for adoption, its treatment of Daniel's embrace of Judaism turns on questions of biological and cultural inheritances as well.[128] As the novel shows, Daniel's conviction that he must take up the mantle of Judaism occurs in several ways. Daniel is given historical proof of his heritage when his mother validates his Jewish origins by passing on to him an archive, "about our family, and where my father lived at various times – you will find all that among the papers in the chest."[129] With this bequest, Daniel suddenly possesses a "family tree" or a genealogical map the likes of which he has desired all his life.[130] As a boy, Daniel overhears the remark that "he features the mother," which propels his fascination with and wonder about the Mallinger family tree.[131] Eliot emphasizes the effect that the remark has on him: "Daniel had never before cared about the family tree . . . But now his mind turned to a cabinet . . . where he had once seen an illuminated parchment hanging out, that Sir Hugo said was the family tree."[132] Despite not having the courage to scrutinize the cabinet, Daniel experiences the absence of such family history as a "sore that had opened in him."[133]

As *Deronda* also makes clear, Daniel's embrace of Jewishness comes from his mother's total rejection of it. His mother, Leonora, is determined to frustrate her own father's desire for a Jewish heir by making sure that his grandson Daniel "should not know [he was] a Jew."[134] Her rejection of Judaism, we're told, catalyzes the racial feeling in Daniel: "It seemed as if her words called out a latent obstinacy of race in him."[135] The multi-generational tensions between father and daughter, and mother and son, underscore an ineluctable force of racialized identity within the novel. By revealing Daniel's Jewish ancestry to him, Leonora ultimately fulfills her father's design, a fact she well knows: "Well, I will satisfy him, I cannot go into the darkness without satisfying him."[136] In relinquishing her desire to suppress her Judaic heritage, Leonora unburdens herself of this secret and enables Daniel to passionately affirm the very identity that she previously hid. Still, by linking the racial feeling Daniel asserts to the ebbs and flows of familial loyalties, Eliot leaves the basis for such identification open to change. Will Daniel someday follow Leonora's scorn for the racial basis of Judaic identification? Will he come to believe, as his other parent Sir Hugo does, that choosing to identify himself as a Jew bears too much risk? These questions remain deferred in the novel, but the possibility of such outcomes is raised by the example of Leonora and Daniel.

In the end, despite validating Daniel's turn to Judaism through the biological fact of his birth, the novel disavows a purely essentialist notion of racial or ethnic identity. Daniel's Jewishness eludes any singular experience and remains tied to multiple forms of inheritance. It is historically verified, as well as psychologically and socially produced. In Jan-Melissa Schramm's terms, "The power of the inheritance plot lies not only in its capacity to align gradual change and individual choice, but in its dense web of metaphoric associations."[137] As Schramm reminds us, inheritances consist of both "chattels and legacies" as well as "the transmission of culture and faith, and post-Darwin, the unwilled determinism imposed upon individual lives by biological imperatives."[138] When Leonora presses him on whether he would "turn [himself] into a Jew" like his grandfather, therefore, Daniel's response is telling. He acknowledges that taking on an exclusively Jewish identity "is impossible" because his prior "education can never be done away with." With "increasing tenacity of tone," Daniel remarks on his hybridity, averring that the "Christian sympathies in which my mind was reared can never die out of me."[139] Daniel rejects the notion of ethnic or religious purity, as his life with the Mallingers has had an enduring influence on his identity. The revelation of Daniel's origins calls forth his "filial imagination," but it also triggers the parallel realization that "the filial yearning of his life [is] a disappointed pilgrimage to a shrine where there were no longer the symbols of sacredness."[140] At the heart of Daniel's experience of blood and communal kinship, there is a foundational absence that has structured his life's search for meaning and identity. As Cynthia Chase observes, Eliot never omnisciently confirms Daniel's origins, nor does she verify the ultimate resolution of his quest. According to Chase, "Both the origin of Deronda's history (the fact of his birth) and its goal (the act of restoration) are excluded from his history."[141] Given this absence, Daniel's identification with his "hereditary people" is always tenuous and necessarily limited. Daniel declares, "But I consider it my duty – it is the impulse of my feeling – to identify myself, *as far as possible*, with my hereditary people, and if I can see any work to be done for them that I can give my soul and hand to I shall choose to do it".[142] Rejected by his mother, Daniel turns toward his heritage as a self-conscious response, and he is aware of its limits. His desire to "identify" himself with his people carries with it the caveat that any identification can only be made "as far as possible."[143]

The constitutive limitations of Daniel's identity are figured in his status as an orphan. Cheryl Nixon makes an important point about the figure of the orphan in relation to the family. Writing about Charlotte Smith's *Emmeline, the Orphan of the Castle* (1788), Nixon asserts that the orphan "calls attention to the law's construction of the family through last wills, inheritance agreements, marriage settlements, and guardianship deeds."[144] In order to secure recognition, "without biological bonds to rely on, the orphan needs these legal bonds to be clearly defined." By materially standing in for the parents, these "legal documents not only record, but create the family."[145] But, as we have seen, the legal interventions of wills and other documents only approximate the dominant narrative of biological kinship that the law typically affirms. In *Daniel Deronda*, Eliot shows how the orphan's legal status with regard to the inheritance of property remains vexed under English family laws.

As a presumed orphan, Daniel is not a viable legal male heir to Sir Hugo. One of the impediments to Daniel's integration into the Mallinger family is the "ancient and wide" law of primogeniture that governs Sir Hugo's inheritance and property.[146] Because Sir Hugo has no natural born sons, the ancestral home, Diplow, and other Mallinger estates, pass to his nephew, the debaucher Henleigh Grandcourt.[147] The informally adopted orphan, Daniel, has no legal claim to any inheritance in this scenario. Despite Sir Hugo's affection and even "a certain pride in Deronda's differing from him," it is Daniel's difference that sets him apart legally.[148] Although Sir Hugo "brought him up from a child," the intimacy between them cannot legally satisfy the "want of a son to inherit the lands."[149] Mrs. Davilow's dismissal of Daniel as a prospective suitor for her daughter Gwendolen because he will "not inherit the property, and he is not of any consequence in the world" highlights his double disinheritance, economically and socially.[150] Importantly, and perhaps as a sign of their deeper connection, Daniel's orphan status works to disinherit both him and Sir Hugo. Sir Hugo assures Daniel that "whatever happens to you must always be of importance to me," but his affection cannot remedy his "despair of a son" to ensure that his own line of descent remains legally intact.[151]

Love and the Sacred Inheritance

The narrative arc of *Daniel Deronda* thus draws various instances of inheritance into conversation with one another. Daniel's inability to inherit property from Sir Hugo, for example, must be seen in tandem with his reclamation of his identity from his mother.[152] Daniel can inherit nothing from Sir Hugo other than the monetary gift of sixteen thousand pounds that he receives from him.[153] Sir Hugo's generous gift testifies to their affective kinship even as it marks the absence of a legally recognized one. Daniel's inheritance of family lineage from Leonora, however, supplements the financial gift he receives from Sir Hugo. Arguably Daniel also inherits Leonora's rebellious temperament. He is determined to accept his Jewish heritage, reversing the trajectory she sought for herself. Beyond these affective and genealogical inheritances, Eliot depicts another powerful legacy that beckons to Daniel. Ezra Mordecai schools him on "the sacred inheritance of the Jew." Mordecai, who is dying of tuberculosis, charges Daniel with the task of carrying on his spiritual mission:

> You will be my life: it will be planted afresh; it will grow. You shall take the inheritance; it has been gathering for ages . . . You will take the inheritance

> which the base son refuses because of the tombs which the plow and harrow may not pass over or the gold-seeker disturb: you will take the sacred inheritance of the Jew.[154]

Rejected by his mother and dispossessed by English family law, Daniel turns to Mordecai to claim a different "inheritance." Daniel is riveted by Mordecai's impassioned advocacy of a proto-Zionism. Mordecai's words have a mesmeric effect on Daniel, as they make available to him new legacies of community, homosocial brotherhood, and political citizenship. These forms of belonging displace the partial inheritances he receives from all of his parents. Through Mordecai's fevered assertions, he is endowed with a sense of purpose. Mordecai's invocation of a spiritual kinship supersedes the secular terms of biological and adoptive relations.

But Daniel's relationship with Mordecai does not merely transcend other modes of kinship categories, it unsettles their founding assumptions. The queer subtext of Daniel's affection for Mordecai challenges the heteronormative terms upon which both biological kinship and inheritance through primogeniture are based. Eliot seems to deliberately feminize him and critics have noted Daniel's exceptional and self-conscious beauty. Margaret Rowe, for example, has commented on Eliot's "androgynous characterization" of Daniel, while Sarah Gates notices that he is "ambivalently gendered."[155] Gates, as well, shows how the bond between Daniel and Mordecai is "figured at first as libidinal cathexis" and ultimately "becomes an icon through which Daniel's contradictory gendering is resolved – according to the generic conventions of divine scripture."[156] In Gates's reading, the sexual charge of the relationship is routed into a narrative of religiosity and the quest for a Jewish homeland: "Daniel as cathected beloved becomes instead a divinely chosen 'second soul' whose task will be to bring new life to his people by creating for them a new national self."[157]

Yet, the text is also explicit about the homosexual desire between the two. As Daniel is listening to Mordecai, "the two men with as intense a consciousness *as if they had been two undeclared lovers*, felt themselves alone in the small gas lit book-shop and turned face to face, each baring his head from an instinctive feeling that they wished to see each other fully."[158] How does Daniel's queer kinship with Mordecai resonate with the various other modes of kinship it confronts?

Eliot paints a clear portrait of homosexual desire, but ultimately channels the passion between the two men toward religious rather than sexual ends. For instance, Eliot provides an alibi for Daniel's heterosexuality in the form of Mirah, Mordecai's sister. In the novel, Daniel marries Mirah, who interrupts the intense magnetism between Mordecai and Daniel, sublimating a scarcely disguised libidinal intensity between the men into a normative heteromarital promise.[159] Drawing on Eve Kosofsky Sedgwick's thesis that the modernist impulse was to abstract male homosexuality, Jeff Nunokawa suggests that Eliot resolves the problem of transgressive sexuality through an effort "to conceal the male body freighted with homoerotic potential."[160] "The nervous drama of intimacy between Daniel Deronda and Mordecai," Nunokawa explains, "is safely routed through a female vessel."[161] Once Daniel marries Mirah, he is able to overcome his hesitation to Mordecai's physical touch, as "the press of flesh that everywhere marks the intercourse between Deronda and Mordecai is cast as the mere expression of a metaphysical communion."[162] In other words, the homoerotics between Mordecai and his pupil are cathected into Daniel's spiritual and ethnic future.

Mordecai, as Susan Meyer observes, is a proto-Zionist and Eliot's incorporation of a narrative of ethnic restoration and return within the text can be seen as an allegory for the broader question of Zionism. Eliot's portrait of Daniel's personal reclamation of his ethnic origin parallels early Zionist goals of restoring, or claiming, Palestine as a Jewish homeland. In this respect, *Daniel Deronda* frames the dilemma of the orphan's exclusion from the family as a metaphor for Jewish exclusion from the nation. Daniel's hybrid upbringing is central to the staging of this allegory. Daniel's alienation from his adoptive family propels him toward both an affective relationship with Mordecai, as well as an embrace of his lost ethnic and religious roots. And for Mordecai, Daniel's hybridity is an asset rather than an impediment as he envisions the possibility of citizenship outside of Europe. Imploring Daniel to promote the dream of the diaspora's return to the homeland, Mordecai critiques the incompleteness of Jewish citizenship in England. In so doing he allies Daniel's personal alienation with questions of "national fellowship." Mordecai asks, "What is the citizenship of him who walks among a people he has no hardy kindred and fellowship with, and has lost the sense of brotherhood with his own race?"[163] Reflecting the undertones of self-hatred that Eliot's characterization of him resonates throughout, Mordecai argues that in England, the Jew "is an alien of spirit, whatever he may be in form; he sucks the blood of mankind, he is not a man, sharing in no loves, sharing in no subjection of the soul, he mocks it all."[164] At the same time, Daniel's search for community and collectivity marks his failure to embrace the individualism that is increasingly validated within modern England. He is therefore unable to actualize the potential freedoms his status as an adoptee, unburdened by family influences, might afford him. According to Mordecai, Daniel cannot exist as a person of mixed origins, both affective and racial, in England. The fundamental rights of citizenship – including those of kinship and fellow feeling – are denied him. His presence is viewed in vampiric terms and bound to be repelled. Mordecai beseeches Daniel to leave, and he does.

Drawing the novel into explicit dialogue with Britain's imperial project during the late nineteenth century, Susan Meyer argues that Eliot "likens Mordecai, in his attempt to awaken a desire for the Jewish state in other minds, to a British imperialist"[165] (751). Meyer's claim is that, by casting the Jew as a figure of both revulsion and romanticization, *Daniel Deronda* endorses an imperial narrative about the need for Jews to leave Europe.[166] As Meyer shows, Eliot's representation of Jewish hybridity allows her to both rationalize removing Jews from the space of the nation, as well as employing them as agents in the imperial enterprise. In this she echoes Edward Said's assessment that "Eliot's account of Zionism in *Daniel Deronda* was intended as a sort of assenting Gentile response to prevalent Jewish-Zionist currents." For Said, the novel "serves as an indication of how much in Zionism was legitimated and indeed valorized by Gentile European thought."[167] Nuancing the novel's relationship to the historical project of Zionism, however, Meyer shows that "when *Daniel Deronda* is considered within the context of Jewish aspirations in the 1870s, before the crucial switch in Jewish orientation after the pogroms in Russia in the 1880s, the Zionist agenda of the novel emerges as distinctly problematic, not only for the inhabitants of Palestine, but for the Jews as well."[168] "The British gentile proto-Zionist activity of the mid-nineteenth century," which Meyer identifies as the "predecessor to the movement named 'Zionism' by Jews in the 1890s, was something of which the Jews of the time were, with reason, suspicious." In fact, Meyer notes, "[i]t was the English gentiles in this period, not the Jews, who were fascinated with the idea of the Jewish return."[169]

For Meyer, Eliot's embrace of Mordecai's proto-Zionism is reflected in her ambivalent portrait of the figure of the Jew, as well as in her disregard for the material reality of Palestine. Connecting Eliot's resolution of the Jewish question to her portrait of gender normativity discussed earlier, Meyer argues that

> the novel ultimately does with the Jews, the non-English race with its submerged connection to female selfhood, precisely what it does with female transgressiveness: it firmly ushers both out of the English world of

> the novel, it returns those who have strayed and transgressed, it removes them, in the euphemistic language of the novel, 'safely to their own borders.'[170]

Meyer sees Eliot's depiction of both Leonora and Gwendolen's gender transgressions as disparaging, and further connects the portrait of the women to the gender ambivalence that characterizes Eliot's representation of the novel's proto-Zionist project. When taken together, Meyer concludes, both "reveal Eliot's uneasiness about the Jews and about female transgressiveness," reflecting "her desire to conclude the novel with a restoration of hierarchies in race and in gender."[171] While my own reading of the text recognizes ambivalence in Eliot's depiction of gender, it is not clear whether Eliot merely makes available alternative arrangements of various other norms (such as family, religion, ethnicity, etc.) or whether she actually endorses them. What is clear, however, is that the novel reflects the goals of enforced exile, on the one hand, even as it inaugurates a colonial fantasy on the other.

As both Meyer and Edward Said have remarked, the existing inhabitants of Palestine are virtually absent from Mordecai's, and thus Eliot's, vision of a Jewish homeland.[172] Said connects this absence to the novel's colonial mentality, arguing that Daniel exemplifies the Western missionary's ignorance of the actual history of lands and peoples outside the imperial metropole.[173] Importantly, bringing the personal into conversation with the political, Daniel's immersion in the Zionist plan also severs his adoptive relationships. Bidding farewell to Gwendolen and Sir Hugo, Daniel opts to live out his future with Mirah and the novel closes with their preparation for "Eastern travel."[174] Unlike *Silas Marner*, then, the verdict on adoption in *Daniel Deronda* remains undecided. While the novel, to an extent, grants a greater elasticity to conventional understandings of family, it also reveals, and arguably perpetuates, the ways in which adopted children, both literally and allegorically, remain vulnerable to self-doubt, exclusion, and exploitation.

Adoption's Uncertain Horizons

Taken collectively Eliot's novels display an ambivalence to assimilating the orphan completely within established family and community units, thus reflecting the limits of the Victorian era. During the eighteenth and early-nineteenth century, the legal definition of an orphan was patrilineal and limited to "a child who has lost his or her father" because the mother does not have "custodial rights to her 'orphaned' child."[175] Perhaps for this reason, Eliot's focus is mainly on the paternal relation between adoptive parent and child. The adoptive father forms a predictable focal point for Eliot's contemplations on the possibilities and limits of adoption within the social landscape she inhabits.

But her focus on adoptive fatherhood is surprising, as others have noted, because Eliot herself adopted the sons of the critic and philosopher George Lewes with whom she lived. James McLaverty observes that "[a]doption is a major theme in *Silas Marner*, with the conclusion of the novel supporting Silas's claim to his adopted daughter."[176] He further notes, "It seems quite probable that George Eliot was particularly concerned with questions of adoption at this period because it was on 23 June 1860 that she was introduced to the Lewes boys as "Mutter."[177] Gordon Haight links Eliot's exploration of adoptive relations to her own estrangement from her biological family, especially her brother Isaac.[178] Lawrence Dessner also remarks on the "reciprocal tension between text and author" that exists in 1860 as Eliot is writing *Silas Marner*.[179] During the same period, she was newly introduced to her stepsons, the Lewes boys, and apprehensive about their reception of her. Eliot, Dessner explains, "could only hope that the boys would accept her usurpation of their mother's place and rights, and accept their own new difficult social status."[180] Dessner suggests that Eliot's experiences with the boys are central to her portrayal of parental relations of care in *Silas*. At the time she was writing the novel, Eliot's acceptance by the boys "was in doubt, and such doubts are central to *Silas Marner*."[181]

In the end, however, the enthusiasm for adoption in *Silas Marner* mirrors the acceptance Eliot ultimately received from the Lewes boys. It also reflects the love that developed between them.[182] Dessner writes that the scene in which Godfrey returns to claim Eppie "is an imaginative transformation of George Eliot's role" as "Lewes's male children become Eppie."[183] The abandoned child thus provides the occasion for the "new parent's moral regeneration." In this respect, Dessner shows, the "imaginative realm permits, even encourages, a kind of speculative play through which the bounds set by moral imperatives can be freely crossed."[184] Dessner thus suggests that Eliot's personal experience of adoption is a factor in how she maps its redemptive possibilities for initiating freer and more expansive human relationships. Yet the sentiments Eliot represents in her work are also undergirded by some unrelenting social norms.

In the case of *Silas Marner*, *Daniel Deronda*, *Felix Holt*, and others, Eliot is unable to transgress social conventions of gender and ethnicity. In Gillian Beer's view, Eliot was "beset" by "the familiar polarization" between the "intellectual strength of a 'man' and the emotional weaknesses of 'woman.'" Beer observes that Eliot "strove to find ways of collapsing it, though she was well aware of the restrictions of power experienced by even liberated women."[185] (36). When she does depict characters fiercely at odds with prevalent social norms (such as Leonora or Mordecai in *Daniel Deronda*), she is perceptive enough about Victorian society to recognize the artificiality of integrating them back into the social fold.[186]

Ultimately, George Eliot's imaginative portraits of adoption both reflect and refute public sentiments about orphans in nineteenth-century England. In the nineteenth century, as George Eliot makes clear, the social practice of adoption that attaches to the unfamilied child introduces new and important questions about permissible forms of human kinship. As both Eliot's novels and the experience of Begum Sumroo and David Dyce Sombre indicate, by the nineteenth century, adoption was central to the representation of kinship and family. Taken together, the case of Begum Sumroo and the immensely popular novels of George Eliot confirm Marianne Novy's conviction that legal and literary "adoption plots dramatize cultural tensions about definitions of family and the importance of heredity."[187] While Victorian England celebrated the individualism of adoptive narratives, at least when limited to unambiguously English families, colonial law used adoptive kinship to intervene in the public transmission of sovereignty. And, while adoption made way in England for enduring narratives of intimacy, affection, and individuality, in the Indian context adoption could only signify the failure of public claims to title and territory. Within this broad dichotomy, however, within England as well, what matters in the nineteenth century and beyond is how readily the child may be socially integrated, or adopted, into emotional and political discourses about family, nation, gender, and kinship. In this respect, both the Sumroo cases and Eliot's novels enrich our capacity to rethink the bonds of family, in all of their myriad forms.

Afterword

Colonial Law in India and the Victorian Imagination has read the ideological traffic between legal ideas and literary themes during the British colonial era of the nineteenth century. Many of the conceptual frameworks for thinking through the logic of the opinions of the Judicial Committee of the Privy Council (JCPC), I have argued, can be seen in works of fiction. These novels in turn reflect and also shape broader cultural practices, including the law, both in England and in India. What I hope to have constructed is a dialogue between colonial-era law and literature that shows the mutual trace, though not necessarily conscious, of each upon the other.

At its heart, this study has argued that nineteenth-century rhetorics of justice, pursued through the law as well as outside of it, operate both in literary texts and legal ones, shaping the often-divergent paths for English and colonial subjects. Likening the presence of the law in Victorian fiction to Edward Said's remarks on imperialism in the genre, Catherine O. Frank observes that "there is a kind of legalism at work that makes it possible to read for the law even when legal matters don't appear to be part of the novel's immediate subject."[1] Frank's invocation of Said's observation about imperialism illustrates how both law and imperialism provide a crucial subtext of nineteenth-century narratives. Yet, despite the substantial scholarship on both the law and imperialism in nineteenth-century literature, very few studies have brought the two topics together. By looking at the specific archive of appeals to the Judicial Committee of the Privy Council from nineteenth-century India, *Colonial Law in India and the Victorian Imagination* has explored how these legal cases open up new ways of reading the cultural logic represented in canonical Victorian novels.

Relatedly, the colonial relationship between England and India, I have argued, is illuminated in new ways when the archive of the JCPC is considered alongside these literary texts. Sometimes, as in *Confessions of a Thug*, literature serves as a narrative vehicle for the ideological performance of the law. In other instances, the law enacts the cultural ideals and ideology that literature exemplifies. And often, literature reveals the tensions inherent within the law, in relation to questions, for example, of race, gender and sexuality, religion, and place. Placing the legal opinions beside the literary texts thus focuses our attention toward the relationship between law, justice, and the imagination. In other words, while this project considers a specific archive of colonial legal opinions, and relates observations about those cases to the particular novels with which they are paired, it also reveals some broader insights about the relationship between colonial law and Victorian literature.

In the instances I discuss throughout this project, the law both functions as a surrogate for colonial ambitions and provides insight into their potential subversion. As S. K. Acharya, the advocate general of West Bengal during the late twentieth century has humorously remarked, "even when the British wanted to oppress people, they first made a law giving themselves the right to do it."[2] Underlying Acharya's quip is the tendentious relationship between the law and justice in the colonial context. The law, Acharya implies, provides a procedure and a narrative logic for what would otherwise be recognizable as oppression. The mechanism through which the law makes itself appear just is, in my argument, narrative. In different contexts, the various chapters of this book have examined how both colonial law and literature narrativize, whether critically or supportively, nineteenth-century British norms.

To this end, each pair of companion chapters has considered how nineteenth-century novels and the JCPC grapple with common questions. Often, as in the treatment of criminality in *Great Expectations*, we see that literature leads the law in imagining new ways of thinking about ingrained social attitudes. By contrast, in the instance of *Ramaswamy Aiyan* v. *Venkata Achari* the law creates and further entrenches assumptions about difference, cultural relativism, and the methods by which narrative and truth claims are made to appear real. Equally importantly, sometimes England seems to set the standard of progress, as in the teleology put forth in *The Moonstone*, while at other times historical figures such as Begum Sumroo seem far ahead of their time. Sumroo's views on adoption and her own sovereignty, for example, are in many ways more progressive than the norms that governed English society as represented in the novels of George Eliot. If the methodology of this book has been to look at discursive and thematic resonances between a collection of appeals to the JCPC and related Victorian novels, its guiding quest has been to examine how the discourse of colonial justice relates to literary and legal emplotments.

The Discourse of Justice

As this book has argued, the particular revelations inspired by pairing the archive of the JCPC with these Victorian novels enable broader observations about the evolving nature of sovereignty and justice in both England and colonial India. In England, Mithi Mukherjee has shown, the transition from monarchic to parliamentary rule was reflected in the shift from justice as equity to justice under common law. "The discourse of justice as equity," Mukherjee explains, "was dominant in a monarchical polity where the laws had their origin in the person of the monarch and the people related to the monarch as his subjects."[3] By the middle of the nineteenth century, "the discourse of justice as equity had been reduced in Britain to a mere supplementary role" in relation to "the discourse of common law reflective of the rising tide of democratic ethos."[4] By contrast, in India during the same period, following the Queen's Proclamation, "justice as equity became the new discourse of colonial governance," reflecting the figure of the sovereign as the fountain of justice.[5] Under this new paradigm, as Rohit De remarks, "[j]ustice was not rooted in natural law, but was seen as a gift of the British monarch to the people of India."[6] Though it precedes the transfer of control to the Crown, the right of appeal to the Judicial Committee of the Privy Council is, as I discuss in Chapter 1, itself a reflection of this idea of justice as emanating from the sovereign.

As both De and Mukherjee observe, what constituted justice in practice was a complicated question, especially since in many cases, the judges had very little, if any, familiarity with the local laws and cultural practices that were being adjudicated. The JCPC was in the peculiar position, therefore, of administering justice within a myriad of legal frameworks (e.g. Hindu, Muslim, Parsi, etc.) that were often alien to the judges themselves.[7] De relates the theory espoused by the Lord Chancellor Viscount Simon "that it was its *very alienation* from India that made it an effective tribunal for Indians who were divided by caste and religion."[8] Rather than being an impediment, the judges' distance from the local became a sign of their objectivity and impartiality. For Simon, the "fact that the members of the JCPC stood wholly removed from local influence meant that even the most 'violent' politicians had not suggested that their judgments were affected by any consideration apart from 'pure law and justice.'"[9]. In Simon's view, ignorance of local customs and practices rendered the English judges impartial arbiters of "pure law and justice." At the same time, their own cultural and locational biases were made to appear irrelevant.[10]

As this book has argued, however, the notion of "pure law and justice" is a foundational fiction of Indian colonial law. The process of codification cemented the fiction of a positive law that could be adjudicated with objectivity and transparency, thus bringing the colony into the fold of the rule of law. In his capacity as law member in India, a position previously occupied by Thomas Macaulay and Henry Maine, James Fitzjames Stephen furthered the work of codification initiated by his predecessors. "An ideal code," Stephen believed, "should combine the highest qualities of literary skill and technical knowledge."[11] Stephen praised Macaulay's fashioning of the Indian Penal Code, which, "freed from the endless verbiage, circumlocution and technicality of English statutes, became a model of logical precision, and was even entertaining as a piece of literature."[12] Stephen's attention to the literariness of the law was perhaps a product of his early interest in a career as a writer, but it is emblematic of a broader porousness between the two spheres.[13] In his biography of his famous brother, Leslie Stephen writes that for Fitzjames Stephen "professional success at the bar was in his mind always itself connected with certain literary projects" and "from the first he was revolving schemes for a great book."[14] According to his brother, for "Fitzjames himself the legal career always represented the substantive, and the literary career the adjective."[15] In legal terms, the substantive comprises the formal content of the law while the adjectival is the set of procedures by which the law is applied. Within this metaphor, literature functions as a resource by which the logic of the law can be disseminated.

Stephen was the son of James Stephen, the author of the Slavery Abolition Act of 1833, and the paternal uncle of Virginia Woolf.[16] As a member of a family equally illustrious in the fields of law and literature, Stephen saw literary texts as a means to educate the reading public in the "laws of human society." In an editorial for the *Edinburgh Review* in 1857, he critiqued the sentimentalism of contemporary fiction, and affirmed that it is through reading novels that "the springs of human actions are laid bare, and the laws of human society discussed in language intelligible and attractive to young imaginations and young hearts."[17] While the "laws of human society" are not necessarily limited to or identical with judicial or legislative practices, they reflect norms that the apparatus of the law often seeks to formalize. The pedagogical potential of the novel that Stephen identifies is thus suggestive of both the formal as well as the social elements of the law. Stephen's idea that the law should be "entertaining as a piece of literature" while literature should impart the value of laws speaks to the cohesion between the two fields in his thought.

Like Gabriel Betteredge of *The Moonstone*, one of Stephen's favorite novels was *Robinson Crusoe.*[18] Stephen felt that a "novel should be a serious attempt by a grave observer to draw a faithful portrait of the actual facts of life" and in *Robinson Crusoe*, he saw "the life of a brave man meeting danger and sorrow with unflinching courage, and never bringing his tears to market." *Robinson Crusoe* is also, of course, one of the first English novels as well as one of the most explicitly concerned with the themes of conquest and colonialism. Crusoe's narrative, which seamlessly joins British adventure and individual development to the possession of foreign territories, has profoundly shaped the history of the British novel. *Robinson Crusoe* is also one of the first English novels to grapple with questions of the law, as Wolfram Schmidgen notes in his discussion of the text's representation of private property and natural law.[19] The tradition that novels such as *Robinson Crusoe* have established of weaving together legal narratives with literary ones continues to resonate in the postcolonial moment as well.

Fiction and Reality: A Case in Point

Within contemporary South Asian literature, it is common to encounter elements of the law or legal concepts as features of the plot. In examples too numerous to list, from across the subcontinent, the law provides the subtext within which fictional plots continue to arise.[20] We see evidence of this, for example, in the titular character's human rights work in the wake of the Sri Lankan civil war in Michael Ondaatje's *Anil's Ghost.* In Indra Sinha's fictional representation of the Bhopal Union Carbide disaster in *Animal's People*, the lawyers for the "Kampani" persistently attempt to evade laws governing multinationals in order to shirk corporate accountability. And Kamila Shamsie's *Burnt Shadows* entwines the history of World War II with the US war in Afghanistan and the quasi-legality of Guantánamo prison. As these and other novels demonstrate, the law is too often aligned with the interests of those who have access to its levers.

Historically, as well, I have argued that the judicial opinions of the Privy Council have routinely channeled the diverse and unruly sociality of the subcontinent into the normative paths laid out in the law. Yet, to what extent does contemporary law continue to circumscribe the literary imagination? Does literature always exceed the law's capacity to think expansively about imaginative possibilities? Or is the law's imagination at times more capacious than literature? In many respects the Indian Penal Code, a signal achievement of colonial law, continues to exert its influence not only in India but also throughout South and Southeast Asia. But two recent legal developments in the arena of gender and sexuality in India demonstrate the suppleness of the law, allowing for a glimpse of what Jose Munoz poetically describes as the "warm illumination of a horizon imbued with potentiality."[21] The first is the Indian Supreme Court's recognition of the third gender in *National Legal Services Authority* v. *Union of India* and the second is the repeal of Section 377 of the IPC criminalizing homosexuality.

In April 2014, in an opinion delivered just one month before his retirement, Indian Supreme Court Justice K. S. Radhakrishnan detailed the court's reasoning for granting legal and constitutional rights to what it terms a "third gender." The opinion opens with an acknowledgement that society rarely recognizes the "trauma, agony and pain" that trans individuals experience.[22] Radhakrishnan calls special attention to the quotidian aspect of discrimination and ridicule, noting that it often occurs in "public places like railway stations, bus stands, schools, workplaces, malls, theatres, [and] hospitals."[23] Radhakrishnan's opinion begins with the recognition of "the moral failure" that "lies in the society's unwillingness to contain or embrace different gender identities and expressions." "This is a mindset," he argues, "we have to change."[24] The ruling recognizes several categories of the third gender, invoking "transgender" as "an umbrella term for persons whose gender identity, gender expression or behavior does not conform to their biological sex."[25] In addition to the more globally recognized category of transgender, the ruling also references hijras, who "are neither men nor women and claim to be an institutional 'third gender.'"[26] The hijra's historical and cultural specificity within the South Asian context is of particular interest in situating the logic of the Supreme Court's decision.

In Chapter 3 I argued that the Privy Council's opinion in the case of *Ramaswamy Aiyan* v. *Venkata Achari* documented a change in British attitudes toward temporality over the course of the appeals process. While earlier judgments show the courts' willingness to draw on and integrate indigenous conceptions of historical time, the later rulings dismiss evidence based in the ancient past. The effect, I show, was to establish the preeminence of modern legal time, making it the exclusive basis for the evaluation of rights. As though in response to the Privy Council's logic, Radhakrishnan's opinion turns to the mythic past in order to establish the cultural history of the hijras. Citing references to hijras from Hindu texts such as the Ramayana and Mahabharata, as well as from "the royal courts of the Islamic world, especially in the Ottoman empires and the Mughal rule in the Medieval India," Radhakrishnan argues that the third gender was historically accepted, and even revered, in the precolonial era.[27] According to Radhakrishnan, this changed "with the onset of colonial rule from the 18th century."[28] Perhaps the narrative cast by Radhakrishnan warrants the caution that Frantz Fanon famously raised in his discussion of national culture in *The Wretched of the Earth* about the tendency of postcolonial intellectuals to romanticize and reclaim a largely imaginary glorious past. If the Privy Council's opinion invoked fictions of Indian stagnancy and degeneracy, Radhakrishnan's revision perhaps fictionalizes an earlier period of tolerance and respect. Nevertheless, Radhakrishnan's effort to locate the legal question within a broader colonial question is noteworthy. By invoking a historical continuity with the precolonial past, the decision authorizes a different understanding of legal temporality that extends beyond the parameters of modern law and the colonial frame from which it derives.

Not only does the decision look to the precolonial past for a more accommodating history of rights for the third gender, it explicitly locates the origins of contemporary social and legal biases in colonial era laws. In particular, Radhakrishnan highlights the Criminal Tribes Act of 1871, which characterized hijras "as innately 'criminal' and 'addicted to the systematic commission of non-bailable offences.'"[29] The act, which relates to the suppression of thuggee as discussed in Chapter 2, also "provided for the registration, surveillance and control" of hijras, thereby statutorily criminalizing gender and sexual nonnormativity under the sign of biocultural deviance. The Criminal Tribes Act of 1871, Radhakrishnan explains, found an anchor in Section 377 of the Indian Penal Code (1860), which prohibited homosexuality, or in the terminology of the law, "unnatural offences."

In his concurring opinion, Justice A. K. Sikri affirms that by "recognizing TGs as third gender, this Court is not only upholding the rule of law but also advancing justice to the class, so far deprived of their legitimate natural and constitutional rights."[30] Referencing cultural and political theorists such as Immanuel Kant, Jeremy Bentham, Aristotle, John Rawls, Amartya Sen, and others, Sikri outlines the argument for the legal distribution of rights as the imperative of justice. In the final ruling, the court not only recognizes the human rights of hijras and other trans individuals, including the right to freely designate male, female, or third gender, but also grants them an affirmatively protected status under state and federal law.[31] Affirmative action programs allow for preferential consideration for admissions in educational institutions and public appointments. The ruling also provides separate HIV services, proper measures for medical care, separate public toilets and other facilities, "various social welfare schemes for their benefit," and "measures to regain their respect and place in the society which once they enjoyed in our cultural and social life."[32] The court's narrative of restoring rights that have been abrogated by colonial laws provides a fascinating contrast to the Privy Council opinion in *Ramaswamy Aiyan* v. *Venkata Achari*.

But to what extent does *National Legal Services Authority* v. *Union of India* rely upon fiction or mythology in order to justify the ostensible restoration of rights to hijras and other transgender people? The invocation of the uniquely South Asian history of hijras and other regional trans communities situates the decision within a narrative of cultural tolerance that was interrupted by the rule of law under British colonialism. In this respect, the decision repeats the structuring logic, if not the political valence, of many of the cases I discuss in this volume. Despite its very different narrative arc, this case shares with the others the underlying notion of fiction motivating the material outcomes of the law. If, as Jonathan Grossman has argued, "the law courts crucially shaped the formal structures and political aims of the novel," it is equally the case that fiction has shaped the political contours, if not aims, of the law.[33] I have claimed throughout that the law works to shape imaginative possibilities; perhaps different fictions will enliven a brighter future.

Four years after the *NALSA* judgment, in their decision on *Navtej Singh Johar* v. *Union of India*, the Indian Supreme Court struck down Section 377 of the constitution that criminalized homosexuality. In a series of lengthy opinions, citing legal and social theorists from John Stuart Mill and Jeremy Bentham to Eve Sedgwick and Nivedita Menon, the court justified its unanimous rejection of the colonial era law. Arguing that the heterosexism of Section 377 depends upon a foundational gender binary that the *NALSA* case had previously dismantled, Justice Chandrachud extends the stakes of the decision beyond the queer community. "Section 377," he notes, "criminalizes behaviour that does not conform to the heterosexual expectations of society," and therefore "perpetuates a symbiotic relationship between anti-homosexual legislation and traditional gender roles."[34] Because the heterosexism that guides Section 377 derives its logic from normativizing gender roles universally, Chandrachud argues, the interest in overturning Section 377 should also be felt universally. "The effort to end discrimination against gays," he reasons, "should be understood as a necessary part of the larger effort to end the inequality of the sexes."[35] The judgment also, however, maintains a clear focus on the "transformative constitutionalism" necessary to protect the rights of specific minorities. Noting the legacy that the law exerts over the imaginative landscape of its subjects, Justice Chandrachud acknowledged that it "is difficult to right the wrongs of history. But we can certainly set the course for the future."[36] The legal outcomes of these two cases do not necessarily indicate that the law becomes more flexible in the postcolonial moment. Nor is it to say that postcolonial law remains rigidly fixed to, and inevitably derivative of, colonial frameworks. Rather, as Chandrachud remarks, the "shadows of a receding past" continue to shape the present.[37]

The Afterlife of the Judicial Committee of the Privy Council

A final word is due to the current status of the Judicial Committee of the Privy Council. The JCPC was abolished as the final court of appeal in India in 1949, Pakistan in 1950, and Sri Lanka in 1971; and following decolonization throughout Africa and Asia, it has become a largely peripheral institution within the legal world. It does, however, continue to exercise jurisdiction over a handful of domestic British matters, the Crown dependencies, and various commonwealth nations. A consideration of current issues before the JCPC thus takes us away from our focus on the Indian subcontinent but remains entrenched in many of the same concerns. A particular category of cases dealing with Caribbean death row appeals is especially relevant.

Although the death penalty was abolished in Great Britain in 1965 and in Northern Ireland in 1973, the JCPC routinely hears appeals in capital cases from various commonwealth countries, largely as a result of capital punishment laws instituted during the colonial era. In *The Queen* v. *Eduljee Byramjee* (1846), which I discussed in Chapter 1 of this book, the JCPC held that criminal appeals in capital cases should not be entertained because to do so would cause undue delay, resulting in cruelty toward the prisoner awaiting execution. In that instance, the JCPC also worried that lengthy appeals would undermine the deterrent effects of public executions, thus removing "all benefit to be expected from a public example."[38]

Over one hundred years later, similar issues were at stake in a series of cases from the Anglophone Caribbean. In *Riley* v. *Attorney General of Jamaica* (1982) the JCPC decided that a delay in execution while awaiting appeal does not in itself constitute excessive cruelty. In *Pratt and Morgan* v. *Attorney General of Jamaica* (1993), the JCPC reversed its previous opinion and declared that delays in execution greater than five years were "inhuman" and, as a result, unconstitutional.[39] The history of capital punishment in Jamaica is another instance of the shadow cast by a "receding past." Jamaica's capital punishment laws, like those of many other Caribbean nations, are holdovers from the colonial era when crimes such as murder carried mandatory death sentences.[40] There is, in this respect, an irony in the JCPC continuing to evaluate matters pertaining to capital cases. While the constitutions of the now independent nations protect human rights, including the right to life, specific pre-independence laws were "saved" from becoming obsolete under the new constitutions. As James Campbell notes, Jamaica's "constitution prohibited 'torture, inhuman or degrading punishment,' but a special savings clause in the document exempted existing forms of punishment from that requirement."[41] "With Britain moving toward abolition of capital punishment in the early 1960s and the Judicial Committee remaining Jamaica's highest court of appeal after independence," Campbell explains, "the savings clause was designed to protect the death penalty in Jamaica from future constitutional challenges."[42]

Within its narrowly circumscribed jurisdiction, as outlined in Chapter Seven of the Jamaican constitution, one of the main charges for the Privy Council is to consider constitutional questions, such as the constitutionality of capital punishment itself, related to civil or criminal matters. Further, the JCPC can also hear appeals in civil proceedings, "where in the opinion of the Court of Appeal the question involved in the appeal is one that, by reason of its great general or public importance or otherwise, ought to be submitted to Her Majesty in Council" (Ch. 7, Part II). While the type of appeals that the JCPC can hear is limited, therefore, the scope of matters over which it is able to exercise judgment is comparatively broad. The Privy Council typically hears cases of "great general or public importance" that have the capacity to shape the narrative of the law moving forward.[43]

According to Derek O'Brien, there are two primary reasons that the British Caribbean has retained the right to appeal to the Judicial Committee of the Privy Council, despite the advent of the Caribbean Court of Justice in 2005.[44] The first is "that its appellate jurisdiction is available at no cost to the governments of those countries that still subscribe to its jurisdiction."[45] The second reason, echoing Viscount Simon's statement referenced earlier, is "that it is composed of judges who are of the highest calibre and who are judicially independent, being free of the political influence and control that some of the region's governments have been accused of exerting over their national judges"[46].

The fiction of "pure law and justice" still exerts a profound influence over the narrative of the JCPC's legal interventions.

At present, the Caribbean cases represent the most significant international appeals before the Judicial Committee of the Privy Council.[47] Yet, despite these important cases, in the wake of decolonization, the JCPC's influence continues to wane. As this book has shown, however, even as the jurisdiction of the JCPC contracts, its legacy lives on in the various legal narratives it has cast.

Notes

Introduction

1 As Ian Watt reminds us, however, the concurrent rise of the nation and the novel also provides the foundations of individualism. According to Watt, individualism "posits a whole society mainly governed by the idea of every individual's intrinsic independence both from other individuals and from that multifarious allegiance to past modes of thought and action denoted by the word 'tradition'" (p. 60). While for Watt the novel is the aesthetic evidence of larger cultural tendencies toward individualism and progress (hence the popularity of the bildungsroman), Michael McKeon sees the novel as symptomatic of larger epistemological crises around the coherence of truth and representation. The mode of individualism that Watt and even McKeon describe as newly available to the Englishman, though, also has important intersections with the historically simultaneous expansion of colonialism. The kind of freedom that is the precondition for Watt's notion of individualism, for example, cannot be extricated from the rise of colonial and plantation economies. The aesthetic form of the novel and its signature individualist subject must therefore be situated within the concomitant rise of colonialism and slave economies globally. I take up the topic of individualism especially in Chapters 4 and 6, though it is relevant to my discussion throughout the volume.

2 See Diane Kirkby and Catherine Coleborne's *Law, History, Colonialism: The Reach of Empire* for a discussion of the centrality of empire to the development of modern law.

3 P. A. Howell uses the anecdote in the introduction of *The Judicial Committee of the Privy Council 1833–1876: Its Origins, Structure and Development.* Howell's text provides a thorough history and overview of the JCPC during the period considered in this volume.

4 L. Colley, *Britons: Forging the Nation, 1707–1837* (New Haven: Yale University Press, 2005), p. 6.

5 This is not to say that Britain became culturally homogenous after the Act of Union. "The sense of a common identity here did not come into being," Colley writes, "because of an integration and homogenization of different

cultures. Instead, Britishness was superimposed over an array of internal differences in response to contact with the Other, and above all in response to conflict with the Other" (p. 6).

6 Colley, *Britons*, p. 7.

7 See Lennard Davis's discussion of how the novel evolved in reaction to the legal proscriptions on anti-state narratives beginning in the thirteenth century. Likewise, Sue Chaplin argues that for "Britain in the nineteenth century, looking to the past helped consolidate a more unified notion of the cultural, national, and legal present" (pp. 808–809). Britons of the eighteenth and nineteenth centuries looked to the medieval period to provide an origin story for the nation, as well as for its literature and law. "During a period in which notions of national identity and unity had been severely tried," Chaplin explains, "this narrative sought to account for the birth of English law and of the English nation by removing the question of juridical origin from the constitutional maelstrom of the 1600s and casting it back into a more distant, politically safer if quasi-fictive past" (p. 809). The two-pronged invention of an origin story that served to locate both the law and literary culture in a shared narrative of national history cemented British notions of self, which in turn fueled the novels of the nineteenth century. As Chaplin shows, "national myths of the origin of a uniquely English body of law acquired immense hegemonic force in the Romantic era and their emergence and development is inextricably linked to the formation in this period of the idea of a unique English literary tradition with its own narrative of origin" (pp. 808–809).

8 The JCPC continues to adjudicate appeals from a small number of Commonwealth countries.

9 For a detailed history of colonial law, see Anand Banerjee's *English Law in India.*

10 The minimum requirement for suits on appeal to the Privy Council increased over time.

11 I discuss Hastings's judicial plan in greater detail in Chapter 3.

12 The colonial courts ended the practice of consulting pandits and muftis in 1864, shortly after the Queen's Proclamation in 1858.

13 Oyeronke Oyewumi makes a similar point about the invention of gender in the context of Nigerian law.

14 In practice, as Rankin notes, the JCPC shares personnel with the House of Lords, which in the nineteenth century was still the final court of appeals for England (p. 3).

15 The JCPC also heard appeals from various British constituencies such as the Church of England, the Channel Islands, veterinary doctors, etc.

16 G. Rankin, "The Judicial Committee of the Privy Council," *The Cambridge Law Journal*, 7, 1 (1939), 2, p. 3.

17 Ibid.

18 L. A. Benton, *Law and Colonial Cultures: Legal Regimes in World History, 1400–1900* (Cambridge: Cambridge University Press, 2002); *A Search for Sovereignty: Law and Geography in European Empires, 1400–1900* (Cambridge: Cambridge University Press, 2009).

19 *The Canadian Law Times, 37*, 9 (September 1917), p. 625.
20 See, for example, the discussions of a similar reordering of Indian temporalities in Chapters 3 and 5.
21 For an extended discussion, see Radhika Singha's *A Despotism of Law*.
22 J. Burbank, and F. Cooper, "Rules of Law, Politics of Empire," in *Legal Pluralism and Empires, 1500–1850* (New York: NYU Press, January 1, 2013), 261–277, p. 283.
23 Ibid.
24 Judicial Committee of the Privy Council, www.jcpc.uk/about/history.html
25 L. A. Benton, and R. J. Ross, *Legal Pluralism and Empires, 1500–1850* (New York: NYU Press, 2016), p. 8.
26 M. Sharafi, *Law and Identity in Colonial South Asia: Parsi Legal Culture, 1772–1947* (Cambridge: Cambridge University Press, 2016), p. 56. Dissenting opinions have, however, been allowed since the Judicial Committee Order of 1966.
27 R. De, "'A Peripatetic World Court' Cosmopolitan Courts, Nationalist Judges and the Indian Appeal to the Privy Council," *Law and History Review, 32*, 4 (November 1, 2014), 821–851, p. 832.
28 Interestingly, as De points out, the JCPC was "not bound by its own precedent and could reverse its own decisions in similar matters with ease" (p. 832). For this reason, each opinion was something of a sovereign pronouncement.
29 R. Ferguson, "The Judicial Opinion as Literary Genre," *Yale Journal of Law & the Humanities*, 2, 1 (1990), pp. 201–202.
30 Ferguson's essay builds on the work begun by Benjamin Cardozo on the literary language of judicial opinions in his foundational essay "Law and Literature," published in the *Yale Law Review* in 1925. Richard Posner also has a chapter entitled "Judicial Opinions as Literature" in *Law and Literature* (Cambridge, MA: Harvard University Press, 1988).
31 Ferguson, "Judicial Opinion," p. 205.
32 Ibid.
33 Ferguson, "Judicial Opinion," p. 207. In this respect, the judicial opinion shares a common feature with the developmental logic of the novel, as discussed in Chapters 2 and 4.
34 Ferguson, "Judicial Opinion," p. 207.
35 A. Ben-Yishai, *Common Precedents: The Presentness of the Past in Victorian Law and Fiction* (New York: Oxford University Press, 2015), p. 4.
36 For a slightly different reading of the law reports in which judicial opinions were disseminated, see Ayelet Ben-Yishai's *Common Precedents*. For Ben-Yishai, the "law report narratives, though varied, are usually abstract, miserly in detail, devoid of character descriptions, and can best be described as choppy or truncated. In other words, they are as distinct from the naturalized narratives of the period – often connected with the realist novel – as they can possibly be" (p. 22). While I do not disagree with Ben-Yishai's description

of the texture of the narratives, I see the complexities of plot and meaning as complementing the Victorian novel.

37 J. Muñoz, *Cruising Utopia: The Then and There of Queer Futurity*. Sexual Cultures (New York: New York University Press, 2009), p. 19.

38 Ibid., p. 20.

39 E. Sedgwick, and A. Frank, *Touching Feeling: Affect, Pedagogy, Performativity* (Series q) (Durham: Duke University Press, 2003). p. 8.

40 Ibid.

41 Ibid.

42 Ibid.

43 Jacques Derrida plays with the same dual meanings of "*appel*" in *The Politics of Friendship*.

44 P. Brooks, "Narrative Transactions - Does the Law Need a Narratology?," *18 Yale Journal of Law & Humanities, 1-28* (2006), p. 2.

45 A. G. Amsterdam, and J. S. Bruner, *Minding the Law* (Cambridge: Harvard University Press, 2009). p. 122.

46 Ibid., p. 135.

47 J. L. Austin's analysis of the performative force of the law is useful here. Pronouncing a couple married, for example limits the field of imaginative possibilities available to them. In turn, Foucault's discussion of the normative unit of the bourgeois family exemplifies how imaginative possibilities circumscribe material realities. Relatedly, Judith Butler, most directly in "Is Kinship Always Already Heterosexual?" argues that the goal of legal marriage profoundly limits the capacity to imagine alternative possibilities that lie outside of hetero- or homonormativity. It is this type of relationship between legal structures on the one hand, and imaginative possibilities on the other, that I am interested in probing.

48 J. B. Baron, "Law, Literature, and the Problems of Interdisciplinarity," *Yale Law Journal, 108,* 5 (January 1, 1999), 1059–1085, pp. 1064–1066. In Baron's analysis, the humanist approach views the study of literature as a means of injecting moral and emotional wisdom into law, which is otherwise understood as lacking in an appropriately ethical vision (1064). The hermeneutic school takes the position that legal analysis could benefit from the insights offered by literary theory (1065). Finally, the narrative scholars, mostly emerging from feminist and race studies, focus on the uses of storytelling within legal institutions in order to open a space for correcting systematic injustices within the law (1065).

49 Baron, "Law, Literature, and the Problems of Interdisciplinarity," p. 1062.

50 J. S. Peters, "Law, Literature, and the Vanishing Real: On the Future of an Interdisciplinary Illusion," *PMLA, 120,* 2 (2005), 442–453, p. 448.

51 Simon Petch provides a thorough overview of the scholarship on law and Victorian literature in "Law, Literature, and Victorian Studies."

52 U. Chandra, "Liberalism and Its Other: The Politics of Primitivism in Colonial and Postcolonial Indian Law," *Law & Society Review, 47,* 1 (March 1, 2013), 135–168, p. 136.

53 S. Morton, *States of Emergency: Colonialism, Literature and Law* (Ser. Postcolonialism across the Disciplines, 11) (Liverpool University Press, 2013), p. 3.

54 S. Ahmed, *Archaeology of Babel: The Colonial Foundation of the Humanities* (Stanford, CA: Stanford University Press, 2018), p. 18.

55 Ibid.

56 Ibid. See, also Tejaswini Niranjana's discussion of the colonial politics of translation in *Siting Translation: History, Poststructuralism and the Colonial Context.*

57 A fruitful model for bringing legal studies and postcolonialism together is emerging within the discipline of history. Recently, an expanding body of work on legal history has sought to provide a record of the cultural implications of colonial legal structures in South Asia. Scholars such as Mitra Sharafi, Rohit De, Lauren Benton, Elizabeth Kolsky, Martin Weiner, Radhika Singha, and others have laid the groundwork for historical analyses of colonial law. This scholarship examines topics such as local legal practices, differential applications of the law, or the historical evolution of specific legal regimes. While the historical context has important resonances across the humanities, however, equally significant work remains to be done through bringing legal studies into dialogue with postcolonial literary studies.

58 E. S. Anker, *Fictions of Dignity* (Ithaca: Cornell University Press, 2017), p. 13.

59 Anker aims her critique specifically at what she identifies as the postructuralist genealogy of postcolonial theory, dividing the field of postcolonialism into camps that either contest or endorse globalization. This framing of the critical terrain of postcolonialism, however, downplays the diversity of conversations among and across various strands of postcolonial discourse. Moreover, focusing on the question of postcolonialism's affiliation with poststructuralism does more to compartmentalize and contain the possibilities of postcolonialism rather than to engender dialogue across apparent sites of disagreement or divergence.

60 E.S. Anker, "Globalizing Law and Literature," in Meyler, B., and Anker, E. S. editors. *New Directions in Law and Literature* (New York: Oxford University Press, 2017), p. 212. Christine Krueger makes a similar point about the negative depiction of the law in literary analysis more broadly: Both legal and literary scholars (excepting, perhaps, literary historians) have tended to theorize law as an authoritarian, rule-bound, patriarchal disciplinary discourse in need of the antidote of mutltivoiced, subjective, and oppositional literary discourse. Alternatively, law and literature, particularly in New Historicist literary criticism and in Critical Legal theory, are understood as equally complicit in maintaining patriarchal bourgeois hegemony. (2) Krueger, however, argues for an interwoven practice of reading, such that the two discplines, including their well-developed and often divergent strategies, inform one another in a sustained and specific way.

61 Anker, "Globalizing Law and Literature," p. 218. As a literary alternative, Anker directs our attention to Nuruddin Farah's novel *Gifts*, which, she

suggests, "requires a significantly more ambivalent as well as balanced view of law and legality in the Global South" (213). Arguing that in practice the law is more "diffuse" than some theories of it might suggest, Anker looks to "an array of irregular, informal, bootlegged, and extrajudicial spheres of rule making, dominion, and exchange" as "deeply capacitating" examples of law in the Global South (212). For Anker, these "illegal profit centers and renegade authorities" function as alternative instances of the law, and, as such, she suggests that these "nonstate sovereignties are ripe for harnessing and manipulation in ways that escape the reach and parameters of neoliberalism – indexing the limits of neoliberalism as an analytic" (212). Despite an aura of subversive appeal, however, such a representation of postcolonial extralegal formations merely endorses derivative, and inherently less accountable, alternatives to the colonial and postcolonial state's capacity to exercise its power through the rule of law.

62 Moreover, as Alpana Roy remarks, "[f]rom a postcolonial perspective, it is clear that the portrayal of Western legal systems as superior has not been confined to history, but continues in contemporary legal thought in this era of postcolonialism" (329).

63 J. Muñoz, *Cruising Utopia: The Then and There of Queer Futurity* (Sexual Cultures) (New York: New York University Press, 2009), p. 4.

64 In his chapter entitled "Queerness as Horizon: Utopian Hermeneutics in the Face of Gay Pragmatism," Muñoz theorizes the concept of the "horizon" as a political imperative of utopian thinking. What Muñoz envisions is "a queerness that registers as the illumination of a horizon of existence" (25).

65 See, for example, Joseph Slaughter's *Human Rights, Inc.*, Colin Dayan's *The Law Is a White Dog*, and Wendy Hesford's *Spectacular Rhetorics*. Bernadette Meyler analyses these trends in her article "Law, Literature, and History: The Love Triangle," *UC Irvine Law Review*, 5, pp. 365–391.

66 Kieran Dolin's *Fiction and the Law*, for instance, traces the recurrence of legal themes in the nineteenth-century novel. In his wide-ranging study, Dolin argues "that a contextualized study of the fictional representations and appropriations of law, and of the institutions of writing and legal practice will materially enhance our understanding of the nineteenth-century culture and its dominant genre, the novel (4). *Legal Fictions* shares Dolin's interest in uncovering the shared logic that binds literary and legal texts. Lisa Rodensky's *The Crime in Mind* examines the psychological motivations of crime in literary and legal contexts.

67 J.-M. Schramm, *Atonement and Self-Sacrifice in Nineteenth-Century Narrative* (Cambridge: Cambridge University Press, 2012), p. 69.

68 J. H. Grossman, *The Art of Alibi: English Law Courts and the Novel* (Baltimore: Johns Hopkins University Press, 2002), p. 16.

69 My emphasis on narrative also speaks to the one-sidedness of the archive. Indian responses are not as readily available, and while it is important to note this fact, it is not something that can be resolved by turning to the archive.

70 G. Spivak, "The Rani of Sirmur: An Essay in Reading the Archives," *History and Theory*, 24.3 (1985), 247–272, p. 249.

71 Ibid., p. 251.

72 N. Z. Davis, *Fiction in the Archives: Pardon Tales and Their Tellers in Sixteenth-Century France* (Stanford, CA: Stanford University Press, 1987), p. 3.

73 Ibid.

74 In their ruling, the justices of the Indian Supreme Court argued that changing the prohibition on "unnatural acts" instituted by the colonial regime was a matter for the legislature rather than the judiciary.

75 See, for reference Foucault's *History of Sexuality*, Vol. 1 in which he discusses the transformation of acts into identities. While I am interested in rethinking Foucault's account insofar as he transposes his observations onto a historical change that is unique to Europe, I agree with his suggestion that juridical assessments about acts carry the kernel of some truth about identity even when the legal script concerns an act. This is perhaps what a literary reading of the law might add to our understanding of Foucault.

76 In invoking the performative, I mean to reference J.L. Austin's foundational work on the law's capacity to enact what it names and states. In particular, see Austin's discussion of "exercitives" and "verdictives" in Lecture XII of *How To Do Things with Words*.

77 J. Bentham, and C. K., Ogden, *Bentham's Theory of Fictions* (Ser. International library of psychology, philosophy, and scientific method) (Kegan Paul, Trench, Trubner, 1932). p. xvii.

78 R. A. Yelle, *Sovereignty and the Sacred: Secularism and the Political Economy of Religion* (Chicago: University of Chicago Press, 2018) p. 153.

79 A. Stoler, "Colonial Archives and the Arts of Governance," *Archival Science* 2.1-2 (2002), p. 97.

80 Ibid., p. 100.

81 Ibid., p. 90.

82 Blurring the line between fiction and theory, yet reminding us of the capacity of each to call subjects into being, Paul de Man remarks that "Literature as well as criticism – the difference between them being delusive – is condemned (or privileged) to be forever the most rigorous and, consequently, the most unreliable language in terms of which man names and transforms himself" (18).

83 W. Iser, *The Act of Reading: A Theory of Aesthetic Response* (Johns Hopkins University Press, 1978), p. 126.

84 Ibid.

85 G. Spivak, "Ethics and Politics in Tagore, Coetzee, and Certain Scenes of Teaching," *Diacritics, 32* (3/4) (2002), 17–31. p. 23.

86 For a different viewpoint that argues the centrality of empire in the literature of the period, see Bernard Porter's *Absentminded Imperialists*, Daniel Bivona's *Desire and Contradiction*, and Jane Bownas' *Thomas Hardy and Empire*.

87 W. Collins, *The Moonstone* (Oxford: Oxford University Press, 1750/2015), p. 2.

Chapter 1

1 T. Hobbes, *Leviathan* (New York: Penguin, [1668] 1982), pt. 1, ch. 13.
2 M. Foucault," The Body of the Condemned," in *Discipline and Punish: The Birth of the Prison*, trans. Alan Sheridan (Vintage Books, 1995), p. 29.
3 Bombay (India: State), *Gazetteer of the Bombay Presidency* (Bombay: Printed at the Government Central Press, 1877–1926), vol 14, pp. 345–346.
4 Ibid., 346.
5 Ibid.
6 Ibid.
7 Ibid., p. 348.
8 Ibid., p. 350.
9 Ibid.
10 E. Moore, *The Queen, on the Prosecution of the Bombay Government* v. *Eduljee Byramjee and Seventeen Others*, in *Reports of Cases Heard and Determined by the Judicial Committee on Appeal from the Supreme and Sudder Dewanny Courts in the East Indies*, vol. iii 1841–46 (London: V. & R. Stevens and G.S. Norton, 1846), pp. 468–487.
11 Moore, pp. 468–469. Eduljee Byramjee filed this petition on "behalf of himself and eight *Parsees*, also undergoing sentence of transportation at *Singapore*" (Moore, p. 469).
12 Ibid., p. 470.
13 In his testimony, the coroner, Dr. Leith, discusses the size and placement of the stab wounds that caused the death of Muncher-jee Hormusjee. The coroner's report seems to suggest one or two blades involved in the killing:

> all the wounds were in the space of four and a half inches, and in the neighborhood of the shoulder blade; the wounds varied in size from a little more than half an inch to an inch and a half; they appeared to have been inflicted by an instrument shaped like a knife with the broad end downwards; three of the wounds were parallel to each other, but did not penetrate the chest, the other three were parallel to each other. (9)

As the defense attorneys argued, it seems unlikely that a group of eighteen people stabbing would have created such a pattern of wounds. The coroner's testimony goes on to say that only two wounds were life-threatening: "I am of opinion that hœmorrhage from the wound which cut the intercostal vein, caused death; the other wound was dangerous, but was not necessarily a fatal wound" (9).
14 *A Detailed Report of the Proceedings on the Trial of the Eighteen Parsee Prisoners for Murder, Before the Supreme Court, Bombay, on Wednesday July 17, 1844* (London: Samuel Clarke, 1845), p. 111.
15 Ibid., p. 11.
16 Ibid., pp. 19–20.
17 Ibid., pp. 20–21.
18 The ability to hire their own attorneys speaks to these defendants' affluence, pointing to class stratifications within the group of defendants.

19 *Detailed Report*, p. 69.
20 Ibid., p. 99. China Budla was in fact represented by counsel, whom he shared with six other defendants.
21 Ibid.
22 Ibid., pp. 99–100.
23 Ibid., p. 113.
24 Ibid., p. 114.
25 Ibid., p. 9.
26 Ibid.
27 Ibid., p. 102.
28 Ibid., p. 98.
29 Ibid., p. 100.
30 In a different vein, it might also be possible to read the Indian hampering of British justice as a covert mode of resistance. This, however, is not my approach here. Rather, I want to highlight the ways in which a particular representation (portrait and proxy) of Indian behavior was authorized by the colonial record, which, in turn, authorized the practice of colonial justice.
31 C. Robin, *Fear: The History of a Political Idea* (New York: Oxford University Press, 2004), p. 2.
32 A. R. JanMohamed, *The Death-Bound Subject: Richard Wright's Archaeology of Death* (Durham: Duke University Press, 2005), p. 279.
33 See, also, Marx's discussion of death and slavery as the paradigmatic limit points of wage labor.
34 At this point in history, England was far from the imperial giant it would later become. Until the seventeenth century, England lagged behind its European competitors, who had the upper hand in colonial acquisitions and national treasure.
35 J. Robinson, *The Development of Modern Europe*, vol. 1 (UK: Ginn, 1929), p. 172. Letter from Jahangir to King James.
36 L. Colley, "Britishness and Otherness: An Argument," *Journal of British Studies, 31*, 4 (1992), p. 316. For a more sustained discussion of the relationship between colonial expansion and early British nationalism, see Linda Colley's *Britons: Forging the Nation, 1707–1837*.
37 S. Aravamudan, "Hobbes and America," in D. Carey and L. Festa (eds.) *Postcolonial Enlightenment: Eighteenth Century Colonialism and Postcolonial Theory* (New York: Oxford University Press, 2009), p. 59.
38 Ibid., pp. 40–41.
39 See Wallerstein, etc. In *Dominance Without Hegemony*, Ranajit Guha makes the argument that both colonial and nationalist bourgeoisie profited by way of dominating the subaltern classes in India. In Guha's argument, the bourgeoisie secured their dominance through force rather than consent, by suppressing and concealing modes and instances of peasant resistance. For Guha, the insecurity that provides the motivation for hegemony in Sassen's model, for example, is dealt with in India with more direct coercion. More recently,

Vivek Chibber, in *Postcolonial Theory and the Spectre of Capital*, refutes many of Guha's, and the broader subaltern school's, claims about the workings of capitalism in India. Chibber revisits Enlightenment universalism by arguing that Guha and others misdiagnose the effects of capitalism by dwelling on what he sees as the artificial differences in European and colonial efforts to incorporate the subaltern classes within the narrative of the rise of the bourgeoisie. For a response to many of Chibber's critiques, see Gayatri Spivak's review of Chibber's book in *Cambridge Review of International Affairs*, 27, 1, 2014.

40 S. Sassen, *Territory, Authority, Rights: From Medieval to Global Assemblages* (Princeton, NJ: Princeton University Press, 2008), pp. 96–97.

41 Ibid.

42 Ibid., pp. 98–99.

43 Ibid., p. 99.

44 Nathan Hensley engages in a related discussion when he examines Fitzjames Stephen's essays on Hobbes in the context of the Jamaica Rebellion and its aftermath. See "Form and Excess, Morant Bay and Swinburne," in Hensley's *Forms of Empire*.

45 J. Crimmins, "Bentham and Hobbes: An Issue of Influence," *Journal of the History of Ideas*, *63* 4(2002), 677–696, p. 680.

46 Ibid.

47 R. Esposito, *Communitas: The Origin and Destiny of Community*, trans. T. Campbell (Palo Alto: Stanford University Press, 2009), p. 23. In addition to Esposito, see Carl Schmitt's *The Leviathan in the State Theory of Thomas Hobbes*, Jacques Derrida's *The Beast and the Sovereign, Vol. 1* and Étienne Balibar's *Spinoza and Politics*.

48 Ibid.

49 Ibid., p. 27.

50 Ibid., p. 33.

51 B. Massumi, "The Future Birth of the Affective Fact: The Political Ontology of Threat," in *The Affect Theory Reader*, eds. M. Gregg, and G. Seigworth (Durham: Duke University Press, 2010), p. 61. Massumi's discussion of the futurity of the threat provides an interesting counterpart to Muñoz's utopianism as referenced in the Introduction.

52 Massumi, "The Future Birth of the Affective Fact," p. 63.

53 Ibid., p. 54.

54 Ibid.

55 Chapter 3 takes up the question of temporality with regard to the colonial courts' organization of time and history within a teleological narrative.

56 Hussain provides a very useful overview of the history of colonial jurisprudence.

57 British civil servants were encouraged to position themselves against not only Indian criminals, but British ones as well. Elizabeth Kolsky's account of white violence in the Empire provides a fascinating overview of the tensions between

the official narrative of the colonial project, and the white criminality it struggled to conceal. Of course, in terms of the law, there were different provisions for white and native criminality. Martin J. Weiner explores the racial dimensions of colonial law in *An Empire on Trial: Race, Murder, and Justice under British Rule, 1870–1935*.

58 M. J. Wiener, *An Empire on Trial: Race, Murder, and Justice under British Rule, 1870–1935* (Cambridge: Cambridge University Press, 2009), p. 132.

59 T. B. M. Macaulay, *The Complete Works of Lord Macaulay* (United Kingdom: Longmans, 1871), p. 433.

60 Ibid., pp. 433–434.

61 Also of note is the segregation of transported criminals. While Indian transports were sent to Southeast Asia, Australia was reserved for criminals of European ancestry: "it shall not be lawful for any such Court to order the transportation of any person, being a native of the East-Indies and not born of European parents, to the eastern coast of New South Wales, or any of the islands adjacent thereto" (*Asiatic Journal*, 269).

62 E. Kolsky, *Colonial Justice in British India* (Cambridge: Cambridge University Press, 2011), p. 109. Kolsky frames the construction and enforcement of colonial law around tensions between government officials and the sizeable non-official population of Europeans in India. Though official and non-official Europeans shared an interest in racialized protections under the law, as Kolsky shows, their interests were often at odds with one another.

63 For a detailed reading of the construction of colonial criminality and its significance to the ideology of the civilizing mission, see Upamanyu Mukherjee's *Crime and Empire*. Mukherjee's focus is primarily on literary representations of criminality. Though his approach is different, his project shares with mine a central concern with how legal structures intersect with the field of available imaginative possibilities for its subjects.

64 Clare Anderson argues in *Legible Bodies* that "The invention of thuggee was part of the orientalization of India, and a source of seemingly endless fascination to Europeans" (5). Kim Wagner takes a somewhat more ambivalent stance in her book on thuggee, suggesting that while exaggerated, the colonial reports of thuggee cannot be summarily dismissed (7). Amal Chatterjee, in his chapter entitled "Thugs," discusses thuggee as a mode of colonial representation.

65 R. Singha, *A Despotism of Law: Crime and Justice in Early Colonial India* (Delhi: Oxford University Press, 1998), p. 87.

66 Ibid., p. 95.

67 Ibid., p. 129.

68 Ibid., p. 84.

69 The campaign to suppress Thuggee was not without controversy. Singha notes that the campaign generated "institutional friction" between the executive and the judiciary, with each arm struggling for legal control (90).

70 Singha, *Despotism*, p. 85.

71 W. H. Sleeman, *Ramaseeana: Or a Vocabulary of the Peculiar Language Used by the Thugs* (Cambridge University Press, 2011), p. 13. Sleeman's account continues to fascinate, inspiring more contemporary popular accounts such as George Bruce's *The Stranglers* and Nicholas Myer's film *The Deceivers*, based on the historical figure of W. H. Sleeman. In *The Strangled Traveler: Colonial Imaginings of the Thugs in India*, Martine van Woerkens traces the Orientalist representation thuggee from the colonial era through more contemporary iterations such as *Indiana Jones.*

72 Sleeman, *Ramaseeana*, p. 21.

73 A similar pattern unfolds in my discussion of *The Moonstone* and the mystery genre in Chapter 4. In that chapter I show how the suggestion of Indian criminality affirms the certainty of British innocence.

74 Preeti Nijhar's excellent book *Law and Imperialism* maps out the coevolution of nineteenth-century British legal norms and the fear of colonial criminality. For example, she makes the case that:

> Bentham, who had effectively rendered the emblematic public execution redundant, also provided a detailed blueprint for the introduction of criminal justice institutions based on the model of the Panopticon and procedures both in England and abroad, in colonial jurisdictions (as later in the Andaman Islands). Thus, the penitentiary, the new police and the co-terminous changes in criminal jurisdiction, reflected the needs of the propertied classes to suppress imagined criminalities and to instill new forms of civility and discipline on an emerging class of urban criminals. (50)

Nijhar's text examines not only how British fears shaped colonial justice abroad, but also how bourgeois fears of urban criminality in newly industrial metropolitan centers in Britain drove revisions to the penal system at home.

75 Separation from society, where criminals held in isolation instead of being sentenced to work, emerged as a mode of punishment in Britain following American experimentation with this method of penal incarceration.

76 Britain is the only nation that transported criminals abroad (Yang, 185).

77 A. Yang, "Indian Convict Workers in Southeast Asia in the Late Eighteenth and Early Nineteenth Centuries," *Journal of World History, 14*, 2 (2003),179–208, p. 182.

78 Despite the obvious global reach of the project of empire, as Anand Yang points out, British discourse was reluctant to draw connections between various modes of unfree labor:

> Although the prevailing Southeast Asian labor system decisively shaped the colonial framework in which Indian convict labor became imperative, it was rarely factored into the British discourse about labor. Official discourse, in fact, shied away from highlighting the ties that bound together the different systems of coerced labor, almost as if colonial administrators were fearful of their advocacy of convict labor eroding the high moral ground that they had claimed by advocating the abolition of slavery in the region. The two forms of labor were nonetheless closely interrelated: the closing down of the slave trade (banned in theory by the British parliament in 1807) and the subsequent abolition of slavery in many areas of the region exacerbated labor shortages (182–183).

79 C. Anderson, "Execution and Its Aftermath in the Nineteenth-Century British Empire," in Ward, R. (Ed.). *A Global History of Execution and the Criminal Corpse* (Basingstoke, UK: Palgrave Macmillan, 2015), p. 387.
80 Ibid., pp. 388–389.
81 Yang, "Indian Convict Workers," p. 183.
82 Convict workers were not primarily hardened or habitual criminals (Yang 181).
83 Ibid., p. 180.
84 Ibid., pp. 188–190.
85 Ibid., p. 189.
86 Ibid., p. 193.
87 Anderson, "Execution and Its Aftermath," p. 391.
88 Anderson shows that the strategy of using penal transport to undermine political dissidence was used widely throughout the Empire, in response to various rebellions against slavery and colonialism.
89 M. Mann, "Dealing with Oriental Despotism: British Jurisdiction in Bengal, 1772–1793," in *Colonialism as Civilizing Mission: Cultural Ideology in British India*, eds. H. Fischer-Tiné and M. Mann (London: Wimbledon Publishing Company, 2004), p. 33.
90 Moore, *The Queen* v. *Eduljee Byramjee*, 470.
91 Ibid., pp. 471–473. At the same time, as attorneys for the opposition argued, the charter also asserts that in all indictments, informations, and criminal suits, and causes whatsoever, the said Supreme Court of Judicature, at *Bombay*, shall have the full and absolute power and authority to allow or deny the Appeal of the party pretending to be aggrieved, and also to award, order and regulate the terms upon which Appeals shall be allowed in such cases in which the said Court may think fit to allow such appeal. (474)
The controversy of course arises in the fact that the Charter seems to grant absolute power to both the Queen and the Supreme Court of Bombay to decide whether appeals may be heard. This contradiction is at the crux of the case at hand.
92 Ibid., p. 476.
93 Litigants, as well, frequently shopped for the most favorable forum for their claims.
94 Moore, *The Queen* v. *Eduljee Byramjee*, p. 480.
95 Ibid., p. 481. The Privy Council overturned the Eduljee judgment in 1887 in *In re A.M. Dillet*, a case originating from the British Honduras regarding the criminal conviction for perjury of a white British man as a result of his conduct in a property-related civil case.
96 Incidentally, the law did not apply in Scotland.
97 S. Waddams, *Law, Politics and the Church of England: The Career of Stephen Lushington (1782–1873)* (Cambridge: Cambridge University Press, 1992), p. 27.
98 As Preeti Nijhar notes, the prevailing British attitude toward Indians, criminal and otherwise, was one of paternalism. Although they were subject to the

force of the law, they were viewed as unfit to administer justice on their own behalf (102). Race was, of course, the primary factor in demarcating various levels of punishment under colonial law.

99 Moore, *The Queen* v. *Eduljee Byramjee*, p. 475.

100 Ibid., p. 485.

101 Ibid., p. 479.

102 E. Kolsky, *Colonial justice in British India* (Cambridge: Cambridge University Press, 2011), p. 31.

103 In tracing the rise of the colonial project alongside British modernity, Nasser Hussain makes a similar argument in *The Jurisprudence of Emergency* (pp. 22–32).

104 Moore, *The Queen* v. *Eduljee Byramjee*, p. 487.

105 In her overview of capital punishment across the British Empire, Clare Anderson notes that the implementation of death sentences varied considerably during the nineteenth century, both between Britain and the colonies, and between different colonies. Anderson shows that "in the colonies, gruesome forms of mutilation constituted an element of capital sentences for much longer than in Great Britain." Ideas about criminal corpses, Anderson shows, were founded on the principle of "colonial difference, a notion developed that subject peoples thought in particular and different ways about death, compared to Europeans, and this produced distinct and dramatic methods of execution". "Most significantly, though," Anderson argues, "it was the scale of judicial reprisals seen in Empire, including mass executions under martial law, which had no parallel in nineteenth-century Britain" (171). Through her compilation of colonial data, Anderson also reveals the unevenness of the application of domestic British legal reforms of capital punishment across the colonies.

106 M. Foucault, *Security, Territory, Population: Lectures at the College de France, 1977–1978*, M. Senellart (ed.), trans. G. Burchell (New York: Palgrave Macmillan, 2007), p. 1.

107 Dipesh Chakrabarty historicizes the Enlightenment's impact on colonial and postcolonial thought in *Provincializing Europe: Postcolonial Thought and Historical Difference* (Princeton University Press, 2009). Drawing on the contradiction between Enlightenment notions of universal humanism and the brutality of the colonial exercise of power, Chakrabarty writes, "The European colonizer of the nineteenth century both preached this Enlightenment humanism at the colonized and at the same time denied it in practice" (4). Of course, hierarchies of race, religion, nation, gender, etc. always occluded Enlightenment notions of the human.

108 Moore, *The Queen* v. *Eduljee Byramjee*, pp. 482–483. A similar sentiment was expressed by Lord Willingdon, the Viceroy of India, in 1932 regarding the deterrent effect of death sentences for "terrorists" agitating for Indian independence. (privycouncilpapers.org).

109 S. Waddams, *Law, Politics and the Church of England: The Career of Stephen Lushington (1782–1873)* (Cambridge: Cambridge University Press, 1992), p. 27.

110 Ibid., p. 28.
111 Ibid.
112 Hansard, March 27, 1832. https://api.parliament.uk/historic-hansard/commons/1832/mar/27/abolition-of-capital-punishments
113 C. Wynne, *The Colonial Conan Doyle: British Imperialism, Irish Nationalism, and the Gothic* (Westport, CT: Greenwood Press, 2002), p. 106.
114 J. O'Brien, *The Scientific Sherlock Holmes: Cracking the Case with Science and Forensics* (Oxford University Press, 2013), pp. 64–66.
115 George Edalji has been the subject of much recent attention, including Julian Barnes' 2005 novel *Arthur and George*, which was also the inspiration for an ITV miniseries. Catherine O. Frank examines the case in relation to questions of law and literature in "Narrative and Law." In the essay Frank discusses Conan Doyle's use of narrative omniscience in creating a reading public that was able to be empathetic to Edalji without undermining the rule of law. Focusing on the "world-creating potential" of narrative and law, Frank shows that "by comparing individuated, real experiences to a collective ideal, outsider narratives promise to reframe, or in some cases to authenticate, that vision by making it more inclusive" (57).
116 A.C. Doyle, "The Case of Mr. George Edalji," in *The Daily Telegraph* (January 11 and 12, 1907 [UK]). The story was also reprinted in various American newpapers including *The Washington Post* and *The New York Times.*

Chapter 2

1 Moore, *The Queen* v. *Eduljee Byramjee*, p. 478.
2 Ibid.
3 J. Slaughter, *Human Rights, Inc.: The World Novel, Narrative Form, and International Law* (New York: Fordham University Press, 2007), p. 4.
4 F. Moretti, *The Way of the World: The Bildungsroman in European Culture* (Verso, 1987), p. 6.
5 Moretti distinguishes between the "classification" and "transformation" types of novels. For the purposes of my discussion here, I am focusing on the "classification" aspect of the *Bildungsroman.*
6 F. Moretti, *The Way of the World*, p. 7.
7 Ibid.
8 Moore, *The Queen* v. *Eduljee Byramjee*, p. 482.
9 F. G. Kitton, *A Supplement to Charles Dickens by Pen and Pencil: Including Anecdotes and Reminiscences Collected from His Friends and Contemporaries* (United Kingdom: Frank Sabin, 1890), p. 6.
10 Shankar makes the point that the word "*thug*" entered the English language in India in the early nineteenth century from Hindi, where the word meant 'a cheat, swindler.'" In Hindi, the word is not associated with either systematic or ritualistic criminality nor does it refer to murder. Tracing the etymology of

the word, Shankar observes, "In the OED, the entry after *thug* is for the related word *thuggee*, whose meaning is given as '[t]he system of robbery and murder practiced by the Thugs.' … *Thuggee* and *thug* entered the English language, then, as identifications respectively of a monstrous and criminal 'system' and of those who were members of it" (98–99). As for W. H. Sleeman's purported dictionary of terms, as Shankar notes, many of them are ordinary words taken from Hindi, Hindustani, Telugu, and other languages.

11 W. H. Sleeman, *Ramaseeana: Or a Vocabulary of the Peculiar Language Used by the Thugs* (Cambridge University Press, 2011), p. 11.

12 Ibid.

13 Ibid., p. 7.

14 Ibid., p. 27.

15 Ibid., p. 13.

16 Ibid., p. 21.

17 Ibid.

18 The notion of India as timeless and ancient, lacking any firm divisions between modernity and the past is commonplace in novels and films from *A Passage to India, Slumdog Millionaire, Indiana Jones and the Temple of Doom*, etc. See Mrinalini Chakravorty's fascinating discussion of the stereotype in contemporary South Asian literature for a reading of how these historical ideas continue to reverberate in the present.

19 Sleeman, *Ramaseeana*, pp. 7–8.

20 S. Shankar, "Thugs and Bandits: Life and Law in Colonial and Epicolonial India." *Biography – An Interdisciplinary Quarterly, 36*, 1 (December 1, 2013): 97–123. p. 112.

21 M. Ní Fhlathúin, "The Making of a Master Criminal: The 'Chief of the Thugs' in Victorian Writings on Crime," in *Victorian Crime, Madness and Sensation*, eds. A. Maunder, and G. Moore (Ashgate, 2004), pp. 31–44.

22 Ibid., p. 38.

23 P. Meadows Taylor, *Confessions of a Thug* (1858/2001) (New Delhi: Rupa), p. 20.

24 Ibid., p. xi. *Kala pani*, or black water, was the term used to describe both the ocean and the fear of crossing the water. It was also the alternative name of the Cellular Jail on the Andaman Island penal colony, to which political dissidents were sent in the years following the Sepoy Rebellion.

25 Ibid.

26 Ibid., pp. xi, xiii.

27 Ibid., p. xiii.

28 Ibid.

29 Ibid., p. 1.

30 Ibid., p. 252–253.

31 Ibid., p. 2.

32 Ibid., p. 1.

33 Mary Poovey presents a different reading of Taylor's novel in "Ambiguity and Historicism: Interpreting *Confessions of a Thug.*" Poovey reads the novel as offering "an oblique critique of the East India Company and everything it represented: assumptions about the racial superiority of the English, the conviction that Christianity is morally superior to various Indian religions, and the belief that Western bureaucracy is more efficient and rational than its Eastern counterpart" (4). Poovey draws a distinction between the implied author and the real author of the novel, and focuses on the tension between these two positions. "'Taylor'/Taylor, the implied and real author" use "narrative parallels and textual contradictions to encourage readers to subvert the white narrator's 'eye of power.'" Poovey's interpretation of the novel is largely based on a psychological reading of both Taylor and the narrator, whom she sees as a double of Ameer Ali. Poovey identifies in Taylor an animating feeling of resentment toward the East India Company and the Government of India because he worked for the Nizam of Hyderabad and "felt jealous when he learned that a Company official, who enjoyed so much more power than he did, had earned the 'fame' of the discovery" of Thuggee (10). Ultimately, Poovey casts the novel as a critique of the East India Company that takes a more sympathetic stance toward Ameer Ali than would first seem apparent.
34 Taylor, *Confessions of a Thug*, p. 12.
35 Ibid., p. 23.
36 Ibid., p. 72.
37 Ibid., p 189.
38 Ibid., p. 493.
39 Ibid., p. 37.
40 Ibid., pp. 22–23.
41 See Chapters 5 and 6 for an extended discussion of adoption in the Indian and English contexts.
42 Taylor, *Confessions of a Thug*, p. 442.
43 Ibid., p. 443.
44 Ibid., p. 445.
45 Ibid., p. 446–447.
46 Ibid., p. 452.
47 Ibid.
48 Ibid.
49 Ibid.
50 Ibid.
51 Ibid., p. 42.
52 Ibid., p. 43.
53 Ibid., p. 432.
54 Ibid., p. 434.
55 Ibid.
56 Ibid., p. 261.
57 Ibid., p. 544.

58 Ibid., p. 325.
59 This is the only occurrence of the word "sympathy" in the novel.
60 J. Majeed, *Ungoverned Imaginings: James Mill's The History of British India and Orientalism* (Oxford England: Clarendon Press, 1992), p. 90.
61 Ibid., p. 89.
62 As Majeed notes, British views of the insurmountable heterogeneity of the subcontinent "formed the basis for justifying British rule itself." Such considerations were at the heart of a committee on Indian self-rule appointed by Lord Dufferin in 1888 (90). I take up the point about heterogeneity and uniformity in Chapter 3 as well in the context of caste.
63 Majeed, *Ungoverned Imaginings*, p. 88
64 Piya Pal-Lapinski notes, for example, that the novel was "avidly read by Queen Victoria herself" (31).
65 L. Edelman, "The Future Is Kid Stuff: Queer Theory, Disidentification, and the Death Drive," *Narrative, 6* 1 (1998), 18–30, p. 19.
66 Most were transported abroad or died in jail.
67 Taylor, *Confessions of a Thug*, p. 538.
68 As in its prior context, the marker of "thug" becomes a ready justification for racialized violence, by both state actors and private citizens. In "Thug Nation: On State Violence and Disposability," Robin D.G. Kelley argues that this logic of racialization and criminalization renders Black lives disposable. The evidence of this disposability for Kelley is that American society tolerates the routine killing with impunity of unarmed Black men and children including Trayvon Martin, Michael Brown, Jordan Davis, Freddie Gray, Eric Garner, Terence Crutcher, Tamir Rice, and so many more. The term also continues to be used by the American state to criminalize political protest. For example, on May 29, 2020, President Donald Trump used the term to describe protesters against the police killing of George Floyd in Minneapolis, Minnesota.
69 See P. Collins's *Dickens and Crime.*
70 S. Grass, "Narrating the Cell: Dickens on the American Prisons," *The Journal of English and Germanic Philology, 99* 1 (2000), 50–70, p. 51
71 J. Alber, *Narrating the Prison: Role and Representation in Charles Dickens' Novels, Twentieth-Century Fiction, and Film* (Youngstown, NY: Cambria Press, 2007), p. 6.
72 Collins cautions against reading Dickens as too much of a reformist, and points to several passages in Dickens's body of work that "illustrate the harsher side of his attitude to criminals" (90).
73 P. Collins, *Dickens and Crime (Cambridge Studies in Criminology*, ed. L. Radzinowicz) (London: Macmillan, 1965), p. 91.
74 After 1834, returning from transportation ceased to be punishable by death (*The Newgate Novel* 25).
75 C. Dickens and E. Rosenberg, *Great Expectations: Authoritative Text, Backgrounds, Contexts, Criticism* (New York: Norton, 1999), p. 9.
76 F. Moretti, *The Way of the World: The Bildungsroman in European Culture* (Verso, 1987), p. 16.

77 Ibid.
78 Dickens, *Great Expectations*, pp. 10–11.
79 Ibid., p. 18.
80 Ibid., p. 17.
81 In "Spectacularizing Crime: Ghostwriting the Law" Peter Hutchings provides a historical context for this shift toward the subjectivity of the criminal. As the focus of criminal punishment shifted from torture and death to prison and rehabilitation, the target of discipline changed from the body to the subjectivity of the criminal:

> In demonstrating the end of one régime of spectacular corporeal punishment which was to be replaced with a discretely humane incarceration and, as the argument goes, a generalized disciplining of bodies in their scarification and dismemberment before the law, Foucault gives an account of a withdrawal of punishment from a public, spectacular domain into a no less public and yet also private sphere of the prison. It is an account too of the displacement of punishment's point of application from the body to a newly formed subjectivity, interpellated by the disciplinary régime. (30–31)

Pip's tendency to psychologically identify with the criminal can be read as evidence of the shift from disciplining bodies to cultivating and shaping subjectivities.
82 Dickens, *Great Exptectations*, pp. 75–76.
83 Ibid., p. 241.
84 The bildungsroman's investment in centering the normal that Franco Moretti points out is important in this triangulation. Pip and Magwitch, each in their own way, confirm their normality through their triangulation with the bourgeois reading public.
85 Dickens, *Great Expectations*, p. 259.
86 Ibid.
87 G. Moore, *Dickens and Empire: Discourses of Class, Race, and Colonialism in the Works of Charles Dickens* (Burlington, VT: Ashgate Press, 2004), pp. 15–16.
88 Kim Wagner explores the relationship between thuggee and phrenology in "Confessions of a Skull: Phrenology and Colonial Knowledge in Early Nineteenth-Century India." In her article she examines seven skulls held in the Medical School of the University of Edinburgh. "The story of the seven men and their skulls," Wagner argues, "is also the story of the complex correlation between colonial knowledge and the science of phrenology in early nineteenth-century British India" (28). The article uncovers the fascinating stories of the individual skulls, as well as the larger context of phrenology through which they came to be housed at the University of Edinburgh. Wagner has a series of articles on thuggee, in which she examines the history and representation of thuggee.
89 Newgate prison in London was the scene of public executions and torture, and prisoners' fates were documented in the infamous Newgate Calendar.

90 Dickens, *Great Expectations*, p. 131.
91 Laura Gillingham reads the Newgate novel as part of a larger trend to focus on heroic agency within the nineteenth-century novel. Her discussion of the tension between representing the criminal's individualism as well as the social dimension of crime is particularly interesting.
92 K. Hollingsworth, *The Newgate Novel, 1830–1847: Bulwer, Ainsworth, Dickens & Thackeray* (Detroit: Wayne State University Press, 1963), pp. 13–14.
93 In "Twisting the Newgate Tale," Juliet John relates the popularity of Newgate novels to the transformational power of mass media. Focusing on *Oliver Twist* in particular, she reads "the interrogation of the potential of popular culture as a vehicle of power," and shows how the genre is responsible for "the infiltration of 'official' culture by popular cultural modes" (140).
94 H. Worthington, *The Rise of the Detective in Early Nineteenth-Century Popular Fiction* (Houndmills, Basingstoke, Hampshire: Palgrave Macmillan, 2005), p. 7.
95 K. Hollingsworth, *The Newgate Novel, 1830–1847*, p. 27.
96 Ibid.
97 Ibid.
98 R. Filmer, and J. P. Sommerville, *Patriarcha and Other Writings* (Cambridge, England: Cambridge University Press, 1991), p.12.
99 Ibid.
100 This is particularly interesting because the genealogical element of Indian criminality, as Taylor represents it, needs no biological connection between father and son.
101 Dickens, *Great Expectations*, p. 259.
102 Ibid.
103 J. E. Marlow, "English Cannibalism: Dickens after 1859," *Studies in English Literature, 1500–1900, 23*, 4 (1983), 647—666, p. 661.
104 Ibid.
105 Ibid.
106 E. Said, *Culture and Imperialism* (New York: Knopf, 1993), p. xv.
107 Ibid.
108 Ibid., p. xvi.
109 Building on Said's discussion, Hyungji Park claims "Magwitch's return to London in some ways represents the haunting of the English middle class by the criminal and colonial infrastructure upon which Victorian prosperity was built" (708). Identifying the colonial theme as crucial to the development of the sympathetic criminal, Park reads Magwitch's willingness to break the rules of his exile as constitutive of his "'paternal' humanity" (724).
110 The racial politics of criminal transportation are also important here, as the penal colony of Australia was reserved for white criminals.
111 Filmer, *Patriarcha*, p. 12.

112 As Ankhi Mukherjee notes, cinematic adaptations – from David Lean's to Alfonso Cuarón's – restage the "protagonist's avowedly cosmopolitan epiphanies," though Cuarón shifts the setting from the English marshes and London to the Gulf Coast of Florida and New York City. Importantly, Cuarón also forgoes the "dated center-periphery dialectic" and Pip's (or Finn's) travel abroad (111).

113 As Jan-Melissa Schramm rightly observes in *Atonement and Self-Sacrifice in Nineteenth-Century Narrative*, "the target of [Dickens's] critique is primarily utilitarianism (though, inevitably, his satire exaggerates its weaknesses)" (21). Dickens's critique of utilitarianism in the British context would place him at odds with the kinds of legal solutions the government was seeking to implement in India at the same time, further marking the inconsistencies between domestic and foreign policies.

114 Moretti, *The Way of the World*, p. 16.

115 This point is similarly made clear in *Jane Eyre*, one of the most iconic *Bildungsromane* of the Victorian era. At the beginning of the novel, Jane compares herself to a "rebel slave" and a "savage," while by the end of the novel she refuses to become part of a "seraglio" or "harem"and distinguishes herself from a "suttee" (9–11; 229; 233).

116 Slaughter, *Human Rights, Inc.*, p. 99.

117 Ibid., p. 4.

118 Ibid., p. 29.

119 Ibid., p. 94.

120 H. Park, "Criminality and Empire in *Great Expectations*," *English Language and Literature, 49* 4 (2003), 707–729, p. 710.

121 P. Joshi, "Mutiny Echoes: India, Britons, and Charles Dickens's *A Tale of Two Cities*," *Nineteenth-Century Literature, 62* 1 (2007), 48–87, p. 51.

122 Quoted in Park, "Criminality and Empire," p. 710–711.

123 V. K. Acharya, *Thugs of Hindostan* (Mumbai: Yash Raj Films, 2018).

124 Ibid.

125 See, for example, *Mangal Pandey: The Rising*, *The Legend of Bhagat Singh*, and *Manikarnika*, an action-packed film about the Rani of Jhansi whose kingdom, like Begum Sumroo's as discussed in Chapter 5, was annexed by the British.

126 L. Hunt, *Measuring Time, Making History* (The Natalie Zemon Davis Annual Lecture Series) (Budapest: Central European University Press, 2008), p. 51, 63.

127 This is a fundamental aspect, as well, of Sleeman's representation of thuggee as akin to ancient European sacrificial practices.

Chapter 3

1 R. Koselleck, and K. Tribe, *Futures Past: On the Semantics of Historical Time* (New York: Columbia University Press, 2005), p. 197.

2 In Percy Shelley's "Ozymandias," for example, the space and time are mapped onto one another in the phrase "I met a traveller from an antique land," where "antique" stands in for foreign.

3 J. Mill, *The History of British India* (United Kingdom: Baldwin, Cradock, and Joy, 1820), p. 155.
4 Ibid.
5 Ibid., p. 156.
6 Ibid., pp. 156–157.
7 Ibid., p. 159. In accordance with his Utilitarian principles, Mill's critique of caste is part of a larger attempt to streamline and rationalize the law. The connection I draw between caste and precedent on the one hand, and Mill's *History* and the logic of the Privy Council on the other, might seem contradictory in light of Mill's utilitarianism and the Privy Council's invocation of the rule of precedents. Yet the utilitarian critique of precedents within the common law, I would argue, has more to do with their vagueness and imprecision than their connection to the past and future, which is the focus of my analysis here. For a detailed discussion of Mill's *History* in relation to his historical and theoretical context, see Javed Majeed's *Ungoverned Imaginings.*
8 Ibid. Mill's analysis of the "terror" of religion is related to the relationship between terror and power that I discuss in the previous two chapters. If the colonial government used the terror of law and punishment, Mill suggests early Hindu rulers used religion for similar purposes.
9 R. Koselleck, and K. Tribe, *Futures Past: On the Semantics of Historical Time* (New York: Columbia University Press, 2005), p. 197.
10 Ibid., p. 16.
11 D. Davis, "A Historical Overview of Hindu Law," in *Hinduism and Law: An Introduction* (Cambridge University Press, 2010), p. 25
12 S. Ahmed, *Archaeology of Babel: The Colonial Foundation of the Humanities* (Stanford, California: Stanford University Press), p. 19.
13 Ibid.
14 R. Sturman, "Marriage and Family in Colonial Indian Law" in *Hinduism and Law: An Introduction*, ed. T. Lubin, D. Davis, and J. Krishnan, (Cambridge University Press, 2010).
15 L. A. Benton, *Law and Colonial Cultures: Legal Regimes in World History, 1400–1900* (Cambridge, UK: Cambridge University Press, 2002), p. 139.
16 Ibid.
17 See Roy and Swamy for a detailed discussion of motivation and process of adopting religious law in India. Roy and Swamy also provide an excellent overview of the challenges the British faced, including the influx of personal law cases in the colonial courts, the backlogs and delays created by the number of cases, and the difficulties posed by adhering to the Brahminic code books.
18 T. Roy, and A. Swamy, *Law and the Economy in Colonial India* (Chicago: University of Chicago Press, 2016), p. 18.
19 Because it is the basis of the case I examine in this chapter, *Ramaswamy Aiyan v. Venkata Achari,* I will focus primarily on Hindu law. However, the colonial administration of Muslim law was fraught with similar issues. See, for example, Benton on Qadi law in *Law and Colonial Cultures* and Teena Purohit's *The Aga Khan Case: Religion and Identity in Colonial India.*

20 R. Rocher, "The Creation of Anglo-Indian Law," in *Hinduism and Law: An Introduction*, ed. T. Lubin et al. (Cambridge: Cambridge University Press, 2010), p. 80.
21 Ibid.
22 Ibid.
23 D. Davis, (2010) "A Historical Overview of Hindu Law" in *Hinduism and Law: An Introduction*. Cambridge University Press, p. 25.
24 David Washbrook's "Law, State and Agrarian Society in Colonial India" presents a different perspective. Washbrook argues that the implementation of personal law served a strategic economic purpose, which was to "keep society in the structure of relations in which the colonial authority had found it and to construe the moral problems of the present against standards taken directly from the past" (652).
25 R. Lariviere, "Justices and Paṇḍitas: Some Ironies in Contemporary Readings of the Hindu Legal Past," *The Journal of Asian Studies, 48* 4 (1989), p. 757.
26 Ibid., pp. 759–760.
27 J. Duncan, M. Derrett, "The Administration of Hindu Law by the British," *Comparative Studies in Society and History, 4* 1 (1961), 10–52, p. 37.
28 L. Rocher, *Studies in Hindu Law and Dharmaśāstra*, ed. Donald R. Davis Jr. (Anthem Press, 2012), p. 662.
29 R. Rocher, "The Creation of Anglo-Indian Law," in *Hinduism and Law: An Introduction*, ed. T. Lubin, et al. (Cambridge: Cambridge University Press, 2010), p. 88.
30 R. Sturman, "Marriage and Family in Colonial Indian Law," in *Hinduism and Law: An Introduction*, ed. T. Lubin, D. Davis, and J. Krishnan (Cambridge University Press, 2010), p. 9.
31 Ibid., p. 7
32 In *The Stillbirth of Capital*, Siraj Ahmed makes a similar point with regard to the Orientalist construction of Indian property laws. Orientalism, Ahmed shows, "helped fix a rule of property that could turn rent toward war and buried that rule so deeply in India's supposed ancient traditions that its modern logic became invisible" (164–165).
33 L. Rocher, *Studies in Hindu Law and Dharmaśāstra*, ed. Donald R. Davis Jr. (Anthem Press, 2012), p. 636.
34 T. Roy, and A. Swamy, *Law and the Economy in Colonial India* (Chicago: University of Chicago Press, 2016), p. 88.
35 See "Hindu Conceptions of Law," in *Studies in Hindu Law and Dharmasastra.*
36 Ibid., p. 90.
37 See Anindita Ghosh's "Revisiting the 'Bengal Renaissance': Literary Bengali and Low-Life Print in Colonial Calcutta" for a necessary corrective to the notion that the elite *bhadralok* monopolized the literary market in colonial Bengal.
38 A. Mukhopadhyay, *Behind the Mask: The Cultural Definition of the Legal Subject in Colonial Bengal (1715–1911)* (New Delhi: Oxford University Press India, 2012), p. 81.
39 Ibid.

40 See, for example, Gayatri Spivak, Guha, Chatterjee, Sumanta Bannerjee, Tapti Roy, etc.

41 For a detailed analysis of the role of the colonial administration in temple practices and administration, including the collection of taxes and fees, see Arjun Appadurai's *Worship and Conflict under Colonial Rule: A South Indian Case*. In particular, Chapters 3 and 4 provide an excellent discussion of the transition from Company oversight to judicial intervention in the religious and financial practices of temples.

42 Appadurai writes about a similar nineteenth-century temple dispute involving *mirāsi* rights:

> in the discussion of the *mirāsi* question, the fundamental problem was the contradiction between the "extractive" function of British rule (with its abrogation of local economic rights and relationships) and the "investive" functions of British rule (with its wish to preserve local economic rights and privileges in the interests of stability and productivity). This led to a process of "codification" of local rights and privileges, which was necessarily both arbitrary (because the original economic nexus of the relationships in question had been severely disturbed) and stimulative of conflict (because individuals and groups used those fractured categories in order to achieve, consolidate, or legitimize claims in the present). This is the explanation of the turmoil around *mirāsi* positions. (148)

As Appadurai explains, temple *mirāsi* rules impacted revenue collection and were thus of interest to the British. Where possible, the colonial government sought to standardize *mirāsi* rights through codified rules in order to enable more efficient flows of revenue.

43 Roy and Swamy, *Law and the Economy in Colonial India*, p. 167.

44 B. Cohn, *Colonialism and Its Forms of Knowledge: The British in India* (Princeton: Princeton University Press, 1996), p. 65.

45 For a discussion of the dual representation of India as primitive and despotic, see Amal Chatterjee's *Representations of India, 1740–1840: The Creation of India in the Colonial Imagination.*

46 M. Mukherjee, *India in the Shadows of Empire: A Legal and Political History, 1774–1950* (New Delhi: Oxford University Press, 2010), pp. 99–100.

47 Ibid., p. 99.

48 Along similar lines, Nicholas Dirks, in *Castes of Mind: Colonialism and the Making of Modern India*, examines how caste came to signify the ancient essence of Indian civilization:

> [C]aste, as we know it today, is not in fact some unchanged survival of ancient India, not some single system that reflects a core civilizational value, not a basic expression of Indian tradition. Rather, I will argue that caste (again, as we know it today) is a modern phenomenon, that it is, specifically, the product of an historical encounter between India and Western colonial rule … it was under the British that 'caste' became a single term capable of expressing, organizing, and above all 'systematizing' India's diverse forms of social identity, community, and organization. This was achieved through an identifiable (if contested) ideological canon as the result of a concrete encounter with colonial modernity during two hundred years of British domination. In short, colonialism made caste what it is today. (5)

49 S. Bayly, *Caste, Society and Politics in India from the Eighteenth Century to the Modern Age* (New York: Cambridge University Press, 1999), p. 98.
50 A. Appadurai, "Number in the Colonial Imagination," in *Orientalism and the Postcolonial Predicament: Perspectives on South Asia*," ed. C. Breckenridge and P. van der Veer (Philadelphia: University of Pennsylvania Press, 1993) p. 117.
51 Ibid.
52 P. G. Price, "Acting in Public versus Forming a Public: Conflict Processing and Political Mobilization in Nineteenth Century South India," in *Religion and Public Culture: Encounters and Identities in Modern South India*, eds. J. J. Paul, and K. E. Yandell (Abingdon, U.K.: Routledge, 2013), p. 44.
53 Ibid., p. 45.
54 Ibid.
55 As Appadurai also notes, the process of counting was also "generative" of caste based identities (117).
56 E. Moore, "*Ramaswamy Aiyan* v. *Venkata Achari*," in *Reports of Cases Heard and Determined by the Judicial Committee on Appeal from the Supreme and Sudder Dewanny Courts in the East Indies, Vol. IX* (London: V. & R. Stevens and G.S. Norton, 1863), p. 348.
57 R. Mawani, "Law as Temporality: Colonial Politics and Indian Settlers," 4 *UC Irvine Law Review* (2014) p. 71.
58 Ibid.
59 Ibid., p. 73.
60 Ibid., p. 75.
61 Ibid.
62 E. Moore, "*Ramaswamy Aiyan* v. *Venkata Achari*," in *Reports of Cases Heard and Determined by the Judicial Committee on Appeal from the Supreme and Sudder Dewanny Courts in the East Indies, Vol. IX* (London: V. & R. Stevens and G.S. Norton, 1863), p. 358.
63 Ibid. p. 352.
64 A. Barua, "Metaphors of Temporality: Revisiting the 'Timeless Hinduism' versus 'Historical Christianity' Antithesis," *The Harvard Theological Review, 104* 2 (2011), 147–169, p. 148.
65 Ibid.
66 Ibid., p. 158.
67 Moore, *Ramaswamy Aiyan* v. *Venkata Achari*, p. 360.
68 Ibid., p. 361.
69 Ibid., p. 364.
70 U. Kalpagam, *Rule by Numbers: Governmentality in Colonial India* (London: Lexington Books, 2014), p. 141.
71 Ibid., p. 142.
72 Ibid., p. 143.
73 For a fascinating study of the global standardization of time and its relationship to literature, see Adam Barrows's *The Cosmic Empire of Time: Modern Britain and World Literature.* Vanessa Ogle's *The Global Transformation of*

Time places the standardization of time in relation to the processes of globalization.

74 U. Kalpagam, *Rule by Numbers*, p. 148.

75 Ibid., p. 153.

76 Moore, *Ramaswamy Aiyan* v. *Venkata Achari*, p. 370.

77 Ibid., p. 376.

78 See also the discussion of Islamic temporalities in Chapter 5.

79 Moore, *Ramaswamy Aiyan* v. *Venkata Achari*, p. 378.

80 Ibid., pp. 364–365.

81 Ibid., p. 365.

82 R. Rocher, "The Creation of Anglo-Indian Law," in *Hinduism and Law: An Introduction*, ed. T. Lubin et al. (Cambridge: Cambridge University Press, 2010), p. 85.

83 Ibid., p. 87.

84 Ibid.

85 Ibid., p. 85.

86 An important precedent to *Ramaswamy Aiyan* v. *Venkata Achari*, for example, was the 1845 case of *Namboory Setapaty* v. *Kanoo-Colanoo Pullia*. In this case the Privy Council refused to resolve the litigants' complaints, but reserved for itself the right to adjudicate matters of caste.

87 Moore, *Ramaswamy Aiyan* v. *Venkata Achari*, p. 388.

88 A. Ben-Yishai, *Common Precedents: The Presentness of the Past in Victorian Law and Fiction* (New York: Oxford University Press, 2015), p. 3.

89 Ibid., p. 37.

90 R. Rocher, "The Creation of Anglo-Indian Law," p. 86.

91 The caste system was relevant to an array of other laws and regulations. From the designation of certain castes as criminal in the Criminal Tribes Act, to the heightened rigidity of caste in marital choices, to the sexual enforcement of newly defined terms of caste purity, caste served to regulate the field of choices exercised over a broad swathe of Indian life. Caste purity was, and continues to be, secured through policing and regulating desire, sexuality, and, ultimately, sociality at large. In this sense, caste restrictions worked to further consolidate the marital and reproductive norms that I discuss in Chapter 5. And, as marital and sexual norms became more rigid, it follows that social relations more broadly came to be increasingly routed through caste relations as well.

Chapter 4

1 T. Todorov, "The Typology of Detective Fiction," in *The Poetics of Prose* (Ithaca, NY: Cornell University Press, 1995), p. 44.

2 F. Moretti, "Clues," in *Signs Taken for Wonders* (New York; Verso, 1983), p. 138.

3 Ibid., pp. 137–138.

4 Quoted in R. Thomas, "Detection in the Victorian Novel", in *The Cambridge Companion to the Victorian Novel*, ed. by D. David (Cambridge: Cambridge University Press, 2001), pp. 169–191, p. 179.
5 D. A. Miller, *The Novel and the Police* (Berkeley, CA: Univ. of California Press, 1989), pp. 49–50.
6 Ibid., p. 42.
7 Ibid., p. 34.
8 W. Collins, *The Moonstone* (Oxford: Oxford University Press, 1868/2015), p. 1.
9 Ibid.
10 Ibid., p. 2.
11 Ibid.
12 Ibid.
13 Ibid.
14 Ibid., pp. 2–3.
15 Ibid., p. 3. The novel folds the Mughal era into the broader construct of "Mohammedan rule," drawing a continuous line between various geographical, cultural, and temporal contexts.
16 Ibid., p. 4.
17 Ibid.
18 Ibid., p. 6.
19 Ibid.
20 Ibid., p. 33.
21 Ibid., pp. 188; 54.
22 Johannes Fabian's discussion of the ways in which geographical space differentiates temporality is relevant to the discussion here. Similarly, Reinhard Koselleck demonstrates how ideological narratives about time work to create spaces of modernity, while correspondingly exiling others to the past.
23 Collins, *The Moonstone*, p. 76.
24 Interestingly, the novel does not provide independent corroboration of Ezra Jennings's solution of the mystery. The novel hinges upon Jennings's reliability in his narration of events. Dr. Candy, whom Jennings accuses of having administered the opium without Franklin Blake's permission, has since been disabled and cannot provide his own narrative. It is therefore interesting that Collins's puts the reader in the position of having to rely upon, and trust, a socially marginalized figure such as Jennings. This could be read as an intervention into the presumed ease with which Godfrey Ablewhite would be "able" to get away with his theft because he is "white." Collins's recurrent sympathetic portraits of such figures as Limping Lucy, who expresses a queer desire to run away with Rosanna Spearman and Ezra Jennings, whose racial hybridity is both the source of revulsion and the sign of his reliability, suggest that *The Moonstone* cannot be neatly packaged as an unambiguous purveyor of typical stereotypes. Collins's political motivations and interventions are, at best, however, overdetermined.

25 In the historical parallel, Prince Albert had the Koh-i-noor diamond re-cut in Amsterdam.
26 For an interesting discussion of the blackface scene as well as other instances of racial hybridity in the novel, see John Glendening's "War of the Roses: Hybridity in *The Moonstone*."
27 Collins, *The Moonstone*, p. 464.
28 Ibid., p. 465.
29 Ibid.
30 Ibid., p. 466
31 Ibid.
32 Quoted in L. M. Goodlad, *The Victorian Geopolitical Aesthetic: Realism, Sovereignty, and Transnational Experience* (Oxford: Oxford University Press, 2017), p. 141.
33 John R. Reed, "English Imperialism and the Unacknowledged Crime of *The Moonstone*. *Clio* 2, 3 (1973): 281–290, p. 288.
34 L. Nayder, "Robinson Crusoe and Friday in Victorian Britain: 'Discipline,' 'Dialogue,' and Collins's Critique of Empire in *The Moonstone*." *Dickens Studies Annual, 21* (1992), 213–231, pp. 215–216.
35 U.P. Mukherjee, *Crime and Empire: The Colony in Nineteenth-Century Fictions of Crime* (New York: Oxford University Press, 2003), p. 177.
36 Ashish Roy, "The Fabulous Imperialist Semiotic of Wilkie Collins's *The Moonstone*." *New Literary History, 24*(3) (1993), 657–681, p. 658.
37 Ibid., p. 666.
38 R. Thapar, *Somanatha, the Many Voices of a History* (New Delhi: Penguin, Viking, 2004), p. ix.
39 Ibid., p. 164.
40 Ibid., p. 11.
41 Ibid., p. 207.
42 The notion of "Muslim rule" itself reflects the kind of oversimplification characteristic of colonial representations of Indian history. As Thapar notes, "as is usual with rulers of any religious persuasion, the rule varied in quality and intention." "Phrases such as 'Muslim rule' and 'Hindu rule' are," she argues, "historically speaking inappropriate, since much more was involved than the religion of the ruling class, although it was significant in some situations" (164).
43 Thapar, *Somanatha*, 166.
44 Ibid., p. 172.
45 Ibid., p. 174.
46 I make a similar point with respect to the elision of British interests in the case of *Ramaswamy Aiyan* in chapter three.
47 Thapar, *Somanatha*, p. 170.
48 Ibid., pp. 171–172.
49 Collins, *The Moonstone*, p. 466.
50 Ibid.

51 Manavalli makes a similar point in her claim that "the text subtly deconstructs itself" through the "disconcerting analogy between Herncastle's theft of the gem at Seringapatam and that of the military officer in Aurengazeb's army" (75). "Through these more subliminal than overt textual linkages" Manavalli argues, "the British officer Herncastle becomes fused with the figure of the 'rapacious' Muslim invader." For Manavalli, the text's overt claims to an anti-imperialist agenda are undermined by the comparison between Herncastle and Aurangzeb's army.

52 K. Manavalli, "Collins, Colonial Crime, and the Brahmin Sublime: The Orientalist Vision of a Hindu-Brahmin India in The Moonstone." *Comparative Critical Studies*, 4(1) (2007), 67–86, p. 72. See Chapter 3 for a discussion of the legal and social overtones of the type of Brahminization Manavalli identifies.

53 Ibid.

54 Ibid., p. 78.

55 See Chapter 3 for a discussion of how colonial courts and the JCPC used orientalist texts that made the ancient past legible to the modern legal apparatus.

56 T. Todorov, "The Typology of Detective Fiction," in *The Poetics of Prose* (Ithaca, NY: Cornell University Press, 1995), p. 44.

57 For a different approach to detective fiction, narrative and the law, see Peter Brooks's "Clues, Evidence, Detection: Law Stories." Brooks discusses how clues in a narrative function as a "retrospective prophecy," or "a construction of the story of the past by way of its outcome, what it was leading to." For Brooks, "[i]t is in the peculiar nature of narrative as a sense-making system that clues are revealing, that prior events are prior, and causes are causal only retrospectively, in a reading back from the end" (15). In this respect, clues function both as a prophecy of the future, as well as a confirmation of the past when the story is read from the viewpoint of the ending.

58 Todorov, "The Typology of Detective Fiction, p. 45.

59 If narrative is one aspect of detection, scientific investigation was equally important to the Victorian imagination. For a fascinating discussion of science and detection, see Lawrence Franks's *Victorian Detective Fiction and the Nature of Evidence*.

60 See Laura Marcus's "Detection and Literary Fiction."

61 M. Currie, *About Time: Narrative Fiction and the Philosophy of Time* (Cambridge: Cambridge University Press, 2012), p. 88.

62 Ibid.

63 Ibid., p. 89.

64 Ibid., pp. 89–90.

65 Ibid., pp. 103.

66 J. Mehta, "English Romance; Indian Violence." *The Centennial Review*, 39(3) (1995), 611–657, p. 620.

67 Ibid.

68 Ibid., p. 618.

69 Ashish Roy, "The Fabulous Imperialist Semiotic of Wilkie Collins's *The Moonstone*." *New Literary History*, 24(3) (1993), 657–681, p. 657.
70 Collins, *The Moonstone*, p. 2.
71 Ibid., p. 3.
72 Ibid.
73 Ibid.
74 British Library, India Office Records, Mss Eur B276, p. 5.
75 Ibid., pp. 5–6.
76 Collins, *The Moonstone*, p. 4.
77 Lauren Goodlad notes that "Collins prepared for *The Moonstone* by reading Indian history in the Athenaeum library" (115), and Melissa Free adds that Collins's research for the novel has recently been published:

> Collins' s research for *The Moonstone*, conducted in 1867, in which the story began to appear in serial form in *All The Year Round*, has largely survived. Stored at Princeton in the Parrish Collection, it has just been published for the first time (see Baker). Listing as source material the *Encyclopaedia Britannica* (8th ed.); a *History of India*; a biography of the general, Sir David Baird, who led the Siege on Seringapatam; a book on gemstones; and a letter solicited from John William Shaw Wylie, member of a distinguished Anglo-Indian family and of the Indian Civil Service, Collins's "notes suggest that he intended at first" – I would say, from the first – "to emphasize the Indian aspect of his materials." (347)

78 Y. Siddiqi, *Anxieties of Empire and the Fiction of Intrigue* (New York: Columbia University Press, 2007), p. 24.
79 Ibid.
80 Ibid., p. 25.
81 Collins, *The Moonstone*, p. 17.
82 Ibid. Lillian Nayder reads the same scene differently. Nayder emphasizes the fact that the Indians rescued the boy from dire conditions in London, and argues that Collins uses the scene to critique the English for turning a blind eye toward the suffering of their own children. In her reading,

> The Indians use the English boy for their own purposes - to foresee the arrival of the moonstone in Yorkshire; but they do not ill-use him. They treat the boy better than do his fellow Englishmen, who allow children like him to live in marketplaces and sleep in baskets. It is left to the ostensibly savage Brahmins to remove the "hungry, ragged, and forsaken" child from the wilds of London. In this portrait of Anglo-Indian relations, Collins exposes the savagery of the English class system rather than that of the Brahmins. (Nayder, "Robinson Crusoe and Friday in Victorian England 222)

Nayder's broader argument about the novel as a whole also highlights what she identifies as Collins's anti-imperialism.

83 Ibid., p. 18.
84 K. Singh, *Ranjit Singh: Maharajah of the Punjab* (New Delhi: Penguin, 2001), p. 27.
85 Ibid., p. 221.
86 A. Anand, and W. Dalrymple, *Koh-i-Noor: The History of the World's Most Infamous Diamond* (New York: Bloomsbury, 2017), p. 146.

87 Ibid., p. 133. There is an interesting parallel between the reasoning employed by Singh's Sikh advisors and the colonial state in the cases of both Maharaja Duleep Singh and David Ochterlony Dyce Sombre, as discussed in Chapter 5 of this volume.
88 Ibid., pp. 167–168.
89 Ibid., p. 168.
90 Ibid., p. 177.
91 British Library, India Office Records, Mss Eur F 213/23, p. 159.
92 Anand and Dalrymple, *Koh-i-Noor*, p. 200.
93 British Library, IOR, Letter from Lord Dalhousie to John Hobhouse, MSS Eur/F213/24, p. 131.
94 Anand, & Dalrymple, *Koh-i-Noor*, p. 185.
95 The discussion of adoption and inheritance in Chapters 5 and 6 of this book also resonates with Duleep Singh's dispossession of land and family.
96 British Library, IOR, Mss. Eur. F/213/24, p. 134.
97 Anand, & Dalrymple, *Koh-i-Noor*, p. 188.
98 Ibid., p. 243.
99 British Library, IOR F 236/486. See British Library, IOR L/PS/6/514 for a catalog of Rani Jindan's jewels. The catalog lists over 525 significant items of jewelry.
100 In her letter to her son, contained in the India Office Records, Rani Jindan makes a concerted mention of British superiority, ostensibly to appease the censors whom she realized were monitoring her correspondences with her son.
101 British Library, IOR R/1/1/44; R/1/1/46.
102 British Library R/1/1/44 no. 397.
103 Anand, & Dalrymple, *Koh-i-Noor*, p. 268.
104 Maharaja Duleep Singh's tumultuous life has been the subject of several biographies, novels, and films. See, for instance, Navtej Sarna's *The Exile* and Kavi Raz's recent film *The Black Prince.*
105 Collins, *The Moonstone*, p. liii.
106 Ibid.
107 Ibid.
108 Melissa Free reads this statement differently. Free sees Collins as endeavoring "to explore in *The Moonstone* not psychology (the influence of circumstance on human beings) but action: the impact of individuals, and their societies – character, that is – on history – or circumstance" (344). While I agree that "action" is an important object of Collins's analysis, I do not see it as divorced from psychology. Rather, I see "action" as the outcome of psychological desires and motivations. Free also sees a corresponding "move in authorial concern away from subjectivity toward accountability, from personal susceptibility to personal responsibility." It is not clear, however, how such accountability plays out in the text. Niketa Narayan points out that some of the questions might be attributable to confusion over what the term "character" means in this context (791).

109 F. Moretti, "Clues," in *Signs Taken for Wonders* (New York: Verso, 1983), p. 143.
Sundeep Bisla makes a very different argument about the mystery novel in general and *The Moonstone* in particular:

> The mystery novel is In type of protest novel, a protest bemoaning the loss of the author's perpetual proprietary right. Far from being conclusively silenced, a certain conception of the author took up residence, in defiance of the Lords and of late-eighteenth-century legal discourse, in the mystery, where we find it happily residing today. (179)

Distinguishing between the "author-as-creator" and "author-as-disseminator," Bisla situates the novel within evolving Victorian attitudes toward privacy (192). Bisla further reads the colonial elements of the novel discursively rather than literally or historically (201).

110 For a Foucauldian reading of *The Moonstone*, see D.A. Miller's iconic "From Roman Policier to Roman-Police: Wilkie Collins's *The Moonstone*".

111 Moretti, "Clues," p. 145.

112 In Chapter 1 I address the evolution of criminal punishment, both in England and India.

113 J. H. Grossman, *The Art of Alibi: English Law Courts and the Novel* (Baltimore: Johns Hopkins University Press, 2002), p. 4.

114 For a related discussion, see Chapters 1 and 2 on criminality in this volume.

115 Moretti, "Clues," p. 138.

116 Ibid.

117 Ibid.

118 Ibid.

119 Ibid., pp. 138–139.

120 Ibid. p. 155

121 Carlo Ginzburg makes a related point about the process of hunting for clues and narrative teleology in detective fiction.

122 N. Sargent, "Mys-Reading the Past in Detective Fiction and Law." *Law and Literature, 22*(2) (2010), 288–306, p. 289.

123 Collins, *The Moonstone*, p. 54.

124 Ibid., p. 33.

125 Sargent, "Mys-Reading the Past," p. 289.

Chapter 5

1 A. A. Moin, *The Millennial Sovereign: Sacred Kingship and Sainthood in Islam* (New York: Columbia University Press, 2012), pp. 3–4.

2 Ibid., p. 4.

3 D. Gilmartin, 4. "Imperial Sovereignty in Mughal and British Forms." *History and Theory, 56*, 1 (March 1, 2017), 80–88, p. 83.

4 Moin, *The Millennial Sovereign*, p. 212.

5 Ibid., p. 216.
6 Throughout its history, and especially under Akbar's rule, the Mughal court was religiously diverse, and in society various religions coexisted on the subcontinent. Moin notes that much twentieth-century scholarship characterizes the changes instituted by Shah Jahan as evidence of "an explicit break from the 'un-Islamic' ways of Akbar and Jahangir," but, as he shows, the historical record is more complicated. "If the emperor was such a champion of Islamic purity," Moin argues, "it is puzzling that he threw his weight so completely behind his free-thinking son Dara Shikoh rather than his shari'a-minded one, Aurangzeb. Dara Shikoh was well known for his passionate pursuit of a unified understanding of Islam and Hinduism derived from the metaphysics of Sufism and Vedanta" (212–214). Rather than viewing Shah Jahan's rule as a firm break with previous generations, therefore, Moin attends to the "significant threads of continuity in the manners and modes of sacred kingship through the seventeenth century and later" (213).
7 Ibid., p. 216.
8 Ibid., p. 217.
9 This is not to say that each of these cultural/racial/religious positions did not have internally coherent structures of normativity, but rather that none had reached hegemonic stature across the subcontinent.
10 Gilmartin, "Imperial Sovereignty in Mughal and British Forms," pp. 84–85.
11 Michael Fisher notes the year of her birth as 1741/53, while others such as Alka Hingorani use 1750/51. A range of dates appear in the several biographical sketches of the Begum, and she seems to have made no attempt to record her early history.
12 Once again, there is much speculation, but little is known about Walter Reinhardt Sombre. Sombre's name has been documented variously as Walter Reinhardt, Walter Reiner, Johann Reiner and Walter Somer. Some writers have attributed his name to a sobriquet based on his somber countenance, while others suggest that it is a variant of Sommers, an alias he may have taken on after having slaughtered several British soldiers in the service of Kassim Ali. Reinhardt's national origins are similarly uncertain, and he is documented variously as a French, German, British, Austrian, and Luxembourger soldier over the course of his time on the subcontinent.
13 W. P. Andrew, *India and Her Neighbors* (New York: George Munro, 1878), p. 80.
14 In his biographical sketch of the Begum, Brijraj Singh identifies Reinhardt's first "common-law wife" as Bahaar. He uses the same designation of "common-law wife" to describe the Begum, noting that it "was not at all unusual for Europeans in eighteenth-century India to have two or more common-law wives or concubines called *bibis*. The custom was accepted by both Indians and Europeans, and *bibis* enjoyed not only social acceptability but also many legal rights" (14–15).
15 Andrew, *India and her Neighbors*, p. 80.

16 For a detailed nineteenth-century history of the Begum, see Firminger *Bengal, Past and Present: Journal of the Calcutta Historical Society*, Vol. 1.

17 In his *Refutation*, David Dyce Sombre raises the question of Georgiana's illegitimacy. Correspondences between David and various friends and acquaintances suggest Dyce might have fathered Georgiana with a Muslim woman.

18 Indeed, as William Dalrymple notes in his review of a biography of Dyce Sombre by Michael Fisher, "contrary to the professions of faith made by her officers, she chose to convert from Islam to Catholicism and appealed directly to the Pope to send a chaplain for her court. By the time the intriguingly named Father Julius Caesar turned up in Sardhana from Rome, the begum had already begun to build the largest cathedral in northern India, in a style that promiscuously mixed baroque and Mughal motifs, with a great classical dome rising from Mughal squinches decorated with honeycombed Persian murqanas" (Dalrymple, *The Observer*, July 31, 2010).

19 Gilmartin, "Imperial Sovereignty in Mughal and British Forms," p. 87.

20 Ibid., pp. 86–87.

21 Spivak (1985) makes a similar point about reading the absences in historical records.

22 See Guha (1999) where he famously argues the connection between speculation, rumor, and the circulation of subaltern dissent in India around the revolt of 1857. Guha's argument is resonant here because the 'uncontrollable' aspects of rumors about insurgency allowed for rebels, elite nationalists and British colonialists alike to construct narratives suitable to their position. The Begum's person is similarly invented in order to serve as alibi for various ideological positions, those represented by British women, the patriarchal colonial apparatus, as well as the Indian attempt to subvert these.

23 See Chapters 1 and 2 for a discussion of Sleeman's role in the campaign to suppress *thuggee.*

24 W. H. Sleeman, *Rambles and* Recollections *of an Indian Official, Vol. 2* (London: Archibald Constable & Company, 1893), p. 397.

25 Ibid., p. 385.

26 Ibid., p. 398.

27 R. Heber, *Narrative of a Journey through the Upper Provinces of India from Calcutta to Bombay, 1824–1825, Vol. 2* (London: John Murray, 1873), p. 278; G. Hewett, *Private Record of the Life of General Sir George Hewett* (Newport: W. W. Yelf, 1840), p. 56.

28 D. O. D. Sombre, *Mr. Dyce Sombre's Refutation of the Charge of Lunacy Brought against Him in the Court of Chancery* (Paris: David Ochterlony Dyce Sombre, 1849), p. 6.

29 See, for example, Gayatri Spivak's 'Can the Subaltern Speak,' Sen (2002) and Radhika Singha's *A Despotism of Law.*

30 E. Roberts, *Scenes and Characteristics of Hindostan, With Sketches of Anglo-Indian Society* (London: J.L. Cox & Sons, 1825), pp. 156–158.

31 Jenny Sharpe's *Allegories of Empire* (1993) is still one of the most comprehensive analyses of the construction of English femininity in the service of Empire. Sharpe makes the claim that imperial logic invoked normative models domesticity and chastity in order to justify the civilizing and protectionist claims of colonialism that cast the colony as a threat to English femininity. Sharpe illustrates how such narratives circulated in England, and were internalized by colonial actors especially at times of crisis such as the 1857 Rebellion.

32 References to the Begum's clothing abound in English representations of her. While she is usually described as wearing "masculine" attire, it is difficult to discern whether this was actually the case, or if it indicates an English unfamiliarity with various Indian styles of clothing. For example, Michael Fisher cites Lady Nugent's description of the Begum's clothing that was "'more like a man's than a woman's'" (27). In this instance, her dress consisted of "trousers of cloth of gold, with shawl stockings, and Hindoostanee slippers; a cloth of gold kind of dress with flaps to it, coming a little below the knees . . . and abundance of shawls wrapped about her in different ways'" (27). Portraits of the Begum dressed in this manner and smoking a hookah, Fisher suggests, may convey "her intentional adoption of a more traditionally masculine royal demeanor" (27). Yet, as Abraham Eraly observes, descriptions by seventeenth- and eighteenth- century travel writers such as Jean de Thevenot and Niccolao Manucci document the clothing of Mughal women as "virtually the same as that of men" and royal women often "with the emperor's permission" wore "a turban adorned with an aigrette of gems" (139). According to Manucci, "there are dancing-women who have the same privilege." Sumroo's adoption of the turban thus might be more of an assertion of her sovereign independence than a performance of gender non-conformity. It is also possible to read the Begum's demeanor as an indication of courtliness rather than of gender as such. For a detailed discussion of Mughal clothing and customs, see Eraly's *The Mughal World: Life in India's Last Golden Age*. Rosalind O'Hanlon's "Manliness and Imperial Service in Mughal North India" provides a thorough overview of the role of masculinity in the Mughal court.

33 For a nuanced reading of the concept of the stereotype and its historical origins, see Mrinalini Chakravorty's *In Stereotype*. Chakravorty argues that the stereotype plays a profound and amibivalent role within processes of consumption and self-conception. As a "cultural prosthetic that, like a fetish, obscures by reanimating the material and the pscychic investments it engenders," the stereotype propels past associations into the present (27). In this regard, the stereotype functions much like a legal precedent, enabling the endless recasting of the past into the imagination of the future.

34 D. Ghosh, *Sex and the Family: The Making of Empire* (Cambridge: Cambridge University Press, 2006), p. 160.

35 Brijraj Singh writes of the Begum's "multiculturalism" in "Crossing Boundaries: The Life of Begum Samru."

36 Michael Fisher (2004) provides an excellent overview of the strategic uses to which the Begum put her different kinship-like alliances. Fisher details how the Begum invoked kinship relations not only with her designated heirs, but also with her courtiers, other Mughal rulers, Catholic officials, and even the English. In particular, Fisher draws attention to "the circumstances and choices that went into the formation of the 'families' she made through the deployment of kinship terms rather than biology or legal bonds" while exploring "the political and cultural implications of the asymmetrical familial relationships she created" (96).

37 The Begum, during her lifetime, submitted a will declaring her wishes to deed her property to Dyce Sombre upon her death. The British government raised no objection to the transfer until after the Begum's death, at which point they nullified her will (Moore 106).

38 Sombre, D. O. D., *Refutation*, p. 374.

39 Ibid.

40 *The English Reports. Vol. XIV: Privy Council III.* (Containing Moore, P.C. Vol. 8–12).
A. Wood Renton, Esq., editor (London: Stevens and Sons Ltd., 1901), p. 484.

41 Sombre, D. O. D, *Refutation*, p. 375.

42 Ibid., p. 376.

43 See Chapter 3 for a discussion of the various linguistic and religious traditions of the colonial courts. During the Begum's lifetime, Muslim law was used in the colonial courts to resolve matters of personal law.

44 E. Moore, *Troup et. al.* v. *The East India Company and Dyce Sombre* v. *The East India Company*, in *Reports of Cases Heard and Determined by the Judicial Committee on Appeal from the Supreme and Sudder Dewanny Courts in the East Indies*, Vol. vii 1857–1860 (London: V. & R. Stevens and Sons, 1860), p. 106.

45 Sections 2 and 3 of the act read as follows:
"2. The Criminal Courts shall not take cognizance of any offence prior to 27th January, 1836, unless specially empowered.
3. No Civil Court shall take cognizance of any claim previously adjudicated on by a competent Court."

46 See "An Agreement Between George Dempster Guthrie, Esq., On the part of the Honorable East India Company, and the Begum Sombre" in Dyce Sombre et al., *Dyce Sombre's Refutation* (1849). The Agreement consolidates the deal – bartering recognition for protection – the Company and the Begum agreed upon.

47 Sombre, *Refutation*, p. 361. For a detailed record of the East India Company's dealings with the Begum, see Sutherland (1873), pp. 349–359.

48 Ibid., p. 363.

49 Ibid., p. 364.

50 Ibid., p. 369.

51 H. M. Elliott, *Memoirs on the History, Folk-lore, and Distribution of the Races of the North Western Provinces of India: Being an Amplified Edition of the Original Supplemental Glossary of Indian Terms, Volume 1* (London: Trübner & Company, 1869).
52 Sombre, *Refutation*, p. 519.
53 E. Moore, *Troup et. al.* v. *The East India Company and Dyce Sombre* v. *The East India Company*, in *Reports of Cases Heard and Determined by the Judicial Committee on Appeal from the Supreme and Sudder Dewanny Courts in the East Indies*, Vol. vii, 1857–1860 (London: V. & R. Stevens and Sons, 1860), p. 108.
54 Ibid.
55 Larkins, the administrator of Dyce Sombre's estate, died in 1856.
56 H. Cowell, *G.C.W. Forester and Others* v. *The Secretary of State for India in Council*, in *The Law Reports: Supplemental Indian Appeals: Being Cases in the Privy Council on Appeal from the East Indies, Decided Between March, 1872, and November, 1873, and Not Reported in Moore's Indian Appeals* (United Kingdom: Incorporated Council of Law Reporting for England and Wales, 1880), p. 13.
57 Ibid. Interestingly, the same "legal dictum that 'no distinction can be drawn between the public and the private property of an absolute Chief'" was cited as a justification for the refusal by the British government to return the portion of Duleep Singh's estate that he claimed was private as well (Pensionary and Other Claims of Maharaja Dalip Singh, BL R1/1/46 p. 18)
58 Cowell, *Forester* v. *Secretary of State for India*, p. 21.
59 Ibid., p. 23.
60 Zamindaris often calculated dates using fiscal calendars, which might account for the discrepancy. See Betty Joseph's discussion of the rani of Burdwan (134).
61 Cowell, *Forester* v. *Secretary of State for India*, p. 24. Shah Alam II continued to rule until his death in 1806, though he was considerably weakened, especially after 1803 when the British conquered Delhi.
62 Ibid., p. 29.
63 Ibid., p. 32.
64 Dyce Sombre would, in any case, have been the biological heir of Zuffur Yuab Khan, who was his maternal grandfather.
65 Ibid.
66 Stoler (1989) elaborates on the state's effort to introduce Victorian morality into the scene of what it saw as the debauchery of colonial sexual practices.
67 W. Dalrymple, *White Mughals: Love and Betrayal in Eighteenth-Century India* (Penguin Books, 2004), p. 41.
68 Ibid.
69 Cheryl Harris offers what is still the most cogent reading of race and private property in "Whiteness and Property", *Harvard Law Review* 106(8).
70 G. Hewett, *Private Record of the Life of General Sir George Hewett* (Newport: W. W. Yelf, 1840), p. 56.

71 M. H. Fisher, *The Inordinately Strange Life of Dyce Sombre: Victorian Anglo-Indian MP and 'Chancery Lunatic'* (India: C. Hurst, 2010), p. 27.

72 G. Spivak, 'The Rani of Sirmur: An Essay in Reading the Archives,' *History and Theory* 24.3 (1985): 247–272, p. 254. David Ochterlony had several Indian concubines with whom he had at least six children. One of his descendants was George Dyce, David Dyce Sombre's father. Toward the end of his life, Ochterlony was rebuffed by the East India Company for a position he took in a local revolt. Ochterlony "retired to Begum Sombre's mansion in Meerut, where he soon expired" (Fisher, *The Indordinately Strange Life of Dyce Sombre*, pp. 31, 41).

73 Spivak, "Rani of Sirmur," p. 263.

74 Ibid., p. 266.

75 Ibid., p. 249.

76 Ibid., p. 267.

77 Ibid., p. 249.

78 B. Joseph, *Reading the East India Company 1720–1840: Colonial currencies of gender* (New Delhi: Orient Longman, 2006), p. 127.

79 Ibid., p. 125.

80 Ibid., p. 129.

81 Ibid., p. 145.

82 Ibid., p. 147.

83 The backdrop of Queen Victoria's rule must also be highlighted in terms of the divergent narratives about Indian and English women and their fitness for governance.

84 D. Ghosh, *Sex and the Family: The Making of Empire* (Cambridge: Cambridge University Press, 2006), p. 154.

85 U. Dalal, 'Femininity, State and Cultural Space in Eighteenth-Century India', *The Medieval History Journal, 18,* 1 (April 1, 2015), 120–165, p. 122.

86 G. Spivak, 'The Rani of Sirmur: An Essay in Reading the Archives', *History and Theory* 24.3 (1985): 247–272, p. 250. See, also, Jon Wilson's "Anxieties of distance: codification in early colonial Bengal," Nicholas Dirks' "From Little King to Landlord: Property, Law and the Gift under the Madras Permanent Settlement," and Mithi Mukherjee, *India in the Shadows of Empire: A Legal and Political History, 1774–1950.*

87 I. Chatterjee, *Unfamiliar Relations: Family and History in South Asia* (New Brunswick, NJ: Rutgers University Press, 2004), p. 14.

88 M. Sreenivas, "Conjugality and Capital: Gender, Families, and Property under Colonial Law in India," *The Journal of Asian Studies, 63*(4) (2004), 937–960, p. 941.

89 Ibid.

90 Ibid. For a discussion of the transition from land grants to private property, see Nicholas Dirks's "From Little King to Landlord: Property, Law, and the Gift under the Madras Permanent Settlement."

91 In 1834, the Court of Directors for East India Company enacted a policy in which "sanctioning the adoption of an heir should be the exception, not the rule":

> In isolated cases the right of adoption had done no harm; but its frequent repetition in states, where the disappearance of all blood-heirs was proof positive of the degeneracy of the race and the corruption of the Government, only served to intensify the evils of misgovernment that were becoming the scandal of India" (Boulger 180)

This policy brought the inheritance law governing Indian aristocracy into alignment with their English counterparts, for whom adoption was not recognized.

92 M. Fisher, *The Inordinately Strange Life of Dyce Sombre: Victorian Anglo-Indian MP and 'Chancery Lunatic'* (India: C. Hurst, 2010), pp. 226–227.
93 Ibid., pp. 209–210.
94 Ibid., p. 230.
95 Ibid., p. 248.
96 —. *Prinsep and the East India Company* v. *Dyce Sombre and Others* in *Reports of Cases Heard and Determined by the Judicial Committee and the Lords of His Majesty's Most Honourable Privy Council* (United Kingdom: W. T. Clarke, 1856), p. 238.
97 Ibid., p. 237.
98 Fisher, *The Inordinately Strange Life of Dyce Sombre*, p. 247.
99 Ibid., p. 297.
100 Ibid., pp. 288–289.
101 The same justices would preside over *Troup* v. *East India Company* a year later.
102 Mary Ann Troup and Georgiana Solaroli, David's two sisters, were also named in the suit.
103 Moore, *Prinsep and the East India Company* v. *Dyce Sombre and Others*, p. 281.
104 Ibid., p. 282.
105 Ibid., p. 242.
106 Ibid., p. 240.
107 Ibid., p. 241.
108 Ibid., p. 243.
109 Ibid., p. 261.
110 Historical accounts of Mary Anne are far less flattering, describing her as a flirt and as "mad." One account warned of her plans to "entrap" an elder Duke "into marriage by sharing his bed and conceiving his child" (Fisher 149–150).
111 Moore, *Prinsep and the East India Company* v. *Dyce Sombre and Others*, p. 248.
112 Ibid. p. 299. The Counsellors' desire to confirm history as the primary arbiter of truth resonates with my discussion of history and temporality in Chapters 3 and 4.
113 Contemporary scholars continue to revile Dyce Sombre, including in explicitly racialized terms. In her review of Fisher's book, for example, Mary Ellis Gibson marvels that "Jervis married Dyce Sombre, despite his obesity, mixed

ancestry, and philandering." "Why Dyce Sombre imagined that a charming flirt, who had made her way socially on the strength of musical talent," she continues, "would submit to his notion of wifely virtue – a close approximation of purdah – is to me beyond comprehension, unless indeed he had lost touch with reality" (365–367).

114 M. Fisher, *The Inordinately Strange Life of Dyce Sombre* (2010), p. 325.

115 Ibid.

116 British Library, IOR/Z/E/4/15/S984: 1837–1839.

Chapter 6

1 G. Eliot, & D. Carroll, *Silas Marner: The Weaver of Raveloe* (London: Penguin Books, 1861; 1996), p. 169.

2 Ibid. p. 172. In Sarah Abramowicz's clever reading of the same scene, "the novel presents these two fathers as embodying two opposed modes of defining parenthood: law, on the one hand, and, on the other, the child's remembered narrative of her early experience" (4). In this reading biological kinship is the basis for law, while adoption is allied with literature.

3 Adoption remained informal and not legally controlled in Britain until 1920. However, as many scholars have noted, houses for orphans and other such institutions of schooling and care were founded as early as the eighteenth century when Methodists began social reform initiatives. Thomas Coran established the first Foundling Hospital in London in 1739. The first modern adoption law is one implemented in 1851 by the Commonwealth of Massachusetts from whence some of the founding principles of legal adoptions in the West – for example the principle to follow the 'best interests of the child' – still derive.

4 The examples of orphans, foundlings and waifs in ninetieth-century English literature are legion. From Charlotte Bronte's *Jane Eyre,* to Heathcliff in *Wuthering Heights* to numerous central figures in Dickens's books: Oliver Twist, David Copperfield, Esther in *Bleak House,* Pip in *Great Expectations* and others.

5 M. Novy, *Reading Adoption: Family and Difference in Fiction and Drama* (Ann Arbor, MI: University of Michigan Press, 2007), p. 125.

6 The case I make for the ways in which Eliot celebrates but also negates adoptions in this chapter can be extended to her other works, *Romola* (1863) and "The Spanish Gypsy" (1868). These more minor of Eliot's works also depict in the manner of *Daniel Deronda* the violent pitfalls of transnational adoptive relations. In the former, the son murders his adoptive father and in the latter, the female child is first forcibly assimilated to Spanish society after being abducted and chooses to leave it to return to her people.

7 Nancy Henry takes issue with readings of *Deronda* that expose Eliot's imperialism. Eliot's "experiences with money and colonialism between 1860 and 1876," Henry argues, "contributed to her presentation of more shaded moral

pictures. When examined closely, and in the light of her own involvement, such references to British colonialism complicate the 'imperialist ideology' that many critics are eager to expose" (113). In particular, Henry problematizes "[c]riticism of Deronda that searches for an ideology to condemn," and suggests that this form of reading "has narrowed the notion of context to a morally blameworthy imperialism, distorting our understanding of the text's mimetic and moral subtleties."

8 Critics have pointed out how the Victorian orphan's search for a home becomes a metaphor for thinking about the conditions of dispossession and self-hood in the nineteenth century. The recurrent figure of the orphan is seen as a contrary sign for foreignness or exclusion (Peter), detachment and creativity (Auerbach), social stigma (Novy), individuation (Murdoch), and legal definition (Murdoch and Zomchick) and the articulation of normative family bonds (Donzelot and Peter). As Cheryl Nixon observes, "the orphan is a figure of multiple possibilities" (5).

9 L. Peters, *Orphan Texts: Victorian Orphans, Culture and Empire* (Manchester: Manchester University Press, 2018), p. 1.

10 Ibid.

11 T. O'Toole, "Adoption and the 'Improvement of the Estate'" in *Imagining Adoption: Essays on Literature and Culture.* Marianne Novy, editor (Ann Arbor: University of Michigan Press, 2001), p. 18.

12 In such a milieu, as Jacques Donzelot argues in *Policing of Families* (1997), the orphan serves as the vehicle through which to read the political history of the family in the West. The interactions between state and family, Donzelot shows, reduces the heterogeneity of the family and compels a symmetry between state and familiar power structures. John Zomchick makes a similar argument about the salience of the orphan as a juridical subject before the law to enact its expressions of individual and community. See Zomchick, *Family and the Law in Eighteenth Century Fiction* (2007).

13 P. Martin, *Victorian Families in Fact and Fiction* (New York: St. Martin's Press, 1995), p. 135.

John Boswell's *The Kindness of Strangers* provides archival evidence to show that in ancient and medieval Europe, it was common for strangers to raise or foster children. He suggests that this was done to continue lines of inheritance without regard to genealogical restrictions. The practice of wet-nursing in Britain during the renaissance also occurred alongside informal adoptions that took the shape of apprenticeships and service. See Ihana Krausman Ben-Amos, *Adolescence and Youth in Early Modern England* (New Haven: Yale University Press, 1994).

14 J. Wiesenfarth, "Demythologizing Silas Marner," *ELH, 37,* 2 (June 1, 1970), 226, p. 226.

15 Eliot, *Silas Marner*, p. 1.

16 See Lee Edelman's *No Future* for a critique of the figure of the child as an all-encompassing symbol of the future.

17 Eliot, *Silas Marner*, p. 169.

18 Ibid., p. 168.
19 Godfrey's motives for keeping his ties to Eppie secret are shrouded in repression of his affair with Molly, a woman of a lower social class. Whenever he contemplates the consequences of the revelation of his torrid alliance, Godfrey is convinced of "the repulsion the story of his earlier marriage would create," especially if revealed to Nancy after "long concealment" (157). Godfrey's tentative attempt to claim Eppie as an adoptee cloaks this other libidinal economy or traffic in hidden pleasures across class and social lines that nevertheless, as Eliot infers, also has a protracted history of being denigrated and suppressed.
20 Ibid., p. 169.
21 Ibid., pp. 170, 171.
22 Ibid., p. 170.
23 Ibid., p. 171.
24 Ibid.
25 Ibid., p. 172.
26 Eliot, *Silas Marner*, p. 170; J. Wiesenfarth, "Demythologizing Silas Marner." *ELH, 37,* 2 (June 1, 1970), 226, p. 231.
27 James McLaverty in his analysis of Comtean fetishism in *Silas Marner* too bases his claims on the surplus and deficit of "feeling" he sees Eliot as attributing to Silas and Godfrey: "Silas, for all the deprivations of his life at the Stonepits, retains in perverted form the life of feeling which typifies fetishism, while Godfrey, a product of the corrupt life of the Red House, lacks it" (318). Essentially it is this element of 'feeling' nurtured that exists between Eppie and Silas and affirms their kinship, despite Godfrey's 'lawful' pleas to the contrary.
28 I. P. Watt, *The Rise of the Novel: Studies in Defoe, Richardson and Fielding* (Chicago: University of Chicago Press, 2015), p. 13.
29 S. Abramowicz, "Adoption and the Limits of Contract in Victorian Adoption Case Law and George Eliot's *Silas Marner*." 2014. Available at: https://digitalcommons.wayne.edu/lawfrp/216, p. 5.
30 Eliot, *Silas Marner*, p. 172.
31 Ibid., p. 170.
32 B. Swann, "*Silas Marner* and the New Mythus," *Criticism*, 18, 2 (1976), Article 1. Available at: https://digitalcommons.wayne.edu/criticism/vol18/iss2/1, pp. 115, 117. See McLaverty's argument in "Comtean Fetishism in *Silas Marner*" that develops the idea that Eliot's depiction of Silas's labor, as well as his concern with hoarding his money, reflects a Positivist developmental model where human fetishism indicates struggles to move from stages of primitive into settled life (323). Silas's ability to 'heal' others, his homeopathic knowledge, is itself seen as an aspect of his unknown origins and deemed occult: "when a weaver, who came from nobody knew where, worked wonders with a bottle of brown waters, the occult character of the process was evident" (18).
33 Swann, "*Silas Marner* and the New Mythus," p. 103.

34 Ibid.
35 Ibid.
36 Eliot, *Silas Marner*, p. 15.
37 Ibid., p. 16.
38 Ibid., p. 5.
39 Ibid., p. 6. Eliot reinforces this idea that Silas's cultivated knowledge – his ability to cure diseases – rather than leading to admiration for him in Raveloe, "heightened the repulsion between him and his neighbors, and made his isolation more complete" (19). Raveloe, as the book shows, is a place where social caste is entrenched so much so that only Dr. Kimble, the village doctor, is seen as a true physician by virtue of having descended from a medical family, a doctor "by hereditary right" (98).
40 Ibid., p. 17.
41 Ibid., p. 20.
42 Ibid., p. 42.
43 J. Nunokawa, "The Miser's Two Bodies: 'Silas Marner' and the Sexual Possibilities of the Commodity," *Victorian Studies, 36*, 3 (April 1, 1993), 273–292, p. 273.
44 Eliot, *Silas Marner*, p. 21.
45 Swann, "*Silas Marner* and the New Mythus," p. 117.
46 It is also possible to read this scene differently, as foreshadowing the fatherly care that Silas will offer Eppie when she materializes as a replacement to the money Silas loses. In this reading, as developed below, the money serves as a placeholder for the real affection Silas will invest in the child. The portrait of Silas resonates interestingly with Dickens's representation of Magwitch in *Great Expectations* as discussed in chapter two of this volume.
47 Eliot, *Silas Marner*, p. 76.
48 Swann, "*Silas Marner* and the New Mythus," p. 117.
49 Nunokawa, J." The Miser's Two Bodies," p. 274. Making the homosexual allusion explicit, Nunokawa goes on to write of this moment: "The miser's self-love suggests one that dare not speak its name, a love whose definition is glimpsed in the shadow of Sodom ... that hovers over "the city of Destruction" from which the miser is saved when the gold is replaced by the girl" (274).
50 Swann, "*Silas Marner* and the New Mythus," p. 104. Silas's fixation on his wealth has also been understood as a kind of religious remainder. David Carroll argues that the novel depicts modernity's secular preoccupation with primitive forms of worship (165–220). James McLaverty supplements Carroll's influential reading by invoking Comtean fetishism in order to understand Silas's transformation from primitive to civilized human within a narrative of progress (318–319).
51 Dunham, R. H. (November 1, 1977), "Silas Marner and the Wordsworthian Child," *Studies in English Literature, 1500–1900, 16*, 4, 645, p. 646.
52 Ibid., p. 647.
53 Ibid., p. 648.

54 Eliot, *Silas Marner*, p. 110.

55 Another such moment occurs later in the text: "Marner took her [Eppie] on his lap trembling with an emotion mysterious to himself, at something unknown dawning on his life . . . he could only have said that the child was come instead of the gold—that the gold had turned into the child" (122). The logic of this chain of substitution is not limited to the replacement of the gold with the child. Silas, for instance, confuses Eppie's blondness with memories of his long dead sister, speculating that the coming of the child was a cosmic harbinger of a kind of message from the dead (111). Indeed, Eppie comes to stand-in for all of Silas's missing links, to his home and to the family he never had.

56 Ibid., p. 122.

57 J. Nunokawa, "The Miser's Two Bodies," p. 275.

58 Ibid., p. 273.

59 Ibid.

60 C. Flint, *Family Fictions: Narrative and Domestic Relations in Britain, 1688–1798* (Stanford, CA: Stanford University Press, 1998), p. 32.

61 Eliot, *Silas Marner*, p. 146.

62 J. Nunokawa, "The Miser's Two Bodies," p. 273.

63 Indeed, the persistent descriptions of Begum Sumroo's gender non-conformity point to a similar queering at the heart of the adoptive relationship in that instance as well.

64 Eliot, *Silas Marner*, p. 115.

65 This scene also restages Silas's previous desire to "cling" to his money.

66 Ibid.

67 L. Peters, *Orphan Texts: Victorian Orphans, Culture and Empire* (Manchester: Manchester University Press, 2018), p. 2.

68 Ibid.

69 Eliot, *Silas Marner*, p. 118.

70 Ibid., p. 122.

71 Ibid., pp. 122, 146. Eliot describes the feelings Eppie and Silas come to share in exalted terms: "Perfect love has a breath of poetry which can exalt the relations of the least instructed human beings; and this breath of poetry had surrounded Eppie from the time she had followed the bright gleam that beckoned her to Silas's hearth" (146).

72 Peters, *Orphan Texts*, pp. 6, 19.

73 Ibid., p. 23.

74 Eliot, *Silas Marner*, pp. 125, 130.

75 Of course there are many examples of orphans in eighteenth- and early nineteenth-century literature, including Delavier Manley's *The New Atlantis* (1709); Daniel Defoe's *Moll Flanders* (1722); Eliza Haywood, *The Distress'd Orphan or Love in a Madhouse* (1726); Henry Fielding's *Tom Jones* (1749); Frances Burney's *Evelina* (1778) and *Cecelia* (1782); Charlotte Smith's *Emmeline, the Orphan of the Castle* (1788); Maria Edgeworth's *Belinda* (1801); Jane Austen's *Mansfield Park* (1814). See Cheryl Nixon, *The Orphan*

in *Eighteenth Century Law and Literature* for a more complete account of this early literature featuring orphans in the context of Lord Hardwicke's Marriage Act (1753), which changed marriage from a religious to a legal contract.

76 N. Auerbach, "Incarnations of the Orphan." *ELH, 42,* 3 (November 1, 1976), 395, p. 396.

77 M. Novy, *Reading Adoption: Family and Difference in Fiction and Drama* (Ann Arbor, MI: University of Michigan Press, 2007), p. 87. Novy's point also gestures toward the isomorphic relationship between Silas Marner and the figure of the orphan.

78 Ibid., p. 89

79 Eliot, *Silas Marner*, p. 146.

80 Ibid.

81 Ibid., p. 141.

82 Ibid., p. 156.

83 Ibid., p. 157.

84 Ibid., p. 155.

85 Ibid., p. 157. In the parlance of the times, being "transported" referred to the expulsion of convicts to the colonies, as discussed in Chapters 1 and 2.

86 Ibid., p. 156

87 Ibid., pp. 162, 163.

88 Ibid., p. 163

89 Ibid., p. 164

90 The novel is about Eliot's attempt to consider the asymmetries between liberal political feeling and class identity that the Reform Act of 1832 attempted to settle.

91 Sophocles, *Oedipus Rex* in *The Oedipus Cycle.* Dudley Fitts and Robert Fitzgerald, trans., 1939. Quoted in Novy, *Imagining Adoption.*

92 See F. R. Leavis's polemic in *The Great Tradition* (1948) where he proposes separating the "good half" of *Daniel Deronda* from the "bad half," "represented by Deronda himself, and by what may called in general the Zionist inspiration" (80).

93 See for example: Jerome Beaty, "Daniel Deronda and The Question of Unity in Fiction" (1959); Barbara Hardy, *The Novels of Eliot: A Study in Form* (London: Athlone Press, 1959); David Carroll, "The Daniel Deronda," (1959); Maurice Beebe, "Visions are Creators: The Unity of *Daniel Deronda* (1955); Harold Fisch, "Daniel Deronda or Gwendolen Harleth?"(1965); Cynthia Chase, "The Decomposition of the Elephants" (1978); Jean Sudrann *Daniel Deronda* and the Landscape of Exile" (1970); James Caron, "The Rhetoric of Magic in Daniel Deronda (1983); Herbert Levine, "The Marriage of Allegory and Realism in Daniel Deronda" (1982).

94 S. Gates, "'A Difference of Native Language': Gender, Genre, and Realism in Daniel Deronda," *Elh, 68,* 3 (January 1, 2001), 699–724, p. 703.

95 See Reina Lewis's claim that "the interpenetrative discourses of Englishness and Jewishness . . . suffuse the novel and its reception" (193). Lewis considers how ideas of Englishness and alienness develop relationally in the novel.

96 A. Mufti, *Enlightenment in the Colony: The Jewish Question and the Crisis of Postcolonial Culture* (Princeton, NJ: Princeton University Press, 2007), pp. 98–99.
97 Ibid., p. 99
98 G. Eliot, *Daniel Deronda* (London, Penguin Classics, 1876; 1995), p. 22.
99 Ibid., p. 165.
100 Ibid.
101 Ibid., p. 333
102 Ibid.
103 Ibid., p. 613
104 Ibid.
105 Ibid., p. 614. Interestingly this moment is preceded by Daniel's direct inquiry about his father: "Is my father also living?" to which Sir Hugo responds "immediately in a low emphatic tone – "No" (613).
106 Ibid., p. 620
107 Ibid.
108 Ibid., p. 638
109 Ibid., p. 170
110 Ibid.
111 Ibid., p. 617
112 M. Homans, "Adoption Narratives, Trauma, and Origins," *Narrative, 14,* 1 (January 1, 2006), 4–26, p. 14.
113 Eliot, *Daniel Deronda*, p. 619.
114 Ibid.
115 Ibid.
116 Ibid., p. 625
117 Ibid.
118 Ibid.
119 Ibid., p. 626.
120 Ibid.
121 Ibid., p. 627.
122 Ibid., p. 634.
123 As a model for feminist resistance, Leonora stands in sharp contrast to Dorothea Brooke in *Middlemarch.* Dorothea, herself an orphan, relinquishes her own scholarly inclinations for the tranquilities of marriage and motherhood. Whatever scandal the suspicion of an affair between Dorothea and her husband's cousin Will Ladislaw causes is resolved when she determines to forego the fortune her husband leaves her only so she can marry Ladislaw and settle into domesticity.
124 Ibid., p. 626.
125 Ibid., p. 628.
126 S. Meyer, "'Safely to Their Own Borders': Proto-Zionism, Feminism, and Nationalism in Daniel Deronda," *Elh, 60,* 3 (October 1, 1993), 733–758, p. 742. To be clear, Meyer argues that the Princess's transgressive feminism is ultimately suppressed in *Daniel Deronda.* She writes: "The novel ultimately

does with the Jews, the non-English race with its submerged connection to female selfhood, precisely what it does with female transgressiveness: it firmly ushers both out of the English world of the novel, it returns those who have strayed and transgressed, it removes them, in the euphemistic language of the novel, "safely to their own borders" (735). While, I don't disagree with this assessment about the book's conservatism with regard to allowing challenges to nation and patriarchy to subsist, I find it useful to acknowledge Eliot's stretch toward imagining positions outside the norm for her characters. By inhabiting an avowed anti-maternal position, the Princess ushers adoption into the social fray as an option in the best interest of the unloved child.

127 Eliot, *Daniel Deronda*, p. 631.

128 Stephen Marcus and Cynthia Chase consider Daniel's likely circumcision in terms of similar questions of gender, sexuality and self-awareness.

129 Eliot, *Daniel Deronda*, p. 659.

130 This historical record also resonates with the law's demand of historical proof as discussed in Chapter 3.

131 Ibid., p. 170.

132 Ibid., pp. 170–171.

133 Ibid., p. 171.

134 Ibid., p. 634.

135 Ibid., p. 635.

136 Ibid., p. 636.

137 J.-M. Schramm, *Atonement and Self-Sacrifice in Nineteenth-Century Narrative* (Cambridge: Cambridge University Press, 2012), p. 183.

138 *Ibid.*, pp. 183–184.

139 Eliot, *Daniel Deronda*, p. 661.

140 *Ibid.*, p. 660.

141 C. Chase, "The Decomposition of the Elephants: Double-Reading Daniel Deronda," *PMLA, 93*(2) (1978), 215–227, p. 223 (661 emphasis added).

142 Eliot, *Daniel Deronda*, p. 661, emphasis added. To his grandfather's friend, Joseph Kalonymous he later says, "I shall call myself a Jew . . . But I will not say that I shall profess to believe exactly as my fathers have believed. Our fathers themselves changed the horizon of their belief and learned of other races" (725).

143 At *other* moments too when Daniel seems more secure in his assertions, Eliot marks the limits of his support of Judaism in terms of sentimental racial feelings. Daniel says, for instance, "You renounced me – you still banish me – as a son . . . But that stronger something has determined I shall be all the more the grandson you willed to annihilate" (663). He later reiterates his feeling for "the expression of something stronger, with deeper, farther-spreading roots, knit into the foundations of sacredness for all men" (663). Daniel's profuse expressions of innate racial solidarities are contextually ungrounded. His embrace of a "stronger something" seems a response to his mother's rejections of the ties that bind them. The text itself drives home this point about Daniel's hollow clinging when Leonora, remarking on

Mirah's Jewishness, comments, "Ah, like you. She is attached to the Judaism she knows nothing of" (665).

144 C. L. Nixon, *The Orphan in Eighteenth-Century Law and Literature: Estate, Blood, and Body* (Burlington, VT: Ashgate, 2011), p. 75.

145 Ibid.

146 Eliot, *Daniel Deronda*, p. 159.

147 In this respect, English legal culture was different from its Indian counterparts, which had always recognized adoption as a mode of property transmission. Importantly, the Company's attempts to intervene in this recognized practice were taking place in India as adoption was entering into legal discourse in England.

148 Ibid., pp. 321–322.

149 Ibid. pp. 322, 158. Through its representation of inheritance between the Mallingers, the novel portrays how English sociality revolves around a series of transactions undertaken to secure property rights. Sir Hugo, for instance, muses about his offer of compensation to Grandcourt for the family home: "If, after all, the unhoped-for son should be born, the money would have been thrown away, and Grandcourt would have been paid for giving up interests that had turned out good for nothing" (159). The heir's presence or absence motivates familial bargains so that a bargain once struck in the absence of the son seems wasteful if he should suddenly materialize. All the while of course there is the adoptive son who can receive emotional, but not material benefit from the parent.

150 Ibid., p. 334.

151 Ibid., pp. 718, 159.

152 For a discussion of inheritance law and legal concepts such as settlement, entail, and primogeniture in Eliot's fiction, see Phoebe Poon's "From Status to Contract: Inheritance and Succession in George Eliot's Late Fiction."

153 In this regard, Daniel's situation is very similar to David Dyce Sombre's. Both men can only inherit cash gifts, but not the broader inheritances of land, title, and lineage.

154 Ibid. p. 500.

155 M. M. Rowe, "Melting Outlines in *Daniel Deronda*," *Studies in the Novel, 22*, 1 (April 1, 1990), 10–18, p. 11; S. Gates, "'A Difference of Native Language': Gender, Genre, and Realism in Daniel Deronda," *Elh, 68*, 3, (January 1, 2001) 699–724, p. 708.

156 Gates, "A Difference of Native Language," p. 715.

157 Ibid., p. 716.

158 Eliot, *Daniel Deronda*, p. 495, emphasis added.

159 See Gates, "A Difference of Native Language," p. 715 and Nunokawa, "The Miser's Two Bodies," p. 281.

160 Nunokawa, "The Miser's Two Bodies," p. 279.

161 Ibid., p. 282. Sarah Gates makes a similar argument about the novel's messianic turn.

162 Ibid., p. 281.

163 Eliot, *Daniel Deronda*, p. 527.
164 Ibid., pp. 527–528.
165 S. Meyer, "'Safely to Their Own Borders': Proto-Zionism, Feminism, and Nationalism in Daniel Deronda," *Elh, 60,* 3 (October 1, 1993), 733–758, p. 751.
166 Meyer also importantly notes the elision of Palestine from the book: "The Arab inhabitants of Palestine are never referred to directly in Daniel Deronda, a fact that is telling in itself, but a few passages in the novel also indirectly suggest Eliot's lack of concern both with the situation of the indigenous population of Palestine and with the inevitable conflict between them and the Jews that the proto-Zionist project would create" (751).
167 S. Said, *The Question of Palestine* (London: Vintage Books, 1979; 1992), p. 66.
168 Meyer, "Safety to Their Own Borders," p. 733.
169 Ibid., p. 748.
170 Ibid., p. 735.
171 Ibid., p. 747.
172 Said reads Eliot's novel as infused with a colonial mentality that converts the East into England by endorsing Daniel's missionary prospects and erasing Palestinian history. "Underlying all this, however, is the total absence" Said writes, "of any thought about the actual inhabitants of the East, Palestine in particular . . . Brightness, freedom, and redemption – key matters for Eliot – are to be restricted to Europeans and the Jews, who are themselves European prototypes so far as the colonizing the East is concerned" (65).
173 In terms of the larger project of this book, a parallel may also be drawn with the justices of the Privy Council adjudicating within unfamiliar legal systems.
174 Eliot, *Silas Marner*, p. 810.
175 C. L. Nixon, *The Orphan in Eighteenth-Century Law and Literature: Estate, Blood, and Body* (Burlington, VT: Ashgate, 2011), pp. 4–5.
176 J. McLaverty, "Comtean Fetishism in Silas Marner," *Nineteenth-Century Fiction, 36,* 3 (December 1, 1981), 318–336, p. 332.
177 Ibid. On this detail McLaverty cites Eliot's *Letters,* III, 308–309.
178 See especially chapters 9, "*Adam Beade*" and 10, "*The Mill on The Floss* and *Silas Marner*" in Gordon Haight's *George Eliot: A Biography*, 1968.
179 L. J. Dessner, "The autobiographical matrix of 'Silas Marner,'" *Studies in the Novel* (January 1, 1979), 251–282, p. 260. Dessner draws out the analogies between the author's life and her work by suggesting that not only did George Eliot adopt the Lewes boys, but in choosing to align herself with George Henry Lewes against the religious orthodoxy of her biological family, Eliot adopts herself out: "By casting her lot with . . . Lewes, George Eliot chose an adoptive family over her natural family" (261).
180 Ibid.
181 Ibid.

182 Again as Dessner observes, Eliot's own experiment with adoptive ties "proves wonderfully satisfactory. George Eliot would not only be accepted but also become the boys' loved and loving 'Mutter'" (260).

183 Ibid.

184 Ibid.

185 G. Beer, *George Eliot* (Bloomington: Indiana University Press, 1986), p. 36.

186 This is akin to Feldama's situation in "The Spanish Gypsy (1868)," Eliot's dramatic poem set in fifteenth century Spain. Feldama, forcibly abducted and assimilated to Catholicism, breaks with social decorum and rejecting the Spanish nobleman to whom she is engaged, casts her lot in with her gypsy race to return them to their African homeland.

187 M. Novy, *Imagining Adoption: Essays on Literature and Culture* (Ann Arbor: University of Michigan Press, 2001), p. 2.

Afterword

1 C. Frank, "Narrative and Law", in Dolin, K. (Ed.), *Law and literature* (Cambridge Critical Concepts Series) (Cambridge, United Kingdom: Cambridge University Press, 2018), p. 1.

2 Quoted in Z. Masani, *Indian Tales of the Raj* (Berkeley: University of California Press, 1988), p. 19.

3 M. Mukherjee, *India in the Shadows of Empire: A Legal and Political History, 1774–1950* (New Delhi: Oxford University Press, 2010), p. 88.

4 Ibid., p. 89.

5 Ibid.

6 R. De, "'A Peripatetic World Court' Cosmopolitan Courts, Nationalist Judges and the Indian Appeal to the Privy Council," *Law and History Review, 32,* 4 (November 1, 2014), 821–851, p. 843.

7 See Mitra Sharafi's *Law and Identity in Colonial South Asia* for an interesting analysis of Parsi legal culture.

8 De, "A Peripatetic World Court," p. 841.

9 Ibid., pp. 841–842.

10 George Rankin cites the following from *Hull* v. *McKenna* (1926) in his overview of the JCPC: "'The Judicial Committee of the Privy Council is not a body, strictly speaking, with any location. The Sovereign is everywhere throughout the Empire in the contemplation of the law'" (11). The notion that the sovereign is everywhere is an interesting corollary to the impartiality of the judges. Yet, as Alpana Roy notes, "while liberal positivism creates the theoretical forum for legal neutrality, formal equality and legal objectivity, its unwillingness to see from Other positions essentially results in the promotion of substantive inequality" (319).

11 L. Stephen, *The Life of Sir James Fitzjames Stephen: A Judge of the High Court of Justice* (London: Smith, Elder, & Co., 1895), p. 248.

12 Ibid.

13 As Kieran Dolin and others have noted, many nineteenth-century authors had dabbled in the law (4). Catherine O. Frank remarks that "one out of every five" Victorian novelists had "failed as barristers" (3).
14 Stephen, *The Life of Sir James Fitzjames Stephen*, p. 135.
15 Ibid., p. 134.
16 1833 is also the year of the Judicial Committee Act, which formally established the Judicial Committee of the Privy Council as the highest court of appeal for the colonies.
17 J. Stephen, "The Licence of Modern Novelists", in *The Edinburgh Review* (United Kingdom: A. and C. Black, July 1857).
18 L. Stephen, *The Life of Sir James Fitzjames Stephen: A Judge of the High Court of Justice* (London: Smith, Elder, & Co., 1895), p. 155.
19 W. Schmidgen, "*Terra Nullius*, Cannibalism, and the Natural Law of Appropriation in *Robinson Crusoe*," in *Eighteenth-Century Fiction and the Law of Property* (Cambridge: Cambridge University Press, 2002), pp. 32–62.
20 See my "The Love Laws: Section 377 and the Politics of Queerness in Arundhati Roy's The God of Small Things" for a discussion of the implicit effects of Section 377 of the Indian penal code on Arundhati Roy's representation of queerness in *The God of Small Things.*
21 J. Muñoz, *Cruising Utopia: The Then and There of Queer Futurity (Sexual Cultures)* (New York: New York University Press, 2009), p. 1.
22 *National Legal Services Authority* v. *Union of India and others,* Writ Petition (Civil) No. 400 of 2012, India: Supreme Court, 15 April 2014.
23 Ibid., p. 2
24 Ibid.
25 Ibid., p. 10.
26 Ibid. In his decision, Radhakrishnan references extensive case law, from colonial and postcolonial Indian courts, as well as from national and regional courts in the United States, Great Britain, Australia, Argentina, Malaysia, Germany, and others. The decision further cites the Universal Declaration of Human Rights (1948), the International Covenant on Civil and Political Rights (1966), and the Yogyakarta Principles (2006).
27 Ibid., p. 13.
28 Ibid.
29 Ibid.
30 Ibid., p. 124.
31 Ibid., p. 128.
32 Ibid., pp. 127–129.
33 J. H. Grossman, *The Art of Alibi: English Law Courts and the Novel* (Baltimore: Johns Hopkins University Press, 2002), p. 5.
34 *Navtej Singh Johar & Others.* v. *Union of India thr. Secretary Ministry of Law and Justice*, Writ Petition (Criminal.) No. 76 of 2016, p. 318.
35 Ibid., pp. 321–322.
36 Ibid., p. 270.
37 Ibid., p. 268.

38 E. Moore, *The Queen, on the Prosecution of the Bombay Government* v. *Eduljee Byramjee and Seventeen Others*, in *Reports of Cases Heard and Determined by the Judicial Committee on Appeal from the Supreme and Sudder Dewanny Courts in the East Indies*, vol. iii, 1841–46 (London: V. & R. Stevens and G.S. Norton, 1846), p. 482.

39 *Pratt and Morgan* v. *The Attorney General for Jamaica and another* (Jamaica) [1993] UKPC 1 (2nd November, 1993)

40 The Indian Penal Code and Section 377 are also examples of colonial era laws that were "saved" after independence.

41 J. Campbell, "Murder Appeals, Delayed Executions, and the Origins of Jamaican Death Penalty Jurisprudence," *Law and History Review, 33*, 2(May 1, 2015), 435–466, p. 437. For a discussion of the JCPC's rulings in a series of cases challenging the constitutionality of the death penalty, especially in reference to "savings clauses," see Tittemore (2005), Schabas (1994), and Antoine (1992).

42 Ibid.

43 Website of the JCPC at www.jcpc.uk/about/role-of-the-jcpc.html. The JCPC hears appeals from the Commonwealth as follows:

> To bring an appeal to the Judicial Committee of the Privy Council, you must have been granted leave by the lower court whose decision you are appealing. In the absence of leave, permission to appeal must be granted by the Board. In some cases there is an appeal as of right and a slightly different procedure applies.
>
> In civil cases, the lower court will generally grant you leave to appeal if the court is satisfied that your case raises a point of general public importance.
>
> In criminal cases, it is unusual for the lower court to have the power to grant leave unless your case raises questions of great and general importance, or there has been some grave violation of the principles of natural justice.

44 See Ezekiel (2013) for an argument in favor of the CCJ.

45 D. O'Brien, The Post-Colonial Constitutional Order of the Commonwealth Caribbean: The Endurance of the Crown and the Judicial Committee of the Privy Council, *The Journal of Imperial and Commonwealth History*, 46 5 (2018), 958–983, p. 976.

46 Ibid.

47 Despite many lawyers and jurists throughout the Caribbean questioning the desirability of maintaining the right of appeal to the Privy Council, the Caribbean Court of Justice has yet to attain widespread support for replacing it.

Bibliography

Abramowicz, S. (2014). "Adoption and the Limits of Contract in Victorian Adoption Case Law and George Eliot's *Silas Marner*." Available at https:// digitalcommons.wayne.edu/lawfrp/216

Acharya, V. K. (2018). *Thugs of Hindostan*. Mumbai: Yash Raj Films.

Agamben, G. (1998). *Homo Sacer: Sovereign Power and Bare Life*, trans. D. Heller-Roazen. Palo Alto, CA: Stanford University Press.

Ahmed, S. (2011). *The Stillbirth of Capital: Enlightenment Writing and Colonial India*. Palo Alto, CA: Stanford University Press.

(2018). *Archaeology of Babel: The Colonial Foundation of the Humanities*. Stanford, CA: Stanford University Press.

Ainsworth, W. H., and Cruikshank, G. (1898). *Jack Sheppard: A Romance*. London: G. Routledge & Sons.

Alber, J. (2007). *Narrating the Prison: Role and Representation in Charles Dickens' Novels, Twentieth-Century Fiction, and Film*. Youngstown, NY: Cambria Press.

Amsterdam, A. G., and Bruner, J. S. (2009). *Minding the Law*. Cambridge, MA: Harvard University Press.

Anand, A., and Dalrymple, W. (2017). *Koh-i-Noor: The History of the World's Most Infamous Diamond*. New York: Bloomsbury.

Anderson, C. (2004). *Legible Bodies: Race, Criminality, and Colonialism in South Asia*. King's Lynn: Berg.

(2015). "Execution and Its Aftermath in the Nineteenth-Century British Empire." In R. Ward (ed.), *A Global History of Execution and the Criminal Corpse*. Basingstoke: Palgrave Macmillan, pp. 170–198.

Andrew, W. P. (1878). *India and Her Neighbors*. New York: George Munro.

Anker, E. S. (2017). *Fictions of Dignity*. Ithaca, NY: Cornell University Press.

(2017). "Globalizing Law and Literature." In B. Meyler and E. S. Anker (eds.), *New Directions in Law and Literature*. New York: Oxford University Press, pp. 210–225.

Anonymous. (1845). *A Detailed Report of the Proceedings on the Trial of the Eighteen Parsee Prisoners for Murder, Before the Supreme Court, Bombay, on Wednesday July 17, 1844*, London: Samuel Clarke.

Antoine, R. M. B. (January 1, 1992). "The Judicial Committee of the Privy Council: An Inadequate Remedy for Death Row Prisoners." *The International and Comparative Law Quarterly*, *41*(1), 179–190.

Appadurai, A. (1993). "Number in the Colonial Imagination." In C. Breckenridge and P. van der Veer (eds.), *Orientalism and the Postcolonial Predicament: Perspectives on South Asia*. Philadelphia: University of Pennsylvania Press, pp. 314–339.

(2007). *Worship and Conflict under Colonial Rule: A South Indian Case*. Cambridge: Cambridge University Press.

Aravamudan, S. (2009). "Hobbes and America." In D. Carey and L. Festa (eds.), *Postcolonial Enlightenment: Eighteenth Century Colonialism and Postcolonial Theory*. New York: Oxford University Press, pp. 37–70.

Armstrong, N. (2006). *Desire and Domestic Fiction: A Political History of the Novel*. New York: Oxford University Press.

Arnold, D. (January 1, 1995). "The Colonial Prison: Power, Knowledge and Penology in Nineteenth-Century India. Subaltern Studies VIII: Essays in Honour of Ranajit Guha." *The Indian Economic and Social History Review*, *32*(3), 392.

The Asiatic Journal and Monthly Register for British India and Its Dependencies, Vol. 26 (1828). London: Black, Parbury, & Allen.

Auerbach, N. (November 1, 1976). "Incarnations of the Orphan." *ELH*, *42*(3), 395.

Austin, J. L., Urmson, J. O., and Sbisa, M. (2011). *How to Do Things with Words: The William James Lectures Delivered at Harvard University in 1955*. Oxford: Clarendon Press.

Bakhtin, M. M., and Bakhtin, M. M. (2017). *The Dialogic Imagination: Four Essays*. Austin: University of Texas Press.

Barnes, J. (2007). *Arthur and George*. New York: Vintage.

Baron, J. B. (January 1, 1999). "Law, Literature, and the Problems of Interdisciplinarity." *Yale Law Journal*, *108*(5), 1059–1085.

Barrow, A. (2011). *The Cosmic Time of Empire: Modern Britain and World Literature*. Berkeley: University of California Press.

Barua, A. (2011). "Metaphors of Temporality: Revisiting the 'Timeless Hinduism' versus 'Historical Christianity' Antithesis." *The Harvard Theological Review*, *104*(2), 147–169.

Bayly, S. (1999). *Caste, Society and Politics in India from the Eighteenth Century to the Modern Age*. New York: Cambridge University Press.

Beer, G. (1986). *George Eliot*. Bloomington: Indiana University Press.

Ben-Amos, I. K. (1994). *Adolescence and Youth in Early Modern England*. New Haven/London: Yale University Press.

Bentham, J., and Ogden, C. K. (1932). *Bentham's Theory of Fictions*. International Library of Psychology, Philosophy, and Scientific Method. London: Kegan Paul, Trench, Trubner.

Benton, L. A. (2002). *Law and Colonial Cultures: Legal Regimes in World History, 1400–1900*. Cambridge: Cambridge University Press.

(2009). *A Search for Sovereignty: Law and Geography in European Empires, 1400–1900*. Cambridge: Cambridge University Press.

Benton, L. A., and Ross, R. J. (2016). *Legal Pluralism and Empires, 1500–1850*. New York: NYU Press.

Ben-Yishai, A. (2015). *Common Precedents: The Presentness of the Past in Victorian Law and Fiction*. New York: Oxford University Press.

Bernard, P. (2006). *The Absent-Minded Imperialists: Empire, Society, and Culture in Britain*. Oxford: Oxford University Press.

Bisla, S. (2002). "The Return of the Author: Privacy, Publication, the Mystery Novel, and *The Moonstone*." *Boundary 2, 29*(1), 177–222.

Bivona, D. (1990). *Desire and Contradiction: Imperial Visions and Domestic Debates in Victorian Literature*. Manchester: Manchester University Press.

Bombay (India: State). (1877–1926). *Gazetteer of the Bombay Presidency*, Vol. 14. Bombay: Government Central Press.

Boswell, J. (1998). *The Kindness of Strangers: The Abandonment of Children in Western Europe from Late Antiquity to the Renaissance*. Chicago: University of Chicago Press.

Bownas, J. L. (2017). *Thomas Hardy and Empire: The Representation of Imperial Themes in the Work of Thomas Hardy*. London: Routledge.

British Library, India Office Records, Mss Eur B276.

India Office Records, Mss Eur F 213/23.

India Office Records, Letter from Lord Dalhousie to John Hobhouse, Mss Eur F 213/24.

India Office Records, F 236/486.

India Office Records, R/1/1/44.

India Office Records, R/1/1/46.

India Office Records, Z/E/4/15/S984: 1837–1839.

Brontë, C. (1847/2001). *Jane Eyre*. New York: Norton.

Brooks, P. (January 1, 1982). Narrative Transaction and Transference (Unburying "Le Colonel Chabert"). *Novel: A Forum on Fiction, 15*(2), 101–110.

(2006). "Narrative Transactions – Does the Law Need a Narratology?" *Yale Journal of Law & Humanities, 18*, 1–28, p. 2.

(January 1, 2017). "Clues, Evidence, Detection: Law Stories." *Narrative, 25*(1), 1–27.

Brown, A. (2003). *English Society and the Prison: Time, Culture and Politics in the Development of the Modern Prison, 1850–1920*, Suffolk, UK: The Boydell Press.

Bulwer-Lytton, E. (1830). *Paul Clifford*, London: Routledge.

Burbank, J., and Cooper, F. (January 1, 2013). "Rules of Law, Politics of Empire." *Legal Pluralism and Empires, 1500–1850*, 261–277. New York: NYU Press.

Campbell, J. (May 1, 2015). "Murder Appeals, Delayed Executions, and the Origins of Jamaican Death Penalty Jurisprudence." *Law and History Review*, 33(2), 435–466.

Cardwell, M. (1972). *The Clarendon Dickens: The Mystery of Edwin Drood*. Oxford: Clarendon.

Carroll, D. (1967). *Silas Marner: Reversing the Oracles of Religion. Literary Monographs*. Madison: University of Wisconsin Press.

Chakrabarty, D. (2009). *Provincializing Europe: Postcolonial Thought and Historical Difference*, Princeton: Princeton University Press.

Chakravarti, U. (2018). *Gendering Caste: Through a Feminist Lens*. New Delhi: SAGE Publications.

Chakravorty, M. (2017). *In Stereotype: South Asia in the Global Literary Imaginary*. New York: Columbia University Press.

Chandra, U. (March 1, 2013). "Liberalism and Its Other: The Politics of Primitivism in Colonial and Postcolonial Indian Law." *Law & Society Review*, 47(1), 135–168.

Chaplin, S. (2017). *Law, Sensibility and the Sublime in Eighteenth-Century Women's Fiction: Speaking of Dread*. London: Routledge.

Chase, C. (1978). "The Decomposition of the Elephants: Double-Reading Daniel Deronda." *PMLA*, *93*(2), 215–227.

Chatterjee, A. (1998), *Representations of India, 1740–1840: The Creation of India in the Colonial Imagination*. London: Palgrave Macmillan.

Chatterjee, I. (2004). *Unfamiliar relations: Family and History in South Asia*. New Brunswick, NJ: Rutgers University Press.

Cohn, B. (1996). *Colonialism and Its Forms of Knowledge: The British in India*, Princeton: Princeton University Press.

(1998). *An Anthropologist Among Historians and Other Essays*, New Delhi: Oxford University Press.

Colley, L. (1992). "Britishness and Otherness: An Argument." *Journal of British Studies*, 31(4), 309–329.

(2005). *Britons: Forging the Nation, 1707–1837*, New Haven: Yale University Press.

Collins, P. (1965). *Dickens and Crime* (Cambridge Studies in Criminology, ed. L. Radzinowicz). London: Macmillan.

Collins, W. (1868/2015), *The Moonstone*. Oxford: Oxford University Press.

Cowell, H. (1880). *G.C.W. Forester and Others* v. *The Secretary of State for India in Council*. The Law Reports: Supplemental Indian Appeals: Being Cases in the Privy Council on Appeal from the East Indies, Decided Between March, 1872, and November, 1873, and Not Reported in Moore's Indian Appeals. United Kingdom: Incorporated Council of Law Reporting for England and Wales.

Crimmins, J. (2002). "Bentham and Hobbes: An Issue of Influence." *Journal of the History of Ideas*, *63*(4), 677–696.

Currie, M. (2012). *About Time: Narrative Fiction and the Philosophy of Time*. Cambridge: Cambridge University Press.

Dalal, U. (April 1, 2015). "Femininity, State and Cultural Space in Eighteenth-century India." *The Medieval History Journal*, 18(1), 120–165.

Dalrymple, W. (2004). *White Mughals: Love and Betrayal in Eighteenth-Century India*. New York: Penguin Books.

(2010). Review of *the Inordinately Strange Life of Dyce Sombre* by Michael Fisher. *The Observer*. July 31, 2010.
Dash, M. (2006). *Thug: The True Story of India's Murderous Cult*. London: Granta.
Davis, D. (2010). "A Historical Overview of Hindu Law." In Timothy Lubin, Donald R. Davis, and Jayanth Krishnan (eds.), *Hinduism and Law: An Introduction*. Cambridge: Cambridge University Press.
Davis, L. J. (1997). *Factual Fictions – The Origins of the English Novel*. Philadelphia: University of Pennsylvania Press.
Davis, N. Z. (1987). *Fiction in the Archives: Pardon Tales and Their Tellers in Sixteenth-Century France*. Stanford, CA: Stanford University Press.
Dayan, C. (2017). *The Law Is a White Dog: How Legal Rituals Make and Unmake Persons*. Princeton: Princeton University Press.
De, R. (November 1, 2014). "'A Peripatetic World Court' Cosmopolitan Courts, Nationalist Judges and the Indian Appeal to the Privy Council." *Law and History Review*, 32(4), 821–851.
Derrett, J. D. (1961). "The Administration of Hindu Law by the British." *Comparative Studies in Society and History*, *4*(1), 10–52.
Derrida, J. (2009). *The Beast and the Sovereign, Volume 1*, trans. G. Bennington. Chicago: University of Chicago Press.
Dessner, L. J. (January 1, 1979). "The Autobiographical Matrix of 'Silas Marner.'" *Studies in the Novel*, *11*(3), 251–282.
Dickens, C. (1838/2003). *Oliver Twist*, Harmondsworth: Penguin Classics.
Dickens, C., & Rosenberg, E. (1999). *Great Expectations: Authoritative Text, Backgrounds, Contexts, Criticism*. New York: Norton.
Dirks, N. B. (January 1, 1992). "From Little King to Landlord: Colonial Discourse and Colonial Rule." In *Colonialism and Culture*. Ann Arbor: University of Michigan Press, pp. 175–208.
(2001). *Castes of Mind: Colonialism and the Making of Modern India*. Princeton: Princeton University Press.
Donzelot, J. (1979). *The Policing of Families*. New York: Pantheon Books.
Doyle, A.C. "The Case of Mr. George Edalji." *The Daily Telegraph* (11 and 12 January 1907 [UK]).
Dunham, R. H. (November 1, 1977). "Silas Marner and the Wordsworthian Child." *Studies in English Literature, 1500–1900*, 16(4), 645.
Edelman, L. (1998). The Future Is Kid Stuff: Queer Theory, Disidentification, and the Death Drive. *Narrative*, *6*(1), 18–30.
Eliot, G. (1861/1996). *Silas Marner: The Weaver of Raveloe*. London: Penguin Books.
(1866/1995). *Felix Holt, the Radical*. London: Penguin Classics.
(1876/1995). *Daniel Deronda*. London, Penguin Classics.
Eliot, G., and Haight, G. S. (1954). *The George Eliot Letters: Volume 3*. London: Oxford University Press.
Elliott, H.M. (1869). *Memoirs on the History, Folk-lore, and Distribution of the Races of the North Western Provinces of India: Being an Amplified Edition of the*

Original Supplemental Glossary of Indian Terms, Volume 1. London: Trübner & Company.

Esposito, R. (2009). *Communitas: The Origin and Destiny of Community*, trans. T. Campbell, Palo Alto: Stanford University Press.

The English Reports. Vol. XIV: Privy Council III. (Containing Moore, P.C. Vol. 8–12). Wood Renton, A. Esq., editor. London: Stevens and Sons Ltd., 1901.

Eraly, A., & Eraly, A. (2008). *The Mughal World: India's Tainted Paradise*. London: Phoenix.

Ezekiel, R. (n.d.). "Courts of Appeal and Colonialism in the British Caribbean: A Case for the Caribbean Court of Justice." *Michigan Journal of International Law, 35*, 1.

Fabian, J. (2014). *Time and the Other: How Anthropology Makes Its Object*. New York: Columbia University Press.

Fanon, F. (1968). *Black Skin, White Masks*, trans. R. Philcox. New York: Grove Press.

(1963). *The Wretched of the Earth*, trans. R. Philcox. New York: Grove Press.

Ferguson, R. (1990). "The Judicial Opinion as Literary Genre." *Yale Journal of Law & the Humanities, 2*, 1.

Filmer, R., and Sommerville, J. P. (1991). *Patriarcha and Other Writings*. Cambridge, England: Cambridge University Press.

Firminger, W. K. ed. (1907). *Bengal, Past and Present: Journal of the Calcutta Historical Society*, Vol. 1. Calcutta: The Calcutta General Printing Company.

Fisher, M.H. (2004a). "Becoming and Making 'Family" in Hindustan.' In I. Chatterjee (ed.), *Unfamiliar Relations: Family and History in South Asia*. New Brunswick: Rutgers University Press.

(2004b). *Counterflows to Colonialism: Indian Travellers and Settlers in Britain, 1600–1857*. New Delhi: Permanent Black,

(2010). *The Inordinately Strange Life of Dyce Sombre: Victorian Anglo-Indian MP and "Chancery Lunatic'*. India: C. Hurst.

Flint, C. (1998). *Family Fictions: Narrative and Domestic Relations in Britain, 1688–1798*. Stanford, CA: Stanford University Press.

Foucault, M. (1995). *Discipline and Punish: The Birth of the Prison*, trans. Alan Sheridan. New York: Vintage Books.

(2007). *Security, Territory, Population: Lectures at the College de France, 1977–78*, M. Senellart (ed.), trans. G. Burchell. New York: Palgrave Macmillan.

Frank, C. (2018). "Narrative and Law." In K. Dolin (ed.), *Law and Literature* (Cambridge Critical Concepts Series). Cambridge, United Kingdom: Cambridge University Press.

Frank, L. (2003). *Victorian Detective Fiction and the Nature of Evidence: The Scientific Investigations of Poe, Dickens, and Doyle*. Basingstoke: Palgrave Macmillan.

Free, M. (2006). "'Dirty Linen': Legacies of Empire in Wilkie Collins's *The Moonstone*." *Texas Studies in Literature and Language, 48*(4), 340–371.

Freitag, S. B. (May 28, 1991). "Crime in the Social Order of Colonial North India." *Modern Asian Studies*, 25(2), 227.

Ganguly, D. C. (1958). *Select Documents of the British Period of Indian History*, Calcutta: Trustees of the Victoria Memorial.

Gates, S. (January 1, 2001). "'A Difference of Native Language': Gender, Genre, and Realism in Daniel Deronda," *Elh*, 68(3), 699–724.

Ghosh, A. (2002), "Revisiting the 'Bengal Renaissance': Literary Bengali and Low-Life Print in Colonial Calcutta." *Economic and Political Weekly*, 37(2), 19–25.

Ghosh, D. (2006). *Sex and the Family: The Making of Empire*, Cambridge: Cambridge University Press.

Gibson, M. E. (2013). *The Inordinately Strange Life of Dyce Sombre: Victorian Anglo Indian MP and Chancery 'Lunatic'* by Michael H. Fisher (review). *Victorian Studies*, 55(2), 365–367. Indiana University Press.

Gillingham, L. (2009). "Ainsworth's 'Jack Sheppard' and the Crimes of History." *Studies in English Literature, 1500–1900*, 49(4), 879–906.

Gilmartin, D. (March 1, 2017). 4. Imperial Sovereignty in Mughal and British Forms. *History and Theory*, 56(1), 80–88.

Ginzberg, C. (1990). *Myths, Emblems, Clues*. London: Hutchinson Radius.

Glendening, J. (2008). "War of the Roses: Hybridity in *The Moonstone*." *Dickens Studies Annual*, 39, 281–304.

GoGwilt, C. L. (2000). *The Fiction of Geopolitics: Afterimages of Culture, from Wilkie Collins to Alfred Hitchcock*. Stanford: Stanford University Press.

Goodlad, L. M. (2017). *The Victorian Geopolitical Aesthetic: Realism, Sovereignty, and Transnational Experience*. Oxford: Oxford University Press.

Gordon, S. N. (July 26, 2016). "Scarf and Sword: Thugs, Marauders, and State-formation in 18th Century Malwa." *The Indian Economic & Social History Review*, 6(4), 403–429.

Grass, S. (2000). "Narrating the Cell: Dickens on the American Prisons." *The Journal of English and Germanic Philology*, 99(1), 50–70.

Grossman, J. H. (2002). *The Art of Alibi: English Law Courts and the Novel*. Baltimore: Johns Hopkins University Press.

Guha, R. (1997). *Dominance without Hegemony: History and Power in Colonial India*, Cambridge, MA: Harvard University Press.

(1999). *Elementary Aspects of Peasant Insurgency in Colonial India*. Durham: Duke University Press.

Haight, G. S. (1968/ 1985). *George Eliot: A biography*. London: Penguin Books.

Hansard. https://api.parliament.uk/historic-hansard/commons/1832/mar/27/abolition-of-capital-punishments

Harris, C. I. (1993) 'Whiteness as Property.' *Harvard Law Review*, 106(8), 1710.

Heber, R. (1873). *Narrative of a Journey through the Upper Provinces of India from Calcutta to Bombay, 1824–1825*, Vol. 2, London: John Murray.

Hegel, G. W. F. (1988). *Introduction to the Philosophy of History*, trans. Rauch, L. Indianapolis: Hackett Publishing Co.

Hensley, N. K. (2016). *Forms of Empire: The Poetics of Victorian Sovereignty*. New York: Oxford University Press.

Hesford, W. S. (2011). *Spectacular Rhetorics: Human Rights Visions, Recognitions, Feminisms*. Durham, NC: Duke University Press.

Hewett, G. (1840). *Private Record of the Life of General Sir George Hewett*, Newport: W.W. Yelf.

Hobbes, T. (1668/1982). *Leviathan*. New York: Penguin.

Hollingsworth, K. (1963). *The Newgate Novel, 1830–1847: Bulwer, Ainsworth, Dickens & Thackeray*. Detroit: Wayne State University Press.

Homans, M. (January 1, 2006). "Adoption Narratives, Trauma, and Origins." *Narrative*, 14(1), 4–26.

Howell, P. A. (1979). *The Judicial Committee of the Privy Council 1833–1876: Its Origins, Structure and Development*. Cambridge: Cambridge University Press.

Hunt, L. (2008). *Measuring Time, Making History* (The Natalie Zemon Davis Annual Lecture series). Budapest: Central European University Press.

Hussain, N. (2003). *The Jurisprudence of Emergency: Colonialism and the Rule of Law*. Ann Arbor: University of Michigan Press.

Hutchings, P. (2014). *The Criminal Spectre in Law, Literature and Aesthetics: Incriminating Subjects*. New York: Routledge.

Inden, R. B., & American Council of Learned Societies (2000). *Imagining India*. Bloomington, IN: Indiana University Press.

Iser, W. (1978). *The Act of Reading: A Theory of Aesthetic Response*. Johns Hopkins University Press.

JanMohamed, A. R. (2005). *The Death-Bound Subject: Richard Wright's Archaeology of Death*, Durham: Duke University Press.

Jeffries, M. P. (2011). *Thug Life: Race, Gender, and the Meaning of Hip-Hop*. Chicago: University of Chicago Press.

John, J. (2006). *Dickens's Villains: Melodrama, Character, Popular Culture*. Oxford: Oxford University Press.

Joseph, B. (2006). *Reading the East India Company 1720–1840: Colonial Currencies of Gender*. New Delhi: Orient Longman.

Joshi, P. (2007). "Mutiny Echoes: India, Britons, and Charles Dickens's *A Tale of Two Cities*." *Nineteenth-Century Literature, 62*(1), 48–87.

Kalpagam, U. (2014). *Rule by Numbers: Governmentality in Colonial India*. London: Lexington Books.

Kelley, R. D.G. (2016). "Thug Nation: On State Violence and Disposability." In J. T. Camp, and C. Heatherton (eds.), *Policing the Planet: Why the Policing Crisis Led to Black Lives Matter*. New York: Verso.

Keay, J. (2001). *India: A History*. New York: Grove Press.

Kirkby, D. E., and Coleborne, C. (2010). *Law, History, Colonialism: The Reach of Empire*. Manchester: Manchester University Press.

Kitton, F. G. (1890). *A Supplement to Charles Dickens by Pen and Pencil: Including Anecdotes and Reminiscences Collected from His Friends and Contemporaries*. United Kingdom: Frank Sabin.

Kolsky, E. (2011). *Colonial Justice in British India*. Cambridge: Cambridge University Press.

Koselleck, R., and Tribe, K. (2005). *Futures Past: On the Semantics of Historical Time*. New York: Columbia University Press.

Krueger, C. L. (2010). *Reading for the Law: British Literary History and Gender Advocacy*. Charlottesville, VA: University of Virginia Press.

Lariviere, R. (1989). Justices and Paṇḍitas: Some Ironies in Contemporary Readings of the Hindu Legal Past. *The Journal of Asian Studies, 48*(4), 757–769.

Leavis, F. R. (1948). *The Great Tradition: George Eliot, Henry James, Joseph Conrad*. London: Chatto & Windus.

Lewis, R. (1996). *Gendering Orientalism: Race, Femininity, and Representation*. London: Routledge.

Macaulay, T. B. M. (1871). *The Complete Works of Lord Macaulay*. United Kingdom: Longmans.

Majeed, J. (1992). *Ungoverned Imaginings: James Mill's The History of British India and Orientalism*. Oxford England: Clarendon Press.

(1996). "Meadows Taylor's Confessions of a Thug: The Anglo-Indian Novel as a Genre in the Making." In B. M. Gilbert (ed.), *Writing India, 1757–1990: The Literature of British India*. Manchester, UK: Manchester University Press, pp. 86–110.

Mann, M. (2004). "Dealing with Oriental Despotism: British Jurisdiction in Bengal, 1772–1793." In H. Fischer-Tiné and M. Mann (eds.), *Colonialism as Civilizing Mission: Cultural Ideology in British India*.. London: Wimbledon Publishing Company.

Manavalli, K. (2007). "Collins, Colonial Crime, and the Brahmin Sublime: The Orientalist Vision of a Hindu-Brahmin India in *The Moonstone*." *Comparative Critical Studies, 4*(1), 67–86.

Marcus, L. (2003). "Detection and Literary Fiction." In M. Priestman (ed.), *The Cambridge Companion to Crime Fiction* (Cambridge Companions to Literature). Cambridge: Cambridge University Press, pp. 245–268.

Marcus, Sharon. (2007). *Between Women: Friendship, Desire, and Marriage in Victorian England*. Princeton: Princeton University Press.

Marcus, Steven. (1976). *Representations: Essays on Literature and Society*. New York: Random House, p. 212, n.

Marlow, J. E. (1983). "English Cannibalism: Dickens after 1859." *Studies in English Literature, 1500–1900*, 23(4), 647–666.

Martin, P. (1995). *Victorian Families in Fact and Fiction*. New York: St. Martin's Press,

Marx, K. (1853). "The Future Results of the British Rule in India." *New-York Daily Tribune*, August 8.

Masani, Z. (1988). *Indian Tales of the Raj*. Berkeley: University of California Press.

Massumi, B. (1993). *The Politics of Everyday Fear*. Minneapolis: University of Minnesota Press.

(2010), "The Future Birth of the Affective Fact: The Political Ontology of Threat." In M. Gregg and G. Seigworth (eds.), *The Affect Theory Reader*. Durham: Duke University Press.

Mawani, R. (2014). "Law as Temporality: Colonial Politics and Indian Settlers." *UC Irvine Law Review*, *4*.

McAuliff, C.M.A. (1986). "The First English Adoption Law and Its American Precursors." *Seton Hall Law Review*, *15*, 656.

McInelly, B. C. (January 1, 2003). "Expanding Empires, Expanding Selves: Colonialism, the Novel, and Robinson Crusoe." *Studies in the Novel*, 35(1), 1.

McKeon, M. (2002). *The Origins of the English Novel: 1600–1740*. Baltimore: The Johns Hopkins University Press.

McLaverty, J. (December 1, 1981). "Comtean Fetishism in Silas Marner." *Nineteenth-Century Fiction*, 36(3), 318–336.

Mehta, J. (1995). "English Romance; Indian Violence." *The Centennial Review*, *39*(3), 611–657.

Meyer, N. (Director) (1988). *The Deceivers*. Merchant Ivory Productions.

Meyer, S. (October 1, 1993). "'Safely to Their Own Borders': Proto-Zionism, Feminism, and Nationalism in Daniel Deronda." *Elh*, 60(3), 733–758.

Meyler, B. (2015). Law, Literature, and History: The Love Triangle. *UC Irvine Law Review*, 5, 365–391.

Meyler, B., and Anker, E. S. (2017). *New Directions in Law and Literature*. New York: Oxford University Press.

Mill, J. (1820). *The History of British India*. United Kingdom: Baldwin, Cradock, and Joy.

Millar, R. M. C. (2012). *English Historical Sociolinguistics*. Edinburgh: Edinburgh University Press.

Miller, D. A., and Miller, D. A. (1989). *The Novel and the Police*. Berkeley, CA: Univ. of California Press.

Moin, A. A. (2012). *The Millennial Sovereign: Sacred Kingship and Sainthood in Islam*. New York: Columbia University Press.

Moore, E. (1846). *The Queen, on the Prosecution of the Bombay Government* v. *Eduljee Byramjee and Seventeen Others*. In *Reports of Cases Heard and Determined by the Judicial Committee on Appeal from the Supreme and Sudder Dewanny Courts in the East Indies*, Vol. iii 1841–1846. London: V. & R. Stevens and G.S. Norton.

(1856). *Prinsep and the East India Company* v. *Dyce Sombre and Others*. In *Reports of Cases Heard and Determined by the Judicial Committee and the Lords of His Majesty's Most Honourable Privy Council*. United Kingdom: W. T. Clarke.

(1860). *Troup et. al.* v. *The East India Company and Dyce Sombre* v. *The East India Company*. In *Reports of Cases Heard and Determined by the Judicial Committee on Appeal from the Supreme and Sudder Dewanny Courts in the East Indies*, Vol. vii 1857–1860. London: V. & R. Stevens and Sons.

(1863). *Ramaswamy Aiyan* v. *Venkata Achari*. In *Reports of Cases Heard and Determined by the Judicial Committee on Appeal from the Supreme and Sudder Dewanny Courts in the East Indies*, Vol. IX. London: V. & R. Stevens and G.S. Norton.

Moore, G. (2004). *Dickens and Empire: Discourses of Class, Race, and Colonialism in the Works of Charles Dickens*. Burlington, VT: Ashgate Press.

Moretti, F. (1983). "Clues," in *Signs Taken for Wonders*. New York: Verso.

(1987). *The Way of the World: The Bildungsroman in European Culture*. London: Verso.

Morton, S. (2013). *States of Emergency: Colonialism, Literature and Law* (Series Postcolonialism across the disciplines, 11). Liverpool University Press.

Mufti, A. (2007). *Enlightenment in the Colony: The Jewish Question and the Crisis of Postcolonial Culture*. Princeton, N.J: Princeton University Press.

Mukherjee, A. (2005). "Missed Encounters: Repetition, Rewriting, and Contemporary Returns to Charles Dickens's Great Expectations." *Contemporary Literature* 46(1), 108–133.

Mukherjee, M. (2010). *India in the Shadows of Empire: A Legal and Political History, 1774–1950*. New Delhi: Oxford University Press.

Mukherjee, P. (2004). *Crime and Empire: The Colony in Nineteenth Century Fictions of Crime*. Oxford: Oxford University Press.

Mukherjee, U.P. (2003). *Crime and Empire: The Colony in Nineteenth-Century Fictions of Crime*. New York: Oxford University Press.

Mukhopadhyay, A. (2012). *Behind the Mask: The Cultural Definition of the Legal Subject in Colonial Bengal (1715–1911)*. New Delhi: Oxford University India.

Muñoz, J. (2009). *Cruising Utopia: The Then and There of Queer Futurity* (Sexual Cultures). New York: New York University Press.

Murdoch, L. (2006). *Imagined Orphans: Poor Families, Child Welfare, and Contested Citizenship in London*. New Brunswick, NJ: Rutgers University Press.

Myer, N. (1988). *The Deceivers*. New York: Cinecom Pictures.

Narayan, N. G. (December 8, 2017). "The Persistence of the Brahmin Priests in Wilkie Collins's *The Moonstone*." *Victorian Literature and Culture, 45*(4), 783–800.

National Legal Services Authority v. *Union of India*, Writ Petition (Civil). No. 400 of 2012.

Navtej Singh Johar and Others. v. *Union of India thr. Secretary Ministry of Law and Justice*, Writ Petition (Criminal.) No. 76 of 2016.

Nayar, P. K. (2012). *Colonial Voices: The Discourses of Empire*. Chichester, West Sussex: Wiley-Blackwell.

Nayder, L. (1992). "Robinson Crusoe and Friday in Victorian Britain: 'Discipline,' 'Dialogue,' and Collins's Critique of Empire in *The Moonstone*." *Dickens Studies Annual, 21*, 213–231.

Neti, L. (May 4, 2017). "The Love Laws": Section 377 and the Politics of Queerness in Arundhati Roy's *The God of Small Things*. *Law & Literature, 29*(2), 223–246.

Ngugi, T. (2011). *Decolonising the Mind: The Politics of Language in African Literature*. London: J. Currey.

Ní Fhlathúin, M. (2004). "The Making of a Master Criminal: The 'Chief of the Thugs' in Victorian Writings on Crime." In A. Maunder and G. Moore (eds.), *Victorian Crime, Madness and Sensation*. Ashgate, pp. 31–44.

Nijhar, P. (2009). *Law and Imperialism: Criminality and Constitution in Colonial India and Victorian England.* London: Pickering and Chatto.

Niranjana, T. (1992). *Siting Translation: History, Post-Structuralism, and the Colonial Context.* Berkeley, CA: University of California Press.

Nixon, C. L. (2011). *The Orphan in Eighteenth-Century Law and Literature: Estate, Blood, and Body.* Burlington, VT: Ashgate.

Novy, M. (2007). *Reading Adoption: Family and Difference in Fiction and Drama.* Ann Arbor, MI: University of Michigan Press.

(2001). *Imagining Adoption: Essays on Literature and Culture.* Ann Arbor, MI: University of Michigan Press.

Nunokawa, J. (April 1, 1993). "The Miser's Two Bodies: 'Silas Marner' and the Sexual Possibilities of the Commodity." *Victorian Studies,* 36(3), 273–292.

O'Brien, D. (2018). "The Post-Colonial Constitutional Order of the Commonwealth Caribbean: The Endurance of the Crown and the Judicial Committee of the Privy Council." *The Journal of Imperial and Commonwealth History,* 46(5), 958–983.

O'Brien, J. (2013). *The Scientific Sherlock Holmes: Cracking the Case with Science and Forensics.* New York: Oxford University Press.

Ogle, V. (2015). *The Global Transformation of Time: 1870–1950.* Cambridge, MA: Harvard University Press.

O'Hanlon, R. (February 1, 1999). "Manliness and Imperial Service in Mughal North India." *Journal of the Economic and Social History of the Orient,* 42(1), 47–93.

Ondaatje, M. (2011). *Anil's Ghost.* London: Vintage.

O'Toole, T. (2001). Adoption and the "Improvement of the Estate." In Marianne Novy (ed.), *Imagining Adoption: Essays on Literature and Culture.* Ann Arbor, MI: University of Michigan Press.

Oyewumi, O. (2005).Colonizing Bodies and Minds. In G. G. Desai and S. Nair (eds.), *Postcolonialisms: An Anthology of Cultural Theory and Criticism.* New Brunswick, NJ: Rutgers Univ. Press.

Pal-Lapinski, P. (2005). *The Exotic Woman in Nineteenth-Century British Fiction and Culture: A Reconsideration.* Durham, NH: University of New Hampshire Press.

Patten, R., Jordan, J., and Waters, C. (eds.) (2018). *The Oxford Handbook of Charles Dickens.* Oxford: Oxford University Press.

Park, H. (2003). "Criminality and Empire in *Great Expectations.*" *English Language and Literature,* 49(4), 707–729.

Pensionary and Other Claims of Maharaja Dalip Singh, British Library R/1/1/46 p. 18.

Petch, S. (January 1, 2007). "Law, Literature, and Victorian Studies." *Victorian Literature and Culture,* 35(1), 361–384.

Peters, J. S. (October 1, 1997). "*Law and Literature: Possibilities and Perspectives* by Ian Ward; *Law and Literature Perspectives* by Bruce L. Rockwood; *Law's Stories: Narrative and Rhetoric in the Law* by Peter Brooks, and Paul Gewirtz." *Cardozo Studies in Law and Literature,* 9(2), 259–274.

(2005). "Law, Literature, and the Vanishing Real: On the Future of an Interdisciplinary Illusion." *Pmla, 120*(2), 442–453.

Peters, L. (2018). *Orphan Texts: Victorian Orphans, Culture and Empire.* Manchester: Manchester University Press.

Poon, P. (January 1, 2012). "From Status to Contract: Inheritance and Succession in George Eliot's Late Fction." *Sydney Studies in English, 38,* 50–80.

Pratt and Morgan v. *The Attorney General for Jamaica and another* (Jamaica) [1993] UKPC 1 (November 2, 1993).

Purohit, T. (2012). *The Aga Khan Case: Religion and Identity in Colonial India,* Cambridge, MA: Harvard University Press.

Rankin, G. (1939). "The Judicial Committee of the Privy Council." *The Cambridge Law Journal, 7*(1), 2–22.

Rao, A. (2009). *The Caste Question: Dalits and the Politics of Modern India.* Berkeley: University of California Press.

Rapson, E. J. (1962). *The Cambridge History of India,* Vol. 1. Cambridge: Cambridge University Press.

Raz, K. (2017). *The Black Prince.* London: Brillstein Entertainment Partners.

Reed, John R. (1973). "English Imperialism and the Unacknowledged Crime of *The Moonstone.*" *Clio* 2(3): 281–290.

Roberts, E. (1825). *Scenes and Characteristics of Hindostan, with Sketches of Anglo-Indian Society.* London: J.L. Cox & Sons.

Robin, C. (2004). *Fear: The History of a Political Idea.* New York: Oxford University Press.

Robinson, J. (1929). *The Development of Modern Europe,* Vol. 1. UK: Ginn.

Rocher, L. (2012). *Studies in Hindu Law and Dharmaśāstra,* Donald R. Davis (ed.). London: Anthem Press.

Rocher, R. (2010). "The Creation of Anglo-Indian Law." In T. Lubin *et al.* (eds.), *Hinduism and Law: An Introduction.* Cambridge: Cambridge University Press.

Rodensky, L. (2003). *The Crime in Mind: Criminal Responsibility and the Victorian Novel.* New York: Oxford University Press.

Rowe, M. M. (April 1, 1990). "Melting Outlines in *Daniel Deronda.*" *Studies in the Novel,* 22(1), 10–18.

Roy, Ashish. (1993). "The Fabulous Imperialist Semiotic of Wilkie Collin's *The Moonstone.*" *New Literary History, 24*(3), 657–681.

Roy, Alpana. (2008). "Postcolonial Theory and Law: A Critical Introduction." *Adelaide Law Review, 29*(2), 315–357.

Roy, P. (1996). "Discovering India, Imagining Thuggee." *Yale Journal of Criticism,* 9(1), 121–145.

Roy, T., and Swamy, A. (2016). *Law and the Economy in Colonial India.* Chicago: University of Chicago Press.

Rushby, K. (2003). *Children of Kali: Through India in Search of Bandits, the Thug Cult, and the British Raj.* New York: Walker & Company.

Said, E. (1978). *Orientalism,* New York: Random House.

(1979/1992). *The Question of Palestine.* London: Vintage Books.

(1993). *Culture and Imperialism*. New York: Knopf.

Sargent, N. (2010). "Mys-Reading the Past in Detective Fiction and Law." *Law and Literature, 22*(2), 288–306.

Sarna, N. (2010). *The Exile: A Novel Based on the Life of Maharaja Duleep Singh*. Gurgaon, Haryana: Penguin Books India.

Sassen, S. (2008). *Territory, Authority, Rights: From Medieval to Global Assemblages*. Princeton, NJ: Princeton University Press.

Schabas, W. A. (October 1, 1994). "Soering's Legacy: The Human Rights Committee and the Judicial Committee of the Privy Council Take a Walk down Death Row." *The International and Comparative Law Quarterly*, 43(4), 913–923.

Schmidgen, W. (2002). "*Terra Nullius*, Cannibalism, and the Natural Law of Appropriation in *Robinson Crusoe*." In *Eighteenth-Century Fiction and the Law of Property*. Cambridge: Cambridge University Press, pp. 32–62.

Schmitt, C. (2006). *Political Theology: Four Chapters on the Concept of Sovereignty*, trans. M. Hoelzl and G. Ward. Chicago: University of Chicago Press.

(2008). *The Leviathan in the State Theory of Thomas Hobbes*, trans. G. Schwab. Chicago: University of Chicago Press.

Schramm, J.-M. (2000). *Testimony and Advocacy in Victorian Law, Literature, and Theology*. Cambridge, UK: Cambridge University Press.

(2012). *Atonement and Self-Sacrifice in Nineteenth-Century Narrative*. Cambridge: Cambridge UP.

Sedgwick, E., and Frank, A. (2003). *Touching Feeling: Affect, Pedagogy, Performativity* (Series q). Durham: Duke University Press.

Sen, Satradu. (2002). "The Savage Family: Colonialism and Female Infanticide in Nineteenth Century India." *Journal of Women's History*, 14(3), 53–79.

Sen, Sudipta. (2016). *A Distant Sovereignty: National Imperialism and the Origins of British India*. London: Taylor & Francis.

Shankar, S. (December 1, 2013). "Thugs and Bandits: Life and Law in Colonial and Epicolonial India." *Biography - An Interdisciplinary Quarterly, 36*(1), 97–123.

Sharafi, M. (2016). *Law and Identity in Colonial South Asia: Parsi Legal Culture, 1772–1947*. New York: Cambridge University Press.

Sharma, U., and Parkin, F. (1998). *Caste*. Milton Keynes: Open University Press.

Shaik, N (2007). Interview with G. Spivak, *The Present as History: Critical Perspectives on Contemporary Global Power*. New York: Columbia University Press, pp. 172–202.

Shamsie, K. (2009). *Burnt Shadows*. London: Bloomsbury.

Sharafi, M. J. (2014). *Law and Identity in Colonial South Asia: Parsi Legal Culture, 1772–1947*. New York: Cambridge University Press.

Sharpe, J. (1993). *Allegories of Empire: The Figure of Woman in the Colonial Text*, Minneapolis: University of Minnesota Press.

Siddiqi, Y. (2007). *Anxieties of Empire and the Fiction of Intrigue*. New York: Columbia University Press.

Singh, B. (January 1, 1995). "Crossing Boundaries: The Life of Begum Samru." *Manushi, 87*, 13–22.

Singh, K. (2001). *Ranjit Singh: Maharajah of the Punjab*. New Delhi: Penguin.

Singha, R. (1998). *A Despotism of Law: Crime and Justice in Early Colonial India*. Delhi: Oxford University Press.

Sinha, I. (2009). *Animal's People*. New York: Simon & Schuster.

Sinha, N. (2008). "Mobility, Control and Criminality in Early Colonial India, 1760s–1850s." *The Indian Economic & Social History Review, 45*, 1, 1–33.

Slaughter, J. (2007). *Human Rights, Inc.: The World Novel, Narrative Form, and International Law*. New York: Fordham University Press.

Sleeman, W.H. (1893). *Rambles and* Recollections *of an Indian Official*, Vol. 2. London: Archibald Constable & Company.

(2011). *Ramaseeana: Or a Vocabulary of the Peculiar Language Used by the Thugs*. Cambridge, UK: Cambridge University Press (first published 1836).

Sombre, D.O.D. (1849). *Mr. Dyce Sombre's Refutation of the Charge of Lunacy Brought against Him in the Court of Chancery*. Paris: David Ochterlony Dyce Sombre.

Sophocles, Fitts, D., and Fitzgerald, R. (1939). *Oedipus Rex*. New York, Harcourt, Brace, and World.

Spielberg, S. (1984). *Indiana Jones and the Temple of Doom*. Los Angeles: Paramount Pictures.

Spivak, G. (1985). "The Rani of Sirmur: An Essay in Reading the Archives." *History and Theory*, 24(3), 247–272.

(1988). "Can the Subaltern Speak?," In Cary Nelson and Lawrence Grossberg (eds.), *Marxism and the Interpretation of Culture*. Urbana: University of Illinois Press, pp. 271–313.

(2002). "Ethics and Politics in Tagore, Coetzee, and Certain Scenes of Teaching." *Diacritics, 32*(3/4), 17–31.

Sreenivas, M. (2004). "Conjugality and Capital: Gender, Families, and Property under Colonial Law in India." *The Journal of Asian Studies, 63*(4), 937–960.

Stephen, J. (1857). "The Licence of Modern Novelists." In *The Edinburgh Review*. United Kingdom: A. and C. Black.

Stephen, L. (1895). *The Life of Sir James Fitzjames Stephen: A Judge of the High Court of Justice*. London: Smith, Elder, & Co.

Stern, S. (2017). "Legal and Literary Fictions." In B. Meyler, and E. S. Anker (eds.), *New Directions in Law and Literature*. New York: Oxford University Press.

Stokes, E. (1959). *The English Utilitarians and India*. Oxford: Clarendon Press.

Stoler, A. (1989). "Making Empire Respectable: The Politics of Race and Sexual Morality in Twentieth Century Colonial Cultures." *American Ethnologist* 16(4), 634–660.

(2002a). *Carnal Knowledge and Imperial Power: Race and the Intimate in Colonial Rule*. Berkeley: University of California Press.

(2002b). "Colonial Archives and the Arts of Governance." *Archival Science, 2*, 1–2, p. 97.

Sturman, R. (2010). "Marriage and Family in Colonial Indian Law." In T. Lubin, D. Davis and J. Krishnan (eds.), *Hinduism and Law: An Introduction*. New York: Cambridge University Press.

Sudrann, J. (September 1, 1970). "Daniel Deronda and the Landscape of Exile," *ELH*, 37(3), 433.
Sutherland, D. (1873). *The Weekly Reporter, Appellate High Court*, Vol. 18. Calcutta: Thacker, Spink and Company.
Swann, Brian (1976). "'Silas Marner' and the New Mythus." *Criticism, 18*(2), Article 1. Available at: https://digitalcommons.wayne.edu/criticism/vol18/iss2/1
Tambling J. (1995). "Prison-Bound: Dickens, Foucault and *Great Expectations*." In *Dickens, Violence and the Modern State*. New York: Palgrave Macmillan.
Taylor, P. M. (1858/2001).*Confessions of Thug*. New Delhi: Rupa.
Thapar, R. (2004). *Somanatha, the Many Voices of a History*. New Delhi: Penguin, Viking.
Thomas, R. (2001). "Detection in the Victorian Novel." In D. David (ed.), *The Cambridge Companion to the Victorian Novel*. Cambridge: Cambridge University Press, pp. 169–191.
Thompson, E.P. (1967). "Time, Work-Discipline and Industrial Capitalism," *Past and Present*, No. 38. Oxford: Oxford University Press, pp. 56–97.
Tittemore, B. (March 30, 2005). "Summary of Comments on the Current and Future Status of Litigation on the Issue of the Mandatory Death Penalty in the Commonwealth Caribbean." *Proceedings of the Annual Meeting (American Society of International Law), 99*, 74–77.
Todorov, T. (1995). "The Typology of Detective Fiction." In *The Poetics of Prose*. Trans. R. Howard. Ithaca, NY: Cornell University Press.
Valverde, M. (2015). *Chronotopes of Law: Jurisdiction, Scale and Governance*. Abingdon: Routledge.
van Wœrkens, M. (2002). *The Strangled Traveler: Colonial Imaginings and the Thugs of India*. Trans. C. Tihanyi. Chicago, IL: University of Chicago Press.
Verne, J. (1956). *Round the World in Eighty Days*. London: Collins.
Viswanathan, G. (2015). *Masks of Conquest: Literary Study and British Rule in India*. New York: Columbia University Press.
Waddams, S. (1992). *Law, Politics and the Church of England: The Career of Stephen Lushington (1782–1873)*. Cambridge: Cambridge University Press.
Wagner, K. (2007). *Thuggee: Banditry and the British in Early Nineteenth-Century India*. New York: Palgrave Macmillan.
(2010). "Confessions of a Skull: Phrenology and Colonial Knowledge in Early Nineteenth-Century India." *History Workshop Journal, 69*(1), 27–51.
Washbrook, D. (1981), "Law, State and Agrarian Society in Colonial India." *Modern Asian Studies*, 15(3), 649–721.
Watt, I. P. (2015). *The Rise of the Novel: Studies in Defoe, Richardson and Fielding*. Chicago: University of Chicago Press.
Wiener, M. J. (2009). *An Empire on Trial: Race, Murder, and Justice under British Rule, 1870–1935*. Cambridge: Cambridge University Press.
Wiesenfarth, J. (June 1, 1970). "Demythologizing 'Silas Marner,'" *ELH*, 37(2), 226.
Williams, H. S. (1909). *The Historians' History of the World*. London: Hooper & Jackson, Ltd.

Wohlfarth, M. E. (September 1, 1998). "Daniel Deronda and the Politics of Nationalism." *Nineteenth-Century Literature*, 53(2), 188–210.

Woodward, E. L. (1949). *The Oxford History of England: The Age of Reform, 1815–1870*. Oxford: Clarendon Press.

Worthington, H. (2005). *The Rise of the Detective in Early Nineteenth-Century Popular Fiction*. Houndmills, Basingstoke, Hampshire: Palgrave Macmillan.

Wynne, C. (2002). *The Colonial Conan Doyle: British Imperialism, Irish Nationalism, and the Gothic*. Westport, CT: Greenwood Press.

Yang, A. (2003). "Indian Convict Workers in Southeast Asia in the Late Eighteenth and Early Nineteenth Centuries." *Journal of World History*, 14(2), 179–208.

Yelle, R. A. (2018). *Sovereignty and the Sacred: Secularism and the Political Economy of Religion*. Chicago: University of Chicago Press.

Young, R. (1995). *Colonial Desire: Hybridity in Theory, Culture and Race*. London: Routledge.

Zomchick, J. P. (2007). *Family and the Law in Eighteenth-Century Fiction: The Public Conscience in the Private Sphere*. Cambridge, England: Cambridge University Press.

Index

Abramowicz, Sarah, 177, 181–182
absolute sovereignty
  appeal in criminal cases and, 55–56
  British transition from, 2–5, 211
  colonial expansion and, 2–5
  fear and reinforcement of, 35
  JCPC colonial judgments and fiction of, 7
  Privy Council and ideology of, 6–7
Achari, Venkata, 109–110
Acharya, S. K., 210
Acharya, Vijay Krishna, 92–94
Acts of Union (Britain), 43–45
Act XVII of 1836, 158–159
Act XXX of 1836, 48–49
Adalats, Hastings's establishment of, 4
adoption narrative
  Begum Sumroo case and, 149–154, 157–159
  children in, 182–185
  colonial law and, 174–175
  in *Daniel Deronda* (Eliot), 192–196
  Eliot's ambivalence concerning, 206–208
  in Eliot's fiction, 22–23, 29
  in *Felix Holt, The Radical* (Eliot), 191–192
  Indian inheritance laws and, 28
  in *Silas Marner,* 176–179, 184–185
  social stigma in, 188–192
  sovereignty and, 160–161
  in Victorian fiction, 178–179
affect, fear and, 41–42, 45–50
Agamben, Giorgio, 91
Ahmed, Siraj, 16–17, 100–101
Ainsworth, Harrison, 85–86
Aiyan, Ramaswamy, 109–110
Akbar (emperor), 150–151
Alam II (Shah), 152, 161–164
Alber, Jan, 78
All the Year Round periodical, 78–79, 123–124
alterity, in *Felix Holt, The Radical* (Eliot), 191–192
Althusser, Louis, 80
ambiguity, legal recourse to, 8–9
American Notes (Dickens), 78–79
Amsterdam, Anthony, 12–13
Anand, Anita, 139–140
Andaman Islands, penal transport to, 51
Anderson, Clare, 50–51, 233n.106
Anglo-Sikh War (1846), 140–141
Anil's Ghost (Ondaatje), 213–217
Animal's People (Sinha), 213–217
Anker, Elizabeth, 17
annexation of property, British colonization of India and, 28
anti-colonial movements, film portrayals of, 92–94
anti-state narratives, novel and, 221n.7
Appadurai, Arjun, 92–94, 108–109
appeals
  foreclosure of reform in rejection of, 89–90
  as literary genre, 8
  reconsideration of, 63–65
  sovereignty and narrative in, 12–14
Aravamudan, Srinivas, 43–45
Archaeology of Babel: The Colonial Foundation of the Humanities (Ahmed), 16–17
archives
  of colonial law, 19–21
  narrative in, 23–25
Arendt, Hannah, 91
Aristotle, 215–217
Arnold, David, 69–79
Around the World in Eighty Days (Verne), 76–77
Arthur and George (Barnes), 234n.116
Article 35 (Hastings), 52
Arya Brahmins, 104–106, 115–118
Auerbach, Nina, 188
Aurangzeb, 122–136
Austin, J. L., 223n.47

Bachchan, Amitabh, 92–94
Bakhtin, Mikhail, 5–6
Barnes, Julian, 234n.116
Baron, J. B., 14

Barua, Ankur, 111–112
Bayly, Susan, 108–109
*Baynes, C.E. (Judge), 113–114
Beer, Gillian, 207–208
Begum Sumroo, 22–23
  adoption narrative and case of, 174–175
  biographical details about, 152
  British narratives about, 154–157
  case involving, 28
  challenges to normativity by, 157–159, 210
  Eliot's adoption novels and case of, 29, 177
  family and kinship in cases of, 207–208
  gender identity and cases about, 167–168, 198–199
  individualism and sovereignty in case of, 149–154
  privacy and property in case of, 164–169
  treaties with East India Company and, 25–26, 159–164
Bengal Regulation of 1803, 161
Bentham, Jeremy, 21–22, 215–217
  Hobbes's influence on, 45
Benton, Lauren, 5–7, 101, 103–104
  on colonial law, 22–23
Ben-Yishai, Ayelet, 9–10, 119–120
"beside," Sedgwick's concept of non-dualism and, 11
Between Women (Marcus), 18–19
Bhagavad Purana, 140
Bhopal Union Carbide disaster, 213–217
bildungsroman
  adoption novels and, 29
  Confessions of a Thug as departure from, 75–76
  criminality in fiction and, 27
  father figure in, 90–92
  fiction as history in, 122–123
  Great Expectations as, 64–65
  historicity and, 92–94
  individual responsibility in, 91–92
  narrative and development in, 63–65
  nation-formation in, 89
  normalization in, 238n.84
  precedential reasoning and, 120–121
  structure of tension in, 79–80
  thuggee narrative compared to, 68
biopolitics
  of fear, 39–42, 57–60
  Indian bureaucracy and, 107–110
  in *The Queen* v. *Eduljee Byramjee* case, 36–39
Bleak House (Dickens), 188
body, Indian criminality and role of, 26–29
Bollywood, thuggee representation by, 92–94
Brahminism
  colonial law and, 104–106
  in *The Moonstone*, 125–130, 132–133, 138–139, 144–146
  in *Ramaswamy Aiyan* v. *Venkata Achari* case, 111–112
Bramho movement, 104–106
British criminality
  biopolitics and, 57–60
  concealment of, 47
  in *Great Expectations*, 78–79, 83–85
  individual responsibility and, 91–92
  in *The Moonstone*, 123–124
British imperialism and colonialism
  Acts of Union and, 43–45
  caste system and, 108–109
  convict labor and, 50–53
  in *Daniel Deronda*, 204–206
  in English literature, 24–25
  fear as strategy in, 42–45, 47
  God-King-Father paradigm in, 73–74, 90–92
  governance associated with, 47
  law and literature and, 1–2
  legal ideology and literary themes and, 209–210
  in *The Moonstone*, 135–137
  Mughal sovereignty and, 149–154
  thuggee narrative in, 76–77
  white violence in, 229–230n.58
Brontë, Charlotte, 188
Brontë, Emily, 188
Brooks, Peter, 12–13
Bruce, Knight (Lord Justice), 115–118
Bruner, Jerome, 12–13
Bulwer, Edward, 85–86
Burbank, Jane, 6–7
bureaucracy in India, biopolitics of, 107–110
Byramjee, Eduljee, 26–29
  criminal transport of, 51
  fear of punishment by, 60
  Privy Council appeal by, 53–57
  transport of, 79
  trial of, 36–39

Cambridge Law Society, 4–5
Campbell, James, 217–219
The Canadian Law Times, 5–6
capitalism, colonialism and, 43–45
capital punishment
  biopolitics of fear and, 59–60
  British reform of, 85–86
  in colonial India, 52
  colonial law and, 22–23, 233n.106
  contemporary appeals of, 217–219
  Judgment of Death Act (1823) and, 55

Caribbean litigation, current JCPC rulings in, 217–219
Carter, M. J., 76–77
Caste, Society and Politics in India from the Eighteenth Century to the Modern Age (Bayly), 108–109
caste system
  bureaucratic biopolitics and, 107–110
  colonial law and, 103–106
  precedential reasoning and, 120–121
  Privy Council cases involving, 27
Chakrabarty, Dipesh, 233n.108
Chakravarti, Uma, 108–109
Chandra, Uday, 14–16
Chandrachud (Justice), 216–217
Chaplin, Sue, 221n.7
Charter Act. *See* Government of India Acts (1833 and 1858)
Charter of Justice of Bombay (1823), 53–57, 232n.92
Chase, Cynthia, 200–201
Chatterjee, Indrani, 22–23, 168–169
Chibber, Vivek, 228–229n.40
childhood terror
  in *Great Expectations*, 79–85
  in *The Moonstone*, 138–139
children in Victorian fiction
  adoption narrative and, 182–185
  in Eliot's fiction, 179–182, 194–195
Children of Kali: Through India in Search of Bandits (Rushby), 76–77
China Budla, 38–41
class conflict
  in *Felix Holt, The Radical* (Eliot), 191–192
  in *Great Expectations*, 82–83
"Clues" (Moretti), 143–145
Code of Gentoo Laws, 101
Cohn, Bernard, 43, 107
Colebrooke, Henry Thomas, 100–104
Colley, Linda, 3, 43
Collins, Phillip, 79
Collins, Wilkie
  colonial historical influences on, 131–132
  Dickens and, 123–124
  English modernity and colonialism in fiction of, 28
  influence of *Confessions of a Thug* on, 76–77
  Koh-i-noor diamond discussed by, 142–146
  Privy Council Judicial Committee and work of, 1–2
colonialism. *See also* British imperialism
  absolute sovereignty and, 2–5
  access to legal remedies under, 18
  Acts of Union and, 43–45
  biopolitics and, 57–60
  British state formation and, 3, 43–45
  caste system and, 108–109
  contemporary film narratives of, 92–94, 240n.112
  convict labor and, 50–53
  economic effects of, 43–45
  in English literature, 24–25
  fear as strategy in, 42–45, 47–49
  God-King-Father paradigm in, 73–74, 90–92
  governance associated with, 47
  in *Great Expectations*, 88–89
  history and, 99–100
  Hobbes's *Leviathan* and context of, 42–43
  Indian inheritance laws and, 28
  individualism and, 220n.1
  law and literature and, 1–2
  literary and legal narratives of, 11–12
  in *The Moonstone* (Collins), 125–130, 135–137
  Mughal sovereignty and, 149–154
  narrative in life under, 13–14
  privacy and property and, 164–169
  subaltern class structure and, 228–229n.40
  subjection to legal policies and prohibitions under, 18
  temporality of law and, 114–118
  thuggee narrative in, 68–77
  in Victorian studies, 18–19
  white violence in, 229–230n.58
colonial jurisprudence (colonial law)
  archives of, 19–21
  caste system and, 104–106
  contemporary judicial rejection of, 216–217
  English selfhood and sovereignty and, 2–6
  heteroglossia of, 5–7
  Indian fear of, 39–42, 49–50
  Indian religious law and, 100–104
  justice discourse and, 211
  as narrative, 12–14
  normativity and, 16–17
  potential for appeal in, 53–57
  precedents established in, 118–121
  Privy Council influence on, 7–12
  property ownership and inheritance in, 153–154
  prosecution of thugs and, 48–49
  racism and paternalism in, 232–233n.99
  religious law and, 100–104
  sovereignty of, in criminal appeals, 47–57
  surrogacy and subversion in, 210
  thuggee narrative and, 68–77
  Victorian novel and, 9–10
Conan Doyle, Arthur, 60–62, 76–77

Confessions of a Thug (Taylor), 27
British fiction and influence of, 76–77
film versions of, 92–94
Great Expectations compared with, 64–65
legal ideology in, 209–210
narrative in, 69–72
Poovey's interpretation of, 236n.33
popular culture legacy of, 77
popularity in England of, 65–68
publishing success of, 69–79
subjecthood and citizenship in, 90–92
Conrad, Joseph, 24–25
contemporary law, literature and, 213–217
convict labor
decline in practice of, 50–53
Indian criminals as source of, 26–29, 35–39, 231n.79
Cooper, Frederick, 6–7
Cornwallis, Charles (Marquess), 159–164
Court of Criminal Appeals (England), 60–62
Cowasjee, Nasserwanjee, 37–38
Criminal Appeals Act of 1907, 60–62
Criminal Court of Appeals, 63–65
criminality. *See also* Indian criminality
in detective fiction, 143–145
fear in narratives of, 34–35
in *Great Expectations*, 78–79, 81–85, 88–89
in Newgate novels, 85–86
in *The Queen* v. *Eduljee Byramjee*, 26–29
racialization of, 64–65, 237n.68
subjectivity framework in, 16
in Victorian fiction, 22–23
criminal justice. *See also* colonial jurisprudence (colonial law)
British *vs.* colonial approaches to, 57–60
English *vs.* Indian comparisons of, 26–29
fear as tool of colonial criminal justice, 35
in *Great Expectations* (Dickens), 78–79
potential for appeal in, 53–57
reconsideration of appeals in, 63–65
thuggee narrative and, 68–77
criminal transport. *See* penal transport
Criminal Tribes Act of 1871, 6, 68, 91–92, 215–217
Crimmins, James, 45
Critical Legal Theory, law and literature and, 224n.60
Culture and Imperialism (Said), 87–88
Curia Regis (royal court), 3
Currie, Mark, 134

Dalal, Urvashi, 167–168
Dalhousie (James Andrew Broun-Ramsay) (Lord), 73–74, 140–141, 160–161, 174–175
Dalrymple, William, 139–140, 164
Damodhur, Manuckchund, 38–41
Daniel Deronda (Eliot), 29
adoption in, 192–196
double plot in, 192–193
Jewish identity in, 192–193, 199–202
kinship in, 177–179
orphan narrative in, 201–202
paternity in, 193–194
unknown mother in, 196–199
Dash, Mike, 76–77
David Copperfield (Dickens), 50–53, 89
Davis, Natalie Zemon, 19–20
De, Rohit, 5–6, 211
on fiction in JCPC judgments, 7
dead children, in *Confessions of a Thug*, 74–77
The Deceivers (film), 76–77
Delhi High Court, 20–21
De Man, Paul, 226n.82
Derrett, J. Duncan, 102–103
A Despotism of Law (Singha), 6
A Detailed Report of the Proceedings on the Trial of the Eighteen Parsee Prisoners for Murder, Before the Supreme Court, Bombay, on Wednesday, July 17, 1844, 36–39
detective fiction, temporality in, 133–134
Dharmaśāstra, legal status of, 100–104
Dickens, Charles
Collins and, 123–124
Confessions of a Thug and work of, 65–66
on criminality, 64–65
on criminal justice, 27
criminal transport in novels of, 50–53
influence of *Confessions of a Thug* on, 76–77
Privy Council Judicial Committee and work of, 1–2
Sepoy Rebellion and, 91–92
Dirks, Nicholas, 108–109
disciplinary model of law, Victorian fiction and, 9–10
Dolin, Kieran, 225n.66
drama, narrative basis of law and, 12–13
Dressner, Lawrence, 206–208
Duleep Singh, Maharajah of Punjab, 124–125, 139–142, 146
Dunham, Robert, 184–185
Durrani, Shuja (Shah), 139
Dyce, George Alexander, 152–153
Dyce, Georgiana, 152–153, 161–164
Dyce Sombre, David Ochterlony, 25–26, 28
Begum Sumroo's adoption of, 141–142, 152–153
as Begum Sumroo's heir, 157–159
British colonial rule and fate of, 149–154
cash inheritance of, 159

death of, 161
East India Company land seizure and, 159–164
estate of, 169–174
family and kinship in cases of, 207–208
lunacy charges against, 169–174
sovereignty issues in inheritance dispute of, 164–169
suit against East India Company by, 153
will drafted by, 171–172
Dyce Sombre, Mary Ann, 152–153, 161–164, 169–174. *See also* Troup, Mary Ann Dyce Sombre

Eastern State Penitentiary (Philadelphia), Dickens's visit to, 78–79
East India Company
Begum Sumroo's treaties with, 25–26, 159–164
colonial expansion under, 42–43
land seized by, 157–159, 161–169
monetization of kinship by, 73–74
in *The Moonstone*, 125–130, 135–137
Mughal Empire incursions by, 153
popular misconceptions of, 14–16
property acquisition by, 151
Punjab seizure by, 139–141
royal charter for, 25–26
economics, British state formation and, 43–45
Edalji, George, 60–62
Edalji, Shapurji, 60–62
Edelman, Lee, 76–77
Edinburgh Review, 212–213
Edwin Drood (Dickens), 76–77
Eliot, George, 1–2
acceptance of adoption in *Felix Holt*, 191–192
adoption and kinship in *Silas Marner* of, 176–179, 184–185
adoption in novels of, 179, 206–208, 210
adoption narrative in *Daniel Deronda*, 192–196
adoption novels of, 22–23, 29
family relations in, 176–179
individualism in novels of, 149–150
Lewes boys as stepsons of, 206–208
Eliot, T. S., 123–124
Ellenborough (Edward Law) (Lord), 130–133
Emmeline, the Orphan of the Castle (Smith), 201–202
English Civil War, Privy Council restructuring after, 3
English law
colonial law and, 4–5, 47–57
criminal justice reforms in, 50–53
verticality in, 6–7
English modernity
colonial justice vs., 57–60
in mystery fiction, 28
Englishness, in *Great Expectations*, 89
English political philosophy, fear in, 42–45
English selfhood, colonial law and, 2–5
Enlightenment, colonialism and, 57–60
Esposito, Roberto, 46–47
European criminality
biopolitics and, 57–60
concealment of, 47
execution, subjectivity framework for, 16

Fabian, Johannes, 92–94
family
adoption and inheritance and, 179–182
British colonial rule and, 149–154
in Eliot's fiction, 176–179, 194–195
English notions of, 207–208
in English political philosophy, 86–92
Mughal theories of, 149–154
in *Silas Marner*, 185–188
Fanon, Frantz, 214–215
Farah, Nuruddin, 224–225n.61
fatherhood. *See* paternity
fear
affect and effect of, 45–50
biopolitics of, 39–42, 57–60
capitalization of, 42–45
modernity and functions of, 57–60
of penal transport, 51
political uses of, 34–35
Felix Holt, The Radical (Eliot), 29
adoption in, 191–192
kinship in, 177–179
felony cases, appeal to Crown of, 53–57
femininity, in *Daniel Deronda*, 196–199
feminism, law and literature in, 18–19
Ferguson, Robert A., 8
Fhlathúin, Máire ní, 69–79
fiction. *See also* bildungsroman
adoption narrative in, 206–208
anti-state narratives and, 221n.7
British Empire in, 2–5, 24–25
colonial appeals to Privy Council and, 9–10
in colonial jurisprudence archives, 19–21
Confessions of a Thug influence on, 76–77
in JCPC judgments, 8
legal and literary forms of violence, 14–16
materiality and, 1–2
orphan archetype in, 188
Privy Council Judicial Committee paired with, 1–2
Fiction and the Law (Dolin), 225n.66
Fiction in the Archives (Davis), 19–20

film
Confessions of a Thug influence on, 76–77
images of thuggee in, 92–94
Filmer, Robert, 86–89
Fisher, Michael, 159, 165, 169–171
Flint, Christopher, 186–187
Forms of Empire (Hensley), 14–16, 18–19
Forrester and Others v. *The Secretary of State for India*, 153–154
Forster, E. M., 24–25
forum-shopping, colonial law and, 6, 103–104
Foucault, Michel, 80, 226n.75
on bio-power, 57–60
on sovereignty, 55–56
Frank, Catherine O., 209–210, 234n.116
Freitag, Sandria, 69–79

Gates, Sarah, 192–193
The Gazetteer of the Bombay Presidency, 33–34
G. C. W. Forester and Others v. *The Secretary of State for India in Council*, 161–164
gender
ambiguity of, in Begum Sumroo narrative, 156–157
in *Daniel Deronda*, 196–199, 203
in *Great Expectations*, 84–85
Indian jurisprudence and, 213–217
sovereignty and, 164–169
genealogy
in *Daniel Deronda*, 202–206
narrative and, 186–187
geopolitics, law and literature in context of, 14–16
Ghosh, Durba, 157, 167–168
Gifts (Farah), 224–225n.61
Gilmartin, David, 150–151, 153
Goethe, Johann Wolfgang von, 90–92
gold, in *Silas Marner*, 184–185
Gordon, Stewart, 69–79
Government of India, absolute sovereignty of, 2–5
Government of India Acts (1833 and 1858), 4–5, 25–26
Governor General of India
creation of, 25–26
'The Proclamation of the Gates' by, 131
Governor in Council, 4
Grass, Sean, 78–79
Great Britain
adoption views in, 207–208
democratic transition in, 211
path to national unity in, 3
unification of, 43–45
Great Expectations (Dickens)
childhood terror in, 79–85
Confessions of a Thug compared to, 64–65, 72–73, 77
crime and punishment in, 78–79
criminality and rehabilitation in, 91–92
criminal justice in, 27, 210
criminal transport in, 50–53
orphan archetype in, 188
Said's discussion of, 87–88
subjecthood and citizenship in, 90–92
Grossman, Jonathan, 18–19, 143–145, 216–217
Guha, Ranajit, 19–20, 228–229n.40

Haight, Gordon, 206–208
Haldane (Lord), 2–5
Halhed, Nathaniel, 101
hanging, Indian fear of, 52
Hardy, Thomas, 188
Hart, H. L. A., 80
Hastings, Warren
capital punishment authorized by, 52
courts established by, 4
Indian colonial courts and, 100–104
Heber, Reginald, 155–156
Hensley, Nathan, 14–16, 18–19
hermeneutics, of legal documents, 14–16
heteroglossia, in colonial law, 5–7
Hewett, George, 155–156
hijra, decriminalization in India of, 213–217
Hindus and Hinduism
caste system and colonial law and, 104–106
decriminalization of hijra and influence of, 214–215
Indian colonial courts and, 100–104
judicial practices in, colonial law and, 4
Mill's analysis of, 97–100
in *The Moonstone*, 137–139
Muslim tensions with, 130–133
as Muslim victims, colonial characterization of, 131–132
thuggee linked to, 66–68
historicism
legal and fictional narratives and, 92–94
in *The Moonstone*, 135–137
history
Collins's reframing of, in *The Moonstone*, 130–133
of India, British representation of, 97–100
legal studies and postcolonialism and, 224n.57
in *The Moonstone* (Collins), 124–130
precedents established by, 118–119
History of British India (Mill), 97–100
Hobbes, Thomas
on fear, 45–50
on state formation, 42–45

Hobhouse, John (Sir), 140–141
Hollingsworth, Michael, 85–86
Homans, Margaret, 196–197
homosexuality
in *Daniel Deronda*, 203–204
in Indian Penal Code, 20–21
repeal of Indian criminalization of, 213–217
Hormusjee, Muncher-jee, 36–39, 227n.13
household, Mughal concept of, 150–151
Household Words periodical, 65–66
House of Lords, JCPC compared to, 4–5
humanist perspective, law and literature and, 223n.48
humanities scholarship, normativization of colonial law and, 16–17
Hunt, Lynn, 92–94
Hutchings, Peter, 238n.81

identity
in *Daniel Deronda*, 198–206
in *Great Expectations*, 82–85
India
atemporality of, in *The Moonstone*, 125–130
biopolitics in, 57–60
British representation of history in, 97–100
colonial cultural and political representations of, 75–76
Great Expectations in context of, 91–92
sovereignty in, British undermining of, 149–154
subaltern class structure in, 228–229n.40
Indiana Jones and the Temple of Doom (film), 76–77
Indian colonial courts
appeal in criminal cases and, 55–56
caste system disputes and, 104–106, 109–110
Privacy Council influence on, 4
religious influences on, 100–104, 151
Indian criminality
appeal process and, 53–57
British criminality *vs.*, 64–65
British legal norms and fear of, 231n.75
British sovereignty and fiction of, 26–29
collective aspects of, 91–92
English fictions about, 6
fear in framework of, 35, 40–41, 47–49
interpersonal relationships and, 71–72
public executions and, 52
in *The Queen* v. *Eduljee Byramjee* case, 36–39
religion and, 97–100
Sleeman's depictions of, 66–68
thuggee narrative and, 68–77
Indian degeneracy rhetoric, British sovereignty and use of, 26–29
Indian inheritance laws, 28
Indian law, religious influences in, 100–104
Indian Penal Code
Bentham's pannomion and, 21–22
continued influence of, 213–217
establishment of, 4–5, 18
influence in Indian life of, 20–21
Macaulay's drafting of, 212–213
privacy in, 165
repeal of homosexuality criminalization in, 213–217
section 377, 20–21
Indian social structure, caste system and, 27
Indian Supreme Court, 213–217
Indian universities, law and literature in, 14–16
India Office Records, 174–175
indigenous law, JCPC adjudication and, 5–7
individualism
in *Great Expectations*, 91–92
novel and emergence of, 220n.1
inheritance
colonial laws concerning, 164
in *Daniel Deronda*, 200–206
in India, 28
in Mughal Empire, 153
in *Silas Marner*, 179–182
Iser, Wolfgang, 23–25

Jack Sheppard (Ainsworth), 85–86
Jahan (Shah), 150–151
Jahangir (Emperor), 42–43
James I (King of England), 42–43
Jamsetjee, Burjorjee, 37–38
Jan, Mohamed, Abdul, 41–42
Jane Eyre (Brontë), 188, 240n.115
Jervis, Mary Anne. *See* Dyce Sombre, Mary Ann
Jewish identity, in *Daniel Deronda*, 192–193, 199–206
Jones, William (Sir), 100–104
Joseph, Betty, 166–167
Joshi, Priti, 91–92
Jude the Obscure, 188
Judgment of Death Act (1823), 55
judicial certainty, narrative of, 63–65
Judicial Committee Act of 1833, 4–5
Judicial Committee of the Privy Council (JCPC)
abolition of, 217–219
bildungsroman compared to, 63–65
biopolitics of fear and, 58–60
colonial expansion and establishment of, 4–5
current status of, 217–219
felony conviction appeals and, 35
fictional reflections of opinions by, 209–210
foreclosure of reform, appeals rejections and, 89–90

Judicial Committee of the Privy Council (JCPC) (cont.)
  ideological framework for narrative claims by, 9–10
  indigenous laws and, 5–7
  Jamaican cases and, 217–219
  judicial certainty narrative of, 63–65
  justice discourse and, 211
  legal texts of, 1–2
  precedential reasoning and, 120–121
  rise of British imperialism and, 2–5
  sovereignty and narrative in appeals of, 12–14
  timeline for cases, 25–26
justice
  discourse in law and literature on, 211–213
  in *Great Expectations*, 81–82
  legal and literary rhetoric of, 209–210
  nonviolence linked to, 16

Kaif, Katrina, 92–94
Kalpagam, U., 114–118
Kant, Immanuel, 99–100, 215–217
Kelly, Robin D. G., 237n.68
Khan, Aamir, 92–94
kingship, Mughal concepts of, 150–151
King's Privy Council, 4
kinship
  in Begum Sumroo case, 157–159
  in British culture, 86–92
  in *Daniel Deronda*, 202–206
  in Eliot's novels, 177–179, 194–195
  English notions of, 207–208
  fiction *vs.* law and, 176–179
  Mughal sovereignty and, 149–154
Kipling, Rudyard, 24–25
Koh-i-noor diamond, 124–125, 139, 142–146
Kolsky, Elizabeth, 6, 22–23, 47–57
Koselleck, Reinhart, 99–100
Krueger, Christine, 18–19

labor, Indian convicts as source of, 26–29, 35–39, 50–51
LaCapra, Dominic, 19–20
land grants *(jaghir)*
  in Begum Sumroo case, 162–164
  East India Company seizure of, 157–164
  Mughal system of, 153
Landon, T. D, 69
language and speech
  gender and, 165–167
  in *Great Expectations*, 89
lapse, doctrine of
  Begum Sumroo case and, 160–161, 174–175
  colonial land annexation and, 73–74
Lariviere, Richard, 102–103
Larkins, John Pascal, 161
law
  colonial surrogacy and subversion in, 210
  discourse of justice and, 211–213
  geopolitics and, 14–16
  literature and, 1–2, 14–19
  in *The Moonstone*, 137–139
  performative force of, 223n.47
  personal development narrative and, 64
Law Commission, institution of, 25–26
legal fiction, characteristics of, 21–23
legal history, postcolonialism and, 224n.57
legal opinions, as literature, 1–2
legal positivism, legal fiction and, 21–22
Legislative Council of India, 158–159
Leviathan (Hobbes), 42–45
  fear in, 46–47
liberatory model of law, Victorian fiction and, 9–10
literary genre
  appellate judicial opinions as, 8
  colonial law and, 21–22
literature
  contemporary law and, 213–217
  discourse of justice and, 211–213
  geopolitics and, 14–16
  law and, 1–2, 14–19
Login, John Spencer, 141
Lowe, Lisa, 19–20
Lushington, Stephen, 55–56, 58–60

Macaulay, Thomas Babington, 4–5, 18, 212–213
  on English criminality, 47
  'The Proclamation of the Gates' and, 131
Madura Civil Court, 113–114
Maharaja of Scindia, 162–164
Mahmud of Ghazni, 122–136
Maine, Henry, 212–213
Majeed, Javed, 75–76
Mann, Michael, 52
Marcus, Sharon, 18–19
Marlow, James E., 87
Martin, Penny, 179
masculinity
  in Begum Sumroo case, 154–157
  in *Confessions of a Thug*, 74–76
  in *Great Expectations*, 89
  sovereignty and, 164–169
Massumi, Brian, 46–47
Mawani, Renisa, 110–111
McKeon, Michael, 220n.1
McLaverty, James, 206–208
Mehta, Jaya, 135–137
Menon, Nivedita, 216–217

Metropolitan Police (London), 85–86
Meyer, Susan, 204–206
Mill, James, 97–101
  on Hindu–Muslim religious conflict, 131
Mill, John Stuart, 216–217
Millar, Robert McColl, 89
Miller, D. A., 124–125
Minding the Law (Amsterdam & Bruner), 12–13
"Minute on Indian Education" (Macaulay), 18
modernity
  British *vs.* colonial approaches to, 57–60
  historicity and, 92–94
  in *The Moonstone*, 199, 200, 137–139
  personal development narrative and, 64
Moin, Azfar, 150–151
money
  colonial jurisprudence and, 115–118
  in *Silas Marner*, 182–185
monologic voice and ideology, in appellate judicial opinions, 8
Montgomery, Robert (Sir), 141–142
The Moonstone (Collins)
  conquest and plunder narrative in, 125–130
  criminality in, 144–146
  criminal justice in, 52–53
  English modernity and colonialism and, 28, 210
  fiction as history in, 122–125
  historical details in, 124–125, 137–139, 146
  historicism in, 135–137
  influence of *Confessions of a Thug* on, 76–77
  opposing temporalities in, 133–134
  Prologue and Epilogue of, 125–130
  psychological aspects of, 142–146
  publication of, 123–124
  reframing of history in, 130–133
  religion and, 97–100
  sectarianism and subjection in, 130–133
Moore's Indian Appeals, 1–2
Moretti, Franco
  on bildungsroman, 79–80, 89, 238n.84
  on citizenship and state formation, 91
  on the detective novel, 143–145
  on fiction as history, 122–123
  on personal development narrative, 64
  on singular guilt, 149–150
Morton, Stephen, 14–16
motherhood, in *Daniel Deronda* (Eliot), 196–199
Mufti, Aamir, 193
mufti/maulvis (Muslim legal practitioner), 4, 101
Mughal Empire
  colonial transition in, 168–169
  East India Company incursions into, 153
  land grant system in, 153
  sovereignty and kinship in, 149–154
Mukherjee, Mithi, 107–108, 211
Mukhopadhyay, Anindita, 104–106
Muñoz, José, 10–11, 18, 213–217
Muslims
  colonial law and judicial practices of, 4
  as Hindu oppressors, colonial characterization of, 131–132
  Hindu tensions with, 130–133
  Indian colonial courts and, 100–104
  in *The Moonstone*, 125–130, 135–139
  sovereignty concepts of, 150–151
mystery literary genre
  Collins's legacy in, 123–124
  fiction as history in, 122–125
  Indian context in, 28
  temporality in, 133–134

narrative
  colonial law as, 12–14
  of fear, Eduljee case and, 39–42
  gender and, 165–167
  genealogy and, 186–187
  of judicial certainty, 63–65
  law as text, 21–23
  The Moonstone framework for, 132–133
  Privy Council's reliance on, 1–2, 7–12
Narrative of a Journey through the Upper Provinces of India from Calcutta to Bombay, 1824–1825 (Heber), 155–156
national culture, decriminalization of hijra and influence of, 214–215
National Legal Services Authority v. *Union of India*, 213–217
nation building
  British unification and, 3
  in *Great Expectations*, 89
  imperialism and, 43–45
Navtej Singh Johar v. *Union of India*, 216–217
Naz Foundation v. *Govt. of NCT of Delhi*, 20–21
New Directions in Law and Literature, 17
Newgate novels, 85–86
New Historicism, law and literature and, 224n.60
Nicholas Nickelby (Dickens), 50–53
Nijhar, Pretti, 231n.75
Nixon, Cheryl, 201–202
nondualism, Sedgwick's concept of, 11
nonviolence, postcolonial discourse on, 14–16
normativity
  Begum Sumroo case as challenge to, 157–159
  colonial law and, 16–17
Novy, Marianne, 177, 188, 207–208
Nunokawa, Jeff, 184, 186, 203–204

obedience, fear as motivation for, 45–50
objectivity, law's claim of, 8–9
O'Brien, Derek, 218–219
Ochterlony, David, 165–167
Oliver Twist (Dickens), 85–86, 89, 188
Ondaatje, Michael, 213–217
orphan narrative in Victorian fiction, 177–179
  in *Daniel Deronda*, 201–202
  in *Silas Marner*, 179–187
  social stigma of, 188–192
Orwell, George, 24–25
O'Toole, Tess, 178–179

pandit (Hindu legal practitioner), 4, 101, 104–106
pannomion, Bentham's concept of, 21–22
Park, Hyungji, 91–92
parliamentary democracy, British embrace of, 2–5, 211
paternity
  bildungsroman father figure and, 90–92
  British imperialism and, 73–74
  in *Confessions of a Thug*, 71, 74–76
  Eliot's focus on, 206–208
  in Eliot's novels, 193–194
  in English political philosophy, 86–87
  in *Great Expectations*, 82–83, 86–87
Paul Clifford (Bulwer), 85–86
Pax Britannica mythology
  in *The Moonstone*, 146
  postcolonial studies and, 14–16
Peel, Robert, 85–86
penal systems
  British *vs.* colonial systems, 57–60
  reform of, 89–90
penal transport
  colonial law and, 22–23
  decline in practice of, 50–53
  in *Great Expectations* (Dickens), 79, 88–89
  Indian fear of, 51
  segregation in, 230n.62
  subjectivity framework for, 16
performative force of law, normativity and, 223n.47
personal development, law and narrative of, 64
personhood, Indian *vs.* English criminals and framework of, 16
Peters, Julie Stone, 14
Peters, Laura, 178, 186–188
Philip, M. NourbeSe, 17
Phillips, A. W. (Judge), 112–113
phrenology, thuggee and, 238n.88
The Pickwick Papers (Dickens), 50–53
policing
  British development of, 85–86
  in *The Moonstone*, 124–125
political economy, colonialism and, 43–45
Poovey, Mary, 236n.33
popular culture
  Indian stereotypes in, 235n.18
  Newgate novels and, 85–86
  thug figures in, 77
postcolonial studies
  law and literature in, 14–17
  legal history and, 224n.57
  resistance to, 17
poverty, criminality and, in *Great Expectations*, 83–85
Pratt and Morgan v. *Attorney General of Jamaica*, 217–219
precedents, temporality and establishment of, 118–121
Presidencies of India, Privacy Council influence on, 4
Price, Pamela G., 109–110
Prinsep, Henry Thoby, 171–172
Prinsep and East India Company v. *Dyce Sombre*, 153–154, 171–172
prison reform
  Dickens's interest in, 78–79
  in English criminal law, 50–53
privacy, colonial property seizure and, 164–169
private property, British colonial rule and, 149–154
Private Record of the Life of General Sir George Hewett, 155–156
Privy Council
  absolute sovereignty and, 6–7
  Begum Sumroo case and, 161–164
  biopolitics and logic of, 58–60
  colonial expansion and role of, 4
  colonial jurisprudence and influence of, 7–12
  criminal case appeals to, 26–29
  Dyce Sombre lunacy case and, 171–172
  knowledge production and archives of, 23–25
  origins of, 3
  precedents established by, 118–121
  Ramaswamy Aiyan v. *Venkata Achari* litigation and, 110–113
  temporality of law and, 114–118
Privy Counsellors, sovereignty of, 12–14
'The Proclamation of the Gates,' 131
property
  East India Company seizure of, 158–159
  Indian inheritance laws and, 28
  privacy and, in Begum Sumroo case, 164–169

punishment. *See also* penal systems; penal transport
in Dickens's fiction, 78–79
Punjab Territory, British seizure of, 139–142, 146
purohitam rights, Brahmin claim of, 104–106, 115–118

The Queen v. *Eduljee Byramjee*, 25–26
appeal to JCPC, 52–53
biopolitics of fear in punishment phase of, 60
Confessions of a Thug in context of, 89–90
contemporary criminal appeals and, 217–219
criminality in, 26–29
fear in context of, 35, 39–42
Great Expectations in context of, 89–90
hanging as threat in, 52
penal transport as threat in, 51
Privy Council appeal, 53–57
racialized criminality in decisions for, 64–65
reconsideration of, 63–65
testimony and issues in, 36–39

racialized violence, thuggee and, 64–65, 237n.68
Radhakrishnan, K. S., 213–217
Ramaseeana: Or a Vocabulary of the Peculiar Language Used by the Thugs (Sleeman), 49, 66–68
Confessions of a Thug and, 71
influence on colonial prosecution of, 69–79
Ramaswamy Aiyan v. *Venkata Achari*, 25–27
adoption narrative and, 174–175
bureaucratic biopolitics and, 107–110
caste system and, 104–106, 108–109
contemporary law and precedents of, 215–217
difference and cultural relativism in case of, 210
litigation of time in, 110–113
The Moonstone and, 123–124, 144–146
precedents established in, 118–121
religion and, 97–100, 109–110
statute of limitations in, 161
temporality of law in, 114–118, 122–123, 214–215
Western historicity and, 92–94
Rambles and Recollections of an Indian Official (Sleeman), 154–157
Rani Bhabhani of Rajshahi, 167–168
Rani Bhishnukumari of Burdwan, 166–167
Rani of Sirmur, 165–167
Ranjit Singh, 139–142
Rankin, George (Sir), 4–5
rationality, law's claim of, 8–9
Rawls, John, 215–217
Reading Adoption (Novy), 188
Reading for the Law (Krueger), 18–19
regenerative sovereignty, incapacity narrative concerning, 73–74
Regulation LIII of 1803, 51
rehabilitation ideology
criminal law and, 22–23
in English criminal law, 50–53
in *Great Expectations*, 91–92
Reiner v. *Marquis of Salisbury*, 153–154
Reinhardt, Walter. *See* Sombre (Walter Reinhardt)
religion
British view of Indian history and, 97–100
Indian colonial courts and, 100–104
in Mughal Empire, 150–151
religious conflict narrative in *The Moonstone*, 130–133
Report of the Committee on Prison Discipline, 51
return, narrative of, in *Silas Marner*, 181–182
rights
alienability of, 115–118
"we" in manifesto for, 10–11
Riley v Attorney General of Jamaica, 217–219
Roberts, Emma, 156–157
Robin, Corey, 40–41
Robinson Crusoe (Dafoe), 213
Rocher, Ludo, 102–103
Rocher, Rosane, 101, 118–119
Romantic literature, history and, 97–100
Romola (Eliot), 29
Ross, Richard, 7
Roy, Parama, 48
on thuggee, 69–79
Roy, Tirthankar, 101, 103–104
Rule by Numbers: Governmentality in Colonial India (Kalpagam), 114–118
rule of law
British colonialism and, 151
colonial transition and, 168–169
Indian indigenous law and, 6
Rushby, Kevin, 76–77

Sadr Diwani Adalat (civil and revenue court), 4, 104–106, 113–114
Sadr Nizamat Adalat (criminal court), 4
Safavid empire, 150–151
Said, Edward, 24–25, 206
on *Great Expectations*, 87–88
Sargent, Neil, 146
Sassen, Saskia, 43–45
sati
campaign against, 47–49
narratives of, 22–23

Scenes and Characteristics of Hindostan, With Sketches of Anglo-Indian Society (Roberts), 156–157
Schmidgen, Wolfram, 213
Schramm, Jan-Melissa, 18–19, 200–201
Second Anglo-Sikh War, 140–141
Sedgwick, Eve Kosofsky, 11, 203–204, 216–217
self-determination, bildungsroman and illusion of, 79–80
self-rule, incapacity narrative concerning, 73–74
Sen, Amartya, 215–217
Sen, Sudipta, 3
Sepoy Rebellion of 1857
  caste system and, 108–109
  legal reforms following, 53–57, 91–92
  The Moonstone in the context of, 135–137
  penal transport following, 51
sexuality
  in Begum Sumroo case, 154–157
  colonialism and, 164–169
  in *Daniel Deronda*, 203
  in *Great Expectations*, 84–85
  Indian jurisprudence and, 213–217
Shankar, S., 68, 234–235n.10
Sharafi, Mitra
  on colonial law, 5–6, 22–23
  on Privy Council in colonial era, 7
Siddiqi, Yumna, 137–139
The Sign of Four (Doyle), 76–77
Sikh Empire, 139
Sikri, A. K. (Justice), 215–217
Silas Marner (Eliot), 29
  adoption narrative in, 176–179, 206–208
  child's presence in, 182–185
  family in, 185–188
  gold in, 184–185
  inheritance as theme in, 179–182
  kinship in, 179–182
  paternity in, 193–194
  social stigma of adoption in, 188–192
Singapore, Indian convict labor in, 50–51
Singh, Khushwant, 139
Singha, Radhika, 6
  on colonial law, 22–23
  on thuggee, 48, 69–79
Sinha, Indra, 213–217
Slaughter, Joseph, 63, 90–92
slavery
  criminal transport and abolition of, 50–51
  dramatization of legal case involving, 17
  fear as strategy in, 41–42
Slavery Abolition Act of 1833, 212–213
Sleeman, W. H., 26–29, 47–49, 66–68
  on Begum Sumroo, 154–157
  criticism of, 68–77
  cultural influence of, 76–77
  film versions of thuggee as counterweight to, 92–94
Smith, Charlotte, 201–202
social legitimacy, in Eliot's fiction, 179–182
social norms, in *Great Expectations*, 83–85
social stigma, adoption and, 188–192
Solaroli, Georgiana Dyce Sombre, 161–164
Somanatha, Temple of, 139
  in *The Moonstone*, 130–133
Sombre (Walter Reinhardt), 152
Sombre, Zafaryab, 152–153, 162–164
South Asian literature, law and legal philosophy in, 213–217
sovereignty
  appeal in criminal cases and, 53–57
  in Begum Sumroo case, 153, 157–164
  British undermining in India of, 149–150
  capitalism and, 43–45
  colonial law and, 2–5
  fear in exercise of, 34–35
  Indian assertions of, 6
  judicial opinion and, 12–14
  Mughal theories of, 149–154
  native *vs.* colonial forms of, 6
  privacy and, 164–169
The Spanish Gypsy (Eliot), 29
"Spectacularizing Crime: Ghostwriting the Law" (Hutchings), 238n.81
Spivak, Gayatri Chakravorty, 11–12, 19–21, 23–25, 165–167
Sreenivas, Mytheli, 168–169
stare decisis principle, precedential reasoning and, 120–121
state formation
  British path to, 3
  colonialism and, 43–45
  history and, 99–100
  in *The Moonstone*, 124–125
states of emergency, postcolonial literary and legal studies, and role of, 14–16
state violence
  as colonial justice strategy, 52
  postcolonial literary and legal studies and, 14–16
  racialization of, 237n.68
  subjectivity framework in, 16
Stephen, James, 212–213
Stephen, James Fitzjames, 212–213
Stephen, Leslie, 212–213
Stoler, Ann, 19–20, 23–25
The Strangler Vine (Carter), 76–77
Sturman, Rachel, 22–23, 103–104
subjectivity framework
  appeal in criminal cases and, 53–57

in bildungsroman, 80
criminality and, 238n.81
fear as tool of, 35
Supreme Court of India, homosexuality cases and, 20–21
Swamy, Anand V., 101, 103–104
Swann, Brian, 184–185
sympathy, *Great Expectations* narrative of, 81–82

A Tale of Two Cities (Dickens), 91–92
Tambling, Jeremy, 82–83
Tatwadi Brahmins, 104–106, 113–114
Taylor, Philip Meadows
on *Confessions of a Thug*, 65–68
on criminality, 64–65
cultural influence of, 76–77
film versions of thuggee as counterweight to, 92–94
on Indian *vs.* English criminal justice, 27
Privy Council Judicial Committee and work of, 1–2
Taylor, Weld, 65–66
Telugu Brahmins, 104–106, 113–114
temple management, Privy Council cases involving, 27
temporality
atemporality of India, in *The Moonstone*, 125–130
in detective fiction, 133–134
in India, 235n.18
Indian concepts of, 22–23
litigation of, 110–113
meaning and, 99–100
in *The Moonstone*, 125–130, 133–134
precedents and, 118–121
Privy Council cases and, 114–118
in *Ramaswamy Aiyan* v. *Venkata Achari*, 97–100, 109–110
Western historicity and, 92–94
terror and example, as colonial justice strategy, 52
text, law as, 21–23
Thapar, Romila, 130–133
thuggee
British imperial fictions concerning, 26–29, 68–77, 230n.65
British information sources concerning, 66–68
in contemporary popular culture, 77
Criminal Tribes Act of 1871 and suppression of, 215–217
fear and suppression by colonial British and, 41–42, 47–49, 52–53, 68–77
film images of, 92–94
justification of racialized violence and, 237n.68
laws relating to, 6
narratives of, 22–23, 66–68
phrenology and, 238n.88
terminology and definitions of, 234–235n.10
Thuggee and Dacoity Suppression Acts of 1836–1848, 91–92
"Thugs and Bandits: Life and Law in Colonial and Epicolonial India" (Shankar), 68
Thugs of Hindostan (film), 92–94
Thug: The True Story of India's Murderous Cult (Dash), 76–77
time, standardization of, 114–118
Timurid culture, 150–151
Tipu Sultan of Mysore, 124–130, 135–137, 146
Todorov, Tzvetan, 28, 122–123, 133–134
Touching Feeling: Affect, Pedagogy, Performativity (Sedgwick), 11
travel journals and travelogues
Begum Sumroo narrative in, 154–157
Dickens's travel narrative, 78–79
Indian criminality stereotype in, 48
thuggee stereotypes in, 69–79
Treaty of Lahore (1849), 140–141
Troup, Mary Ann Dyce Sombre, 152–153, 161–164
Troup v. *East India Company*, 28, 153–154, 161–164
"The Typology of Detective Fiction" (Todorov), 133–134

utilitarianism, Dickens and, 240n.113

Verne, Jules, 76–77
Victorian studies, law and literature in, 18–19
violence
in law, 16
legal and literary forms of, 14–16
white violence in British Empire, 229–230n.58
Viswanathan, Gauri, 14–16
voice, in appellate judicial opinions, 8

Waddams, Stephen, 59–60
Wagner, Kim, 238n.88
Watt, Ian, 181–182, 220n.1
"we," in fundamental right, 10–11
wealth, colonialism and, 43–45
Weiner, Martin, 47
Weinhardt, Walter, 152
Weld-Forester, George Cecil, 161–164
Wellesley, Richard (Marquess) (Governor General of India), 159–164
White, Hayden, 19–20
Wiesenfarth, Joseph, 179
Wilhelm Meister's Apprenticeship (Goethe), 90–92

women
  language and narrative relating to, 166–167
  native misogyny concerning, 167–168
  privacy of, property rights and, 164–169
The Wretched of the Earth (Fanon), 214–215
Wuthering Heights (Brontë), 178–179, 188
"Wyrley Ripper," 60–62

Yang, Anand, A., 50–51, 231n.79
Yelle, Robert, 21–22

zamindari system, 166–167
Zionism, in *Daniel Deronda*, 204–206
Zong! (Philip), 17

CPSIA information can be obtained
at www.ICGtesting.com
Printed in the USA
LVHW080855190622
721603LV00004B/244

9 781108 837484